THE FRANKENSTEIN OF 1790 AND OTHER LOST CHAPTERS
FROM REVOLUTIONARY FRANCE

THE FRANKENSTEIN OF 1790
AND OTHER LOST CHAPTERS FROM
REVOLUTIONARY FRANCE

JULIA V. DOUTHWAITE

THE UNIVERSITY OF CHICAGO PRESS

CHICAGO AND LONDON

JULIA V. DOUTHWAITE is professor of French at the University of Notre Dame. She is the author of *Exotic Women: Literary Heroines and Cultural Strategies in Ancien Régime France* and *The Wild Girl, Natural Man, and the Monster: Dangerous Experiments in the Age of Enlightenment*, the latter published by the University of Chicago Press.

The University of Chicago Press, Chicago 60637
The University of Chicago Press, Ltd., London
© 2012 by The University of Chicago
All rights reserved. Published 2012.
Printed in the United States of America

21 20 19 18 17 16 15 14 13 12   1 2 3 4 5

ISBN-13: 978-0-226-16058-0 (cloth)
ISBN-10: 0-226-16058-0 (cloth)

The University of Chicago Press gratefully acknowledges the generous support of the Institute for Scholarship in the Liberal Arts in the College of Arts and Letters at the University of Notre Dame toward the publication of this book.

Library of Congress Cataloging-in-Publication Data

Douthwaite, Julia V.
   The Frankenstein of 1790 and other lost chapters from revolutionary France / Julia V. Douthwaite.
      p. cm.
   Includes bibliographical references and index.
      ISBN 978-0-226-16058-0 (cloth : alkaline paper) — ISBN 0-226-16058-0 (cloth : alkaline paper) 1. France—History—Revolution, 1789–1799. 2. Literature and revolutions—France. I. Title.
   DC158.8.D59 2012
   809.3'93584404—dc23

                                                            2011050822

TO MY PARENTS,

MARY LOUISE SOMERVILLE

AND GEOFFREY KINGSLEY DOUTHWAITE

CONTENTS

FIGURES

ACKNOWLEDGMENTS

This book was inspired by two brave people (my parents) who made political activism a way of life for me and my brothers as we were growing up in what I now realize was one of the most exciting periods of American history: the civil rights era. The book was fueled by a love of French studies and a desire to make the Revolution come alive to readers of literature, in some small way, as the great historians of French politics and culture have done in years past. It was fed by passionate dialogues with friends and fellow travelers far and near, and helped by many librarians and archivists. Thanks go especially to Ken Kinslow, Linda Gregory, and the staff of the Interlibrary Loan Department at the University of Notre Dame Hesburgh Library. To the Nanovic Institute for European Studies discussion group on war and revolution at Notre Dame, I am grateful for readings of chapter-length drafts. To the John Simon Guggenheim Memorial Foundation, thanks for the primary funding that launched the book in 2007. The Institute for Scholarship in the Liberal Arts at the University of Notre Dame was helpful in many ways: for generous research travel support that made it possible to consult libraries and archives in Paris, Aix-en-Provence, and Vizille over the last thirteen years, for graduate student assistant support, and undergraduate assistant support. The Nanovic Institute also deserves thanks for the conference funding that helped bring the unique Franco-American conference "New Paradigms in Revolutionary Studies / Nouveaux paradigmes dans les études révolutionnaires" to South Bend in 2008.

The following people were instrumental in more ways than I can count. As readers and inspiration, I thank Lesley Walker, Lynn Hunt, Tom Kselman, Alex Martin, Robert Fishman, Tiago Fernandez, Pierpaolo Polzonetti, David Andress, Ron Schechter, Anne Mellor, Greg Kucich, Orley Marron, and Essaka Joshua. For their moral support and willingness to talk through issues over the years—and many more to come, I hope—I am indebted to Laurent Loty, Véronique Tacquin, Catriona Seth, Isabelle Lelièvre, Dominique Lelièvre, Stéphane Thomas, my wonderful mother-in-law, Regina Viglione, and my mentees, Alanda Mason and My'iesha Mason. Thanks also to those people who were generous enough to write in favor of this book before it was much more than a glimmer of an idea: Yves Citton, Joan DeJean, Sarah Maza, and Londa Schiebinger. My student assistants were very helpful, and so I thank Sonja Stojanovic, Daniel Richter, Walter Scott, Marguerite Romosan, Kylene Butler, and Jennifer Mathieu. In loving memory of Isabelle Pottier Thomas, whose republican spirit was a revelation.

I would also like to thank the editors at the University of Chicago Press, Alan Thomas and Randy Petilos, the anonymous readers of the manuscript in its earlier phases, and Pamela J. Bruton, copy editor extraordinaire.

Parts of this book were presented at the University of British Columbia, Brown University, the University of Wolverhampton, Wesleyan University, Hope College, the University of Tennessee, the College of William and Mary, Hobart and William Smith Colleges, and the Université de Rennes 2. For joining in discussion of this material and inviting me into their communities, I thank all the people I met during these visits and especially my hosts, Joël Castonguay-Bélanger, Valentine Balguerie, Bryan Zandberg, Ben Colbert, Andrew Curran, Julie Kipp, Mary McAlpin, Giulia Pacini, Catherine Gallouët, Isabelle Brouard-Arends, and Emmanuel Bouju.

Finally, to my family—my husband, Rich, and our sons, Nick and Max Viglione—thanks for sharing my love of good stories, good conversation, and good living.

All oversights, missteps, and faults in this book remain uniquely mine.

Portions of this book appeared in article form in the following journals: part of chapter 2 appeared as "The Frankenstein of the French Revolution: Nogaret's Automaton Tale of 1790" in *European Romantic Review* 20, no. 3 (2009): 381–411 (with Daniel Richter, MA, University of Notre Dame, 2008, © 2009 Taylor and Francis); part of chapter 3 appeared as "Le Roi pitoyable et ses adversaires: La Politique de l'émotion selon J. J. Regnault-Warin, H.-M. Williams, et les libellistes de Varennes" in *Revue d'histoire litté-*

raire de la France 4 (2010): 917–34; and part of the introduction appeared as "Pour une histoire de la lecture romanesque sous la Révolution" in *Débat et écritures sous la révolution*, edited by Huguette Krief and Jean-Noël Pascal (Louvain-la-Neuve, Belgium: Peeters, 2011), 103–18.

INTRODUCTION

In 1789 François-Félix Nogaret, a well-known courtier and author of occasional verse and slightly salacious fiction, dropped his light-hearted
persona to enter the world of political writing and urged others to join him,
exclaiming: "you cannot wield a sword or a musket; write or speak."[1] The
call to action was timely and echoed the sentiments of many others. Over
1,200 novels were published between 1789, when the Bastille fell, and 1804,
when Napoleon triumphantly declared the Revolution's end. Certain works
within this enormous corpus announce the new shapes of literature to come
in the nineteenth and early twentieth centuries. Whether it is in stylistic
innovation, the rewriting of history, or hybrid forms of documentation and
humor, this fiction reveals strong ties to now-famous authors whose careers
were then in their infancy (Mary Shelley, E. T. A. Hoffmann, and Honoré de
Balzac), as well as a few who had yet to arrive on the scene (Charles Dickens, Gustave Flaubert, and L. Frank Baum). That is one of the meanings of
a "revolution in fiction": the formal developments in fiction writing from
the philosophes to the realists. The larger-than-life personalities, heroes,
villains, horrors, and hopes that marked French life in the period from 1789
to 1794 also left a literal trace on the stories written afterward; that is the
second meaning of a "revolution in fiction." From 1795 through the 1900s
and every now and then still today in a variety of media, these stories resur-
face. By focusing on key moments from the revolutionary tumult as they
were reappropriated after the fact, this book takes readers into the process
by which people literally and creatively transcribed, borrowed, and remod-
eled symbolic scenes and encounters from the past into new stories with
ongoing appeal.

    The Frankenstein of 1790 works on a dialectic that connects print cul-
ture both to the short duration of events from the march on Versailles in

October 1789 to the execution of Robespierre in July 1794 and to the longer duration of intellectual trends from the eighteenth to the early twentieth century, for it is in that politico-literary juncture that we will unearth missing links between the ancien régime and that entity we now call modernity. The four chapters build on events that changed some aspects of French history. I aim to show how fiction and, to a lesser extent, its allies in the visual arts (book illustration and caricature) helped make those moments into an indispensable part of French, English, and, in some instances, American culture. My point is that although the Revolution may have ended in 1794, its symbolic power retained considerable currency for years to come, because the following generations of authors and readers had lived through or were born into a world that remained saturated with the signs, language, and emotional residue of the tumult. Later generations enacted an ongoing struggle with the revolutionary past, trying to put it to rest, mock its ambitions, or keep the momentum going, and in so doing to discern the distinctions between their own identity and inherited traits. Each chapter proceeds in what might be imagined as concentric circles: the core being a summary of key points from the dominant historiography, followed by traces in period newspapers, pamphletry, and popular imagery, then more elaborate fictional renditions that include some classic works by master writers of the nineteenth and twentieth centuries.[2] Whenever possible, I have included related archival and biographical sources and thereby contribute to the history of fiction writing, reading, and publishing during the late 1700s and early 1800s: a field that still proves challenging to researchers.

A REVOLUTION IN LITERARY STUDIES

The accent on political-event writing as a form of storytelling and the long-term focus on the retelling of these stories over the years make *The Frankenstein of 1790* distinct from a political history. Like the positivists of the nineteenth century and the cultural materialists of the twentieth, I contend that (1) there are certain facts (political, biographical) one needs to know to make sense of texts written during a revolution; and (2) the literature of 1789–1803 reveals in its pages the signs of its own production. The reason for the first point is simple: given the neglect suffered by the writers of 1789–1803 in scholarship to date, their lives are largely unknown. Yet the personal is political. It matters whether a certain person was aligned with the Jacobins or with the Girondins, what kind of audience they expected for their work, and, if they were imprisoned, when and under whose orders. Although he or she may disavow such material issues in the writing, this context nevertheless provides the horizon of expectations needed to approximate, at a distance of two centuries, what authors were trying to say and who they were trying to reach. The second point is essential for interpreting texts whose forms themselves wielded a certain meaning for period readers and whose words were tied to the vicissitudes of political change. Just as plots often held ideological significance in their treatment of people and current events, the choice of a genre (or the choice to mix several genres) was a deliberate act aimed at generating what Pierre Bourdieu has taught us to consider as "cultural capital." Cultural capital refers to the knowledge or ability that equips people with the empathetic imagination or the competence needed to decipher artifacts of a culture. The pseudorealism of the "secret history" with its dozens of legalistic *pièces justificatives*, for example, made different demands on the reader and promised a different kind of outcome than did Oriental tales couched in fairy-tale conventions. Whether or not to employ neologisms such as *liberticide* or *terroriste*, and how more anodyne words such as *le peuple* and *pitié* were used, reveal other ways that authors molded every story's message to create particular effects at specific moments in time. The representation of things such as crowds, revolutionary leaders, and bloodshed is equally telling in that it endowed events with a causality that gave the Revolution a sense of logic (or not, as in the case of Flaubert). Such issues, icons, and language constitute the cultural capital that was second nature among literate audiences of the 1790s. Knowing how to interpret them is essential to a program of revolutionary reading.

In adopting this approach, one need not reduce literature to societal types such as were embraced by the archetypal positivist Hippolyte Taine (1828–93) nor flatten the dazzling diversity of revolutionary media into "spiritual principles" of nation building such as his successor Ernest Renan celebrated in his famous 1882 lecture. Despite the dictates of Auguste Comte, one need not—and the present volume emphatically does not—refuse to speculate on the sociopolitical origins, results, or meanings of literature either. Yet I insist on the positive aspect of this study—partly to differentiate it from a tendency that is alas too widespread in literary criticism, that is, the obsession with clever readings that reveal more about the critic than the object of study. Interpretation is of course central to my work, but it is grounded in an epistemological framework carefully constructed to appreciate period terminology, social expectations, vernaculars, and the chronology of a time wracked by rapid and sometimes drastic changes (in legislation, public confidence, and security). This method of qualitative and, to a certain extent, quantitative content analysis is not an approach for interpreting all literature. A decade of study has convinced me, however, that the prerequisite to any literary history of the Revolution must be to establish at least one verifiable, literal meaning for the texts in question. As Stanley Fish points out, "there always will be a literal reading, but 1) it will not always be the same one and 2) it can change."[3] The potential parameters of that change in meaning—real or imagined, present or future—are among the things pursued in this book. Whence the "new" positivism.

Any revolutionary history worth its salt must go beyond content analysis, however. Although fascinating to specialists, it is not enough to show readers what was codified, inscribed, or otherwise hardwired into cultural products of the 1790s; a truly revolutionary praxis looks beyond traditional author-reader relations to prompt interlocutors to develop their own skills and eventually transcend the teacher. The end-of-chapter codas and the book's conclusion are designed to that end. By departing from tightly hewn historico-political analysis and venturing afield from the original terrain, readers will see how symbols, semantics, and plot arcs that originally enlivened debate in turn-of-the-century France and England eventually drew in constituents that their authors could not have dreamed of. The conclusion points to some recent results of this cultural reappropriation in genres as far-flung as Egyptian poetry and American film. It is my hope that readers of *The Frankenstein of 1790* will go on to identify and enjoy many more references to revolutionary culture wherever they may be found, from sexy styles in men's fashion to mass demands for a constitution. For whatever one's attitude toward the Revolution's role in human history, one thing cannot be denied: it is not over yet. The implications of democracy come alive in our acts: by doing right by the people close by us, we each realize the dream of the Revolution on a daily basis. Indeed, the issues raised here may be anchored in eighteenth-century problems, but they remain urgent. Which members of the population should join policy debates? At what point does strong leadership verge into dictatorship, and how can one arrest such a development? How should democratic entities balance the loyalties that people feel they owe to other identities—religious, ethnic, or regional? Under what conditions must a state punish its own citizens, and what constitutes a fair punishment? These are tough questions, as a glance at any daily newspaper will show. Delving into the ways that they were debated and realized in another age may give us some perspective.

This project may raise eyebrows in its combination of political and literary reflection. It may seem too historical to some readers and not historical enough to others. The claims of influence or reverberations between the authors of the revolutionary corpus and the authors analyzed in the

codas, who are separated by long stretches of time and space, are specu-
lative. There are some links missing between the missing links. Furthermore, the primary analyses are deeply implicated in French political issues
of the revolutionary era. In keeping with what I call (with tongue slightly in
cheek) the new positivism, the analysis endeavors to avoid the jargon fashionable among some literary critics; it does not invite parallels between the
Revolution and postmodern commonplaces such as the terrorist nature of
language, nor do the readings attempt to produce exhaustive plot summa-
ries or character analyses that are typical of more traditional literary studies. Instead of taking authors' claims at face value (a risky business in the
best of times and fatal during a revolution), I checked the archives for publishing traces and pored over political records, with results that are sometimes eye-opening. I seek to allow readers to see what has been unseen until
now and to intrigue them enough to keep reading and thinking about the
revolutionary heritage on their own, for study or just for fun. I had a great
time tracking down all the sources and stories that fueled this book and believe that they have much to teach us. Some of this material is quite funny,
outrageous, and entertaining, as readers of the "Colonial Sex Comedy" and
"Flaubert's Chronicle of Banality" will see. Dare I hope that readers will
take pleasure from this book?

PRECURSORS

The Frankenstein of 1790 builds on a multilayered edifice of revolutionary
literary history. Nineteenth-century scholars such as Eugène Maron (*Histoire littéraire de la Révolution*; 1856) and Georges Duval (*Histoire de la
littérature révolutionnaire*; 1879) laid the groundwork with their research
on revolutionary oratory and journalism. Maron, however, dismissed fiction
published during the Revolution as unworthy of serious study, and Duval
claimed that none of the novels contemporaneous with events bore any
traces of the tumult anyway.[4] A disparaging or melancholy attitude toward
revolutionary literature ran through the influential works of nineteenth-
century literary critics such as Sainte-Beuve and the Goncourt brothers as
well and conspired to keep this corpus fairly untouched by readers until the
mid-twentieth century.[5] At that moment, inspired by the linguistic turn
in historiography and supported by new reference tools and databases, a
first wave of revisionist historiography began excavating this material and
chiseled it into some finite patterns. Malcolm Cook's 1982 book-length
study launched this development by offering a compact framework for
revolutionary fiction organized by genre. Henri Coulet, Béatrice Didier,

Lynn Hunt, and Allan Pasco took the next step by investing in study of "second-rate" authors and proving their importance to the cultural history of the 1790s. Filling in the mortar between history and literature, Stéphanie Genand has unearthed connections between the *roman noir* and emigration. Working with similar materials, Geneviève Lafrance has shown how the gift economy that sustained émigrés during the Terror grew out of ancien régime ideals of *bienfaisance* and pity. Also notable are the inventories of women authors constructed by Huguette Krief and Carla Hesse. Krief's recent synthesis of political fiction from the 1790s, Joël Castonguay-Bélanger's incursion into the relations between science and literature, and collections edited by Catriona Seth (on the French Gothic) and by Isabelle Brouard-Arends and Laurent Loty (on the concept of political *engagement* in literature) are more signs of the field's coming-of-age.

As is the case with any first wave, some of these books have elicited resistance or even hostility for what critics perceived as the inadequate methodology of historical contextualization and the dubious literary quality of the texts in question. Malcolm Cook's techniques of close textual analysis made perfect sense when applied to the masterworks of "greats" like Bernardin de Saint-Pierre, but the corpus of uneven quality covered in his 1982 study produced a catalog of themes that left unanswered the question of significance. Lynn Hunt depicted revolutionary literature as a powerful nexus of tortured family relations, applying Freudian theory and political analysis to fictional motifs, but she was roundly berated by Philip Stewart for misappropriating literature as historical evidence. Carla Hesse made a case for women's publishing during the 1790s, but she failed to explain what those writers contributed to longer-term developments in literary history. As Joan DeJean noted in a review of *The Other Enlightenment*, "Hesse could have been more convincing had she demonstrated not only the statistical significance of [women's writing] . . . but also the innovativeness of their work and its impact on the way in which French literature was given a radically new shape in the early nineteenth century."[6] Some of these judgments are valid; others less so. The field is still emerging from its infancy and the birthing has been difficult. Revolutionary literature is devilishly difficult to understand, and suitable methods have been long in coming. Perhaps the present volume will help a bit.

ON REVOLUTIONARY FICTION: DEFINITIONS

Based on study of about three hundred politically inflected fictions published originally in French from 1789 to 1803, varying in length from eight pages to more than a thousand, in editions that cover the gamut from cheap, hastily printed pamphlets to elaborately illustrated tomes, I contend that the materials selected here represent a noteworthy combination of relatively elevated literary craftsmanship and in-depth sociopolitical reflection on major events of the French Revolution.[7] The criteria of literary craftsmanship and sociopolitical reflection are defined loosely since my ultimate goal is not to argue for any one unknown masterpiece or author's genius but rather to show how the Revolution produced a body of work that prompted later writers to retell the same stories. Readers will search in vain for some of the mainstays of the period in French letters, such as Isabelle de Charrière, Benjamin Constant, or Germaine de Staël. Others who may be less well known feature prominently: the British writers Edmund Burke, Helen-Maria Williams, and William Godwin and the German novelist E. T. A. Hoffmann. The sociopolitical criterion also made for hard choices: although some novels were prized by their earliest readers, they did not make the cut into this corpus if they left no trace on later generations. I thus left out an interesting little cluster of novels surrounding the July 1790 Festival of the Federation, despite their appeal for specialists.[8] The July 1790 Civil Constitution of the Clergy (which imposed allegiance to the nation over allegiance to the church) and other acts of dechristianization that changed the French cultural landscape in 1791–94 do not feature in any one chapter, yet they can arguably be felt throughout as part of the psychic turmoil. Scant attention is paid to revolutionary drama, songs, or poetry, apart from one important royalist anthem ("Ô Richard, ô mon roi") that puts a surprising spin on a familiar tale.

SIGNIFICANCE FOR READERS OF 1789–1803

The question of readership for fiction published during the 1790s is slippery because our expectations about reading practices do not necessarily jibe with period realities. First of all, the rates of literacy in revolutionary France varied from region to region. Although the national average in 1786–90 was 37 percent (as based on marriage signatures), there were tremendous regional variations. Historians typically speak of a "literacy line" running from Saint-Malo to Geneva to designate the separation between the highly literate north (where male rates attained 80 percent in 1786–90) and the rural areas of the southwest where male rates did not surpass 29 percent. There was also a discrepancy between male and female literacy. Although surveys have shown that female literacy grew from one-half of male literacy in the 1680s to more than half (26.8 vs. 47.4 percent) by 1786–89, such claims may be skewed by the small proportion of peasant populations that had marriage contracts and by the broad variety of skills designated by the term "literacy." Urban areas wield evidence of higher overall rates. In Paris during the reign of Louis XVI (1774–92), 66 percent of men and 62 percent of women could read; even in the working-class Faubourg Saint-Marcel, the literacy rate was approximately 68 percent. Toulouse and Marseille also enjoyed rates over 50 percent, and Lyons, a publishing center, had a rate of 60 percent. The practice of reading embraced people from all walks of life; as Emmet Kennedy reminds us, as early as 1700 Parisian domestic servants had a literacy rate of 85 percent.[9] This does not mean that they necessarily owned the religious books, almanacs, or fairy stories that were the publishers' stock-in-trade before the Revolution, however. Other practices, such as borrowing books (including across class lines, as between domestics and their mistresses), lending libraries (*cabinets de lecture*), and oral readings were popular and widespread ways of enjoying print culture that would not leave a trace in the inventory of a person's possessions after death. For my purposes, then, I define a "readership" as a group of people who availed themselves of their access to print culture broadly writ, whether by listening to a broadside, a newspaper article, or a story read aloud by a neighbor, political clubman, or priest or by buying and reading materials alone at home.

After King Louis XVI signed the order lifting censorship laws in July 1788 and did away with the traditional process by which publishers would have to receive a *privilège du roi* before selling a book, an astonishing number of new kinds of reading material suddenly became available. From 1788 to 1792, thousands of newspapers, posters, broadsides, and brochures went into print and represented all angles of the political spectrum from extreme-right-wing Bourbon loyalism to extreme-left-wing anticlerical and antiaristocratic egalitarianism. (The range of opinion constricted after the devastating events of June 1791 and August 1792 ousted the king from office and ushered in the Convention government in fall 1792. The press remained muffled until 1795, when moderate freedoms alternated with intermittent repressions until Napoleon's regime reinstituted a formal policy of censorship.) It appears that the rate of literacy went up at the same time as this initial rise in political publishing. That does not necessarily mean that people learned to read because of their desire to read these materials. But it does suggest that the stage was set for new kinds of social practices to take root, in which private citizens started mindfully using their skills—of reading, discussing, and intelligent debate—for civic or political purposes.[10] From now on, history would be made, in part at least, by the people. Gradually in

1788 and then with greater urgency in 1789–92, millions of people who had hitherto felt indifferent or helpless to change the course of events started contributing—largely by happenstance, neighborhood networks, or local organizations—to the making of modern France.

Now, disseminating reading materials to the "people" is a primary goal of political leaders during any upheaval, and in the early years of the Revolution this role was wielded with particular aplomb by Jacobin clubs. Unlike their later association with left-wing radicalism or even anarchy, the original club at its founding in 1789 was primarily defined by the well-to-do professional men, priests, and nobles who made up its membership and who were dedicated to creating a constitutional monarchy, whence the original name, the Société des amis de la Constitution. With an extensive and apparently efficient network in place by 1790, the Jacobin clubs made reading rooms available to their members and held weekly meetings that were punctuated by the reading of newspapers and bulletins from the mother club in Paris.[11] These practices may seem far divorced from novel reading, and it is true that literature of all sorts underwent a brusque fall from favor in 1789 concurrently with the spectacular growth in periodical sales.[12] Yet there remain intriguing hints that some people understood and sought to exploit fiction's potential for mass communication.[13]

Although largely unknown today, *La Boussole nationale* (The national compass) by a certain A. Pochet,[14] was well received by the press of 1790 and went into a second edition in 1791 with the title *Voyages et aventures d'un laboureur descendant du frère de lait d'Henri IV* (Travels and adventures of a laborer, descendant of the foster brother of Henri IV). The editors' instructions for its dissemination are tantalizing. The preface describes Paris mayor Jean-Sylvain Bailly's support for the book—deemed "the work of a good citizen"—and exhorts compatriots to stage public readings of it as soon as possible. Moreover, grandiose instructions aiming for wide distribution follow:

> Our only wish is for the village district leaders, country priests, army officers, and leaders of industry to imitate the citizens who have formed Friends of the Constitution societies in Besançon and Strasbourg by setting up Reading Societies and reading aloud there the adventures that befall the imprudent family of the descendant of our good king Henri's foster brother; may this story be for them the eye of the master, with which they will acquire the knowledge [*lumières*] that every good citizen needs.[15]

Even if this lengthy little book (over 950 pages in three volumes in octavos) was not read aloud as the editors requested, it was apparently promoted among the Jacobins and in the public at large. Four book reviews appeared in June–October 1791 in leading Parisian newspapers, where *La Boussole* was praised as a "very useful" book which offered not only a "faithful and lively tableau of the happy life in France" but also warned of the "evils found in foreign lands by those unwise enough to betray their country in guilty emigrations."[16]

The agricultural lessons of *La Boussole* may be banal borrowings from didactic publications such as the rural newspaper *La Feuille villageoise* (whose fifteen thousand subscribers made it one of the most influential newspapers of 1790), but this novel's characters and adventures reveal that even among the king's constitutional supporters he was not exempt from criticism. Most of the novel relates the travails of the Protestant peasant-hero Jaco as he travels through Holland, Russia, Poland, Germany, and England; wherever he goes, he is duped by swindlers, welcomed by fellow Freemasons, learns from them about new agricultural methods, and tries to locate lost relatives. His goal is to convince his cousins to return to France, where they are now welcome thanks to the king's lifting of restraints against non-Catholics, and to join him in building a model family farm. When Louis XVI is mentioned, his name is invariably coupled with the hero's great-great-grandfather's foster brother King Henri IV, and Louis's policies are compared with the religious tolerance and agrarian reforms of that illustrious forebear (as seen in fig. 1, where Henri plows a field among his adoring peasants).

That this book was well received in the press and among the Jacobins is a significant clue to one kind of novel that enjoyed favor in 1790–91: the uplifting, morally and technologically progressive peasant tale. Moreover, the instructions included in the preface suggest an unexpected reciprocity between literature and the activism of groups that would eventually wield a huge role in events, namely the Jacobins and, perhaps less visibly, the Freemasons. The cities where *La Boussole* is to be sent—in imitation of the good work being done in Besançon and Strasbourg—will by association join with what Daniel Ligou labels the "rationalist" lodges of the Freemasons, which were trying to distinguish themselves from their more mystical confederates by setting up academies to educate local folks.[17] Clearly, the Freemasons and Jacobins appeared to some Frenchmen as wielding the potential to assist the rural citizenry—perhaps more effectively than the nation could do for itself. This kind of bold politicking is not unusual in revolutionary fiction.

1. King Henri IV plowing a field with peasants. "Without a model, without the master's eye, no farm can prosper." (Sans l'exemple, sans l'œil
du maître, aucune ferme ne sauroit prospérer.) A. Pochet, *La Boussole
nationale* (1790), 1:36. Bibliothèque nationale de France, Paris.

Where the ideal reader of *La Boussole* is a literate peasant or progressive artisan, most of the novels in question target audiences with more urbane tastes in entertainment and employ more complex literary-political
rhetoric and forms to win them over. (The readership of this corpus may
well have lived outside France during at least part of the period in question.)

Witty satire—of political women and swaggering men—brings the humor
to chapter 1. Although today's reader may find the sexist mockery offensive, one cannot deny its bite. The complex form of an esoteric, learned,
and historical allegory organizes the automaton tale of chapter 2 into a parable with multiple meanings. *Le Cimetière de la Madeleine* (The Madeleine
Cemetery), analyzed in chapter 3, is a baggy hybrid of assorted fictional and
juridical genres, which explains Regnault-Warin's ability to confound readers with (fake) reality claims still today. But the messy conjuncture of memoirs, letters, state secrets, and "supporting evidence" in this book may not
be as accidental as it seems; on the contrary, the author may have counted
on the reader's impatience with his techniques to overlook the subtle digs
against both the Bourbons and the First Consul himself. Chapter 4 analyzes
the Terror through the genres of prison memoirs and crime narratives: two
forms that existed since time immemorial but that took on new function
and significance in 1793–94. While much of the shock value in these books
may be attributed to the readers' presumed sympathy for the condemned,
the candid republicanism expressed by the Bourbon princess in Madame
Guénard's novel *Irma* (Year 8; ca. 1799–1800) demonstrates that what earlier readers have taken for a royalist text actually cloaks a more pragmatic
message for the transitional moment of Year 8.

Several of the novels studied in *The Frankenstein of 1790* had real impact in their day as measured by book reviews, successive editions, translations, print runs, and advertisements.[18] The more ephemeral brochures
left scant traces among reviewers or in archives, but they are interesting
as pieces of a puzzle that was unfolding immediately after events under
the eyes of readers. Illustrations, whether simple woodcuts or elaborate engravings, added expense to bookmaking; their presence suggests that the
publisher expected good sales. The scenes chosen for illustration, the characters' body language and clothing styles, and the captions of the words
spoken provide additional clues to the publisher's and illustrator's ideas of
the book's appeal or message. Other insights into the material's value for
actuality can be read in the implicit or explicit dialogues that run between
fiction and the political caricatures that were circulating at the time and
whose history has been written by scholars such as Michel Vovelle, Antoine
DeBaecque, Claude Langlois, Rolf Reichardt, and Hubertus Kohle, to whom
I return in individual analyses. Police records can also shine some light
on reading practices of those bygone days. The ire provoked by the most
famous novel in question, *Le Cimetière de la Madeleine*, launched a campaign of police repression that lasted almost two years and targeted booksellers and printers located all over the country, from Orléans and Bordeaux

to Marseille and Avignon. Using these kinds of archival sources on fiction, its readers, and the spies, gendarmes, and commissioners who sought to put the brakes on such reading, *The Frankenstein of 1790* adds to the little-known history of censorship and repression from the Convention to the Consulate (1792–1804).

The most obvious significance of the literature I have chosen to highlight lies in the events, of course. With one exception—the 1790–91 decrees on invention that subtend the automaton tales of chapter 2—all the people, events, and dates featured here would have been immediately recognizable to contemporaries. Indeed, the October 1789 march on Versailles, the royal family's flight to Varennes, the execution of King Louis XVI, and the Reign of Terror form part of the French patrimony and remain familiar to French people in all walks of life. Given their notoriety and sensation value, these events are widely known outside France as well.

SIGNIFICANCE FOR READERS OF OUR TIME

Raymond Williams's adage that "a culture can never be reduced to its artifacts while it is being lived" is borne out in these texts, which present partial, if any, "truths" about history.[19] The adage nevertheless begs the question of timing: if not then, when? After the revolutionary fictions, the question of timing is raised and embraced with signature gusto by their successors discussed in the codas—Baum, Shelley, Balzac, Dickens, and Flaubert. "Now is the time!" all five authors seem to say, in works published from 1818 to 1910. Nevertheless, the central issues organizing the chapters of *The Frankenstein of 1790* continue to plague modern democracies still today. Akin to the work of Margaret Somers, my study can be seen to contribute to the historical sociology of concept formation. Like Somers's book on citizenship, this book is designed as an empirical exploration of the networks within which concepts—such as innovation, justice, or pity—are framed and constrained; I too accept that "social processes are intelligible only in the context of their cultural mediation."[20]

But where Somers argues that one must seek to understand the meaning of books or events as relating to a synchronic social system with internal rules, in the codas I show how writers reworked earlier concepts to create new objects on the fly, after the fact, and outside original contexts. They forged new meanings for old concepts. This missing-link principle works both ways: many of the themes and literary devices used by the authors of the 1790s hearken back to the Enlightenment or even the Renaissance, as in the world-upside-down of gender relations studied in chapter 1. Chapter 2 reveals the importance of mechanical philosophies of cognition and sympathy not only in political writings of 1790 but also in the popular automaton shows and "mechanical theaters" of Paris and London from the 1730s to the 1800s and in Shelley's third edition of *Frankenstein* (1831). Similarly, the discussion of Robespierre-the-criminal in chapter 4 sketches out an evolution in medical thinking from mechanistic principles to the more "scientific" focus on physiognomy that marked the early nineteenth century. Such analysis touches not only on philosophical concepts but also on formal principles of literary technique. The symbolic stories of the king and the Terror take on unexpected meanings when conveyed through understated irony, as in Flaubert's *Dictionnaire des idées reçues* (Dictionary of received ideas), or through an elaborate fictional realism that is superposed on a banal human-interest story, as in Balzac's *Père Goriot*.

The main concepts that are worked and reworked in this book are gender, technology, representation, and justice. Chapter 1 takes on the role of women as political players and shows how ridicule and satire were astutely wielded by critics to make individual leaders and followers and any women who dreamed of active citizenry in 1789–94 feel abashed by their aspirations. Technological advances provide food for thought in chapter 2, where characters debate the suitable ways to use invention and ask at what point research and development should pull back, lest progress turn into a monstrous force. This chapter also presents my most spectacular discovery in the person of an inventor named Frankénstein who built a life-size automaton twenty-eight years before Shelley published her Gothic thriller. Representative government—its nature, limits, and demands on citizens—frames the stories of King Louis XVI in chapter 3. Finally, chapter 4 takes on the enormous issue of making a new judiciary and asks how it is possible for the state to ensure justice for all. While clear (and ideologically charged) answers to that question abounded during the heyday of the Revolutionary Tribunal, 1793–94 was not a period when literature flourished. The initial focus of chapter 4 is on newspaper reading, then, until the period post-Thermidor. After the execution of the "Incorruptible" and his confederates, some literary texts were published—including biographies of Robespierre— that reveal intriguing traces of how the Terror was lived, remembered, and rehashed by those closest to events. The narratives beg the main issue of causality or blame the evil on Robespierre, but they did provide some catharsis for a citizenry that had witnessed the country's astonishingly cruel judiciary turn against its own people. The codas reveal how these dilemmas later produced awful, droll, and hilarious stories under the pen of great writers who retooled their plots for audiences distant in time and space.

This book thus commemorates the efforts of ordinary citizens who tried to wrench their country out of an exploitative system in the name of more equitable principles for the future. The ideal of civic equality was and still is an arduous business, however. Mistakes were made then and still are made, horrible mistakes that wield catastrophic consequences for innocent citizens. But if there is one thing that I hope the reader will take away from this book, it is that the experiment was worth it, and that the tales are worth retelling, because one day we may get it right.

I have undertaken this project as a literary historian, not as a critic per se. Literary criticism, as I understand it, is a form of communication that chiefly concerns living, working writers and their readers. Whether their work is televised, printed in magazines, newspapers, and trade journals, or transmitted through blogs and electronic list-serves, book critics serve their audiences by bringing relevant titles to light just as film critics or art critics do for their clienteles. They are useful for writers seeking to improve, respond to, or enjoy their readers' views, as well as for future scholars seeking to locate a text's meaning for its first audiences. I have borrowed from scores of critical writings to piece together the reception histories presented here before delving into interpretation. As Pascale Casanova has aptly noted: "Writing the history of literature is a paradoxical activity that consists in placing it in historical time and then showing how literature gradually tears itself away from this temporality, creating in turn its own temporality, one that has gone unperceived until the present day."[21] The codas are designed to show how that sinuous process of meaning making took place, repeatedly and over time, thanks to the creative energies of authors who hailed from places far from revolutionary France. In the conclusion I bring this reflection full circle with a glance at current traces of revolutionary culture in film, advertising, and styles of the present.

But the last word on the French Revolution remains out because each generation has to find its own meaning in events. Whether one reads for pleasure, intellectual curiosity, or advanced learning, all students of revolutionary literature share a common goal: we decipher texts written to entertain, instruct, and/or provoke a public that died years ago and whose preoccupations were very different from our own. Through historically contextualized interpretation and careful study of a work's reception, we sometimes have the good fortune to stumble upon traces of phenomena that underline the *strangeness* of revolutionary France. In the unexpected alignment of characters unearthed in this book—the Amazons, fishmongers, and suffragists of chapter 1; the automatons and statesmen of chapter 2; the kings proud and pitiful of Chapter 3; and the uncertain "terrorists" and reluctant republicans of chapter 4—I hope that strangeness will feel potent and poignant for readers again today. Some efforts have been made to follow French traces into the New World and especially into France's favorite colony, Saint-Domingue, whose devastating insurrections of 1791–1804 and eventual liberation as Haiti were deeply invested with symbolic significance borrowed from the French example. But that nexus of influences also awaits further study. If the corpus of revolutionary materials unearthed in *The Frankenstein of 1790* cannot yet aspire to global geopolitical scrutiny, given the dearth of primary research and aesthetic evaluation of their place in world canons, they are nonetheless worthy of our attention. As Napoleon Bonaparte once remarked, "Thus, the truth of history, on this point as among others, will probably lie, not in what happened, but only in what continues to be told."[22] *The Frankenstein of 1790* aims to retell some of the greatest stories ever lived and in so doing to renew readers' appreciation for how the cataclysmic events of the 1790s changed the world—for the better.

CHAPTER ONE

From Fish Seller to Suffragist: The Women's March on Versailles

According to the classic historiography of George Rudé, Albert Mathiez, and Munro Price, the march on Versailles that took place on October 5–6, 1789, evolved out of discontent over the shortage of food in working-class neighborhoods in Paris.[1] Such discontent was not a new occurrence; a subsistence riot focusing on bread prices had erupted to spectacular effect in what is now known as the flour war of 1775, and fourteen women were among those arrested.[2] Frustration about the scarcity of flour and the high price of bread had been simmering for weeks in autumn 1789; what finally decided the so-called patriots to act were rumors of the king's imminent departure for (or kidnapping to) the eastern city of Metz, which were inflamed by the display of royalist arrogance at a military banquet at Versailles on October 2. Reports circulated that soldiers of the elite Flanders Regiment, summoned by Louis XVI to cope with disorders in Paris, had enjoyed a lavish evening at court and capped the festivities by trampling the national cockade underfoot while singing a loyalist anthem ("Ô Richard, ô mon roi") and swearing allegiance to His Majesty. The incident splashed across the leading left-wing newspapers; calls for vengeance immediately followed.

It appears that on the morning of October 4 a large group of women gathered at the Palais Royal. Most of them were not poor wretches but rather merchants: *poissardes* (fish sellers) from the central market of Les Halles, working women of the faubourgs, smartly dressed bourgeois, and wealthy *femmes à chapeau* (bonnet-wearing ladies). They accused the queen of being the source of their problems and cheered, "Tomorrow things will go better, because we'll be in charge!"[3] On the morning of the fifth, a mob formed together as planned; witnesses say that the crowd swelled to six or seven thousand people and converged first on the Hôtel de Ville looking for hidden stores of flour, arms, and ammunition. The few soldiers guarding the

building quickly opened ranks and the women invaded, seizing muskets
and bags of money. They carried whatever weapons they could find and
belittled the men who refused to join, calling them cowards and bad citizens. Despite the rain, they set out for Versailles in the early afternoon and
chanted as they marched: "Allons chercher le boulanger, la boulangère, et
le petit mitron!" (Let's go fetch the baker, the baker's wife, and the little
bakerboy!). It was supposed that the king, by his presence among his subjects, would ensure a plentiful supply of bread. After making the six-hour
trek in a drenching rain, they found the gates of the palace closed. So they
took refuge in the National Assembly hall alongside the startled deputies,
who listened to their concerns before adjourning for the night. Many set up
makeshift beds and slept on the soggy ground. During the night General Lafayette learned of the uprising and brought a contingent of twenty thousand
National Guards to Versailles. The next morning a group somehow found
an opening in the gate, invaded the chateau, and ran through the corridors,
going so far as to ransack the queen's bedchamber while Marie-Antoinette
narrowly escaped through a secret passage. Two palace guards were killed
and their heads impaled on pikes. Some claim that hooligans vandalized
the palace and terrorized the royal family with shouts of "Death to the
Austrian." Others allege that the crowd was inflamed after seeing one of
their own being killed, another woman wounded, and a third trampled by
the horses of the Swiss guards. The crowd was eventually calmed by the appearance of Louis XVI on a balcony, followed by Marie-Antoinette and Lafayette. The king vowed to uphold the revolutionary decrees, including the
Declaration of the Rights of Man and of the Citizen, and faced with a crowd
shouting, "The king to Paris!" he submitted to popular demand.

The marchers thus forced the royal family to move permanently to Paris
on the afternoon of October 6. Louis and his intimates rode in a carriage surrounded by market women and National Guards and entered the capital in
early evening before setting up housekeeping in the Tuileries palace. From
November 1789, the site of state power would reside in the capital, with
the monarchy and the assembly side by side on the right bank of the Seine.[4]
More significantly, the king would effectively spend the rest of his days
under house arrest, under the watchful eye of the National Assembly, the
Paris city government, and *le menu peuple* (commoners) who so vigilantly
brought him back to town.

This event has posed a lasting enigma to historians of the French Revolution because the evidence points to wildly different conclusions. Three interpretations dominate present-day historiography: it was either (1) a spontaneous march of thousands of women who, denied formal rights as active

citizens, seized power nonetheless as de facto citizens,[5] (2) a march of common people exercising direct democracy,[6] or (3) a calculated and planned assault on the royal family by organized agents of conspiracy who used fish sellers and prostitutes as cover.[7] Literature reflects historiography to some extent, but the most striking imagery and the most riveting plots focus on the first, a predominantly female tale of political action.

The march on Versailles was arguably the first moment when the nation realized the potency of its own people to rewrite the time-honored structure of the French state. By physically confronting the king in Versailles and forcefully displacing the site of authority from royal court to capital and from monarchy to National Assembly and, by extension, to the people through their elected representatives, the participants in the October Days drove a stake through the heart of the Bourbon legacy. French politics and government would never be the same. The consequences unleashed by this event constitute an example of what anthropologist Ernest Becker labeled in 1975 the *causa sui* project, that is, an oedipal attempt to displace the father in order to invent a new genesis and identity for the self. As Becker writes, this impulse "sums up the basic problem of the child's life: whether he will be a passive object of fate, an appendage of others, a plaything of the world or whether he will be an active center within himself—whether he will control his own destiny with his own powers or not. . . . it is the flight from passivity, from obliteration, from contingency: the child wants to conquer death by becoming the *father of himself*."[8] The eschatological undercurrent was noted by earlier commentators too. Alexis de Tocqueville (1856) remarked, "No nation had ever embarked on so resolute an attempt as that of the French in 1789 to break with the past, to make, as it were, a scission in their life line and to create an unbridgeable gulf between all they had hitherto been and all they now aspired to be."[9] Whether couched in psychoanalytic terms of father-child conflict or epic terms of human struggle, one can easily see why commentators interpreted the events of October 1789 as representing a break—if only symbolic—with the existing order.

But the question of intention remains. While some claim that the Versailles marchers sought to usurp the authority of the king-father and even to kill the queen, most interpret the women's actions as a request for succor, seeking a renewal of traditional bonds and sustenance. My evidence supports this second interpretation but reveals how the women's plea was over time, by recurrent representation in the media, made into an icon of radicalism. As the homely fish merchant was increasingly conflated with an armed and dangerous Amazon, she appeared to be out of place, out of line. Criticism of this kind of woman is tucked inside weighty tomes such as Burke's hugely influential *Reflections on the Revolution in France* (appearing in 1790 in both English and French), where it doubled as a diatribe against the rabble, and the pseudodocumentary travelogue *Le Château des Tuileries* (1802), where a witty Frenchman and his urbane English friend record little-known anecdotes of Parisian life during the Revolution with a particularly snide rendition of the Versailles march and its leader. By interpreting this moment in revolutionary history as an attempt to pervert natural relations and then pushing the wayward back into the fold, writers kept the *causa sui* impulse at bay. Later women's actions for political rights fell into a similar trap—their reasoned petitions were recast as wild-eyed militancy—and the weapons of ridicule and burlesque were used against them too.

The marchers did have partisans. Some major newspapers of 1789 embraced the women's cause and inscribed the marchers in a dignified lineage reaching back to Joan of Arc. Mary Wollstonecraft strongly advocated for the marchers and held them up as exactly the kind of women who deserved better education and enfranchisement. In a more humorous vein, one of my most intriguing findings is a mock-heroic novel called *Melchior ardent* (ca. 1800), where the women warriors and their would-be royal victim are all ridiculed in gendered clichés. The hero staunches the revolt of so-called Féminensiennes with an army of monkey-men and eventually succeeds in remasculinizing the land. Yet he is ultimately hoisted on his own petard when his whole life is explained as an attempt to overcompensate for castration anxieties. Whether *Melchior*'s author was an early and little-known woman satirist or a man pretending to write as a woman remains up in the air. *Melchior ardent* is a fun read, and its retelling of the October Days as the battle of wimpy Amazons versus strutting monkey-men is surely one of the most preposterous renditions that exist.

In an effort to track the retelling of this story in the years that followed, the coda at the end of this chapter notes how French women during the uprisings of the nineteenth century were inspired by their predecessors in 1789, 1830, and 1848 to plead for women's emancipation in a number of protests. Unfortunately, these women also saw themselves caricatured: as coquettish young warriors, or Vésuviennes, during the Revolution of 1848 or, worse, as the mythical viragoes known as Pétroleuses who allegedly set the fires that destroyed some of the most famous buildings in Paris during the 1871 Commune.[10] Narrating even a brief account of the long and painful battle for women's enfranchisement in France would take us beyond the bounds of this study because the conflicting interests of republicanism, Catholicism, and workers' rights thwarted the cause of female suffrage well into the twentieth century. The French were inspired by their sisters-in-battle across the Atlantic, however, and the correspondence between some French and American suffragists has revealed warm sympathies and relationships during the formative years 1848–1900. So we end on a light-hearted note that is consonant with the somewhat-cartoonish nature of this material by a look at the suffrage writings of American novelist L. Frank Baum (1856–1919).

Beloved by children for the fantastic creatures he brought to life in *The Wonderful Wizard of Oz* (1900), Baum was also and first a newspaperman who created an equally endearing character, especially to suffragists, in the plainspoken columnist he called Our Landlady (1890–91). If Our Landlady, as I contend, represents a latter-day *poissarde*, her alter-ego Amazon would surely be General Jinjur, leader of the Army of Revolt in *The Marvelous Land of Oz* (1904). Under Baum's kindly pen both figures do some good cultural work: Our Landlady makes the men listen and General Jinjur makes them work, if only for a while. Taken together they articulate a transitional moment when women's reason was finally gaining ground against the vain froth of misogyny and ridicule.

THE ANXIETY OF AMBIVALENCE: THE JOURNALISM OF OCTOBER 1789

The first reports of the march in the Parisian press reveal the ambivalence that the specter of armed female activism would evoke for generations to come. Sympathetic communion dominates Louis-Marie Prudhomme's account in the leading newspaper of the Left, *Les Révolutions de Paris* (week of October 3–10): the "women of the people" are said to ensure the "salvation of the fatherland" with their enthusiastic recruitment of marchers on the way to Versailles, and the ultimate success of this crowd of four thousand is chalked up to the efforts of *nos brave amazones, ces braves françoises,* and *ces femmes courageuses.* More apprehension marks the rival *Chronique de Paris,* where we read of a "great multitude of armed women" running through the streets and the ruckus they caused in forcing other women to follow them and in shouting out furious slogans. The editor does not deny the event's historical impact and results, however, and notes in the edition of October 7: "It was a truly new sight [*spectacle*] to see the numerous troops of women, soldiers, and armed citizens going by without end, carrying ribbons, tree branches, and loaves of bread on their bayonets." By the third day, the threat dissipates into light-hearted merriment, as the article of October 8 notes: "the lighted windows, the cries of joy . . . the ribald and warlike songs, everything lent a particular feeling to the festival." The article concludes that "this second revolutionary flare-up [*accès de révolution*] will doubtless accelerate the work of the National Assembly [and] animate the generous minority, which now knows it is supported by the people's will [*toute la force populaire*]."[11]

Shortly thereafter both papers made the women's attempt on the royalty explicit by printing transcripts of what the women marchers said to the king at Versailles or what their representative would have said to the queen given the chance. The comments range in tone from deferential to slightly threatening. In the *Chronique* one finds a paragraph-long paean to a beloved king-father, whom the women humbly request to witness the misery of their poverty-stricken neighborhood. In the rival *Révolutions*, one reads a more sharply worded critique by "an ardent citizen" who reviews France's many bad queens of the past and demands that Marie-Antoinette publicly avow her patriotism—a rhetorical tactic that Olympe de Gouges would take up in her 1791 *Déclaration des droits de la femme et de la citoyenne*.[12] This dual role of the female politico runs through all Versailles literature: the first, of the poor market woman seeking food for her babes, was a traditional ploy of both propagandists and female protesters, notably wielded by authors of the Mazarinades of 1648–54.[13] The second, however, proved more perplexing: the fiery, lowbrow orator stating the serious concerns of a female crowd was a voice that was rarely, if ever, heard in French political history.

Apprehension toward female aggression was perhaps unsurprising, given the widespread imagery which hit the streets of women riding astride cannons: hardly an "innocent" pose (fig. 2).[14] The sight was not necessarily condemned: in 1793 it became an official part of Jacobin lore at the Festival of Unity thanks to its semblance of Greco-Roman heroism. But in the circumstances of 1789, it also reminded people of those controversial public figures who seemed to be usurping male prerogative, that is, the so-called *femmes-hommes* (female men) such as Olympe de Gouges and Marie-Jeanne Roland (to whom we return in chapter 4) and the prolific novelist and governess to the Orléans family Stéphanie-Félicité de Genlis, whose opportunism and moralistic persona were mocked in a 1790 tract calling her "Mme Brulard, formerly de Sillery, formerly de Genlis, formerly agreeable."[15] This group was clearly less palatable to popular taste than suffering maternity. Most infamous was the striking Théroigne de Méricourt, whose legend as a rabble-rousing courtesan would persist well into the nineteenth century thanks to Thomas Carlyle's wrathful pen. Based on his own historico-sexual phantasms more than any actual referent, Carlyle's portrait of Méricourt captures multiple commonplaces of the Amazon motif: "The seized cannon are

Le Retour triomphant des Heroïnes Francaises de Versailles a Paris le 6 Octobre 1789.

2. *The Triumphal Return of the French Heroines from Versailles on October 6, 1789* (*Le Retour triomphant des heroïnes françaises de Versailles à Paris le 6 octobre 1789*). Engraving, eighteenth century. Bibliothèque nationale de France, Paris.

yoked with seized cart-horses: brown-locked Demoiselle Théroigne, with pipe and helmet, sits there as gunneress, 'with haughty eye and serene fair countenance'; comparable, some think, to the *Maid* of Orléans, or even recalling 'the idea of Pallas Athene.'"[16] It is hard to imagine that Baum did not have this in mind when sketching his portrait of the raven-haired General Jinjur and her Army of Revolt. Both women are haughty, emasculating, and due for a comeuppance.

This less-sympathetic Amazonian motif conflated the *poissarde* with radically revolutionary verve: a linkage that was exploited in newspapers as varied as the lowbrow *Mère Duchesne* and the archroyalist *Actes des apôtres*. Like its supposed pendant *Le Père Duchesne, La Mère Duchesne* is liberally peppered with feisty rhetoric; its sansculotte heroine Pétronille Machefer (Petronilla Chomp-Bit) declares in signature bravado: "I offer my services to the nation as a warrior . . . at the first roll of the drum, I will take up arms, raise a squadron of Amazons, and lead the way . . . cutting a swath through our enemies like a knife slicing through butter."[17] The universal alliance of women touted in *La Mère Duchesne* was largely fictitious, however, and did not embrace elite society. Madame de Genlis and Madame de Staël circulated in an orbit far removed from Les Halles; as for working women, some eventually joined political clubs in the years 1790–93, but the merchants of Les Halles likely identified more with family, neighborhood, and guild than with the kind of protofeminist solidarity seen here. Of the four *femmes-hommes* targeted in counterrevolutionary libels, Théroigne de Méricourt had the shadiest past and was reportedly most implicated in the October Days.[18] *Les Actes des apôtres* fed such fears by publishing an elaborate engraving that represented her as the conductor of a motley orchestra at the "Revolution Club" (*L'Ouverture du Club de la Révolution*) (fig. 3). Hereafter Théroigne de Méricourt would be canonized as the chief among radical women, to be found wherever unrest was greatest.

This image and the commentary that accompanied it in *Actes* merge a number of motifs running through counterrevolutionary caricature of 1789–92. Although the opinions published here are not representative of any majority, the newspaper yields unique insights because the interpretations accompanying its engravings are miniature masterpieces in themselves. Moreover, the sequential way in which the different parts of *Actes* were sold testifies to the publishers' confidence that readers would appreciate the running dialogue between text and image. As Claude Langlois explains,

> When a quarter's issues were nearly published, the reader was asked to hold off binding the copies into a single volume until he had received an engraving to place at the beginning of the book as a frontispiece. . . . In order to assist the unskilled reader in deciphering the image and to help him to detect all the malicious allusions—as well as for the pure pleasure of fabricating stories based upon the engraving—the newspaper furnished, along with the frontispiece, an explanation that could run over ten pages in length. In this text, the author, caught up in the game, allowed his imagination to wander freely on the bases for the visual fiction, and, so to speak, to redouble its image with his verbal delirium.[19]

The authors and artists behind *Actes* seem to have taken particularly malicious pleasure in inventing tropes of gendered confusion.

Cast as a final scene from a Rabelaisian farce, Méricourt and her revolutionary club feature prominently in the frontispiece and eight-page exegesis published in volume 2 (November 10, 1789).[20] The characters' bizarre appearances signify their distasteful essence. Beginning with Méricourt's androgynous outfit—a scarlet riding habit, or *amazone*—which stands in for the doubtful respectability of the Versailles warriors, a list of outrageous costumes ensues. As they parade across a stage, one deputy is dressed in drag, another hides behind a shark mask, and a third wears a false leg: these disguises symbolize their will to fool the people. Other unnatural ele-

3. *Opening of the Revolution Club* (*L'Ouverture du Club de la Révolution*). *Actes des apôtres* 2 (November 10, 1789): frontispiece. Reproduced from the original held by the Department of Special Collections of the Hesburgh Libraries of the University of Notre Dame.

ments that crowd the stage include female politicos, cavorting monkeys, and a courtier dancing a minuet with a leopard. Overhead, two uneasy tight-rope walkers—including the chubby Deputy Target dressed in a sailor suit and the radical Abbé Sieyès—balance an upside-down obelisk representing the still-unfinished constitution, which seems ready to topple over, and a note directs the reader to another issue of *Actes*, which details its fall. The commentary adopts a mock learned air: an opening line from Horace's satires admonishes spectators to stick to the golden mean, while the travesty clearly flouts any such wisdom. Two other Latin citations, from the *Aeneid*, liken Méricourt to Aeneas's enemy Queen Camilla: she too orchestrated female warriors into a formidable foe.[21] The Revolution becomes a grotesquerie, presaging what Friedrich Schlegel would call "a terrible chaos, a bizarre mixture, a colossal tragicomedy of all mankind."[22] Although it seems a jump from caricature to political history, this combination of motifs—drawing upon Rabelaisian farce, grotesque combinations, and mock-heroic satire—dominates narratives of the Versailles march in serious literature as well.

Such vitriol was not an exclusive prerogative of the Right. The fishwife was already a stock figure in the propaganda brought against Anne of Austria's reign (the Mazarinades of the civil war known as La Fronde, 1648–53), and in the eighteenth century she became a commonplace distinguished by her ethnographic realism and vivid, grammatically incorrect speech.[23] Her malapropisms are often hilarious, as Catriona Seth has pointed out in commentary on *Grande Motion des citoyennes de divers marchés* (1792?), where the clueless merchants pronounce *aristocrat* as *istocrate* and *convention* as *contravention* and slur their speech so that even insults sound funny (*Que sacrenom pas de Dieu!*).[24] The characteristic rhetoric of *poissard* literature is the *engueulade*, or dressing-down, a rough form of teasing that connotes both affection and malice. The butt of the insults could be a political figure, a henpecked husband, an aristocrat, or a snobbish colleague in the marketplace, but the fishwife—invariably cast with a colorful name such as Madame Salmon or Madame Scold (Madame Engueule)—wins out in the end and convinces listeners of a critical lesson.

What kind of lesson? It may surprise readers that the first issues of the periodical featuring the most famous cousin of the *poissardes*, Jacques Hébert's newspaper entitled *Lettres bougrement patriotiques du véritable Père Duchêne* (September 1790), supported a constitutional monarchy, not the anarchy for which it would later be renowned. Père Duchesne (or Duchêne) shocked people with his vulgar language and rough manners, but in this early version he was still a good Catholic and loyal subject who regularly went to Mass.[25] It was only in spring and especially summer 1791 that *Père Duchêne* adopted an uncompromising Jacobin stance. On the other hand, some writers who originally sided with the women of 1789 later changed their tune. Prudhomme's *Révolutions de Paris* in 1791 denounced women's aspiration to revolutionary heroism and declared outright that "civil and political liberty is, so to speak, useless for women and in consequence ought to be foreign to them." He also issued a scornful critique of Condorcet's support for women's rights and condemned the activities of women's political clubs as a "plague to the mothers of good families" and as enemies of "good housekeeping." Reversing his earlier sympathy for what he called *nos braves amazones*, he chastised Louise de Kéralio, editor of a rival publication, as a poorly informed *amazone politique*.[26]

POISSARD AND AMAZONIAN PAMPHLETRY

Pamphletry in the *poissard* vein resists easy classification. If Louis XVI must go, as one post-Varennes pamphlet suggested in 1791, the fishwives would gladly see the scepter transferred to his brother the comte de Provence; the essential thing was to keep the monarchy afloat.[27] Jacobin rule was held up to rude scrutiny by two fishwives in *V'la c'qui s'est dit* (That's what they say; ca. 1791–92), but their primary complaint was against the state's prohibition against presenting bouquets to the king and queen on their saint's day. One of the most widely cited *poissard* pamphlets, *Le Falot du peuple* (The people's lantern; ca. 1792–93), stages a shadow trial for the king wherein a fishmonger (Tender Ma) and a public writer (Father Style) counter the allegations against the king made by the antagonistic Madame Salmon and in so doing present an alternative history of events such as the Versailles march, the 1790 massacre at Nancy, and the flight to Varennes. A maliciously virulent strain exists as well, as, for example, in the *Grande Motion des citoyennes de divers marchés*, where the queen is called a damned Austrian monkey (*sacrée guenon d'Autriche*) and accused of misdeeds great and small, including extortion, distributing rotten food to the poor, and abetting the Flanders guards. After hearing the truth on these and other crimes, the highbrow Mamzelle Javotte agrees with the fish sellers that Marie-Antoinette must die and seeks their pardon by joining them for a drink. The *poissarde* character created the impression of truth-telling and allowed propagandists of various political persuasions to claim to represent the masses, as pigheaded and reactionary as they might be. Such texts regale readers with multiple voices involved in rough-and-tumble, often vulgar-worded quarrels, but it is invariably the lowly *poissarde*, not her Jacobin or aristocratic interlocutor, who gets the last word. Her target is primarily the scurrilous deputy or plotting courtier . . . although it is sometimes the royalty itself.

Like the *poissarde*, the Amazon carried an ambiguous charge in revolutionary parlance: meanings divide unevenly along gendered and partisan lines and change over time. Left-wing women activists used the term to celebrate extraordinary achievement, whereas under the pen of a conservative it could be an insult connoting libertinism, excessive ambition, or violence. Joan Landes has documented this ambiguity in the weeks following the October Days by discussing imagery of the triumphal women's army returning to Paris, as in figure 2. In the images discussed by Landes, the patriotic goodness of the marchers is symbolized by the poplar branches and loaves of bread they carry, and their respect is seen in their conciliatory attitude toward the guardsmen riding along with them on the return to Paris. As well-dressed matrons, they bear little resemblance to the bare-breasted warriors of ancient lore. But the splayed legs of the cannon-riding woman center stage in figure 2 point out the "strong sexual and martial appetites underscoring their Amazonian nature," notes Landes.[28] Opposition to this kind of politicized Amazonia is found in the 1790 *Anecdote*

historique traduite du turc (Historical anecdote translated from the Turk-
ish), which concludes with a sour forecast of social leveling. As the narrator
acidly comments after attending a meeting of the National Assembly that
was crowded with women spectators:

> Women used to be merely amiable, and their duty was only to please.
> They have abandoned that little genre, and now they know how to make
> noise, to agitate, and pass motions in politics, finance, and legislation.
> But they are particularly brilliant at leading revolutions; they shy away
> from nothing when it is a question of vigor, blood, and executions. . . .
> We have eliminated all distinctions [of rank]; we need only eliminate
> the difference between the sexes.[29]

Such anxieties of permeability found a convenient outlet in tales of long-
suffering male victims. Typical of that vein is *Le Roi trompé et détrompé*
(The king abused and disabused; 1790), which resolves problems by staging
an auto-da-fé of a female courtier and declaring a nationwide ban on women
in politics.

For its startlingly prescient conceit of a headless king, no pamphlet can
rival *L'Histoire véritable de Gingigolo, roi du Mano-Emugi* (True history of
Gingigolo, king of Mano-Emugi; ca. 1789). Thinly veiled in Oriental names,
this brochure recounts the misfortunes of a kindly yet naive king at the
hands of his sly courtiers and lewd wife. Foremost among his enemies is the
wily prime minister from the land of Dadas (a stand-in for the influential
Genevan finance minister Jacques Necker), who owns a magical genie that
in response to religious incantations (Necker being a Protestant) changes
the king's head at will. The first scene shows Le Dadas being frustrated by
the people's resistance to his fiscal reforms and demanding that Gingigolo
be transformed into a "popular prince." Having eaten a big meal, the king
conveniently falls into a deep sleep, during which the genie slices off his
head and puts a sheep's head in its place. Upon awakening the next morning, the queen is surprised at the change but merely takes him for their
general (in a jibe at the queen's reported dalliances with Lafayette).[30] Gingigolo himself simply laments the metamorphosis and submits to Le Dadas,
who, in imitation of Machiavelli, gives the king a manual of "popular conduct" to follow.

The October Days are explained here as a result of kingly cowardice
and ministerial treason. After reducing the monarch to a dopey ruminant,
Le Dadas incites his lowbrow partisans (*la canaille*) to capture the palace
and prepare his rise to power. Swarming through the grounds, the howl-

ing masses do not even let the king finish his speech of surrender before they break down the palace doors, disembowel his guards, and carry the monarch off to prison. Depicting the king's naivety in bitter irony, the text depicts Louis offering to do whatever his "good friends" might like, before the mob drags him and his family back to Paris "in the friendliest manner" (très-amicalement).[31] Le Dadas calls for a ball, where the king dances with the fishwives, but their camaraderie does not last long. When the king later ventures into the streets, people heap reproach upon him for his fiscal ineptitude, culminating in the ultimate insult during a visit to a workshop: a worker dumps a chamber pot on his head. Through it all, the sheep head placidly maintains his love for the people. The next transformation replaces the sheep with five new heads quarreling constantly among themselves, in a satirical dig at Necker's proposed Bureau général des dépenses de la maison du roi and its five constitutive members, who were supposed to put an end to infighting among the king's ministers.[32] Then King Gingigolo loses his head entirely, before a deus ex machina saves the day. Reconstructed as a truly regal character, the monarch ultimately sentences his would-be rival to public humiliation and regains the love of his people.

THE *POISSARDE*'S CULTURAL HERITAGE

L'Histoire véritable de Gingigolo, roi du Mano-Emugi shocks by its recurrent image of a headless king. But what interests us most is the scene with the fishwives, because it leads to different conclusions than those made by Carla Hesse in her work in the field. Hesse's chapter on the *poissarde* in *The Other Enlightenment* (2001) reproduces a period engraving entitled *La Folie des hommes* (The folly of men) to underline the radical political connotations in both the *poissard* genre and the world-upside-down motif. Scant exegesis follows, apart from the legend, which reads: "The wife carries the rifle / The husband holds the child on his lap. The Hunter hunts on sea and fish fly in the air."[33] But the attentive viewer sees an image impervious to partisan analysis. Its flat perspective, simple line drawings, and misspellings recall the illustrations found in the chapbooks and fairy tales sold by peddlers and inscribe it in a folksy tradition that would be aped by the faux-populist *Mère Duchesne* newspaper. The parallel represented here is between domestic disorder, symbolized by a pipe-smoking, rifle-toting wife and her emasculated husband (who spins wool and cares for their infant), and an unnatural outdoors where hunters chase fish in the air and livestock in the sea. Hesse claims that images like this one constitute a "rhetorical form of popular legitimacy." But one can also read it as a cautionary tale against presumably female demands for change. The madness would be to wish for either unnatural state in the picture, for both are preposterous: fish do not fly and women are not on top. Just as Natalie Davis warned in her 1975 study of the Renaissance charivari, and Lisa Tickner has noted since in art such as "Is Your Wife a Suffragette?" (a postcard from ca. 1908 showing an overwrought husband struggling with laundry), one cannot attribute to images of inversion any clear-cut sociological intent. Davis comments that "they afforded an expression of, and an outlet for, conflicts about authority within the system; and they also provided occasions by which an authoritarian current in family, workshop, and political life could be moderated by the laughter of disorder and paradoxical play." Tickner adds that "the humor in role reversals is at the expense of both parties. If there was nothing wickeder than a woman deserting her family, there was little funnier than a husband attempting to cope."[34] They may visualize contestation, as Hesse argues, but they also reinforced the reigning order of things.

Hesse is correct in asserting that some artifacts in the *poissard* style did challenge social boundaries. A brochure entitled *Les Jupons de Madame Angot* (Madame Angot's skirts) was sold by the same hawkers who marketed the radicalized *Père Duchesne* and left-wing Jacobin prints during the Terror.[35] Consider as well the exchange between Fanchon and Monsieur Supreme Good Taste, protagonists in one of Vadé's most popular pieces of *Poissardiana*. Irritated by his impolite stare, the pretty fish seller uses her wit to ridicule the foppish manners of her noble client, who mutters banalities in return. With colorful invective and approximate grammar, she conquers him through speech and teaches the aristocrat to treat merchants such as herself with more respect.[36] The comic persona of the fishwife was based on a real-life model of fluid political relations between the aristocracy and the common folk that changed over time.

Since the reign of Louis XV, market women had traveled twice a year to meet with the king at Versailles, and they also appeared on special occasions such as royal marriages or births. But the nature of their politics— or even the existence of a dominant political consciousness among these people—remains unclear. As Pierre Ronzeaud has noted, the foul-mouthed *harangère*, or herring-monger, was already a well-known figure in the Mazarinades of the 1650s where she was cloaked in a cartoonish vulgarity that proved remarkably consistent. A similar ventriloquism runs through revolutionary-age pamphletry; we do not have much access to the women's own words or reliable portraits of their mores. (Rétif's chapter "La Nuit des Halles" in *Les Nuits de Paris*, ca. 1767–88, which describes a *monstre femelle* forcing eau-de-vie on a beautiful young virgin, typifies market portraiture.) True, the market women's absence from festivities on the eve of the Assumption in 1787, when they had been expected to present flowers and compliments to Queen Marie-Antoinette, provoked anxiety at court. A police injunction two days later forced them to comply. True, a number of market women expressed their displeasure with King Louis XVI in early 1789 by participating in a performance of the *Souper de Henri IV* (Henri IV's supper) at a Parisian theater and drinking a toast to Henri IV. It is also true that an early revolutionary song, "La Motion des harangères de la Halle," satirized the deference shown by the market women on their visits to Versailles.[37] As further evidence of the radicalization of the market women in 1788–89, Hesse points to a missive issued by Louis XVI in August 1789 barring merchants of the Saint-Martin market from visiting him on his saint's day. In fact, the text stipulated that the prohibition was against Saint-Martin merchants alone. *Les dames de la Halle* were to be welcomed to court as usual, thus preserving their privileged relationship and revealing that Louis XVI, at least, believed the merchants of Les Halles remained on his side.[38] While such incidents suggest that the women's traditional bond to the Crown was under pressure, one must admit that economic considerations, as well as the *poissard* literary tradition, point to a more complex situation.

Indeed, when we look forward to the period after the Revolution, the *poissarde* lives on. Aligned with the class of nouveaux riches in comic operas of the Directory and Consulate periods, she continued to regale audiences but for different reasons. Madame Scold's most famous lineal descendant was Madame Angot the upstart fishwife. A volume of Madame Angot's inadvertent puns and a fashion plate showing the incongruously haughty attitude of this market woman were published in 1798–1800 (fig. 4). She appeared in play after play from the late 1790s through the 1850s and provided a never-ending source of mirth with her misuse of fine-sounding words and social faux pas. So influential was the clownish character that her name became synonymous with social arrivism. Or, to put it in other words, she served as a none-too-subtle warning to uppity elements of the working classes to stay in their place.[39] Later in the century, however, a light-hearted romance featuring her "daughter" took the stage in a comic opera that was set during the Directory and entitled *La Fille de Madame Angot* (Madame Angot's daughter). Evacuated of the malicious wit and verve which marked the earlier versions, this story is merely a marriage plot. It enjoyed a good run in 1872–73 in Brussels and Paris and then in an English version in London and New York. Filmed in 1935, the opera remains in circulation today (one can purchase a CD recording of a 2002 performance in Paris). A spin-

(133.)

4. *Madame Angot, or the Upstart Poissarde (Madame Angot, ou La Poissarde parvenue)*. Plate 133 of *Costumes parisiens* (An 7; ca. 1798–99). Musée Carnavalet, Paris. Reproduced by permission of The Image Works, Inc.

off newspaper of theater reviews and society news entitled *La Feuille de Madame Angot* published nineteen numbers between 1873 and 74. By the 1870s, the *poissarde* lost whatever link she once had to revolutionary politics (although a spoof by comic singer Julien Petitjean is putting it back into popular parlance on YouTube).

But what exactly was a *poissarde*? In the eighteenth century, the terms *dame de la Halle* and *poissarde* were used to evoke roughly the same group of women: the Parisian market sellers of flowers and foodstuffs such as fish, fruit, vegetables, and dairy products. Other related terms include *harangère, femme de la Halle*, and *marchande de la marée*; but these labels covered a highly diverse group, from comfortable bourgeois shop owners to lowly fruit hawkers. Commentators on the October Days capitalized on these semantics. The royalist journalist Rivarol refused to believe that the market women had turned on the king and argued instead that they were merely "false *poissardes*," by which he may have meant the men disguised as women who were thought to be behind the uprising, possibly underwritten by the duc d'Orléans, or simply disloyal subjects.[40] As Mathiez reminds us, the king and queen enjoyed a great upsurge of popularity among the merchant classes in the days and weeks following the October Days; a letter from Marie-Antoinette to the Austrian diplomat Mercy-Argenteau on October 7 mentions the warm sympathies of the fishmongers who came to visit her at the Tuileries.[41] On October 8 the right-wing *Journal de la ville* underlined this resurgence of monarchical sentiment, noting a petition presented by *les dames de la Halle* in which "authentic merchantwomen" repudiated the rioters' actions and furthermore denied any relation between themselves and the marchers, whom they described as courtesans and prostitutes.[42] An influential historiographical tradition claims that during the interval following the Versailles march the entire course of the Revolution could have been overturned, so strong was the king's sway over the people.[43]

Similarly, the narrative of *L'Histoire véritable de Gingigolo* ends with king and monarchy intact. The joke is ultimately on Necker, who is saddled with a collar of bells to punish him for making too much noise, is forced to attend church and pray for forgiveness, and must read six pages a day of his own books so that he suffers the same boredom he inflicted upon the Mano-Emugiens. The event thus morphs from an episode of royal humiliation into a gesture of royal control, echoing the sympathy for the king and queen that closely followed the October Days and the conciliatory attitude that was not unusual in *poissard* literature of the early Revolution.

FICTIONS OF AMAZONIAN AMBITION

The media portrayal of the Versailles marchers did not end in 1789. When the commission charged with investigating the event finally published its findings eleven months later, it reopened old wounds, and new icons of folksy bravado and warnings against lowbrow disorder hit the streets. The

left-wing *Révolutions de Paris* expressed horrified indignation over the
treatment of the so-called conspirators and claimed that the commission
unfairly cast suspicions on the women marchers: "What! Some women give
voice to insults against the queen, and two hours later the queen comes
peacefully into Paris, surrounded, protected by these same women!" But
editor Prudhomme's main complaint was against the derogatory class signifiers associated with the march: "What! In 20 depositions, the words 'populace,' 'vile populace,' 'women from the dregs of society' . . . hit your ears,
and you said nothing! Have you forgotten the respect due to the people?"
Most vilified by the media was a woman named Audu or Audru, nicknamed
Louise-Reine-le Duc. Her untrustworthy character was stressed by the trial
coverage on October 7, 1790, where she allegedly waffled over her presence
at Versailles in October 1789 and pleaded to the jury that she was "a good
P[rostitute] . . . who always plied her trade with honor." The audience was
shocked; we read that "[the public] broke the silence only to show its disapproval of this woman's indecency."[44] Whether or not she committed the
deeds alleged against her is less relevant than the publicity lent to her case
and the unsavory image of a lying prostitute as leader of the march.

     Three and a half years later, perhaps seeking to undo the dishonor that
this trial cast on republican fervor, the Convention government reportedly
passed a special decree honoring the women "citizen patriots of October 5
and 6" with a reserved place for them at public ceremonies, where a banner
would signal their presence by announcing that "they made the tyrant flee"
(elles ont chassé le tyran devant elles). The decree further proposed that the
women attend such events with their husbands and children in tow and
that they bring their knitting with them. As Camille Granier noted in 1906,
however, this decree is ironic given that the public ceremonies in question
were executions and that the "patriotic citizens" would later go down in
revolutionary infamy as the *tricoteuses* of the Terror.[45]

     Controversies in political theory were sparked by the October Days as
well. Edmund Burke described the Versailles encounter between the royal
"captives" and the marchers as a terrifying sort of bacchanalia; this imagery
left an indelible impression on readers and sparked what later seemed to be
prescient concerns about French popular politics among right-wing sympathizers in Britain and across the Continent.[46] But Burke's *Reflections* did
not go unchallenged. One of his most influential commentators, Mary Wollstonecraft, shrugged off the facile sensationalism of *Reflections* and took
him to task for what she saw as an unfair class and gender bias. In the *Vindication of the Rights of Man* (1790) she condemned his portrayal of the dem-
onstrators as "furies of hell, in the abused shape of the vilest of women,"

and noted, "Probably you mean women who gained a livelihood by selling vegetables or fish." By situating people in a precise niche like this, Wollstonecraft aimed to show how individuals were necessarily formed by their socioeconomic milieu. The "abominable deformity" of the fishwives, she calmly states, would likely have dissipated if these citizens "had had any advantages of education."[47] Wollstonecraft's efforts in that text and the *Vindication of the Rights of Woman* (1792), where she lays out a proposal for female education and employment, inspired generations of women, including the British and American suffragists discussed in the coda. But in the short term, French women would see most gains made by the Revolution gradually disappear until the Napoleonic Code suppressed the very concept of political rights for women.

THE SATIRE OF A PSEUDOHISTORIAN: ROUSSEL'S *LE CHÂTEAU DES TUILERIES* (1802)

Two of the most striking scenes of Amazonian politicking to emerge from the October Days legend are found in a curious documentary novel written by Pierre-Joseph-Alexis Roussel, *Le Château des Tuileries* (The Tuileries castle; 1802). As one might assume from a book that is subtitled *Récit de ce qui s'est passé dans l'intérieur de ce Palais* (Account of what has happened inside this palace) and that purports to reveal little-known facets of palace life, this narrative is couched in a framework combining one part historical reconstruction and one part gossip.[48] Roussel's knack for spinning hybrid narratives out of the interstices between rumor, archive, and fiction is evident in the dozen "secret histories," correspondences, annals, and novels that he wrote or edited from 1793 to his death in 1815, including a study of the Revolutionary Tribunal. The truth-value of his writings has confounded readers for years; biographers classify him as both a *littéraire* and a historian. Born in 1757 or 1759, Roussel originally worked as a lawyer in Épinal before moving to Paris during the Revolution. He became secretary of the Commission of the Convention government, then a member of the Légion d'honneur, before dedicating his later years to writing. Thanks to his work in the Commission, Roussel reportedly enjoyed privileged access to the kinds of documents cited in *Le Château des Tuileries*, including letters from courtiers that had been hidden in the king's secret wardrobe, or *armoire de fer*. The kinds of indiscretions revealed by Roussel in *Le Château des Tuileries* apparently displeased Napoleon's police. His projected publication of *Les Mémoires de Louis XVI* resulted in a prison sentence under the Empire; the manuscript was confiscated and the book never published.

Many of Roussel's works claim to tell the untold stories of high-ranking courtiers and royalty, but *Le Château des Tuileries* also purports to relay the author/narrator's own eyewitness experience as a foot soldier. Sent from his native Lorraine to represent the province in the 1790 Festival of the Federation, the narrator revels in relating two brief exchanges that he enjoyed with the queen during his stint as a palace guard. While inspecting the royal bodyguards with her husband, the queen notes his foreign-looking uniform and asks the soldier where he comes from, to which he replies, "The province of your ancestors. [We are] your faithful Lorrains." The queen nods in pleasure (1:66). Not only does his regiment hail from a region near her native Austria, but he also speaks German. This allows him to scare some disrespectful courtiers with a few well-placed words when he is stationed near her bedchamber one night. When she meets him again in the garden, she stops politely to say hello before strolling off with her children, as immortalized in the elegant frontispiece to volume 1 of Roussel's work (fig. 5). These incidents stress his chivalrous respect for royalty and complicity with the queen. Comparing Marie-Antoinette's strength of character with the weak will of Louis XVI, he insinuates that the whole Revolution could have been stopped early on if the king had used federalists such as himself to staunch radical elements of the National Assembly. The brief glimpses of a pretty queen walking in the garden and reviewing the troops underline the horror of a later eyewitness passage which draws the reader on a tour of her blood-soaked apartments following the August 10 attack (1:163–70).

It is not impossible that Roussel really did meet the queen on these occasions or that he visited the palace in the wake of the August 1792 uprising. But by placing himself in the story as a sympathetic observer of the royal family, he blurs the boundary between the impartiality expected of a historiographer and the emotionally charged narration of a novelist. The frontispiece, with its pictorial echo of Roussel the young soldier gazing wistfully at his queen, further complicates things. The placement of his image within a passage from the story instead of in a stand-alone portrait makes the author appear to be joining the tale (of populist betrayal) as a critic and loyalist. That undermines his self-proclaimed authority as witness to historical truth.

Other moments that blur the boundaries between history and fiction emerge when the narrator relates anecdotes from secondhand sources, such as, for example, the amusing amorous exploits in the palace rose garden that he reconstructs from police reports (1:25–42) and a titillating tale of barbarity in a Masonic temple, relayed from a friend who went through the initiation (2:48–57). Significantly, the narration of Masonic initiation fol-

5. Frontispiece of volume 1 of Pierre-Joseph-Alexis Roussel, *Le Châ-teau des Tuileries* (1802). Reproduced by permission of the Charles Deering McCormick Library of Special Collections, Northwestern University Library.

lows on the heels of the narrator's guided tour of a women's political club at the Church of Saint-Eustache: both assuage the reader's curiosity for hard-to-access secrets about notorious sects. Both also weave hostility toward radicalism right into the text of revolutionary events—a trait that marks this book from the beginning. Indeed *Le Château des Tuileries* presents a

curiously truncated account of the revolutionary period, ignoring the Bastille and other important events because the narrator is loath to memorial-
ize those "awful days that scandalized Europe" (je n'entrerai dans aucun
détail de ces affreuses journées qui firent le scandale de l'Europe; 1:47). The
Versailles march, however, is covered: the narrator's insider information on
it constitutes one of the secrets that justify the book.

Roussel sums up the October Days in a horrid portrait of a "fanatic
femme forte": Reine Audu (1:48). Alluding to the allegations brought
against the duc d'Orléans and his partisans in the months following the
event, Roussel supposes Reine Audu to be d'Orléans's partner-in-crime.
She is described as a terrifying bandit whose eight hundred women warriors surrounded the assembly on October 5 and forced the guardsmen and
deputies to take a civic oath lest they be decimated by cannon fire. After a
skirmish with the palace guards, she received a wound in the breast—appropriate for an Amazon! Although they did not accomplish their real target
of murdering the queen, she and her troops demanded of the king "what
everyone knows" (1:49), before exiting the palace in triumph. Recalling the
caricatured image of the women marchers seen in figure 2, the narrator
claims that she spent the night sleeping astride a cannon barrel, "glorious in
her success" (1:49). Jumping forward in time, the narration concludes that
Reine Audu went insane in prison awaiting her 1790 trial and died in ignominy in 1793—a portrait that hardly squares with a recent history which
stresses her ongoing bravura.[49] Roussel reduces the march on Versailles to a
violent episode of Orleanist plotting gone askew, led by a madwoman since
deceased. Its results endure in the humiliating sojourn of the royal family in
the Tuileries and their tragic demise at the hands of a radical mob.

That ordinary women are unfit for political life is moreover made explicit in the oft-cited chapter of *Le Château des Tuileries* where Roussel
describes a meeting at a women's club in the Church of Saint-Eustache near
Les Halles. The scene opens when an earthy *poissarde*-like speaker takes the
floor and celebrates women's bravery in language that appears to be lifted
right out of a gallery of women worthies. The actual *femme forte* genre,
which flourished in the 1640s and 1650s before reaching its apogee during
the civil wars of the Fronde, typically highlighted the prowess of women of
antiquity and compared them favorably to heroines of modern-day France.
Employing the epithets *généreux, héroïque, illustre,* and *fort,* these writings express an aesthetic delight in the strong, independent female and an
implied devaluation of men; they made a major contribution to the battle
over women's political enfranchisement that marked the regency of Anne
of Austria. Although adapted to a new political situation and couched in

a rhetoric of rights rather than virtue, the feminist pamphlets of 1789–90 pursued a similar logic and both are roundly ridiculed in *Le Château des Tuileries*.[50]

On the surface, the *républicaine*'s speech seems a straightforward account of female heroism. Although Sister Monic hails from obscure origins (a note identifies her as a milliner), she declaims a most erudite genealogy of female achievement running from the Bible (Debora) and antiquity (the Scythian queen Thomyris) to modern French history, beginning with Joan of Arc and ending with those "new Romans" who engaged in such heroic deeds as the siege of the Bastille and the Versailles march. Concluding this stirring tirade—which was frequently interrupted by applause from the all-female audience, the narrator notes—she declares that women not only are as capable fighters as men but also are better suited than men to rule.[51] The women warriors presently fighting in Lille, she notes with signature panache, face their assailants without flinching and laugh in the face of danger.

If the words of this woman seem too eloquent to be true, that is most likely because they are not. Satire of female pretension was commonplace in revolutionary journalism. From 1788 on, a flurry of satires mocked women's demands as they were articulated in *cahiers de doléances* (grievances generated by the Convocation of the Estates General), divorce petitions, and requests to serve in the military. An entire subgenre of novels lampooned such ambitions with images of separatist sects and female Quixotes. *Le Château des Tuileries* belongs to this tradition. Yet scholars such as Lynn Hunt, Joan Landes, and Dominique Godineau have repeatedly fallen for the novelist's ploy and have referenced Roussel's book as an accurate historical source, considering this scene as "the only full record" extant of a meeting of a women's political club, presumably the militant Society of Revolutionary Republican Women.[52] The influence of genre may be invisible to researchers seeking only documentary evidence, but for literary scholars the connection is obvious. Like two other best sellers of the day, Élisabeth Guénard's *Irma, ou Les Malheurs d'une jeune orpheline* (1799–1800) and J.-J. Regnault-Warin's *Le Cimetière de la Madeleine* (1800–1801), Roussel's work is an elaborately crafted historical fiction. And like these other texts, *Le Château des Tuileries* contains abundant evidence—"unpublished documents," inventories, and conversations—that explain its ability to fool readers even today.

One hint of *Le Château des Tuileries*'s unreliable truth-value lies in the condescending laughter that runs through the narrative of revolutionary events. Telling the story of a would-be adulterer who fell in love with a prudish republican, the narrator notes, "we laughed about that a lot" (1:106). While sitting in a royalist café the narrator quotes a man who burst in while "laughing his head off" and regaled the group with a hilarious account of a so-called republican baptism (1:234). After visiting the Hôtel de Ville and seeing the pitiful state of the people's militia, the narrator sardonically warns his friend, "Watch that you don't laugh; those are our respectable sansculottes" (2:24).

But no scene generates such mirth as the women's political club. The *républicaine*'s imperfect speech is particularly amusing, Roussel's narrator comments: "Nothing seemed more comic to us than to hear passages from history recounted by a woman who muddled [*écorchoit*] all the words with a confidence that defies description" (2:41). Laughter can unite people; the camaraderie generated by a shared joke is one of the most indelible forms of social bonding. But the laughter running through this book is not a generous, communal release; rather, it is a weapon wielded by the in-group aiming to marginalize its enemies. Critics regularly used ridicule to discredit the Revolution; the *poissarde* comes in for scathing treatment in the commentary of Earl Gower, English ambassador to Paris, and the marquis de Ferrières. *Raillerie* (mocking laughter) was also the favorite weapon of right-wing journalists who thought they could beat their adversaries with witty sarcasm. Thirty years later, Alfred de Vigny used the same technique in his description of the *dames de la Halle* who came to watch the prisoners of Saint-Lazare awaiting their doom. His narrator notes with repugnance that "I became aware of their entrance by an odor of fish which spread [through the room] and made it difficult for some women to eat in front of those princesses of the gutter and the sludge [*ces princesses du ruisseau et de l'égout*]."[53] That Roussel's narrators are winking at this tradition emerges right before the end of the scene in the Saint-Eustache political club, where we find the following exchange:

"You must admit," said the Englishman, "that those extravagances are very funny." "I agree, but in retrospect, the women's effusiveness worries me. If their heads heat up too much, you know how stubborn they can be; they are capable of attempting any nature of excess." "Your nation has the remedy: the arms of ridicule and persiflage, which you know so well how to deploy, will destroy their comic pretensions."[54]

There, in a nutshell, is Roussel's method: it is the classic method of satire. As J. A. Cuddon reminds us, "the satirist is a man (women satirists are *very* rare) who takes it upon himself to correct, censure and ridicule the follies and vices of society and thus to bring contempt and derision upon aberrations."[55] Although cloaked under a veneer of archival reportage, Roussel's *Château des Tuileries* forms a scathing indictment of republican politics and wields a sophisticated array of literary tools to do so.

One might consider Roussel's narrator as akin to a Voltairean "bumbling chronicler" whose goal is to provoke doubt, were it not for the heavy-handed sarcasm laid onto the narration.[56] Roussel and his cohort lacked the confidence in their public that Voltaire enjoyed; the writers of the period 1790–1800 were the first generation to experience the effects of writing for a mass market with all that it entailed, that is, the sense of anonymity and the competition for individual readers rather than the support of a cultured elite. Where the earlier ironist could elicit his reader's rueful smile with a wink of complicity over the follies of their age, Roussel superposed a laugh track right onto the text, inciting the readers' scornful indignation quite explicitly by showing what should anger them, who was at fault, and how events transpired to undo the monarchy. As unwitting agents of a mock-heroic script, the *républicaine* and the Amazon of *Le Château des Tuileries* leave a legacy that is part farce, part tragedy, and entirely regrettable.

A COLONIAL SEX COMEDY:
SUREMAIN'S *MELCHIOR ARDENT* (CA. 1800)

What might happen if a woman were to satirize the politics of the Versailles march? One answer may lie in *Melchior ardent, ou Les Aventures plaisantes d'un Incroyable* (Ardent Melchior, or the pleasant adventures of an Incroyable; ca. 1800). This book, which is little known today, went into at least two editions and was also known as *Les Aventures plaisantes d'un Bordelais*. *Melchior*'s appeal among aristocratic readers may be deduced from a note following the title page of the first edition, which announces its availability in a reading room/lending library near the Louvre ("Se trouve au Cabinet de lecture de Martinet, Libraire et Marchand d'estampes, rue Coq-Honoré, no. 124"; rue Coq-Saint-Honoré is present-day rue de Marengo). It makes fun of gendered norms by pushing sexual clichés to their logical, ridiculous extremes. The title alone sets up a coy play on words: *incroyable* in French means "incredible," something unbelievable, but in the years of the post-Thermidorian Directory government (1795–99) an Incroyable was also a type of foppish gentleman whose extremely high collar and tight breeches put him at the apex of postrevolutionary fashion (fig. 6). Like their female counterparts the Merveilleuses (or marvelous ones), the Incroyables' politics tended toward militant royalism; they represented a vehement opposi-

6. *Incroyable*. Engraving by B. F. Pieters, 1796. Musée Carnavalet, Paris. Reproduced by permission of The Image Works, Inc.

tion to republicanism and a nostalgia for the ancien régime. Although many were in fact only recently ennobled, they were usually depicted wielding a club or walking stick, and they were notorious for their street violence against anyone suspected of being a Jacobin. The terms "incredible" and "marvelous" are used interchangeably in *Melchior*; the real purpose of the novel is to make readers laugh.[57]

Laugh readers did, to judge by the reviews of *Melchior* and their praise for the work's "gay new genre," but contemporaries also picked up on the novel's satire of sexual stereotypes. One critic admired how the author twisted the "marvelous" to signify not fairies or ghouls but rather an upside-down world of gender relations; another focused entirely on the episode among the Amazons discussed below.[58] Much of the humor in *Melchior* derives from the bodily extravagance and sexual prowess of the hero: he is conceived during a marathon sex act that leaves his father dead, and like Gargantua, he refuses to be born the usual way. The casual cruelty of the male's supremacy over females informs much of the plot: Melchior emerges from his mother's esophagus instead of her womb, for instance, and leaves her dead as she gives life to him. He is suckled not by a wet nurse but by a hunting dog, and he attributes to her his randy instincts, claiming to have had no fewer than 2,499 mistresses. After a feud with a rival nearly gets the young man castrated and lands him with the nickname "almost Abelard" (*Abélard manqué*), he flees his hometown in shame and heads off to sea. A shipwreck leaves him on a desert island of Amazons, and that is where the gendered politics become most interesting.

This island, he learns, is called Féminensis and it is home to a colony of radical feminists who have never seen a grown man nor raised a male child, whence their surprise at discovering him in their midst (fig. 7). The women's discovery of Melchior proceeds through a metaphorical seduction. As they undress him in a drawn-out scene of group foreplay, the hero enjoys every minute: "Fingering my garments, turning me this way and that, stealing my clothes right off my back, was done in a matter of minutes; they undertook the task with perfect speed and agility; all eyes were on me. Such attention could only bring favorable results, so I withstood it without complaint, indeed with pleasure."[59] Although their cult supposedly does not admit of carnal knowledge, these women smile knowingly. As if to underline the book's tongue-in-cheek eroticism, the engraver pictured a foursome of strapping monkey-men handling phallic fishing poles in the background and set the whole scene against a volcanic peak. The sexual ignorance of the Féminensiennes is, of course, a joke. And Melchior, unlike his literary cousin Candide, who botched an analogous encounter in his South American odyssey, immediately understands.[60] In characteristic machismo, he reacts by fretting about the competition for sex: "what services could these monkeys provide the ladies? Were they husbands or slaves? Would they be my masters or my rivals?"[61] Madame Suremain leaves no stone unturned in this satire of male anxiety.

Indeed, the author's name seems almost too fitting for this book. French

7. "Fingering my garments, turning me this way and that." (Palper mes habits, me retourner dans tous les sens.) Frontispiece of volume 1 of Madame S*** [Louise-Marie Sure-
main], *Melchior ardent, ou Les Aventures plaisantes d'un Incroyable* (ca. 1800). Reproduced courtesy of the Lilly Library, Indiana University, Bloomington.

for "Sure Hand," Suremain may very well be a pseudonym; at the very least it adds to the smirk-inducing humor. (Although bibliographers include Suremain in their lists of revolutionary-period novelists, no conclusive evidence has been unearthed on this person's identity one way or another.) I think it likely that *Melchior* was penned by a man writing about both sexes in a satirical vein. Whoever Suremain was, she or he nailed the anxieties of sexual performance with spot-on accuracy.

Melchior's seduction at the hands of a group of man-hating feminists was not an original conceit: this scene mirrors the masculine angst displayed in Révéroni Saint-Cyr's 1798 novel *Pauliska*. As Béatrice Didier has pointed out, *Pauliska* itself rewrote—in a somewhat milder vein—the hostilities of male-female relations in Sade's works.[62] Like *Melchior*, *Pauliska* recounts its hero's accidental foray into a cult of Misanthrophiles, who lock him up naked in a cage. During a ritual initiation ceremony he is subjected to a group striptease that causes him to get an erection, a disgrace recounted in a similarly titillating register: "My sight grew dim at the view of so many beauties, I was practically delirious," he admits, while the repressed *philosophes femelles* look on indifferently in a sensorial sterility that they learned in this camp (*Pauliska*, 115–16). Where both authors make fun of Amazonian sects, Révéroni leaves the cult intact: the man-haters recede from view but remain in the reader's mind, like the other bizarrely threatening secret societies—dastardly priests and evil scientists—that foment trouble in this Gothic landscape. As for Suremain's hero, Melchior, he considers the very existence of the Féminensiennes as an affront to his sex and his national pride. Instead of seeking to flee, he wages a military campaign to abolish their pretensions and enforce French laws on the colony. This absurd ambition, which can only be dubbed "Napoleonic," must have struck a chord with readers in 1800.

Legend has it that the female-only policy on the island dated from a king's betrayal. Ever since that fateful day the country swore to annihilate all men (*Melchior*, 53). Luckily for the Féminensiennes, they apparently needed no males because their native tree allowed them to procreate by eating its fruit, which one can see hanging overhead in the frontispiece and which resembles the exotic flora of period botanical illustrations. Dancing and singing around this tree unites the women in their hatred of and independence from men. Other peculiar gestures and rituals govern this society, Melchior learns, having to do with salutations and signs of respect. He submits—all the while plotting when he might take over and bring this country into conformity with "natural order," that is, obedience to male rule.

A colony that was born out of resentment over a king's betrayal and that worships a magical tree and insists upon newfangled social practices: the features of this odd group echo the innovations foisted upon the French in 1789–93, when a new government was invented, when so-called liberty trees were planted to much ceremony and applause, and when age-old customs were forcibly replaced with new place-names, new salutations, a new calendar, and new egalitarian titles. As a satirical image of Jacobin rule, the Féminensiennes claim to adhere to an impossible code of physical and moral purity as well. But the narration casts an ironic eye on such aspirations by letting us in on their secret. The fertility of the special fruit finds potent support amid the Féminensiennes' companions, the robust monkey-men; these women are surely not as abstemious as they claim. The dismantling of this colony by a diehard Incroyable makes a certain political sense. But the means to that end are truly incredible!

The first step to the hero's victory over the Amazons is his pregnancy and childbirth, announced de facto in a chapter entitled "J'accouche" (I give birth). The marvel is explained, sort of, as the consequence of eating the magical fruit; the birthing proceeds painlessly and Melchior awakens from a deep sleep to find an infant son at his side. He then convinces the queen that they must change the country's constitution to protect his son, and he enlists the monkey-servants to join a militia created to that end.

Rewriting the atmosphere of October 1789 in a rocambolesque spirit, Madame S*** depicts a group of Amazons plotting to overthrow the government. Although couched in a legalistic rhetoric—they accuse the queen of treason (parjure) and claim that she is breaking ancient laws of sovereignty—the women's real complaints focus on male rule: "A man is among us! A man is associated with our queen's power! Oh horrors!"[63] When the battalion surrounds the palace shouting "we want the man" and brandishing weapons, the queen, with Melchior by her side, tries to calm the masses but in vain. To save these "nuts" (folles) from committing regicide, Melchior leads the monkey-militia in a cartoonish repression that quashes the upheaval with a minimum of bloodshed: by shooting water into the women's rifle barrels, they dampen the gunpowder and thus disarm the rebels, who swoon at the sight of blood. After a speedy surrender, the rebel leaders are placed in the custody of the most vigorous monkeys on the island—prompting the narrator to slyly note, "Perhaps this punishment was not cause for complaint; but who can read a woman's mind?"[64]

Like that of his allies the monkey-men, Melchior's political success revolves around sexual performance. Although this theme was well exploited by libels of the 1790s depicting Lafayette coupling with Marie-Antoinette and various other prominent ladies, the plot of *Melchior* departs from precedent in significant ways by transforming the hero into a biologically bizarre *homme-femme* endowed with a womb, a will, and an heir apparent. Melchior not only trumps the Amazons at politics but also betters them at the one task for which they traditionally held preeminence, that is, childbirth. Jokes about male childbirth had earlier circulated regarding the ill-fated Constitution of 1791.[65] But where royalist caricatures of 1790–91 depicted the travails of Deputy Target to underline the Constitution's monstrous genesis, this text presents male childbirth as an effortless means to restore male prerogative over an unnatural matriarchy. The child he engenders grows to prodigious size and strength in just a few days (in an echo of *Gargantua*); he too uses girth to good effect by copying his father's strutting machismo. After the failed rebellion, the mutinous few are handed over to monkey-men for who knows what sort of libidinous exploits. The old laws are burned and a new law stipulates that henceforth the Fémininsiennes will desist from waging war against men; rather, they will help recruit males to "restore the natural order on the island" (76). Mocking another familiar trope of revolutionary rule, Melchior seals the deal with an oath: "As for me, I swore a king's oath, as did my son, to masculinize to the best of my abilities the inhabitants of Féminensis regardless of their rank: and twice-weekly public audiences were established to that end" (76). A lewd pun sums up the regime change: the narrator notes that public opinion soon came around once the women began *feeling* the difference of coupling with men instead of a tree ("il fallut peu de temps pour que les féminensiennes commençassent à *sentir la différence* d'un être animé comme un homme, à un être inanimé comme un arbre"; 77, my emphasis). When a nearby island is discovered to be inhabited by Frenchmen, a lively exchange of favors is soon established. The episode ends with a scene of thriving sexual commerce in which whites assert control over the indigenous primates and Frenchmen dominate the now-docile Amazons.

Melchior presents many more ribald episodes involving a visit to a mysterious Peruvian tribe, a ride in a hot-air balloon, and encounters with the Inquisition, a charlatan, and a slave trader. Mixing genres in a typically fin-de-siècle hybridity, *Melchior* borrows from Françoise de Graffigny's *Lettres d'une Péruvienne* (1747) and Rétif de la Bretonne's *Découverte australe* (1781), among other favorites, before culminating in the creation of a prodigiously fertile family unit back in the hero's native France. The most incredible truth of this fantastic tale, the author notes ironically in closing, is that Melchior settled down and became a faithful husband to his devoted wife, Sophie, who as a consequence bore him a child every ten months. It is hard to imagine that author "Sure Hand" did not intend for these libidinous exploits to come across as a stylishly risqué commentary on male insecurities. To this reader the many seduction scenes are so outlandish as to be comical, as are Melchior's arrogant attitudes toward patriarchy and conquest of every kind. By portraying a hero so swaggering, Madame S*** was doubtless mocking the pretensions of the Incroyables in her or his day, whose exaggerated dress and affected speech made everyday living into an elaborate kind of performance.

One element of the plot may not seem quite so humorous to modern readers, and that is the forced breeding of the Féminensiennes with their new white masters. Although this episode was doubtless meant to be as laughable as the women's trysts with the monkey-lovers, it seems jarring today because of its apparent complicity with colonial politics. Indeed, *Melchior* explicitly underlines the superiority of the Frenchmen's lovemaking over indigenous practices. Alluding to the monkeys' brutality, the narrator notes, "if some toothless old women dared to complain, fearing they wouldn't get any action, the group's disapproval, and their fear of being submitted to the monkeys, quickly reduced them to silence."[66] The new regime ushered in by the hero of *Melchior ardent* puts an end to mixed breeding, in what may or may not have been a comment on colonial life, where creolization was a social reality. By 1800, mixed-race relations carried sinister connotations to many people, thanks to the news of the racial insurrections on Saint-Domingue relayed in the press of 1791–1804, which pinned much of the violence on unreliable *gens de couleur*, or mulattoes. With white-on-white coupling ensured by Suremain's narrator, the women's commerce with the monkey-men effectively ends, as does their error of what the colonial administrator Moreau de Saint-Méry called *amalgamation* (since the more scientific-sounding terms "miscegenation," *croisement entre races*, and *métissage* were not yet coined).[67] The result for Féminensis is a racially pure colony: a fantasy enjoyed by many whites in the New World as well as the Old. Is it too "presentist" to read the whimsical put-down of female insurgency and self-sufficiency in this novel as veiling a colonial agenda? Perhaps. Until we know more about the real identity of Madame S***, the exact satirical intent behind *Melchior* will remain one among many tantalizing puzzles.

CODA: HOW THE FISH SELLER BECAME A SUFFRAGIST, THANKS TO L. FRANK BAUM

The imagery of *poissardes* and Amazonian warriors that emerged from the 1789 march on Versailles was intricately tied to assumptions about male political dominance and anxieties over the working people and their will.

Whereas the earliest pamphlets asserted continuity between past and present in the person of the loyal *poissarde*, later narratives featuring bellicose Amazons with grandiose ambitions were fed by fears of democratic leveling, that is, of a people who dared to break with the past and engender their own political identity (a populist version of Becker's *causa sui* project). Existential meanings abound. Is it any surprise that this age, which saw the overthrow of so many fundamental tenets of daily life, would witness a rise of anxiety over basic gendered prerogatives?

Satires of female politicking form a subgenre in French literature of the late eighteenth century. Consider the proposal for a female army, complete with details on the stylish uniforms they would wear, which circulated in 1792. The *citioyennes* who took this initiative and presented it to the Convention announced their intention to distinguish themselves by their courage and patriotism and "to renounce the seductions of love, until our menfolk [*citoyens*] have brought home laurels of glory." A steep order to be sure! Few signed up.[68] Although the texts in this vein generally show female characters laughably attempting and failing to conduct men's business, as in *Lettres de la comtesse de . . . au chevalier de . . .* (1789) and *Le Réveil des dames* (1791), or forming erotically appealing separatist societies, as in *Les Chevalières errantes* (1792), *Charmansage* (1792), and *Melchior ardent* (1800), some do prove impervious to masculine domination. The leaders of the all-female communities depicted in Révéroni Saint-Cyr's *Sabina d'Herfeld, ou Les Dangers de l'imagination* (1797) and *Pauliska* (1798) are allowed the opportunity to air their complaints about male domination— several paragraphs, at least—and inspire serious reflection among the male protagonists and by extension, one assumes, among readers. The women's groups in this corpus usually lose a member or two to the heroes' wiles but, with the exception of *Melchior*, their secret gatherings live on, hidden in the clouds, the mountains, or the salons of European high society. Such texts pay indirect homage to women's efforts to join serious debate alongside men or, more precisely, in the absence of men. They deserve to be seen as a positive consequence of the Versailles march and the unprecedented, albeit short-lived, women's political clubs that flourished during the first years of the Revolution.[69]

Better known to period audiences and still today, however, is the misogyny of fin-de-siècle writers such as Edmund Burke. In a 1795 letter to Mrs. Crewe, Burke made it clear that his scorn for the Versailles marchers was no less vehement than his distaste for the *femmes-hommes* of the upper classes, that is, all the "Mesdames de Staals, and the Mesdames Rolands and the Mesdames Sillery, and the Mrs. Helena Maria Williams, and the Mrs. Woolstencrofts [*sic*], and all that clan of wicked and mischievously ingenious women, who have brought, or are likely to bring ruin and shame upon all those that listen to them."[70] Meddling with matters beyond their ken, went this argument, was patently the lot of the political woman. Best then to remain quiet and let men run the game.

Transgressions against standard gendered behavior were no laughing matter to the forces of order either. When a new fashion for female *travestissement*, or cross-dressing, was brought to the attention of the Paris police in spring–summer 1799, the response was dead serious. Police archives from germinal to thermidor Year 7 reveal that an important number of agents and spies were mobilized to suppress this vogue among Parisian women. Why? Because it was alleged that (1) such women could be potential émigrées, (2) *travestissement* was bad for public morals, and (3) it was against the law. One agent nevertheless challenged the minister's order. His arguments seem ironclad to us, yet they resulted only in stricter enforcement. Citing a law dated August 1, 1789, which condemned women to fifteen days in prison for wearing men's clothing (and three months for repeat offenders), he argued that such a law could not be upheld because it was created by a provisional government and thus was no longer valid. He also reminded his superior that women were authorized to wear men's clothing if they had to ride horses for their health and had a doctor's order. He agreed that public morality was a crucial preoccupation, yet he implicitly refused to arrest the women who had been seen strolling through the Tuileries gardens *en travesti*. A year and a half later, a new law was published to quell such tergiversation. Disseminated to all police commissioners in the country in November 1800 (brumaire Year 9), the law formally declared it illegal for women to wear men's clothing.[71] The brief loophole of female emancipation closed for a long time to come.

Despite the myriad, positive ways that women contributed to advance the Revolution and the demand for women's political rights voiced by Olympe de Gouges's *Déclaration* of 1791 and others, progress would be slow until French women were allowed full participation in public life. After a divisive series of efforts from 1848 to 1938 failed to enroll women of various political and religious persuasions in a united movement for suffrage, France was one of the latest European countries to give women the right to vote. In 1944, under General Charles de Gaulle, French women finally received suffrage. During the repressive regime of Napoleon's Empire, Olympe de Gouges and the promise of female activism were largely forgotten. The pursuit of political and civil rights in France during the nineteenth century was a long, hard battle and made less progress than in the relatively progressive climates of the United States and Britain.[72] As Patrick Bidelman reminds us, by the late nineteenth century in France, the Anglo-Saxon and Scandinavian countries appeared as beacons with respect to both organized feminist efforts and practical legislative gains.[73]

One legacy of the Versailles march is the large-scale demonstrations and the dramatic suffrage pageantry of Great Britain in 1907–14. In the parades of women worthies that organizers brought to the streets of London, women dressed as famous heroines of bygone times and cited mordant quotes of foremothers such as Joan of Arc, Mary Wollstonecraft, and Mary Somerville as proof of women's dedication to the cause of liberation from traditional gender roles.[74] But these figures and many of the marchers hailed from an elite political culture that enjoyed privileges of education; furthermore, they foresaw the impact that their words and acts would leave on women's history. To retain the focus on the populism of the October Days and the surprising way that this event mobilized a newly politicized, uneducated mass of working women and militants, one must turn instead to a more homespun American example.

The reader with some knowledge of American women's history may recall that the French vocabulary of rights was already appropriated and used in the 1770s by a pioneer of feminism in the United States, Abigail Smith Adams (1744–1818). She may be most famous for writing to her husband, John Adams, then in the Continental Congress, and threatening rebellion unless the rights of her sex were secured. But Abigail Adams's efforts on behalf of women's independence and education continued for years. She was held up as an exemplar by leaders of the American suffrage movement that emerged in the 1830s and took on its greatest momentum in the years 1860–90.[75] The first Women's Rights Congress, held at Seneca Falls, New York, in 1848, appeared to make a dent in the barriers to women's political organization. Despite being ridiculed in their local news media and churches—to such a point that many of the one hundred signers of its Declaration of Sentiments withdrew their names in embarrassment—the event was an international landmark.[76] Embattled French activists were cheered; in 1851 two leading French militants, Jeanne Deroin and Pauline Roland, wrote from their cells in Saint-Lazare prison: "Your courageous declaration of Women's Rights has resounded even to our prison, and has filled our souls with inexpressible joy. . . . Your socialist sisters of France are united with you in the vindication of the rights of woman to civil and political equality."[77] More contact ensued: French leaders Olympe Adouard and Élie Reclus paid visits to the United States in the 1860s and 1870s; Susan B. Anthony visited Paris in 1883; Elizabeth Cady Stanton spent six months in Paris in 1887.

What is less well known is how a related current of feminist politics and populism made its way into the work of American novelist L. Frank Baum (1856–1919). Baum's sympathy for the cause of female suffrage was likely due to the influence of his wife, Maud Baum (née Gage) and her mother, Matilda Joslyn Gage (d. 1898). Matilda Gage was a leader of women's suffrage rallies and speeches of the 1870s, a high point of which was her address at the Centennial Exhibition of 1876 in Philadelphia, where she appeared before thousands. She was instrumental in drafting the Women's Bill of Rights and was a coauthor, with Elizabeth Cady Stanton and Susan B. Anthony, of the massive *History of Woman Suffrage* (1881).[78]

Both nationally and locally, 1890 was an interesting year in the history of women's suffrage. That year found the Baum family in Aberdeen, South Dakota, where they shared their home with mother-in-law Matilda Gage and welcomed the visits of her friends and collaborators such as Susan B. Anthony. During the fifteen months that Gage's son-in-law spent as publisher of the *Aberdeen Saturday Pioneer* (1890–91), one can see multiple signs of editor Baum's support for suffrage. Not only did he allocate space to Gage's occasional articles and prominently feature news of the suffrage organization NAWSA, led by Gage and Anthony, but he also wrote regular editorials of his own; out of the fifty-nine editorials that he wrote, twenty-eight expressed his support for suffrage. The April 26, 1890, number put it very clearly; Baum wrote, "If our politics are to be masculine forever, I despise the republic."[79]

Most interesting for the literary history of the *poissarde* is his regularly featured column, Our Landlady, which appeared in forty-eight numbers of the *Aberdeen Saturday Pioneer* from January 1890 to February 1891. Our Landlady represents the views of a voluble small-town busybody, Mrs. Sairy Ann Bilkins, whose name itself is a pun on her parsimonious ways: bilking, or cheating, was what she did to her boarders. She is a comic semiliterate figure who speaks in a rustic dialect full of malapropisms that bespeak her lack of education and proper upbringing. In weekly columns supposedly reporting dinner table conversations, Mrs. Bilkins argued against topics such as Prohibition and organized religion, and for issues such as women's rights, to an audience of meek but grammatically correct lodgers. This lowbrow commentator is in my view a distant cousin of the fishwife persona of the revolutionary press. Like the repackaged fishwife Madame Angot, who amused audiences in the 1850s with her class-conscious foibles, this figure's more or less realistic reflections on the travails of small-town life in the American West are emphasized over her capacity to incite a belly laugh.[80]

8. André Boratko, cover illustration for L. Frank Baum, *Our Landlady* (1941).

But the columns are not devoid of humor. In fact they abound in slap-stick, outrageous puns (one Mr. Barrett is called "grin and barrett"), and rib-ald imagery, such as the spectacle of the love-struck three-hundred-pound Mrs. Bilkins landing on the lap of a flummoxed boarder who she believed, wrongly, had just proposed marriage (fig. 8). Or consider the scene where the citified boarders try to help Mrs. Bilkins milk a cow and end up instead lying prostrate in the hay. Even silly episodes like that one tell a lesson, as the landlady concludes: "A woman is allus a fool when she asks a man to help her to do anything. If I'd a been alone, that Klokettle an' I would a had it out, and I'd a milked her or broke her neck. But the men-folks spiled it all. . . . A cow is a female, an' she wants her rights, an' after all, I dunno as I blame her so much as I do Doc. fer bein' such a fool as to pull her tail" (*Our Landlady*, 90). Although her enemies tend to be local public officials and sanctimonious churchgoers instead of aristocrats or rival merchants, they suffer the same kind of tongue-lashing that animated the brochures featur-ing Madame Engueule and her ilk in the 1780s and 1790s. Moreover, Mrs. Bilkins always gets the last word.

The female complicity hinted at in the *poissardes* — when they were not brawling, they often shared a drink and a good laugh together—emerges as a deliberate theme under Baum's pen. Consider how Our Landlady deliber-ately threw in her lot with a militant branch of female politicos. In a review of the all-female Aberdeen Guards' first performance in May 1890, Baum (aka Mrs. Bilkins) notes:

> Them Aberdeen Guards kinder knocks the spots off'n anything you
> men folks kin do. Now, the time was when the Amazons was celebrated
> throughout the world as the fiercest lot o' sodjers to tackle there was,
> an' the men folks was skeert to go near 'em, an' them 'air Aberdeen
> Guards is built on the same promisin' lines. I tell you, nobody need be
> 'feered fer the country's safety while them Aberdeen gals is aroun' to see
> things slide like they orter. (73)

These young women meant business. Each had a spear and had been instructed how to impale traitors to the country. As Our Landlady exclaims,
they were "fierce an' furious warriors . . . every one was thinkin' of their
country's enemies an' how they'd like to scratch their eyes out" (74). Although people murmured that one of them had a beard, Our Landlady defends their bellicose spirit and concludes, "You can bet one thing, and that
is that these gals will make their mark 'afore you hears the last of 'em" (74).
As Baum's biographer Katharine Rogers notes, "While Editor Baum bases his
opinions on reason and information, Mrs. Bilkins presents the same opinions based on feelings or rough intuitive common sense."[81] A similar tactic
was employed in the *poissard* tradition, as we saw in the division between
the well-informed public writer "Father Style" and the kindly "Tender Ma"
of *Le Falot du peuple*. Together they made a formidable team.

The author's left-leaning politics came out in passages where Our Landlady dismissed those people who disapproved of her ideas, as in "Fiddle-
sticks! If folks don't like my style they needn't listen to me," or "If only
every man would say 'I will do suthin' instead of sayin' 'why don't somebody else do suthin'?' things would change mighty quick." When her boarders told her to stay out of public affairs, she replied, "it's the conceit o'men
as is the biggest stumblin' block ter universal sufferin' o' women!" (98, 109,
43). As one will see from comparing these exchanges with the dialogue of
Fanchon and Monsieur Supreme Good Taste noted above, *Our Landlady*
compares favorably to the populist vein that ran through *poissard* texts of
the 1790s. The feminism of Baum's editorials also had some precedents in
that genre. Although they are frequently seen to come to fisticuffs, the *poissardes* stand up for each other. Consider the fishwives' defense of divorce—
a radical attitude—in a verse pamphlet from 1797, which one might render
thus: Madame Salmon says, "For virtue ya hafta be free; / Ourz is the only
choices tha' count," and her friend Madame Scold agrees, "With th' divorce
bein' legit, my rascally ol' man / won' give me so much harass'n; / Cuz he'll
be knowin' that I kin leave 'im; / That'll surely teach 'im."[82] Their language
and politics hail from distant milieus, but the sentiments that animate

these fictional market woman and landlady show a continuity of feeling: both transmit sympathy for working people and especially for the women.

But what about Baum's fiction? Critics have praised the feminism of Oz, declaring, for example, that "the condition of being female [in Oz] is exalted in exposition as well as example," or that "Oz is beyond all doubt a little girl's dream-home."[83] Typical of Baum's supposedly feminist slant are the many queens and good witches who people the fourteen-book series, and the kindliness and pacifism of its principals, not to mention the heroine of *The Wonderful Wizard of Oz* (1900), Dorothy, who incarnates self-reliance, generosity, and plain-speaking good sense. But when Baum imagined an all-woman insurrection in *The Marvelous Land of Oz* (1904), he cast it as a farce. In what I see as a distant spin-off of the October Days, this rocambolesque episode gathers together multiple stereotypes of female weakness, yet ends up admitting—in ironic understatement—that a few of the women's complaints are legitimate.

When Baum's pretty brunette General Jinjur and her knitting-needle-wielding militia—shades of Théroigne de Méricourt and the radical *tricoteuses*—attack the castle of Oz, the episode should seem familiar to readers of this chapter. As should their foe. The king of this country garners no awe or respect and cannot even motivate his army to a proper defense. As General Jinjur charges: "When the Wonderful Wizard reigned the Soldier with the Green Whiskers was a very good Royal Army, for people feared the Wizard. But no one is afraid of the Scarecrow, so his Royal Army don't count for much in time of war."[84] Given such a paltry obstacle, no fancy military tactics are necessary: when they point their needles menacingly, the mob of beauties simply scares the Guardian and his Standing Army of one into letting them into the castle (fig. 9). "In this way was the Emerald City captured without a drop of blood being spilled," the narrator explains. "The Army of Revolt had become an Army of Conquerors!" (*Marvelous Land*, 95). Once the king, also known as the "stuffed monarch," receives word of their march, their success is equally easy: King Scarecrow and his entourage immediately flee to safer climes. But General Jinjur and her army, it turns out, have few demands for reform. They seek only an updated world-upside-down where they might live in leisure like the men. This explains Jinjur's coup d'etat. When scolded by the Scarecrow for taking his place, she cavalierly replies: "The throne belongs to whoever is able to take it. I have taken it, as you see; so just now I am the Queen" (173). Their idea of the good life is somewhat appalling to the serious-minded: it revolves around light-hearted chatting, gem hunting from the Emerald City's bounteous civic monuments, eating bonbons, and reading novels.

9. General Jinjur and her Army of Revolt take the castle. Illustration by John R. Neill in L. Frank Baum, *The Marvelous Land of Oz* (1904).

But the social transformation of Oz into a gendered world-upside-down proceeds without a hitch, as the Scarecrow learns upon his return.

> "What has happened?" the Scarecrow asked a sad-looking man with a bushy beard, who wore an apron and was wheeling a baby-carriage along the sidewalk. "Why, we've had a revolution, your Majesty—as you ought to know very well," replied the man; "and since you went away the women have been running things to suit themselves. I'm glad you have decided to come back and restore order, for doing housework and minding the children is wearing out the strength of every man in the Emerald City." "Hm!" said the Scarecrow, thoughtfully. "If it is such hard work as you say, how did the women manage it so easily?" "I really do not know," replied the man, with a deep sigh. (170–71)

This unanswered paradox makes a subtle dig at male superiority.

The problem is that General Jinjur is no better a ruler than the Scare-crow and is probably worse. Neither she nor he rules by popular consensus or inherited right. When Glinda the Good Witch is eventually called in by the Scarecrow to resolve the conflict, he has to admit that his claim to the throne is weak: it was given to him by his predecessor the Wizard of Oz (a humbug), who had seized power from the previous ruler (239–40). In other words, his rule was equally as illegitimate as Jinjur's, and the rule of men was just as arbitrary as the rule of women. The story ends with the surpris-ing revelation that its erstwhile hero, the young boy Tip, is actually an en-chanted version of the country's rightful monarch, Ozma. When returned to her original appearance by witchcraft and restored to her rightful role by Glinda's impressive female army, Ozma assumes wise leadership over the nation and sends General Jinjur and her girl soldiers back home to their mothers, where they resume lives of household drudgery. "At once the men of the Emerald City cast off their aprons. And it is said that the women were so tired eating of their husbands' cooking that they all hailed the conquest of Jinjur with joy" (282–83). Edmund Burke could not have wished for a bet-ter denouement.

General Jinjur and her army represent the stereotypical features of anti-suffrage satire. They are lazy, greedy, and empty-headed gossips who are afraid of trivial things like mice, have no notion of government or leader-ship, and simply covet the leisure that is associated with men's lot in life. Given Baum's feminist leanings, how do we explain the choice to include this episode in what he had reason to expect would be another best seller? Biographer Rogers admits difficulty in reconciling Jinjur's revolt with the enlightened feminist views Baum published elsewhere but explains the epi-sode nonetheless as part of the author's plans for a stage production. This thesis makes a certain sense: *The Wizard of Oz* had made the transition from page to stage with aplomb, and its proceeds provided a tidy fortune to the writer. Moreover, the ranks of comely women warriors would transfer easily to a chorus line, and the burlesque of an unpopular cause would pan-der to conventional audiences. But in fact, this second reason is even more convincing than the first. I suspect that the author mocked female politicos quite simply because they were good game. Gender jokes have long been sporting in the genre of fantasy–fairy tale; the fathers in his audience would probably enjoy the none-too-subtle specter of Jinjur's undoing, the mothers would tolerate it in silence, and the children would appreciate the episode's silliness. As one of Baum's first critics noted (wistfully?) in 1929, "it was still safe to ridicule the suffragettes in 1904."[85] Are things so very different from that today?

The brief world-upside-down caused by this uprising does segue into a
sly critique of male domination and female inferiority by the end. Although
men still rule the roost and leave the home and child care to women, it is
avowed that girls do possess many useful and even intellectual qualities.
When the principals are trying to reassure Tip over his imminent transformation into femininity, they tell him that girls are "nicer than boys"
and "equally good students" (272). Moreover, when order is restored and
the dust settles, careful readers note that Oz's new queen actually reigns
better than any of the men who came before her. As elsewhere in the Oz
series, Amazons join forces with working girls to get the job done, and their
world—for better or for worse—does not seem so very distant from our own.

CHAPTER TWO

The Frankenstein of the French Revolution

W hat author wrote a parable about an inventor named Frankenstein
and his life-size artificial man? If you answered Mary Shelley, you are
half right. Long before Mary Shelley published her "Modern Prometheus"
in 1818, an author penned a tale that resembles Shelley's in more ways than
one. Contrary to the assertions of critics such as Annie Amartin-Serin, who
declared in 1996 that there exists no such thing,[1] my research has uncovered
a number of fictions about artificial creation from the 1790s: the most spectacular being the inventor named Frankénsteïn in François-Félix Nogaret's
novella *Le Miroir des événemens actuels, ou La Belle au plus offrant: Histoire à deux visages* (The looking glass of actuality, or Beauty to the highest
bidder: A two-faced Tale; 1790). This alignment of circumstances presents
an intriguing coincidence. Indeed, it is simply astonishing to find a story
about an inventor named Frankenstein who builds an artificial human during the French Revolution, especially since the Revolution and its attempt
to make a "new man" and a new nation have long been a central lens for
viewing not only Shelley's work but also the very concept of social engineering.

Nogaret's original story of kindly automatons conflates technology and
politics in a manner befitting French political debates of 1789–90: the characters employ state-of-the-art tools in microscopy, astronomy, and aeronau-
tics to tell a tale that elegantly supports scientific progress and industrial
innovation in a state governed by talent, not tradition. The plot is set up as
a contest in which six inventors compete to win a young woman's heart.
This heroine-nation allegory is a common enough motif in revolutionary
materials, and it was signaled as such by Huguette Krief in her 2005 article,
the only critical mention of *Le Miroir* to date.[2] Even Krief did not notice
the pertinence of Nogaret's inventions and their makers for literary history,

however; her admittedly brief treatment of the novella focuses on the feminine body as the signifier for a political message. But the courtship plot is not just a comedic device; it also serves to advance technology in the sluggish economy. And the novella's denouement is not only a marriage but also an arresting example of human-humanoid interaction set in motion by inventors with significant names: Wak-wik-vauk-on-son-frankénsteïn (a combination of the name of the great French engineer Vaucanson and the Teutonic-sounding Frankénsteïn) and Nicator (read "Necker," Louis XVI's finance minister). Explicitly labeled a phenomenon of "animal economy," the two automatons that carry the contest debunk observers' belief in a "divine hand," prove the triumph of science over superstition, and demonstrate the author's familiarity with the latest developments in automation.[3] There is more to this book than meets the eye.

To explain the surprising prescience of Nogaret's tale, this chapter focuses first on the events that gave rise to it: the agitation concerning trade guilds and inventors' rights of 1790–91. From the petition submitted to the National Assembly in August 1790 and the committee work and behind-the-scenes lobbying that were doubtless undertaken by its principals—one of whom was a highly visible *ci-devant* (former aristocrat) with an extensive network at court and among the wealthy—emerged the new patent laws passed in January 1791. The in-depth newspaper reportage of this decree, which might seem like a technical matter, should alert us to the impact that it was thought to have on the French economy. Following that section is a history of some of the most celebrated inventions of the day, especially the automaton, considered in their relevance to debates over mechanical and vitalist philosophies of sympathy and cognition. Next, we delve into analysis of *Le Miroir*, aiming to explain the meaning behind this complex allegory and to reveal how the author's initial enthusiasm for social engineering faded in the five years between the first and second editions (1790, 1795). Situating the two versions of the tale in the larger context of street culture and politics should demonstrate how revolutionary events brought a new urgency and pathos to the theme of artificial creation. Other popular literature and entertainment featuring automatons such as the Marquis de Condorcet's satirical "Lettre d'un jeune mécanicien" (Letter from a young mechanic; 1791) and E. T. A. Hoffmann's novella *Der Sandmann* (The sandman; 1816) are also considered part of this trajectory. This chapter thus charts out an alternative genealogy for Frankenstein's creature, focusing on revolutionary politics and the technology of the automaton as the precursors to Shelley's masterpiece.

The coda at the end of the chapter analyzes Mary Shelley's *Franken-*

stein (1818) accordingly as a parable of invention. Readers may recall that the novelist made frequent use of mechanical metaphors in the third edition (1831). Explaining the rationale that she used to make the creature move, Shelley argued that "extraordinary means" were not what she had in mind but rather a mechanical procedure like galvanism or "the working of some powerful engine."[4] This apparent modification of Frankenstein's famous "spark of life" and the vitalist theories it relied upon may confound readers. Perhaps the cautionary tale implicit between the two editions of Nogaret's novella can offer a clue to Shelley's choice. By stressing the painstaking work involved in manufacturing a creature from what Shelley called "component parts," the present analysis puts blame for the ensuing tragedy squarely in the hands of humans and notably the creature's inventor—an imperfect technician—instead of some external source, be it Providence, divine wrath, nature, or a conspiracy of some sort. That designation of human responsibility was a provocative move in Shelley's age, and it shines a cold light on the meaning of *Frankenstein* as a fable of revolutionary social engineering too.

LEGISLATING INVENTION IN 1790–91

The history of French invention during the Revolution, as historians Maurice Daumas and Charles Gillispie have noted, is hard to come by. Why? First of all, because its terminology was imprecise, as reflection on words such as *science, invention,* and *machine* will reveal to any reader of period texts.[5] But perhaps even more important were the unprecedented demands on industry during the Revolution, when the traditional truism— that science governs the mechanical arts—was under bold attack from a hitherto-apolitical class of skilled artisans.[6] All accounts point to summer 1790 as the turning point in state support of French genius.

Under the ancien régime, inventors benefited from a basic patent system of *brevets* whereby the Crown through its institutional apparatus authorized worthy artisans to profit from exclusive control over their discoveries for a certain time. But beginning in August 1790, the government was forced to consider redefining its role and even to relinquish traditional controls in order to keep technical talent in France. On August 22, at the very time when the budgets of the Jardin des Plantes and the academies were under careful scrutiny, the National Assembly made an amazingly grandiose allocation of two million livres to be disbursed annually in awards for "useful discoveries."[7] Meanwhile, a group of self-avowed *artistes-inventeurs* later called the Société des inventions et découvertes was taking form. They first met in the euphoric days of summer 1790, when Paris was inundated with delegates from all the provinces who came to celebrate the July 14 Festival of the Federation. From the outpourings of fraternity they witnessed in the streets and the media, these men doubtless picked up a sense of urgency about their own status in an economy that was daily looking less familiar. They decided to push for a new system of brevets to protect their own and the nation's productivity.

Inspired by article 17 of the Declaration of the Rights of Man and of the Citizen, this group's petition argued that man's intellectual work and creativity should be covered by the same rights as his property.[8] On September 6 the petition was referred to the Comité d'agriculture et de commerce, which named Deputy Chevalier Stanislas de Boufflers (1737–1815) to prepare a report on it for the assembly. As Gillispie remarks, this choice "could scarcely have been more incongruous or more fortunate" because the onetime colonial administrator of Senegal, despite his reputation as a roué and a saucy raconteur, had turned over a new leaf since his 1788 election to the assembly.[9] He took on the mission with great seriousness and drew up a powerful proposal. The broad network of friends and associates he enjoyed in the assembly and at court could not have hurt the cause either.[10] When Boufflers presented the fruits of his labor to the assembly on December 31, it was a roaring success: the *Chronique de Paris* noted the next day that his report, draft decree, and speech were "often applauded." The king's assent made the decree into law on January 7, 1791.

An anxious awareness about the fragility of French industry was the founding assumption of the society's request, Boufflers's report, and the new law. Citing the Rights of Man, the report argues that useful ideas and discoveries must belong to their originators and predicts that woe will befall the state that does not protect individuals accordingly. In terms that resonate with Nogaret's *Miroir* and other writings of the day, the Boufflers decree insinuates that failure to recognize this right "may well have contributed to discouraging French industry, to have led distinguished artisans to emigrate, and to have expatriated from France a large number of inventions from which France should have had the initial advantages."[11] The exodus of skilled craftsmen was clearly a major concern in winter 1790–91. Prudhomme's *Révolutions de Paris* sought to staunch the flow by printing all eighteen articles of the new law, more than four pages, in January 1791. A month later the paper reiterated the good news—"Today . . . the freedom to practice one's trade is accorded to all"—and laid out some favorable outcomes to be expected from the new system of patent registry.[12] The February 5 *Chronique de Paris* echoes this attitude; it transcribes a speech by a deputy defending a new hydraulic machine with fervent patriotism, claiming: "Mr. Trouville's invention is attracting much attention abroad; we must not lose a useful discovery which may honor the nation." The assembly decreed in his favor.[13]

Another victory for inventors followed on February 16, 1791, when the assembly abolished craft guilds and with them the control that those ancient bodies exercised over industrial procedures, and again on May 25, when the assembly decreed that examination of patent requests would henceforth no longer be judged by the burdensome Académie des sciences but instead by a new group headed by the leader of the Société des inventions et découvertes. This move ridded inventors formally of the final great impediment to their freedom, that is, the academy's power to advise government agencies on the merits of machines and processes submitted for review.

The results of this legislation vindicated the *artistes-inventeurs* who lobbied for it: some 750 patents were issued in the next twenty years in fields ranging from chemistry and engineering to medicine and industrial design. Moreover, the original award monies were redirected toward an egalitarian model of disbursement by a second decree in September 1791, so that the state could benefit aged and indigent artists as well as aspiring inventors in need of start-up funds.[14] Along with legislation facilitating patents and suppressing the trade guilds, the expansion of mechanization constitutes the other fundamental event of the period. From the steam engines digging trenches for Paris sewers to the machines making interchangeable gun parts and the mechanized looms that promised to weave cotton in record-breaking time, new technologies of automation contributed the most to the acceleration of the great political, social, and economic upheavals of the late century.[15]

INVENTORS AND INVENTIONS IN THE PUBLIC EYE

THE EVIDENCE OF PRINT ADVERTISEMENTS

In the popular imagination, however, and arguably in the international marketplace as well, the French inventor was still steeped in an artisanal tradition more aligned with the concept of fine craftsmanship or scientific study than the large-scale manufacturing that was jump-starting an economic boom across the Channel. A glance at period newspapers affords some idea of the technology and devices marketed during the early phase of the Revolution. Advertisements announcing the availability of telescopes, chemistry classes, hydraulic machines, balloon launchings, agricultural tools, magic lantern shows, and methods of automatic writing abound in the pages of the *Journal de Paris* and the *Moniteur*. Inspired by Caroline Herschel's discovery of a comet and by the transit of Venus during February 1790, the *Moniteur* of winter–spring 1790 carried numerous articles stressing the utility of instruments such as the orrery and the telescope and promoting courses in chemistry and astronomy.[16]

Other entrepreneurs attempted to capitalize on the balloon mania set off by the 1783 ascension of Pilâtre de Rozier and the controversy it unleashed about air travel and its potential military applications.[17] The Festival of the Federation gave rise to stiff competition for spectators to the show: two ads appear in the July 13, 1790, *Moniteur* and *Journal de Paris* announcing "aerostatic experiments," one in a twenty-eight-foot balloon with silken wings "in the national colors" that would demonstrate a new method for steering the craft. The price of admission to view these experiments was three livres.[18] Seeking to spur flagging interest for this "most magnificent of arts," another entrepreneur launched subscriptions for a Compagnie aéronautique: for just five hundred livres, an individual could purchase one share of a flying frigate, watch its construction, and participate in preliminary experiments of a technology that promised new means for shipping heavy loads, transporting passengers, and circumnavigating the globe.[19]

Other devices offered for sale or exhibit include an *aéro-clavicorde* (a harpsichord with a human voice), a hydraulic machine promising to allow a man to remain submerged for minutes under the Seine, and two mechanical mills for grinding flour.[20] A method of coded writing—so secret that even the inventor would not be able to crack its code—was also for sale, suggesting that people's fears of unstable political alliances and neighborly suspicion had already created a market for clandestine communication.[21] An ad for steel razors resonates with Boufflers's concerns about French trade: it promotes the razors not only for their superiority over English models but also because patriots have an obligation to help the nation battle foreign, especially British, competition.[22]

AUTOMATONS AND THEIR MAKERS

The most popular invention was the automaton. Although they were not much like other mechanisms of the day—weaving looms or grinding mills—these machines were the most prominent and most beloved by contemporary audiences. By 1790 automaton shows were a familiar sight in London, Paris, other capital cities, and provincial cities. Similar to the shows hosted in London at Cox's Museum and Mr. Haddock's Mechanic Theatre were the automaton shows of Paris: all featured a lineage reaching back to the 1730s alongside state-of-the-art inventions. Cox's Museum drew audiences in the 1770s with its spectacles of mechanical music and jeweled clocks.[23] The museum features in literary works as well, where the automaton is an easy target for satire: its empty gadgetry dazzling the eye for no particular purpose. (As Burney's naive heroine admits during her visit to Cox's in *Evelina* [1778]: "It is very fine, and very ingenious . . . and yet—I don't know how it is—but I seem to *miss something*.")[24] Filling in that need for significance perhaps, in the 1790s Haddock's theater advertised a mechanized spectacle that mirrored the urgent need for British militia: one volunteer soldier robot performed the manual of arms in front of a Temple of Mars while another kept time on his drum. The demand for shows held in a theater on the boulevard du Temple hosted by M. Perrin (or St. Perrin), "Mechanic-Engineer and Demonstrator of Amusing Physics," was high enough to warrant thirteen ads running in two Paris newspapers from March to June 1790 alone. It was also lucrative: tickets ranged from three livres to twelve sols a seat, a costly outing for most Parisian workers, who earned between one and three livres a week. Under the rubric Physics, Perrin awed audiences with the latest in pseudoscientific phenomena and legerdemain, showing aeronautic and electrical experiments as well as magic tricks with intriguing titles such as the Prophet of China, the Dancing Ring, and the Sympathetic Windmill. His most popular automatons were the Hunter, who read minds and shot arrows into a target, and the Oracle of Calehas, who did "most extraordinary things."[25] For all his extravagant claims, Perrin's machines nevertheless marked a decline from the sophistication of earlier models.

England was known for its eminence in clockwork manufacture, yet the most noteworthy master craftsmen of the late eighteenth century were Frenchman Jacques Vaucanson (1709–82), his reclusive compatriot Abbé Mical (1730–89), the brilliant Genevan team of Pierre Jaquet-Droz (1721–90) and his son Henri-Louis (1752–91), and Abraham-Louis Bréguet (1747–1823), who held more patents than any other inventor and made a number of watches for the French royal family before fleeing to Geneva in 1793. Foremost among their creations were Vaucanson's flautist who was first displayed in Paris in 1738 before a wildly successful run in London in 1742. His soft lips, dexterous fingers, and functional windpipe and lungs allowed him to play virtually any flute. Also notable was Vaucanson's mechanical duck, which, while not humanlike, was considered a crowning creation that supposedly demonstrated digestion and other animal behaviors. The lady musician created by the Jaquet-Droz group was first displayed on the Continent in 1773 (fig. 10); she not only played the harpsichord with a delicate touch

10. Jaquet-Droz, harpsichord-playing automaton, 1773.

but also responded to her music with audible sighs and a bobbing head. By 1776, the Jaquet-Droz family exported their wares to London and opened the Spectacle mécanique in Covent Garden, where one could admire a four-foot-square mechanized Swiss garden and three nearly life-size automatons, including the Musical Lady, a draftsman, and a scribe. One commentator marveled over the draw of this curiosity and speculated that it must have been "very lucrative" for the ingenious artists.[26] Unknown abroad but no less remarkable were Abbé Mical's talking heads, which were first exhibited before the Académie des sciences in 1783 and which were able to articulate several cogent phrases in French (fig. 11). Modern readers are struck not only by the ingenuity of these inventors but also by the simple materials that made up the machines: parchment, cork, papier-mâché, leather, and metalwork.[27]

Philosophical interpretations help explain how automatons could incite emotional responses like those imagined in *Le Miroir*, where we see the heroine flutter, faint, and reawaken under the influence of a bronze flautist,

11. Abbé Mical, talking heads (*têtes parlantes*), 1783.

and in E. T. A. Hoffmann's *Sandman*, where the (albeit mentally unhinged) hero swoons over the "adoring glances" of a wooden doll.[28] Some argue that the eighteenth-century automaton teeters on the boundary between the traditional Cartesian conception of an animal-machine and the vitalist paradigms that were already challenging it in the 1750s.[29] But it is more accurate to describe the automaton as incorporating an ambiguity at the heart of Enlightenment thought, since many materialist thinkers who espoused vitalism did not make any distinction between spirit and matter. In works as varied as Condillac's *Traité des sensations* (1754), Buffon's *Histoire naturelle* article "De l'homme" (1750), and Rousseau's *Émile, ou De l'éducation* (1762), authors struggled to prove precisely that man is not preordained to operate in a mechanical way, yet their explanations of human functions rely on a mixed bag of analogies including nerve "fibers," "sensible" body parts, and a mysterious "life force," that is, an epistemology at once mechanistic, vitalist, biological, and Christian.[30]

Simple automatons worked on a Cartesian system of pulleys, levers, or gears, so that force equaled movement, but the more sophisticated models such as the Jaquet-Droz musician could be seen to demonstrate vitalist principles. A central tenet of vitalism is the irreducibility of living processes to laws of physics and chemistry: some external principle must superpose itself on the living body to endow it with a vital property. Emotions and intuition, for instance, may derive from the realm of spirit or even the sacred rather than from physical laws of cause and effect. Now think of the sensitive harpsichord player. As she played music, her chest filled with air and her eyes seemed to fix on her listeners in sympathetic feeling.[31] So convincing was this movement that one visitor to the Musical Lady exclaimed: "she is apparently agitated with an anxiety and diffidence not always felt in real life; her eyes seem intent on the notes, her bosom heaves."[32] This emotional connection between animate and inanimate would be exploited to most disturbing effect in *The Sandman*; however, it is not until Shelley's work that the life of a man-made creature will be explained as resulting from explicitly vitalist principles. Thanks to the spark of being that jolts the creature into consciousness, in *Frankenstein* inert matter seems to take on an energy and willpower that even the most sophisticated eighteenth-century inventions lack. Yet Shelley returned to mechanical principles in a later edition of *Frankenstein*.

Perhaps the mechanical paradigm was less outmoded than we may think. In 1790 a book hit the market promising to teach people how to harness their mental powers like an engine. Called *La Méchanique* [sic] *morale* (Moral mechanics), the book offered the secret to making the human mind

into a "victorious instrument" capable of imparting to man "a veritable om-
nipotence." Before we scoff, let us recall that this now-forgotten book was
promoted on the front page of the *Chronique de Paris*, July 31, 1790, at a
time when newspaper reading and national optimism were at their height.[33]
Should not that tell us something about the purchase that the mechanical
metaphor had on people's imaginations? Surely, such hopes were not unrelated to the support for mechanical processes in industrial applications
noted above.

Although I argue that Nogaret's novella was the first to depict a politicized automaton serving a revolutionary cause, he had a precursor of sorts
in Abbé Mical's talking heads. Mical's mechanism was ostensibly intended
to demonstrate the processes by which human vocal chords produce intelligible phonemes, but its mechanism lay hidden behind a spectacle of royalist propaganda. As seen in figure 11, the device consisted of two life-size
heads of serious-looking, bearded gentlemen, wrought in bronze and gilded
in gold, whose lips moved as they spoke their lines. One wore a crown.
Together they perched atop a stage framed by Corinthian columns, under
which a curtain presented the script of their dialogue. By turning a lever,
one could look behind the curtain and see the mechanism that made them
talk. The machine's reputation was such that Louis XVI himself invited
Mical to an audience, and journalist Antoine Rivarol wrote extensive praise
of the artist and his work.[34] Much to the machinist's dismay, however, his
creation received most renown not for its scientific accuracy but as a side-
show attraction. Part of the appeal lay in the heads' dialogue: it was a stirring credo of royalist loyalty, applauding King Louis XVI for extricating the
French from the recent, ruinous foreign wars.[35] Although the machine pro-
cured some financial gain for the impecunious priest, rumor has it that he
either sold the regal heads or destroyed them in a fit of rage before dying in
poverty in 1789.

By 1789, most Parisian audiences were no longer in the mood for a propaganda machine that touted Louis XVI's military prowess. By 1792, a carica-
turist would cast a mocking commentary on Mical's invention by showing
Louis XVI and Henri IV as two heads balanced on a pedestal and watching a
procession of woeful aristocrats and clergymen pay their respects (fig. 12).[36]
Where Mical's monarchs held forth with grandeur, these heads regard the
scene in mute concern. Although buttressed by the beloved Henri IV on his
right, it is the king's brothers on his left—the émigré princes—who emerge
as the true heroes of the day, as they rally the group to pledge a counter-
offensive against the Republic. Louis's credibility as father of his people had
already slid considerably since the heyday of Mical's machine. Politics are

12. "We will follow, Sire, your august brothers: They come from the school of adversity. Without it Henri IV would not have attained greatness. Like him, they want to retake the kingdom as victors and, as a father, to put it back into your hands." (Nous suivrons Sire, vos Augustes frères: Ils viennent de l'école de l'adversité. Sans elle Henri IV n'eût pas été le grand. Comme lui, ils veulent reconquérir le Royaume en vainqueur & en père pour le remettre entre vos mains.) *The Oath of the French Nobility* (*Le Serment de la noblesse françoises* [sic]), 1792.

at stake here, despite the rudimentary technology of these objects. Bereft of the free will that gives meaning to human action, these automatons function as moving caricatures, with all the simplicity and power that caricature brought to political debate.

A modern-day reader might ask why I have gone into such depth about gadgets of little lasting utility. Would it not be more important to explore the cultural role of engines used in cotton manufacturing, say, or the technology behind mass-produced gauges for cannon ball production rather than one-of-a-kind curios such as the automaton? But if that person could go back two hundred years or so, he might realize that such curios were perceived very differently than they are today. A no-less-distinguished commentator than Dr. Samuel Johnson asserted as much in the *Rambler* (1751), where he explained:

To collect the productions of art, and examples of mechanical science or manual ability, is unquestionably useful, even when the things themselves are of small importance, because it is always advantageous to know how far the human powers have proceeded. . . . It may sometimes happen that the greatest efforts of ingenuity have been exerted in trifles, yet the same principles and expedients may be applied to more valuable purposes, and the movements which put into action machines of no use but to raise the wonder of ignorance, may be employed to drain fens, or manufacture metals, to assist the architect, or preserve the sailor.[37]

French writers of the eighteenth century had a similar appetite for invention, but their work also hinted of worries over the control of technology. At the end of the 1780s, the popularity of the unsound experiments of characters like Franz Anton Mesmer and the comte de Cagliostro created a divide between academicians and amateur scientists and provoked an avalanche of pamphlets challenging the academies' monopoly over defining scientific knowledge.[38] In a gesture that some interpret as spite for his own failings as a doctor and experimentalist, the radical journalist Jean-Paul Marat published in 1791 *Les Charlatans modernes*, which presented a devastating attack on the Académie des sciences and its supposed obscurantism. Among those demanding greater surveillance of swindlers who hawked pseudoscience to the masses was Henri Decremps (1742–1814), whose book *La Magie blanche dévoilée* (The conjurer unmasked; 1785) was translated into English and Italian and found a ready public among readers wanting to understand the maneuvers deployed to beguile them in shows such as the automaton spectacles mentioned above.[39]

The mystique of aerial locomotion, already implicit in works such as Cyrano de Bergerac's *Histoire comique des états et empires de la Lune* (1656) and Fontenelle's *Entretiens sur la pluralité des mondes* (1686), received a tremendous resurgence of interest following the balloon launchings of the Montgolfier brothers and their competitors. The most elaborate fiction to explore this concept was Rétif de la Bretonne's *Découverte australe par un homme volant* (1781).[40] Air travel proves exploitative in Rétif's tale because the winged hero and his family mastermind a eugenic mixing with all the inferior race-species that are under their command. The hero's will and wherewithal to meddle in communities worldwide give the reader pause. A similarly cavalier attitude toward human subjects characterizes the heroes in Robert Lesuire's *Charmansage, ou Mémoires d'un jeune citoyen faisant l'éducation d'un ci-devant noble* (1792) and L.-M. Henriquez's *Voyage et adventures* [sic] *de Frondeabus, fils d'Herschell, dans la cinquième partie du monde* (An 7 [ca. 1798–99]); both novels combine a fascination, à la Rétif, with air travel, sexual voyeurism, and a strong-arm approach to social engineering under the aegis of revolutionary activism. Echoing the conceit, albeit in a more earnest mode, is a 1793 tale by Olympe de Gouges where an air traveler named Toxicodindronn transmits a crucial warning to humans from his vantage point on high.[41]

But the most probing and timely fictional exploitation of technology from the revolutionary period has to be Nogaret's *Miroir des évenemens actuels* (Looking glass of actuality): this novella does more than simply exploit the potential of period inventions; it weaves them into the warp of its plot so that they motivate the action. Echoing Johnson's hopes but in a political vein, the art of statesmanship and the craft of metalwork combine in this tale to present an allegory perfectly suited to the revolutionary decrees on invention of 1790–91.

AN OBJECT LESSON ON AUTOMATON POLITICS

NOGARET'S *LE MIROIR DES ÉVÉNEMENS ACTUELS* (1790)

François-Félix Nogaret (1740–1831) was a recognized writer in the 1770s and a regular figure at court.[42] He worked as librarian for the king's sister-in-law the comtesse d'Artois and attracted the attention of scientists such as Buffon and Adanson for his dabbling in natural history. During the Revolution, he directed a provincial saltpeter manufacture and served the Department of the Interior. He was drama censor under the Consulate and Empire governments until 1807, when his liberal attitudes conflicted with those of the police, to whom that administration was conferred. His independent spirit, intellectual eclecticism, and relish for the esoteric make him an appealingly minor author as the category is conceived by critics Gilles Deleuze and Félix Guattari.[43] That is, Nogaret wore his marginal status as a kind of sociopolitical virtue; he saw himself as an icon of resistance and sensual dynamism even at an age when most people have given up the fight, penning his last work at eighty-nine!

No longer a young man in 1789–93, Nogaret dismissed his once-frivolous style and brandished an engaged persona, claiming to wield his pen as others bear arms.[44] During the Revolution he experimented with various genres: he penned a sarcastic letter of condolences to an aristocratic landowner (*À Louis-Xavier*; 1791), a diatribe against Abbé Raynal (*Extrait*; 1791), and a hymn in honor of the Versailles metalworkers (*Cantique*; ca. 1793). A play published in 1804 reveals the author's sympathies for Freemasonry.[45] But

Nogaret's career as a writer-activist proved short-lived. A self-proclaimed Jacobin in 1793, by 1807 the author had shrugged off philosophical interpretations of his work and cultivated the air of a jovial yet rather esoterically inclined libertine until the publication of his last book, *Dernier Soupir d'un rimeur de 89 ans, ou Versiculets de Nogaret (Félix) sur la métaphysico-néologo-romanticologie* in 1829.[46] The year 1790 marks the release of his most elaborate political fiction, *Le Miroir des événemens actuels, ou La Belle au plus offrant: Histoire à deux visages* (The looking glass of actuality, or Beauty to the highest bidder: A two-faced tale; figs. 13 and 14).

Le Miroir is a complicated allegory that can be read on four levels of significance, three of which are designated in the dedication, where the author calls his work an "erotico-political-patriotic historiette."[47] They include (1) a tale of Syracuse during the Roman occupation (ca. 241–211 BC); (2) an indictment of the Catholic Church (announced on the frontispiece with an apostrophe to the reader, this theme remains a subtext until the end of the story, discussed below); (3) an allegory of the nation seen as a young woman whose actions trace a political meaning; and (4) a comment on the current state of invention and technology and an appeal for French technicians to regenerate the national genius. The last two paths are most germane for a comparison with *Frankenstein* and I therefore focus primarily on them.

Like the National Assembly, which launched a series of decrees to protect inventors in the course of 1790–91, Nogaret's heroine—a seventeen-year old orphan named Aglaonice—decides to try and "spur all these geniuses to action." To launch the plan she asks Marcus Cornélius, a Roman senator-magistrate (*préteur*), "if he wouldn't see with pleasure all these great makers of machines, inactive for such a long time, finally take flight and bequeath some monument of their knowledge to Syracuse."[48] She offers her hand in marriage to the man who can create the most ingenious machine that appeals to a woman's heart. As for his nobility of birth, she could care less: *Nobilitas sub amore jacet* (*Le Miroir*, 5). Although skeptical, the senator agrees to help. Perhaps he was swayed by the heroine's unusual name; combining the Greek words *agla* (grace) and *nice* (victor), it bodes well for her success.[49] The contest begins.

If the young woman represents the French nation, one should see a reflection of current political attitudes in her actions. Six suitors present themselves, each symbolizing a trend in science and technology as inflected by controversies of the day. The first suitor offers a walking steel tripod. But the practical heroine refuses up front because, as the narrator notes, "a tripod that does not *bronche* in carrying the pot is preferable to a tripod that can leave the hearth" (un trépié qui ne bronche pas en portant la marmite,

*Si vous ne voulez que vous amuser, parcourez
moi. Si vous voulez éclairer le peuple & le servir,
passez vîte à la page 69 de cet ouvrage, lisez
& suivez le conseil que je vous donne. Ainsi les
pénitens bleux, les pénitens gris, les pénitens
blancs, les pénitens verts & tous les masques
de cette espece seront moins à redouter.*

13. Frontispiece of François-Félix Nogaret, *Le Miroir des événemens actuels ou la Belle au plus offrant* (1790). Bibliothèque nationale de France, Paris.

LE MIROIR
DES ÉVÉNEMENS ACTUELS,

OU

LA BELLE
AU PLUS OFFRANT,

HISTOIRE A DEUX VISAGES.

. . . . Ridendo dicere verùm.
Quis vetat ?

A PARIS,

Au Palais-royal , fous les colonnes en face du Petit
Dunkerque ; & chez les Marchands de Nouveautés.

L'AN DE NOTRE SALUT

1790,

Et le deuxieme de la LIBERTÉ.

---

14. Title page of François-Félix Nogaret, *Le Miroir des événemens actuels ou la Belle au plus offrant* (1790). Bibliothèque nationale de France, Paris.

est préférable à un trépié qui peut quitter le coin du feu; 6). In employing the multivalenced verb *broncher*, the narrator layers this clause with three meanings: the preferred tripod would not stumble or encounter difficulties or complain about its task; rather, it would stand still by the hearth and hold the pot. An allusion to Vulcan, the god of metallurgy and fashioner of tripods, is patent. It should also be recalled that the revolutionary period was heavily marked by tripartite imagery, as in the iconography of Masonic triangles: an analogy for the three estates. The three legs of the tripod, each moving on a hidden system of gears, form a timely parallel to the deputies of the three estates, each responding to the will of their constituents. Like the tripod, the assembly was not supposed to follow its own caprices but rather to stand firm in service to the nation.

Named Mymecide (combining *mime*, "to imitate," and *cide*, from the Latin *cædere*, "to kill," summing up this self-defeating effort), the second suitor arrives with luxury objects: a minuscule chariot and a tiny ship wrought from precious ivory. But when the heroine harnesses the chariot to a housefly, it disappears out the window. When she floats the ship in a vase of water, it vanishes and leaves only a green film behind: a phenomenon that prompts a lesson on freshwater polyps.[50] Musing over this ephemeral spectacle, the senator murmurs that the great ship of Lutecia would not sink so easily. Although Aglaonice does not understand these cryptic words, she shares his scorn for the fragile and futile knickknacks. Too delicate to be useful, they are quickly lost and forgotten.

The third inventor is a magician with a long name ending in Law-bar-cochébas: a baroque Greco-Hebrew designation signifying "false prophet, speculator, and swindler," according to a footnote. He offers a telescope that allows one to see "a throng of objects that escape the view" and of which "no one can have a perfect knowledge without [its] aid" (10). After an erudite discourse on the plurality of worlds, he invites Aglaonice to view them with his machine. While she peers into the telescope searching for lunar inhabitants, the inventor vanishes, having stolen all her money and jewels. This shocking turn of events alludes to the suspicion of charlatans—both in finance and in science—that was prevalent at the time and casts the vender of optics in a shady light that prefigures the fiendish Coppola of *The Sandman*. But this one is not only a fraud but also a public enemy, like his namesake the Scottish economist John Law, whose innovations wreaked havoc in French finance during the 1720s. Both deplete the nation's treasury either figuratively or literally.

The fourth suitor bears a name that combines the surnames of two infamous officers in the royal army—Brogli and Lambesc—and the designation "aristo."[51] Counting on the avarice of the heroine, who is, after all, a poor commoner, he presents an enormous hot-air balloon and invites her to climb in, join his conspiracy, and ascend the social hierarchy as his wife. Nicknamed Aristos, and being "unable to stand the idea of a perfect equality, he had not yet lost hope for the success of a tyrannical plot" (21). He thus conspires to overthrow Roman rule and establish an oligarchic regime. Like a fairgrounds showman, Aristos exaggerates the virtues of his machine, claiming it will revolutionize planetary travel and benefit the military by allowing generals to recruit on the moon. In this outrageous portrait of a balloonist-conspirator, Nogaret was responding to the widespread balloon mania noted above. Aglaonice rebuffs both Aristos's political and his amorous overtures and defends the Syracusans' hopes for a constitutional monarchy. When the machine takes off, it becomes obvious that the nobleman's incompetence matches his arrogance: his basket rises too high in the sky and disappears. Later, one learns that Aristos drowned in the sea. Hence, "the aristocratic machine," the conspiracy, and its author come to an untimely end.

It is the last two inventors who win: one marries Aglaonice and the other marries her sister. The first describes himself as a "good Gaul, free man," and gives his name as Wak-wik-vauk-on-son-frankénstein. This composite features *wik*, pronounced *vic* (for Victor?), the surname of the renowned automaton builder Jacques Vaucanson, and Frankénstein, which may have been drawn from a German legend of alchemical prowess.[52] This adroit machinist is self-taught: he "excelled in the divine art of harmony, without ever having learned music." He presents a life-size statue cast in bronze and dressed as a Sicilian (as is appropriate for the Syracusan setting) and sitting in a chair with a flute in each hand. Along with the twenty-two melodies that this flautist can produce, the inventor offers his devotion, telling Aglaonice: "you will see, Mademoiselle, that there is not a man alive who does not worship you. Ask, and the metal itself will obey" (42). Without further ado, the machine bows to the group and starts to play. Magic seems to be in the air.

This interlude contains multiple elements of the Frankenstein legend. The inventor is described with awe and admiration: he is a handsome man of learning and culture whose gifts are compared with those of Prometheus ("un artiste dont l'Olympe pourrait être jaloux, comme on assure qu'il le fut autrefois de Prométhée"; 46). While initially known by the clumsy Wak-wik-vauk-on-son-frankénstein, he is shortly thereafter called Frankénstein. His machine seems to transcend the existential boundary between animate and inanimate: although the flautist startles and frightens observers at first sight, the music it plays creates intimacy. Even the learned senator is thun-

derstruck at the view of an invention that replicates mankind ("il n'avait
jamais ouï dire que l'homme eût, pour ainsi dire, créé son semblable"; 42).
Moreover, the flautist's harmony creates an emotionally charged atmosphere. The first song it plays, a poignant ballad "of a heart ravaged by love,"
fills the heroine with such bliss that she faints clear away. On a word from
the master, the automaton then switches to a livelier air and brings her back
to awareness. Sympathy passes like an electrical current from automaton to
heroine; the inventor's passion seems to transfuse right into her breast. But
lest one interpret these scenes as validating a vitalist philosophy, we must
remember that even if it is deemed "prodigious," the shiver connecting
Aglaonice and Frankénsteïn's flautist (like that of Nathanael and Olympia in *The Sandman*) is not a transcendental force. Rather, it is manifest
entirely in the human actor, in what Edmund Burke called "the mechanical structure of our bodies" and the "natural frame and constitution of our
minds."[53] The machine's impact is serendipitous, generated by the human's
own heightened state of excitement rather than the machine's simulacrum of feeling. This reminder is brought home by the senator's warning to
Aglaonice to "take heed against her senses" before choosing a husband (44).
Indeed, the modest Frankénsteïn invites the heroine to weigh other options,
and so, despite her inclination toward him, she calls for the last inventor.

Given his association with foresight and prosperity, this fellow named
Nicator must stand in for the Swiss financier Jacques Necker, who served
for years as finance minister under Louis XVI, played a pivotal role in the
Estates General, guided the fiscal policies of the early Revolution, and was
associated in popular imagery with the cornucopia (as seen in a 1781 caricature; fig. 15). Although not lacking in controversy, Necker's stolid service
to the treasury elicited such trust among the people that upon hearing news
of his dismissal on July 11, 1789, angry crowds forced the king to rehire
him. His visibility was never greater than in the fall and winter of 1789–90.
Like Necker during this brief honeymoon with the French public, Nicator
incarnates finance and wealth.[54] Described as a Chaldean shepherd who,
like his ancestors, understands the stars and is able to predict the future, he
brings an invention symbolizing abundance: a beautiful female automaton
holding a cornucopia stuffed with precious jewels. As she gracefully rolls
into the room and curtsies to the audience, the textual register switches
from comedy to vaudeville, and a child dressed as Cupid emerges from the
doll's skirts and shoots a rosebud-tipped arrow at Aglaonice's heart. When
the smitten heroine asks if Nicator truly loves her, the automaton/inventor
answers, "Yes." When asked if it can do anything else, the machine rolls forward and offers an armful of golden fruits. Although the technical prowess

15. "Great Necker your wise caution / Will make all our hearts delight; / You bring abundance back to us / By doing the will of LOUIS." (Grand Necker ta sage prudence, / Va rendre nos cœurs réjouis; / Tu nous ramènes l'abondance / Sous le bon plaisir de LOUIS.) Caricature of Jacques Necker, 1781.

of this engineer falls short of that of his rival, and the confederate hiding in the skirts suggests that Nicator may be something of a charlatan, the heroine is nevertheless dazzled by his wealth. Supported by her mentor (who displays a shrewd eye for his protégée's fortune), Aglaonice accepts Nicator and proposes that her sister marry Frankénstein.

What interests me is how Nogaret yokes the political impetus to science and manufacturing and makes mechanical devices tell a normative lesson on how technology could support the new nation. The unwieldy tripod designer is dismissed for his excessive ambition. The elaborate handicraft of the artisan in ivory is the product of a shortsighted focus on luxury and artifice instead of utility. The duplicitous telescope operator sneaks off and warns against lending credence to charlatans. The hot-air balloon operator floats above the heads of the heroine and her mentor to disappear far away, like the treacherous but ill-fated counterrevolutionary sympathizers abroad. Both of the successful inventions are based on a human image and perform human functions. They play music, bring gifts, and offer to serve. Like Vaucanson's expertise in mechanization, which gained him a prominent post in silk manufacturing, their inventors' technical skills bode well for the nation's industry. The heroine's acceptance of the devices from abroad symbolizes France's wish to collaborate with neighboring countries that display congruent political sympathies; her choice of the sixth suitor over the fifth reveals a pragmatic concern for financial stability. The last scene depicts the heroine and her sister married to the two automaton builders and making plans with their father figure to replace the oppressive Roman hierarchy with a secular meritocracy.

Yet in a chapter ostensibly relating the wedding banquet and called "Le Souper," there is scarce talk of food. Instead, the narrative becomes a tirade on the atrocities committed by the Catholic Church and the clergy's manipulation of the common folk. This theme was signaled already in the frontispiece announcing the book's double intention. As Frankénstein narrates the history of his country, called Lutecia, he shows how anticlerical activism can improve a nation's well-being. But the movement between these different allegorical meanings—of the marriage plot, French revolutionary politics, and the historical similarities between the Syracusans and the Lutecians under Roman rule—is rather confusing. It is particularly difficult to piece out the distinction between the Lutecians and the French, since their shared historical origins make them virtually synonymous. But that similarity is the point: what has been done once can be done again.

While the tale of Beauty to the Highest Bidder closes on page 61 with an image of this happy composite family in a group hug, the book continues for another fourteen pages that reveal an urgent effort to address present-day concerns. Lest the reader miss the double meaning of his "Two-Faced Tale," Nogaret appends a two-page clarification explaining how he sees his allegory functioning: like "one of those paintings which from a distance seems to represent one thing, but which changes and looks totally different the closer one gets to it; [I am] happy to think that it may contribute in some way to stop my brothers from killing each other" (62). Moreover, he anchors the text in an actual debate, warning readers to act immediately because *le furieux Bergasse* is already mounting an effective Catholic propaganda campaign to stir up the peasantry. The clarification ends with a confrontation between Deputy Bergasse and other traditionalists, seen as cold-hearted Tatars, battling against the wily writer and his pen. Nogaret declares: "Fatal partisan of a hated power / Monster, jealous of the very air we breathe; / Succumb; die at last" (63). The author and his confederates win, and the nation faces a bright future free of the church.

Following this note are twelve pages of appendices containing numerous endnotes on Roman and Syracusan history, followed by a five-page article describing clerical misdeeds. The last five pages reproduce Voltaire's article "Massacres" from *Questions sur l'Encyclopédie* (1770) and a final exhortation demanding that priests stage public readings of this tract. Nogaret thus follows in the footsteps of the philosophes and contributes to the battle over state control of church properties and functions that was already well under way. But even the philosophes did not go as far as Nogaret in demanding action from the reader.

In what must be one of the most outrageous moments in publishing history, Nogaret demands that readers destroy his own book! This move is unprecedented in revolutionary France, as far as I know, and has few imitators. The only other writer approaching Nogaret's radical disregard for the book-as-object is perhaps novelist David Shields. Shields announced to readers of his so-called free-appropriation manifesto *Reality Hunger* (2010): "If you would like to restore this book to the form in which I intended it to be read, simply grab a sharp pair of scissors or a razor blade or box cutter and remove pages 210–218 by cutting along the dotted line."[55] Why? So that one will not see the appendix that the publisher's lawyers required him to include and that lists his many sources. But while Shields's free-market libertarianism served him and his book sales alone (under the specious notion that "reality cannot be copyrighted"), Nogaret's was an attempt to give away learning for free. The frontispiece (fig. 13) lays out two modes of reading: if one seeks only diversion, one should read the whole book. If one seeks to help the revolutionary cause, one should turn directly to page 69, where there is a reproduction of an anticlerical article by Voltaire and the startling advice: "Informed reader, you know [Voltaire's article]; but the common people are not familiar with it, and it is they who must be enlightened. The common man . . . does not have the means to buy sixty volumes to read the twenty lines. . . . *Rip these useful pages out of my book, give them to him, they should not cost him a cent. Thus, you and I, we will have done some good*" (69, my emphasis). Nogaret's *Miroir* is the only book I know that tells readers to rip out its pages and give them away. Perhaps that is why there are so few copies in existence today.[56]

Nogaret's "Aglaonice, ou La Belle au concours" (1795)

The second edition of *Le Miroir*, published in 1795, destabilized the political message, however. A new framing device and a number of textual omissions transformed the tale from a timely allegory and vehicle of enlightenment into a frivolous love story. First, the novella "Aglaonice, ou La Belle au concours" (Aglaonice, or Beauty in the contest) was no longer published as a stand-alone pamphlet but was tucked inside a collection of mildly erotic tales.[57] Second, the author shortened the title, eliminated the reference to actuality, and focused the tale on the traffic in women. Third, he eliminated the frontispiece that proposed the two alternative modes of reading and called for the reader's involvement. Fourth, the tale no longer bears a dedication in which the beautiful orphan/book is placed in the care of an honest government official. Fifth, the most significant inventor's name is truncated, and the allusion to Vaucanson eliminated (he is now called Wak-wik-vauk-an-frankenstein). Sixth, pages 69–75 are deleted and with them the reproduction of the article "Massacres." Instead, the narrative of clerical abuse in "Le Souper" simply includes a footnote that indicates: "See the article *Massacres* in the questions of Voltaire on *l'Encyclopédie*."[58] But perhaps the most glaring change lies in a passage that was left unchanged but that would have created a completely different effect in 1795 than it did in the original. Describing the good works of the Lutecian king who brought in grain to feed the common folk, abolished unjust taxes, and eliminated the influence of "druids" and nobility, the narrator concludes with a celebration of mutual gratitude between the king and his people. Showing a medallion commemorating the reciprocal sacrifices made by the king (pictured as a pelican) and his capital city (shown as a female suckling her father), Frankenstein declares: "The people here do for their King, what he has done for them. . . . Behind them one espies all the other cities of the kingdom, anxious to enjoy the same good fortune as Lutecia."[59] This evocation of optimism for monarchical reform in a novella published two years after the execution of Louis XVI deepens the divide between "Aglaonice" and the "Actuality" of 1790. The variants and anachronisms make the story read like an antiquarian fable rather than a polemic on current events.

Along with these jarring discrepancies is the suppression of Nogaret's most acid anticlerical vitriol, that is, the comment "Whatever you may think, you are the descendant either of assassins or victims. Choose and tremble" (*Le Miroir*, 75). Nogaret returned to political propaganda in a 1798 publication in which he described himself as a martyr to the republican cause: "If I am poor, it's because after losing everything, I refused to gain it back by writing for the court; if I exist, it's because France is saved."[60] But already in "Aglaonice" and later with increasing frequency, the author describes himself as the French Aristenet, a pleasure-loving old man who eschews politics for more earthy concerns and urges his readers to enjoy life, *carpe diem*.

Such pragmatism was not uncommon during the mid-1790s. Although there was a striking uptick in novel publishing during the last years of the century, in 1794–95 the industry remained constrained by inflation and unpredictable governmental policies claiming to protect freedom of speech but aiming to control cultural production. It made sense in this context for Nogaret to recast his allegory as a titillating romance; the genre was highly favored and apparently sold well. Nevertheless, the changes made to this tale between the 1790 and 1795 editions cast the automatons' role in a new light. By suppressing his demand for political involvement, the author disavows the projects of improving upon nature (in the making of automatons) and remaking society (in the convergence between narratives of revolutionary French and Lutecian history). When shorn of their actuality the winning inventions of "Aglaonice" look futile. The technology appears to work less as a means of satisfying human desires for improvement and more as a symbol of the inanity of those desires (a lesson perhaps even more apropos in today's gadget-cluttered landscape). The heroine's final choice could be considered an empty-headed mannequin: after all, the robots do not fulfill any really useful purpose like assembling tools or manufacturing weapons; they are merely accoutrements of gracious living whose bows and curtsies smack of ancien régime gentility. It is possible that Nogaret, in keeping the basic narrative of the 1790 edition in the 1795 version, was reverting to a genre and philosophy he had cultivated to acclaim in the 1770s when he served as librarian to the king's sister-in-law: a hedonism valorizing pleasure, beauty, and love over more serious or sobering aspects of human existence. But it is also possible that, after witnessing the gruesome fate of Louis

XVI and the ravages of the Terror, the author had second thoughts about the notion of remaking society along political lines. (His later comments certainly suggest that he changed his mind about using literature in ideological warfare.) Without the paratextual attack on the clergy and the call to arms against Deputy Bergasse, the urgency dissipates. The closing scene of courtship and marriage holds interest only as a relic of the long-lost Syracusan civilization. There can be no hopes for constitutional monarchy, no return to the time when a fatherly king might have established a more just society. The formerly two-faced tale deflates to a single meaning.

This not-so-subtle shift in emphasis underlines the turn in the five years between 1790 and 1795 from a conception of literature as a moral and political force capable of intervening in history, and the author as a speaker of truth, to a conception of literature as merely a leisure pursuit and the author as entertainer. Where the fictional writers in tales such as *Le Falot du peuple* (The people's lantern; ca. 1792–93), *Les Aventures de Jérôme Lecocq* (The adventures of Jerome Lecocq; 1794), and *Amin, ou Ces derniers temps* (Amin, or These last times; 1797–98) all endeavor to make themselves useful to their fellow men by writing, the last character, Amin, is less sure that it will do much good.[61] Such tensions were tied to political trends in France during the years after Thermidor, when a *politique de bascule*, or see-saw politics, catapulted the country between strong-arm militarism and populist revolt.[62] Hence, the hero of *Amin* is seen to do the most good when his writing career is interrupted by a call from the government and he becomes an army general (*Amin*, 155–63). Many other works of the post-Thermidor period explicitly eschewed the political or focused on its traumatic effects on individuals or families. Obscene and libertine fiction enjoyed an upsurge of interest as well, much to the dismay of civic-minded critics like Louis-Sébastien Mercier. This tension between the concept of author-as-prophet and author-as-entertainer would torture the generation of writers who came of age in the 1830s and continues to plague readers today.[63] Is it any surprise that when the specter of political or environmental crises proves too intimidating, audiences seek a retreat from reality?

THE AUTOMATON BETWEEN *LE MIROIR* AND *FRANKENSTEIN*: CONDORCET, DOPPET, AND HOFFMANN

As a metaphor in philosophy and literature, the term "automaton" (*automate*) was invariably pejorative and suggestive of "puppet" or "monkey": an empty-headed creature of habit. Denis Diderot famously articulated the link between automatism and obedience in *La Religieuse* (begun in 1760; published in 1796) with its scathing portrayal of convent life. Reform-minded writers celebrated innovations such as the freedom of the press for transforming the people from automatons into citizens and criticized the clergy for treating men as machines. Metaphors of automation applied more widely as well. A Saint-Domingue newspaper of 1791 cites a loyalist complaining that naysayers were criticizing the new "political machine" of constitutional monarchy; the loyalist used an extended analogy of cogs, bolts, and gears to defend King Louis XVI: "You present a barely built mechanism to the man expected to turn its lever and you tell him that its constitution requires him to turn it right away, even though it is only half-built. What happens? He turns it [the lever], and inevitably he disturbs and bends its very first gearwheels."[64] Stressing the importance of treating people as individuals or the time it takes to construct a smooth-running apparatus, these writers reveal the power of mechanical metaphors to make a political point.

Six months later, the famous mathematician Condorcet turned the logic of this last example on its head when he wove the automaton metaphor into an amusing critique of Louis XVI in "Lettre d'un jeune mécanicien" (Letter from a young mechanic). Claiming to be trained by Vaucanson, Condorcet contacts a left-wing newspaper with a solution for the problems revealed by His Majesty's escape attempt of June 1791: a new royal family crafted out of clockwork. Cognizant of His Majesty's spiritual needs, the machine would include a special interface allowing the king to bow, kneel, and worship before a detachable icon, "so as to facilitate the substitution of another, in case of a change in religion." Extending the satire to the very principles of the Bourbon monarchy, the narrator argues that his invention is preferable to the present model because it would simultaneously save money and protect the citizenry, since "my king would pose no danger to freedom, and yet, if one carefully maintained the mechanism, he would live forever, which is even better than being hereditary. One could declare him inviolable without injustice, and infallible without absurdity."[65] From the January 1791 defense of the man "who is expected to turn the lever" to this spoof on a wind-up toy, the public image of the king's role had shrunk precipitously.

The term "automaton" would take on more bitter and widespread connotations in Mercier's account of the Revolution published in Year 8 (1799–1800). Mercier applies the moniker across the board; *automates* are the duc d'Orléans (supposed to be a puppet of the English court), the imprisoned and useless King Louis XVI after the flight to Varennes, and the imperturbable Robespierre in front of the guillotine. Unlike the marionette-like duc

d'Orléans or the mechanical Capet, Robespierre is endowed with a diabolical intent: "he was an automaton straight out of hell sent to punish the
humans."[66] Whoever failed to fight for the right cause, supported the wrong
cause, or remained indifferent to the revolutionary cause was deemed an
automate.

Quite literally, some automatons actually did serve—or seem to serve—
the enemy. A fascinating example of automaton espionage emerges in a
Jacobin novel from 1792, where one reads the adventures of a courier who
takes messages and commissions for the aristocracy back and forth between
their camps and homes in France, Italy, and Prussia. Written by a general
in the republican army, François-Amédée Doppet (1753–1800), *Le Commissionnaire de la Ligue d'Outre-Rhin* (The commissioner of the Trans-Rhine
League) claims to recount the repentance of a former counterrevolutionary
who has rejoined the nation and now reveals the tricks and secrets of its
enemies. On one occasion the hero is assigned the task of carrying a life-size
automaton resembling a thirty-year-old woman to its owner in Turin. The
owner is none other than the king's brother, the much-hated comte d'Artois,
who had fled Versailles and abandoned the monarchy two days after the
Bastille fell. Upon arriving at the border, the courier writes: "The visitors
were struck with astonishment and . . . took the automaton for an emigrating aristocrat." Most amusing—but not without peril—was the movement
the doll made when the customs agents opened the carriage door and the
reaction of the startled onlookers: "the springs bounced and the automaton
sat up as soon as they [the customs agents] opened the case. A crowd of
people gathered around, each Piedmontese made his own stupid comment,
and I barely got away before they charged that the Count d'A*** was a wizard, his automaton was the devil's wife, and I myself was the devil incar-
nate. Others . . . argued that the automaton was only a pretext used by the
French to sneak out jewels, gold, and aristocratic correspondence."[67] This
passage is remarkable for the multiple valences surrounding the automaton
and its companion in the volatile political context of France in 1792: the
lifelike mannequin signifies devilry and a traditional religious superstition,
but it also makes people think of aristocrats and their plots against the Republic. While the idea of a grown man owning a doll surprises modern readers, it was apparently not uncommon in early-modern Europe for wealthy
people of both sexes to own and display life-size porcelain mannequins; the
practice is noted in Lesuire's catchall novel *Charmansage* (1792) as well.[68] It
is striking how the narrator shows the doll piercing the boundaries between
banal and uncanny and inspiring a sense of malaise in onlookers. As Terry
Castle has noted, "the eighteenth-century invention of the automaton was

also (in the most obvious sense) an 'invention' of the uncanny," that encom-
passing sense of strangeness and unease.[69]

The psychological ramifications of this theme would receive most stunning treatment by the German author E. T. A. Hoffmann in his portrayal
of a conspiracy between two scientist-technicians who dupe a naive student with an automated doll in *The Sandman* (1816). Although Hoffmann's
narrative owes less to the politically utilitarian ethos of *Le Miroir* or Doppet's *Le Commissionnaire* than to the German genre of fantasy-horror, his
extraordinary depiction of human-humanoid sympathy places *The Sandman* firmly within the automaton tradition. Hoffmann also penned an 1814
article entitled "Die Automate" and a number of later works featuring brilliant scientists who produce copies of life that cross boundaries between
realism and possibility.[70] Transmitted through the words of a narrator who
is visibly enthralled by the volatile mental states of the protagonist, *The
Sandman* depicts a diabolical inventor named Spalanzani and his confederate, the instrument seller Coppola (also known as Coppelius), who together
represent the most notorious traits of turn-of-the-century pseudoscience.
First, the name Spalanzani would conjure up a biologist's threat to the Great
Chain of Being, since the Italian scientist Abate Lazzaro Spallanzani (1729–
99) was best known for making worms in his laboratory demonstrate spontaneous generation. Second, Spalanzani's hidden laboratory, with its vials,
retorts, and flasks, suggests an alchemist's single-minded pursuit of the forbidden. And last but not least, the perverse pleasure that Spalanzani and
Coppola take in fooling the hero Nathanael reveals their malevolent intent.

The life-size doll Olympia, we learn, was the product of twenty years
of Spalanzani's labor and includes the most modern facets of period invention—speech and movement—as well as one component unknown among
real-life inventors: realistic clockwork eyes. When the eyes are knocked out
of Olympia's head in the climactic scene of her destruction, and Nathanael
sees them "staring up at him from the floor," the discrepancy between the
eyeless dummy and his imagined beloved moves him to rage. Screaming,
"Wooden doll, whirl around!" he would have strangled Spalanzani but for
the intervention of others, who restrain him and take him off to a mad-
house. While some townspeople claim this incident was a drawn-out allegory on the limits of technical knowledge, most find it profoundly disqui-
eting. They begin questioning their own powers to discern animate from
inanimate objects and puzzle over the possibility of knowing what it means
to be human at all.

What saves *The Sandman* from descending into Gothic horror or tiresome metaphysics is the irony and humor that run through the narration

as meaning shuttles back and forth between matter-of-fact literalism and the fanciful, terrifying language of metaphor. Sometimes the debunking is explicit. In one of the three letters that frame the story, Nathanael claims that his father was burned alive by a mysteriously malevolent figure known as the Sandman (who he thinks was actually his father's lawyer, Coppelius). But his girlfriend, Klara, counters that the fire was probably caused by an alchemical experiment of his father's own making. When Nathanael divulges his belief in what sounds like a vitalist philosophy, claiming that "creation comes not from within us but results from the influence of a higher external principle," because all men are naught but "the horrible plaything of dark powers," Klara brushes off the claim as "mystical nonsense" (*Sandman*, 285–91). Sometimes the demystification is merely implied. Thus, when Nathanael describes the sympathetic vibrations emanating from Olympia's presence, his emotional investment is relayed through verbs of emotion and perception instead of logic or description. Recalling his first peek at the doll through Spalanzani's curtains, for instance, Nathanael reflects that "she did not seem to notice me; indeed, her eyes seemed fixed, I might almost say without vision" (288). Gazing at her later through a spyglass that he bought from the vendor Coppola, we read: "It seemed as if the power of vision were only now starting to be kindled; her glances were inflamed with ever-increasing life" (297). Note the reliance on the verb "seem" and the modifier "almost" and "only now," which demarcate Nathanael's distorted perception from the domain of the real.

Hoffmann's two-page description of the ball at Spalanzani's home and its social repercussions is where the clash between Nathanael's conviction of Olympia's sympathy explodes into public with tragicomic results. In words that can convey either small-town ostracism or neutral description, the narrator notes that there was "something stiff and measured about her walk that struck many unfavorably," and that her singing voice sounded "high-pitched, bell-like, almost shrill." For Nathanael such details make her all the more desirable: overcome with emotion, he cries out her name. "Everyone looked at him; many laughed." He seeks only her eyes in the crowd, and "he saw that they shone at him with love and longing; and at that moment the pulse seemed to beat again in her cold hand, and warm life-blood to surge through her veins." Even though the "peculiar rhythmical evenness" of her dancing confuses him, he shields the newcomer from hostility and speaks to her of love "in words that no one could understand, neither he nor Olympia. But perhaps she did, for she sat with her eyes fixed on his, sighing again and again, 'Ah, ah, ah!'" (299–300).

Deflecting the criticism of a well-meaning friend, Nathanael construes his relationship as an ideal of which most humans can only dream: "Olympia may indeed appear weird to you cold and unimaginative mortals [but] I discover myself again only in Olympia's love." So he pursues the object single-mindedly and tells her "about mutual sympathy kindled into life," to which the narrator ironically chuckles: "Never before had he had such a splendid listener" (302). Once the hoax is made public, however, and Spalanzani is expelled from the city, the ludicrous implications of this situation become apparent. The menfolk, seized with "a horrible distrust of human figures in general," insist that their wives and girlfriends converse with them "in such a way that it would prove that they really were capable of thinking and feeling" (306). The results are mixed, as one might expect![71]

The final scene of cognitive confusion in *The Sandman* arrives when Nathanael—now healed from his breakdown—visits a clock tower with his fiancée, Klara, and accidentally peers at her with a spyglass. This bizarre episode underlines the double meaning running through the story between scientific mastery, on the one hand, and human intuition, on the other, and the fear that the former may usurp the latter. Seeing Klara magnified through the scope, Nathanael does not recognize her humanity but rather thinks he sees her true identity at last: she is another freakish doll foisted upon him by an evil conspiracy. Screaming, "Whirl wooden doll!" he tries to throw her over the edge to her death. Although they have known each other since childhood, there is no intuitive recognition of his sweetheart in Nathanael's shortened vision. Technology clouds his judgment. Conversely, one might note that there never was any understanding between Nathanael and Olympia, despite the technicians' superlative skills in making that state-of-the-art automaton. There was only an intuition of sympathy, sown by meddling tricksters in the fragile mind of an unstable youth. There too the results are horrendous. Indeed, perhaps there is no magic or vital resonance behind any of these events, which can all be understood as a series of unfortunate causes and effects in a tragic provincial anecdote.

Or can they? Sigmund Freud was inspired by this tale to create the psychic contours of what he called the uncanny—a feeling of uncertainty about whether objects are living or inanimate—and it is true that, even after Olympia's mechanical origins are resolved, the final scene introduces new doubts into the universe.[72] Nathanael's final fiery burst of energy, when he becomes unhinged by the sight of a moving bush below the clock tower and the lawyer Coppelius's laughing face peering up at him, deals a jolt to readers and makes us wonder. Perhaps someone really was conspiring to push him into the abyss by making inanimate objects look alive. Perhaps some occurrences really do elude rational exegesis, only we cannot bear

their sight. An 1817 review of *The Sandman* dismissed it as a Gothic tale—
a *schauderhaftes Nachtstück*, or a ghastly night piece—but the reviewer
got it all wrong, according to Hanne Castein, because he missed this crucial
aspect of Hoffmann's irony, the suspension of disbelief.[73] Unlike the Gothic
novelist, who elicits passion and excitement before staging a final accom-
modation with social norms, Hoffmann leaves the situation unclear, suggesting that irrational or evil forces may not only exist but may also seek
deliberately to thwart our attempts to maintain order or make meaning out
of life. The uncertainty over what Nathanael saw in the moment before
jumping to his death confounds easy answers and makes this tale a powerfully unsettling link in the chain of otherwise-rational, utilitarian automaton sightings leading up to *Frankenstein*.

   Mical's talking heads, Nogaret's flautist, Condorcet's clockwork king,
Doppet's emigrating lady, and Hoffmann's moving doll form a literary tradition that shows how mechanics can be put to sociopolitical purposes. The
ideological impact of Nogaret's tale fades between the 1790 edition and its
1795 reprint but the original presented a resounding message. Although the
technology that made them move was vaguely sketched, the fact that the
objects were presented by technicians in a contest to promote invention
removed the automaton from the realm of the supernatural and reinforced
its ties to Enlightenment science. In their genesis and ultimate political
function, Nogaret's automatons mark the trends that characterized 1790:
skepticism toward the church inherited from Voltaire and Diderot, utopian
politics inherited from Rousseau, and pragmatic concern for fiscal reality
inspired by Necker. Hoffmann digs deeper into the psychological chill conjured up by the sight of inanimate animation and forces us to realize the inherent strangeness of automatons. With his clumsy physiological makeup,
his artificial origins, and especially his failure to achieve "sympathy" with
humans, Shelley's creature belongs to this lineage too, though his meaning
is less easy to discern.

   But perhaps such prismatic illusions are inevitable, double meanings
being implicit in the mechanism of automatism. For turn-of-the-century
audiences the automaton incarnated both aesthetics and industry: the
dumb beauty of a doll and a simulacrum of human intelligence. By imagining a mechanical being that walks and talks like a human, bears an uncanny
resemblance to a human, and nevertheless remains entirely subservient to
the will of its maker, *Le Miroir* and *The Sandman* belong to the mechanical
tradition. Whether cast as elements of an anticlerical morality play, a classic marriage plot, or a mysterious conspiracy, all of these robots function in

stark simplicity and hail from a cartoonish universe far removed from the unreliable landscape traversed by Shelley's creature.

It is only with *Frankenstein* that we see an author imagining not only how to replicate a human appearance but also how to simulate a totally believable human psychology and subjectivity. This shift was one of Michel Foucault's major insights in *The Order of Things* (*Les Mots et les choses*; 1966), where he wrote that in the beginning of the nineteenth century, "man" was invented, that is, as a subjective consciousness that was also and necessarily an empirical object.[74] Automatons being representations of human beings, the fact that Nogaret and others were able to depict only the outward appearance of a human being falls into Foucault's framework, which describes classical man as a fashioner of tables of knowledge, as yet incapable of representing himself as both subject and object of knowledge. The preeminence that Nogaret and Hoffmann gave to the automaton was a step toward the realization of our selves as subjects and objects, but it would take Shelley to flesh out this idea to its fullest potential.

CODA: FRANKENSTEIN'S CREATURE IN THE MECHANICAL MOLD

A tension between enthusiasm and disdain for remaking mankind resonates profoundly in *Frankenstein*. Twenty-some years after *Le Miroir*, Shelley's post-Waterloo dystopia struggles mightily over the potential of collaboration between humans and humanoids and the political hopes that it incarnates. Significant to Shelley scholarship are the questions: what went wrong with the Revolution, and with Victor Frankenstein and his creature? Since the answers are legion, the moral that emerges from *Frankenstein* is fundamentally unstable. We can, however, discern a continuity of meaning issuing from the automaton's tale.

Driven by the changing interests of Shelley's readers, hundreds of interpretations have been proposed for *Frankenstein* over the years—including theories of "lesbian panic," Kantian aesthetics, vegetarianism, and obstetrics—but the French Revolution remains a crucial component for political interpretations.[75] Although I have yet to find traces of *Le Miroir* in their journals, it is important to realize the ambitious readings undertaken by Mary and Percy Shelley in the years 1814–17. Ronald Paulson and Pamela Clemit have shown how a tragic awareness of the suffering caused by ambition loomed large in their conversations and readings. They were at once filled with admiration for Mary's famous parents William Godwin and Mary

Wollstonecraft and tortured by their own experience of coming of age in a country traumatized by years of violent conflict with the French military. In wide-ranging studies that included the counterrevolutionary diatribes of Abbé Barruel as well as the utopianism of Godwin, the young couple sought "an intelligible explanation of how the progressive ideals of the French Revolution had collapsed in despotism, both at home and abroad."[76]

How then can the automaton's tale help illuminate *Frankenstein*? In two ways: on the metalevel of the plot's sociopolitical significance and on the microlevel of the artificial man's story. On the metalevel, there is a parallel between the narrative movement in *Frankenstein* from idyll to suffering and the chronological movement of the Revolution that we saw punctuated by automaton tales. The happiest moment of *Frankenstein* occurs when the creature coexists invisibly with an impoverished family of French émigrés (vol. 2, chaps. 3–7). As months go by, he enjoys watching the De Laceys through the window of their cottage: he learns their language, listens to their readings, and dreams of joining their fireside chats. Touched by their poverty, he secretly offers them gifts of wood. When a beautiful foreigner arrives, he watches as they greet her warmly and usher her into their home, where she joins their quiet life of subsistence farming. One might read this episode as Shelley's model of what a reformed nation might look like, that is, a liberal, egalitarian, and protofeminist family led by a kindly, albeit blind, father figure.[77] This ideal is explicitly articulated in the text, as the creature/narrator praises the group's intergenerational harmony, admires their loving embrace of the stranger, and hopes that he too may one day enjoy their esteem: "Benevolence and generosity were ever present before me, inciting within me a desire to become an actor in the busy scene" (85). But when the creature finally tries to enter their fold, he is rudely cast out. The narrative pivots here from utopian potential to dystopian reality, thus following the progression in the French Revolution from the "happy year" of 1790 captured by *Le Miroir* to the terrifying juxtaposition of authoritarianism and anarchy that marked 1793–94.[78] Just as the French later looked back on the year of the Federation with nostalgia for the unity that did not endure, the creature in *Frankenstein* stresses what might have been. But since it cannot be, he spitefully vows to burn the De Laceys' cottage and sets off his decline into murder and mayhem.

In destroying this idyll, Shelley marks the end of functional family life in *Frankenstein*. The narrative alternation between a commitment to believing utopia to be achievable and a commitment to thinking it not achievable was typical of English literature in the 1790s–1820s, as seen, for instance, in Charlotte Smith's *Desmond* (1792) and William Godwin's *Caleb*

Williams (1794). No family can withstand the tensions in *Frankenstein*. All the families in the novel are destroyed, estranged, or dysfunctional for some reason; guilt and pain hang heavy over them. The adorable Elizabeth, through no fault of her own, is abandoned by her father upon his second marriage. Despite avowing warm affection for her and the rest of his family, Victor seems to take every opportunity to leave them—for Ingolstadt, for Scotland, or for the North Pole—any place is better than home.[79] In the scene of the lonely creature peeking in on communal life that he can never enjoy, the novel casts a starkly pessimistic comment on the possibility of caring and of community.

One might interpret this disillusionment as an allusion to the failed fathers and broken homes that marked French writings after Varennes. In the history of automatons above and more thoroughly in chapter 3, I show how the royal family's escape attempt in June 1791 elicited an avalanche of derision and disappointment. By 1792 Louis XVI had been reduced from a regal colossus to a puppet of émigré princes, and the earlier hopes for a constitutional meritocracy faded as news of his betrayal spread. Years later, having survived the trials of emigration, rationing, and Terror, people narrowed their visions to home and hearth and discarded republican ideals for a new ethos of self-interested survival. The literature of 1795–99 reflects this inward focus in the decline of politically engaged writing depicting individual sympathies that culminate in collective actions, as in *Le Miroir*, and charts instead an increase in Gothic, pastoral, and libertine genres, all of which pull the solitary subject into a kind of day-dreamy detachment. In the creature's interaction with the De Lacey family lies a parable of the failed republican ideal. While initially sympathetic, the king-father proves ultimately incapable of understanding, and their heartfelt conversation, in which the old man pledges to help the creature, climaxes in an unanswered question. On the verge of disclosure, after hearing his litany of sorrow and complaint, old man De Lacey calls out to the creature: "Great God! . . . Who are you?" (91). But he never hears the reply.

At the microlevel of the creature's story, the automaton tradition proves relevant as well. Consider the novel's treatment of invention and inventors. Echoes of the ambivalence toward inventors' abilities to provide the kind of "useful discoveries" decreed in the 1790–91 patent legislation, and exemplified by the editorial changes between the 1790 *Miroir* and its later edition, resound in *Frankenstein*. Initially, young Victor is praised by his colleagues, who envision a brilliant future for him. After just a few years at university, one teacher praises "the astonishing progress [he] made in the sciences," and another declares the pupil "has outstript us all" (42). One cannot deny that he creates life. And yet criticism dogs his every step in the later parts of the novel. Some claim that the very name "Frankenstein" would have recalled an ancient legend of failed science for Shelley, stemming from a chance encounter on a trip to Germany. Others claim he is best understood as a misguided amateur whose obsession gets in the way of his studies.[80]

Victor's plan for animating dead matter relies on his ability to capture the so-called principle of life: a premise that would have been subject to no little controversy had he actually conversed with peers in the London scientific world of 1815–18. Known as the Vitalist Debate, the issue garnered publicity in a series of public lectures that pitted two experts at the Royal College of Surgeons against each other and culminated in a book by William Lawrence published June 1816. Rebuking belief in inorganic particles, Lawrence reduced biology to strictly material principles. His now-famous proposal for rejuvenating mankind was to be enacted through biological, not artificial, means: marriage and sexual intercourse between strong and handsome people. Lawrence ridiculed the notion that the life principle was some kind of extraneous element analogous to electricity that could be added or extracted from bodies and argued instead that animation was an integral component of organic life, to be studied only by close observation of living creatures' actions over time. Apart from the mechanical distribution of desirable traits (i.e., eugenics), there was no way to create a new species.[81] The project hatched by Shelley's scientist thus operates on a quixotic theory that a real-life physician (and friend of the Shelley-Godwin circle) publicly disproved during the writing of *Frankenstein*. One could argue then that Victor Frankenstein fails because his training is insufficient if not entirely misguided.

It is interesting to note that the influence of Victor's professor at Ingolstadt (vol. 1, chap. 2) was written in considerably more emphatic terms in the 1831 edition. After listening to the eminent chemist enthuse about the "new and almost unlimited powers" of modern science, Victor becomes a puppet in Waldman's hands. He later recalls: "Such were the professor's words—rather let me say such the words of fate, enounced to destroy me. As he went on, I felt as if my soul were grappling with a palpable enemy; one by one the various keys were touched which formed the mechanism of my being: chord after chord was sounded, and soon my mind was filled with one thought, one conception, one purpose."[82] It is as if he were unable to shrug off an invincible force controlling his mind. Moreover, Shelley herself in the 1831 introduction claims to have sought out a mechanical tool to make the creature move, as noted above. Anne Mellor contends that these revisions are so complete as to constitute a paradigm shift whereby the earlier organic conception of creation gives way to a mechanistic one: "She now portrays nature as a mighty machine, a juggernaut, an 'imperial' tyrant."[83] Victor's downfall thus seems to depend less on his ignorance or failure to love than on a chain of consequences set off by his teacher's irresponsible panegyric on chemistry's potency to alter life.

The component parts of the invention were likely defective as well. The scientist's plan to create a new species out of random yet handsome body parts found in sites such as charnel houses and paupers' graves forms an apt analogy for the French legislators' dream of creating a regenerated man (*l'homme régénéré*) out of a French citizenry that was idealized as virile, dedicated, and hardworking.[84] No more unified than the monster's parts, this group turns out to be a motley assortment of superstitious, vengeful, barely literate, barely French-speaking, impoverished wretches. Mary Shelley's distaste for the common people is no secret. Recording her trip to Germany in September 1814, she speaks with disgust of the "horrid and slimy faces" of her coach companions (whom she calls loathsome "creepers"), and she notes: "Our only wish was to absolutely annihilate such uncleanly animals, to which we might have addressed the Boatman's speech to Pope— 'Twere easier for God to make entirely new men than attempt to purify such monsters as these.'"[85] Although torn by the political hopes of those around her, especially Percy Shelley and her parents, Mary Shelley's writings suggest that she was not entirely cynical about the revolutionaries' attempts at social engineering; rather, she was poignantly aware of the vast task. Whether one tried to effect abrupt change through vitalist, mechanical, or political means, efforts to create a new man would inevitably be fraught with difficulty.

Continuing the analogy with the automaton, let us consider the destructive drive that animates Shelley's creature in his later actions. Even the most highly sophisticated machines often reflect unintended aspects of their designers: humanoid qualities include character traits such as shyness as much as physical traits like head and arms. As one researcher in robotics has noted, "A lot of the inspiration for the robots seems to come from some kind of deficiency in being human."[86] Like a Pygmalion scenario gone awry, Frankenstein's creation bears the mark of its inventor too, that is, an adolescent vision of superhuman energy and ambition. In his single-minded pursuit to find a way of infusing life into an inanimate body, the scientist apparently forgot to think through the consequences, such as the body's potential to procreate. He belittles those who fall short of his notion of greatness, as when he exhorts Walton's crew—stuck on the polar ice cap—to disregard personal safety and strive toward the impossible: "Oh! be men, or be more than men!" he scolds them. "[This ice] cannot withstand you, if you say that it shall not. Do not return to your families with the stigma of disgrace marked on your brows. Return as heroes who have fought and conquered" (149–50). A frenetic striving toward ill-conceived and irresponsible goals is Victor's tragic character flaw, and it is incarnated in the being he creates as well.

But it is not the creature's fault. Rather, he is a victim of all that which made him. Physically, he is an amalgam of random body parts, and mentally, he is a product of his creator's indifference and society's ill-will. In this he recalls Godwin's hero Caleb Williams, who at the end of his tortuous saga is described by his oldest friend as "a machine . . . not constituted, I am afraid, to be greatly useful to your fellow men; but you did not make yourself; you are just what circumstances irresistibly compelled you to be."[87] In Shelley's depiction of the hapless creature struggling against a society and a creator that he perceives to be aiming for his extinction, isolationism is a temporary, failed answer to social anomie, and all-out anarchy seems right around the corner. In this she reveals her debt to the post-Waterloo age when monarchical control was reimposed throughout Europe but spontaneous mob actions made violence a real threat. By the last scene, when the characters face off among the Arctic ice floes, one realizes the ultimate instability of the *Frankenstein* story—about science, about technology, or about politics.

◦≫◦

The coincidences of name and action linking *Le Miroir* and *Frankenstein* point to an important and original epiphenomenon in literary history. Where the family stands in as a metaphor for the ideal state in *Le Miroir*, in *Frankenstein* it is but a fragile icon of a lost age of innocence and hope. Unlike the docile machines of Nogaret, whose function is to help their creators find a wife and, by extension, to aid in the establishment of a secular and prosperous society, and unlike the equally artisanal automaton of Hoffmann, which perishes in a scuffle between rival inventors, Shelley's lonely creature has a mind, a will, and a biology of his own. He needs a partner to mate with and to bring meaning to his existence. When thwarted, he systematically murders Frankenstein's loved ones and annihilates the scientist's hopes for the future. This complex technological innovation in the biological sphere is fraught with moral pain and heartsickness, whereas the simple and hand-crafted inventions of the earlier texts fully realize their inventors' ambitions. The humanlike brain, emotions, and longings of Shelley's creature make all the difference.

I interpret the male characters surrounding this chapter's automatons—the inventor-husbands and the caring senator of Nogaret, the shifty physicist-technicians of Hoffmann—as useful interlocutors for unpacking the process by which the modern age came to be seen as such. As Marie-Hélène Huet has noted in describing the Romantic period (1790–1830), the break with the ancien régime depended upon the "silent father" regaining his place: "simultaneously, the status of the model will become problematic, and an idea of the artist as father will be advanced with force and passion as that influence which pervades and motivates signs, norms, and monstrosities."[88] Huet claims that the literary renaissance of monster figures such as Shelley's Frankenstein marked the resurgence of a male agency that replaced earlier genesis narratives that relied on maternal imagination. The stories of Nogaret's heroine Aglaonice and her automaton-bearing suitors and of Nathanael's misguided affair with the automaton Olympia are transitional narratives that shuttle between premodern and modern concepts of creation. Although we are talking about technological, instead of biological, agency here, what is significant is that creation is already projected as a masculine prerogative.

These analogies suggest a literary ancestry rooted in different ideological homes and political moods, but all share a fascination with the impact that technology and its artificial creations have on the world, for better or for worse. Although Nogaret's and Hoffmann's transitional narratives animate the "silent father" in intriguing ways and articulate a tentative movement from Cartesianism to a more biological conception of life, like Shelley's creator they too proved incapable of sustaining the "spark of life" into a durable future. That work was left for future statesmen, thinkers, and artists and the phantasms they left in their wake. In our own day audiences are still struggling with the unease that results from blurred categories between androids and humans, thanks to the uncanny villainess of Ridley Scott's science-fiction film *Blade Runner* (1982) and the creepy Japanese robot model Mimu unveiled in 2009. As robots infiltrate more aspects of our daily life and simulate increasingly human affects, we may one day realize that these early authors got it right. Controlling technological creation may take on altogether different and much scarier dimensions when the robots do what we do, but better.

CHAPTER THREE

The Once and Only Pitiful King

He who establishes a dictatorship and does not kill Brutus, or he who founds a republic and does not kill the sons of Brutus, will only reign a short time.

—Machiavelli, *Discorsi*

Man, man, one cannot live quite without pity.

—Dostoevsky, *Crime and Punishment*

Given the magnitude of events, this chapter takes a two-part approach to the king's fate. Part 1 relates his spectacular fall in public esteem after the failed escape attempt of 1791. Part 2 concentrates on how his touching good-byes and brutal execution in January 1793 prompted efforts to redeem Louis XVI as a martyred father figure. Both sections analyze the king's actions as they were depicted in the news, pamphlets, novels, and his own writings published from 1791 to 1803. As in other chapters, the coda follows these threads into the next generation and reveals how Honoré de Balzac put a satiric spin on the concept of kingly fatherhood thirty years later in *Le Père Goriot*.

The king's disgrace on the night of June 21, 1791, sent immediate shock waves through Europe as news of his humiliating arrest at the eastern town of Varennes, his long trip back to Paris, and his subsequent confinement under armed guard burst into polemic, fiction, and caricature. Guilt is an essential theme of all Varennes narratives, but pardon and blame trade sides depending on the observer's perception and politics. The sentimental rhetoric and appeal to the reader's pity, for example, both of which figure prominently in accounts of the famous recognition scene at Sauce's inn, appeared to some witnesses as character flaws denoting the king's coward-

ice and profiteering, while to others they evoked a touchingly human connection between the king and his people. Whatever the observers' initial
thoughts might have been regarding the so-called kidnapping, when they
heard of the incendiary proclamation left in the Tuileries palace on the eve
of the king's flight—and learned that it was written by the king himself—
a deepening schism divided the loyal from a newly invigorated opposition
in the National Assembly, the clubs, and the media. In his public acts and
published autobiographical portrait, the king inadvertently cast doubts on
his own legitimacy that rapidly devolved into proof of national betrayal.
But he nevertheless held on to the notion of himself as a loving father of the
people to the end, as a glance at his last will and testament shows. When
transposed into the bourgeois setting of Le Père Goriot, the failed father and
his unreciprocated love cloak the Bourbon legacy in bitter irony.

By condemning the monarch to death eighteen months after Varennes,
the revolutionary government announced its hostility to a Rousseauian
kind of compassionate justice and forcefully shifted public debate away
from terms of emotional intent to starker signifiers of identity. The Constituent Assembly's hopes for a nation built on loyalty oaths and fellow feeling gave way to a less confident Convention government, whose troubled
status at home and abroad prompted a more militaristic attitude toward
civic engagement with the republican cause. But patrolling people's feelings
then, as now, was no easy task. As soon as the Terror ended and censorship
loosened a bit, a new genre emerged to redeem the martyr-king.

Countering the harsh invective that followed Varennes, narratives of
Louis's last hours (a genre called Adieux) coupled popular tropes of sentimentalism with codified rituals of mourning. By 1795 and into the early
1800s this genre propelled writers and artists to produce artifacts of an in-
triguingly hybrid emotional-political valence with proven market value.
Through trompe l'oeil pictorial strategies and double-voiced narration, they
recast Bourbon history as an ongoing affair and shifted attention away from
nightmares of dripping heads or furious sansculottes to more comforting
thoughts of Louis's piety and familial devotion. In an adept sleight of hand,
the treasonous villain of Varennes was thus redeemed as the tender paterfamilias—to his two young children and to the twenty-six million subjects
awaiting the Bourbons' return. The emotional reactions inscribed in these
texts shift accordingly. Where the post-Varennes pamphlet literature sought
primarily to elicit righteous indignation and republican solidarity against
the Throne, the memorials of Louis's last months conjure up a more complex response.

One might expect such material to exploit the reader's ability to identify with the king by emphasizing his human traits as a father and a husband, and there is certainly a good deal of familial pathos. But equally present is a current of what Edmund Burke in 1757 called "the effects of sympathy in the distresses of others" or what Sigmund Freud labeled *Schadenfreude*, that is, the enjoyment obtained from the troubles of others. As Burke wrote,

> I am convinced we have a real degree of delight, and no small one, in the real misfortunes and pains of others . . . for terror is a passion which always produces delight when it does not press too close, and pity is a passion accompanied with pleasure, because it arises from love and social affection. . . . There is no spectacle we so eagerly pursue, as that of some uncommon or grievous calamity; so that whether the misfortune is before our eyes, or whether they are turned back to it in history, it always touches with delight.[1]

If the violent death of an exemplary ruler like Scipio Africanus affects readers most deeply, as Burke contends, one might assume that the fall of Louis XVI would affect readers as well. Indeed, some of the memorials studied here inscribe Louis in a tradition alongside other famous victims of misfortune. But many commentators elude the issue with subtle ambivalence or profess indifference or even amusement over the king's plight on grounds of the Bourbons' despotism or the king's own prevarication. The crucial distinction lies in whether or not the observer admires the prince; as Burke points out, "Our delight in cases of this kind, is very greatly heightened, if the sufferer be some excellent person who sinks under an unworthy fortune."[2] Despite the king's efforts in his June 1791 *Déclaration du Roi adressée à tous les Français à sa sortie de Paris* and the efforts of memorialists ever since, Louis never quite achieved the response he wanted most from his people—that is, unabashed and heartfelt pity.

Part of the problem may lie in the semantic confusion that surrounds the word pity (*pitié*). The word connotes a primal sort of humanity in Jean-Jacques Rousseau's *Discours sur l'inégalité* (Discourse on inequality; 1754); Burke built on this connotation in his concept of an instinctive social bond in *A Philosophical Enquiry into the Origin of Our Ideas of the Sublime and Beautiful* (1757), as seen above. But the signifier carries within it two diametrically opposed connotations that emerge most visibly in the adjectival locutions. The English adjective "pitiful," like its close cousin "pitiable," can mean either to be full of pity and compassion (synonymous with "humane"), to elicit compassion or tender fellow feeling (syn. "miserable"), or to elicit contempt (syn. "despicable"). Similarly, the French term *pitoyable* means to be compassionate (syn. *humain*), to inspire pity (syn. *malheureux*), or to inspire a "contemptible pity" (syn. *piteux, lamentable*). Although the etymology of "pity" links it to "piety" (from the Latin *pietas*)—from whence it derives the aura of divine kindness and grace (or *miséricorde*)—there is no avoiding the worldly, wobbly implications of "pitiful," *piteux,* and *pitoyable.* In the king's lexicon it is compassionate fellow feeling that he sought. The *Déclaration* speaks at length about the "afflicting tableau" of his sufferings at the hands of the market women in October 1789, the "outrages endured" upon his aborted departure for Saint-Cloud in April 1791, and the insults and ingratitude that were the "sole reward for so many sacrifices."[3] Yet few were the readers who responded as he wished. Why did his public image plunge from one of sovereignty to contempt in those few short months of 1791?

This chapter presents an overview of the dominant historiography on the events of June 20–21, 1791, and January 20–21, 1793, but instead of professing to "tell it like it was," it tells it as it may or may not have been. Why? Because even the most distinguished work of modern-day experts is shot through with the same dilemmas that confronted those who witnessed the events firsthand. Literature proves as reliable as history; that is to say, neither is entirely reliable but they complement each other. My most significant findings lie in how the post-Varennes discourse of dehumanization was nuanced with clever narrative asides, first by an ambitious young novelist and second by a left-wing British expatriate who edited the king's correspondence. The former is the hotly contested work by J.-J. Regnault-Warin, *Le Cimetière de la Madeleine,* a massive opus (four tomes in octavos) that pretends to reveal the secret history of Louis's last years. Following its various printings in 1800 and 1801, *Le Cimetière* unleashed a nationwide police repression; both the publisher and the author were accused and imprisoned for what was considered rabid incivility (*incivisme forcené*), and the printer's plates were ordered to be destroyed. A look at the king's correspondence as edited by Helen-Maria Williams (1803) seems to set the record straight, by providing proof—or the semblance thereof—that shows why Louis XVI inspired both pity and contempt. In the juxtaposition of the king's letters, speeches, and decrees and Williams's own observations, the editor establishes Louis's humanity at the same time as she alludes to the hypocrisy and poor judgment that drove him into the ground. The effects, while humorous on occasion, are harsh. Thanks to its long shelf life, this version marked people's ideas of what King Louis XVI was like for the next generation at least. But Williams's *Correspondance politique* was also charged with fraud: some claim that the letters were entirely invented. A comparison of key passages with the "official" correspondence published in 1864–73 (whose flaws in turn have been denounced by critics of the twenty-first century) reveals differences of tone and vocabulary, but the fatherly self-image and rhetoric of self-sacrifice remain. Ultimately, it matters little which letters were actually penned by the king or his imitators, for it is the public image of Louis XVI that circulated in these years that interests me most. Whether we consult the "hoax" of 1803 or the "flawed" version of 1864–73, the theme of unrequited paternal love dominates to the end.

The coda shows how Honoré de Balzac reworked these currents in *Le Père Goriot* (1835), which is still considered one of the best novels of all time. Unlike his predecessors, who told readers what to think or feel with their sentimental and didactic stagecraft, the Balzacian narrator forces readers to decipher the meaning of characters' actions for themselves. But he also insinuates an often-amusing irony into the narration. Particularly interesting is Balzac's portrait of the relations between Père Goriot and his children. Goriot's struggle with ungrateful daughters Anastasie and Delphine conjures up memories of tragic King Lear, but his loving complicity with an effusive "son," Eugène de Rastignac, evokes an idealized image of filial loyalty. That Goriot is a far cry from the monarch in exile that Rastignac imagines him to be, however, comes to the reader in a melody sung to the father-son pair by a shrewd observer. The song is not just any song but the royalist anthem "Ô Richard, ô mon roi," first popularized during the October Days in 1789. When combined with other subtle allusions to history, these textual clues add up to a tragicomic parable of royal failure.

To bring back to life an amusing corpus of kingly and not so kindly tales about French identity in the twilight of the Bourbon dynasty, this chapter thus embraces the cacophony of dissonant voices that from 1791 to 1803 spoke about the king and his actions. The coda shows how Balzac cast a jaded gaze on the memorializing impulse in the postrevolutionary, post-Napoleonic, and soon to be post-Bourbon world of France in the 1830s.

PART 1: VARENNES

THE VARENNES OF HISTORIANS: A COMEDY OF ERRORS

"Nothing," reads the king's journal entry for June 20, 1791.[4] Yet while going through the routine ritual of "Le Coucher" that night, surrounded by the usual cluster of well-organized servants, Louis was plotting the move that would inalterably shift the course of history. Minutes after midnight, slipping out of his darkened bedchamber, the king dressed in a green riding coat, brown vest, gray wig, and round hat—such as might befit a merchant or a banker—and thus transformed himself from monarch to commoner. He proceeded calmly through the long corridors, stopping to fix a loose buckle on his shoe, and walked right by guards before exiting the main gates onto the place du Carrousel and mounting a carriage waiting around the corner.[5] The banality of the journal entry and the ease of his transit through the long palace halls, which contrary to rumor involved no subterranean passages or secret staircases, create a bizarre impression of normalcy. Did Louis really think the preparations were so unimportant? Or was his laconic style a subterfuge to hide secrets from posterity? Although historians have pored over the documents for centuries, the king's feelings and allegiance remain unclear. Was he aiming to set up a temporary satellite government until a modified constitution could be worked out? Was he an active plotter seeking foreign assistance? Or was he swept up in a virtual kidnapping fomented by agents of counterrevolution led by his wife and her entourage?

What intrigues readers seeking the truth about Varennes is the disparity running through historians' detailed accounts of the events and the wildly different claims of royal motivation that they imply. Scholars have painstakingly reconstructed the logistics, route, and timing by which the five members of the royal family and their six servants and guards (in one large and one small carriage with two equestrian outriders) made their way through the sleeping capital, exited at the Clichy toll-gate, and slowly traversed the gentle terrain of the Île-de-France and Champagne. Thanks to the testimonials of eyewitnesses, we have ample access to names, locations, and reactions of people claiming to have seen the party roll past. But such testimonials, like almost every other detail in this historiography, are subject to debate. The appearance of the royal family's black-and-yellow coach (*berline*) itself is up in the air: whereas the French academician E.-A. Ancelon in 1866 described it as "comfortable, but nothing extraordinary," the American historian Timothy Tackett claimed in 2003 that the carriage was "exceptionally large" and "poorly conceived for inconspicuous travel."[6] Since the convoy stopped (only once or several times, depending on sources), some eyewitnesses (many or very few) had the opportunity to see or even converse with His Majesty when the family took meals (or not) at way stations along the road.[7]

Glimmers of recognition must have punctuated this journey. Princess Marie-Thérèse, then aged thirteen, recalled mixed feelings of hope and fear when their incognito was discovered, noting, "We were recognized by

everybody," especially at Châlons, where passersby "thanked God on seeing the King, and prayed that he might escape."[8] In her account and that of
later commentators one senses a certain anxiety over the king's assurances.
It seems that Louis grew increasingly confident as the afternoon gave way
to dusk, sensing that each mile that separated the travelers from the capital
brought them closer to a familiar landscape of loyal subjects whose love of
tradition outweighed their allegiance to newfangled Parisian politics. Although such confidence seems ill-founded on political grounds, given the
staunch patriotism of many provincial assemblies, the king had reason
to expect compliance when one remembers the military might that had
been sent ahead to lead the party to safety. Nevertheless, when the convoy
alighted at an evening stage stop at Sainte-Ménehould, it took only one
observer—a former deputy with fond memories of the Festival of the Federation—to suspect subterfuge and raise the alarm in the next town down
the road, before the journey was abruptly aborted. Where were the troops,
the menacing heft of the German hussars under the command of Colonel
Choiseul and General Bouillé? Who was to blame for the king's arrest?

  Early nineteenth-century writers sought to make amends for their own
or their family's shortcomings and published diaries and letters to silence
critics and bury the blame.[9] Ever since, historians have elaborated upon
such sources to argue various theories on what went wrong or who was at
fault. Ancelon (1866), Castelot (1951), and Loomis (1971) point the finger at
the queen's lover, Axel Fersen (supposed to be a double agent for the Swed-
ish Crown), or at General Lafayette (described as a wily politico) or explain
the fiasco through the mixed signals received by the high-ranking army
officers who were supposed to be preparing the king's passage: Choiseul,
Bouillé, and Goguelat.[10] Biographers of Louis XVI continue to rehash what
is known about the incident. Petitfils directs particular reproach at the marquis de Bouillé's younger son François, who despite having sixty dragoons
under his command failed to liberate the king from Sauce's inn, where he
was guarded only by Sainte-Ménehould postmaster Drouet, three Jacobins,
and two upturned carts of furniture![11] Hardman emphasizes the king's own
hesitation as the crux of the matter. In fact, the most telling order made by
Louis XVI at Varennes was a non-order. Speaking to Captain Deslons, who
had come into town to receive his orders, the king said: "I am a prisoner
and have no orders to give." Being a prisoner gave King Louis XVI the ex-
cuse for what Hardman calls the "constructive inaction" that characterized
his conduct since October 1789: it was "an inaction which implies action
by others on his behalf."[12] Similar to what a Shakespearean king might say

to his servant or a coy mistress to her suitor, it implies mind reading and discretion instead of straightforward communication. But it also leaves the king free to prevaricate while waiting for someone to act upon his unspoken wish. So perhaps the king himself was ultimately to blame for what happened at Varennes.

For all the delays, errors, and cowardice of Louis's officers that are displayed in these works, and the insinuations of conspiracy among the monarch's enemies, there exists the unresolved issue of Louis's motivation and future plans. Petitfils puzzles over Louis's determination to reach the garrison town of Montmédy, noting that neither of his closest advisers, Bouillé and Breteuil, had a clue what he planned to do there. Although Viguerie applauds the establishment of a well-armed satellite court in Montmédy as a first step toward wresting control away from the assembly, he too admits bafflement concerning exactly how Louis XVI planned to accomplish that audacious second step.[13] Unless a complete overhaul was effected of the assembly's legislation to date, and a new, more authoritarian definition was adopted for the notion of "representative government," these plans would invariably constitute treason. Hardman underlines the good initial thinking behind Louis's plans and seems to agree with the duc de Choiseul that, once Louis had reached Montmédy, the rest would fall into place. The problem lay less with the monarch's intentions than with the unreliability of the troops and civilian militants. "Whatever Louis's good intentions," Hardman notes, "if things turned nasty he would be forced to rely on Austrian troops."[14]

More recent historiography on Varennes proves equally perplexed and explains the king's motivations either through a critical scrutiny of the king-as-villain that denounces the disparity between his public face and private thoughts or a light-hearted even comic attitude toward the king-as-fool that highlights the "marvelous" facets of this debacle recounted as a fairy tale or thriller. In *Varennes* Mona Ozouf reminds readers that the perpetrators of Varennes had to answer twice for their misdeeds, first during the Revolution when those unfortunate enough to still be in France sought to exonerate themselves and then during the Restoration when memoir writers speculated on why the attempt failed. Her inventory often verges on the burlesque in its enumeration of the accidents and arrogance that led to the ultimate disgrace.[15] Tackett's sober reckoning looks at the event from a longer perspective and argues that Varennes was a watershed moment not only for the king but also for the nation's elected representatives. After June 1791 deputies in the assembly increasingly sanctioned strong-arm methods that departed from the people's will and presaged the repressive decrees that would characterize 1793–94, as political allegiances hardened into concern for the safety of the state. Here too however the sources and tensions remain the same: royal hagiography opposes populist rage, and personal recrimination devolves into family feud.

THE PITIFUL KING IN HIS OWN WORDS

The king brought reproach on himself because of the manifesto that he left in the Tuileries. Entitled *Déclaration du Roi adressée à tous les Français à sa sortie de Paris* (The King's declaration addressed to all the French upon his departure from Paris), this sixteen-page manuscript in his own handwriting by all accounts accurately sums up his view of the situation on leaving town. Hardman describes its message: "Louis intended, from a place of safety, surrounded by loyal troops, to negotiate his return with the Assembly in return for changes to the constitution along the lines he indicated . . . he would then take up residence in Compiègne and translate the Assembly there."[16] But this document does more than communicate the king's plans; it also paints a telling self-portrait of the monarch. Emboldened perhaps by a brochure campaign that in 1790 had disseminated the notion of the king's crucifixion and resurrection, the text makes unabashed and frequent comparisons between Louis XVI and Jesus Christ. Not only is the king forced to bear silent witness to the wrongdoing of his enemies, but he is also forced to "drink to the dregs of the chalice" in service to the cause.[17] Moreover, the king claims that he has had to *sacrifice* everything—a concept reiterated no fewer than seven times in the first eight paragraphs—yet the more he sacrifices for the people's happiness, the more his adversaries belittle him.[18] For all this appeal to fellow feeling, the king's identification with the people is strained because he also describes himself among the ranks of the aristocracy and complains about living in the Tuileries palace because it lacks those comforts and commodities that "any wealthy person" (tout particulier qui a de l'aisance) would expect (*Déclaration*, 50).

This surprising document exhibits an emotionalism and peevishness that clash with the traditional sangfroid expected of a sovereign. Hardman notes the "necessary difficulty of speaking his mind" that made it so important for Louis XVI to write it but admits that the results are "somewhat bad-tempered." Explaining his reasoning on the days when military intervention could have reversed the course of events such as July 14 or October 5–6, 1789, the king stresses his *sensibilité* and the choice he made to suffer rather than exert force or fire upon the misguided people (*la multitude égarée*).[19] He lays out a five-point structure of governmental functions (e.g., justice, finance) and explicitly articulates how a French king is supposed to provide leadership: this is contrasted with actions taken by the people's representatives in the assembly. But the tone here is ultimately resigned rather than indignant. Instead of refusing the "simulacrum of monarchy" that has been handed to him by the greedy assembly and their confederates the Jacobins (who are quickly usurping the judiciary), he gives up.[20]

But this is not the end. Instead, the manifesto presents a more personal appeal to the people:

> Frenchmen, is that what you wanted when you sent your representatives to the National Assembly? . . . Did you want to see your King heaped with insults and deprived of his liberty while he was exclusively occupied with establishing yours? The love for their Kings is one of the virtues of the French, and His Majesty has personally received such touching signs of this love that he will never forget them. The factious men realized that as long as that love subsisted, their work would never succeed; they felt as well that to weaken it, it would be necessary to annihilate if possible the respect that has always accompanied it; this is the source of all the outrages suffered by the King over the past two years.[21]

What follows are more "afflicting tableaux" that display the regal resignation with which the king and his family have suffered events such as the October Days, the Festival of the Federation, and their aborted visit to Saint-Cloud for Easter 1791. With melancholy and not a little resentment for the status he seems to have lost, Louis XVI explains how "factious men" have taught the people to disrespect the royal family over the past two years. The one line that may be interpreted as a warning—where he foretells his return to a France restored to its former reason—sounds more like wishful thinking.[22] Indeed, the document as a whole reads like a reductio ad absurdum of insult and injury from which the victim's only recourse is escape. From the once-mighty perspective of a sovereign power, the king sounds like a frightened subaltern when he concludes: "given the impossibility of the king's doing good and preventing the evils around him, is it any wonder he sought to regain his freedom and seek safety [*se mettre en sûreté*] with his family?" (82). Ultimately, Louis's suffering serves no effective end because he himself abandons his disciples and their cause. The final plea explodes the illogic behind the text: how is it possible for the people of Paris to "return to their King, who will always be their father, their best friend," when he is no longer in their midst?![23]

Varennes in the News from Paris to Cap-Français

The differing accounts of the royal family's absence from the Tuileries reveal the French newspapers' partisan loyalties and the time lag between
the official announcement of kidnapping and the growing awareness of an
escape attempt. The moderate-right dailies, the *Moniteur* and the *Journal
de Paris*, maintained the fiction of the king's kidnapping for three days and
smoothed over the king's return to Paris by reprinting a letter he wrote
to his cousin, the émigré leader Condé, wherein Louis XVI expresses his
support for the constitution and commands Condé to return to France as
soon as possible. (Needless to say, this demand was not respected.)[24] The
Chronique de Paris is probably more representative of majority opinion.
Although it too announces the kidnapping of the royal family at the beginning of an article on June 22, two pages later it cites a conspiracy that helped
the royal family and concludes with a scathing dig at Louis XVI: "Yesterday
morning, we learned that the king had just fled with all his family, leaving—by the most cowardly of cruelties—his ministers and all those who
served his court exposed to the initial fury of the people's resentment."
Moreover, refuting the king's oft-repeated aversion for bloodshed, the paper
declares: "What regret can we feel for a prince who abdicates voluntarily,
and who, to regain all the privileges of the Crown, blithely sends 25 million
men into the horrors of war."[25]

Immediately after its discovery in the Tuileries palace on June 21, the
Déclaration was delivered to Alexandre de Beauharnais, the president of
the National Assembly, who read it to the deputies when the assembly con-
vened that morning. By afternoon it was being excerpted in Parisian newspapers as the Manifesto of June 20 and stirred up a firestorm of reaction.[26]
Despite its generally sympathetic attitude toward the monarchy, the report of the assembly in the *Journal de Paris* expresses ironic disbelief over
the plaintive tone of Louis's *Déclaration* and his long list of complaints,
commenting, for instance, "This will become a monument added to all the
others to prove the extent to which truth is foreign to kings. . . . At each
phrase, along with many other emotions, we suffered to see this misfortune
which besieges kings, and which casts a veil between their eyes and the
world."[27]

The topical pamphlets published in the days and weeks after projected
an even greater animosity toward the king and rewrote the mainstays of
Louis's text—his penchant for emotion rather than action, his aristocratic
sense of entitlement, his self-pity—to underline the king's illegitimacy or
at least redundancy for the French state. In a significant break from the

sympathetic *poissard* literature studied in chapter 1, these tracts coupled truth-seeking with a demand for political action that did or *did not* include the monarch. Radicals blamed him for refusing the principles of secular governance as outlined by the assembly, while monarchists denigrated his impotent threat of reprisal. Add to this the king's incredible imprudence in publicizing the manifesto before safely relocating outside Paris and one can see why the document created such explosive effects, almost all of them opposed to the original intention.[28]

Suspecting no doubt that his plans had gone awry, by September 1791 the king issued a request that these events be forgotten and that the National Assembly annul all the procedures relative to the events of June 20–21.[29] That request notwithstanding, the people's angry indignation is palpable in the print culture left behind. Consider the anonymous *Lettres de deux habitans des frontières à tous les François* (Letters from two people living near the border to all the French; 1791), which purports to be written by a mother who relays with disgust what she saw at Sauce's inn, where the king threw himself at the innkeeper and tried to convince him to help by babbling promises such as "Yes, my friend, it is your king who is in your power, it is your king who implores you. . . . Save me, I am in your hands. . . . I promise you an immense fortune, for you and your family. I will make your town more important than all other towns in the kingdom."[30] Just as offensive as this illicit bartering for power is the recourse to sentimentalism, seen in the queen's desperate plea for Sauce's sympathy ("elle emploie ce qu'elle croit de plus propre à l'attendrir"). Mr. Sauce, depicted as an honorable and faithful patriot, refuses both appeals and reminds them of their vow to the nation. Imagine his shock, and the reader's, in hearing the king's vulgar reply: "So much for f——ing freedom" (Voilà bien la f—— liberté)!

A similar warning against a cowardly, derelict ruler rings out in the *Grand Jugement rendu par le peuple français contre Louis Seize* (Great judgment of the French people against Louis the Sixteenth; ca. 1791), where the king is also seized in *flagrant délit*. In reply to Mr. Sauce, who says, "I believe I have the honor of addressing Louis the Sixteenth, king of the French," the narrator describes a monarch who "stood immobilized, and his blood froze in his veins. All he could say were these words, hardly worthy of a king . . . WILL THEY HURT ME?"[31] The fear that blurts from the king's lips is dishonorable because it reveals cowardly feelings that would have been better left unsaid: kings are supposed to act nobly, with cool reserve and dignity. In conclusion, the writer detaches the nation from this king— in a sarcastic remake of Henri IV's song—and calls for citizens to take a new national vow of freedom or death.[32]

Louis XVI was thrown in with an odd lot after Varennes and implicated in actions occurring as far away as the Antilles. Critics from the colony of Saint-Domingue held him responsible for the massacre of whites by black slaves in August 1791. In what may be a quirk of fate or evidence of concerted action, the slave uprising that decimated settlements in the north of Saint-Domingue occurred just about seven weeks after the king's failed flight—that is, the time it took for news of Varennes to travel abroad and reach the interior of the island. In other words, the fateful night when slave insurgents took arms and burned down Cap-Français (August 21, 1791) was just a few days after the agents fomenting unrest might have learned of the king's debacle. This timing and the impassioned yet politically inchoate pronouncements of the slave leaders have prompted much speculation about the sympathy between the black rebels and King Louis XVI. Historian Philip Curtin reminds us that the king's attempt to flee was interpreted by slave populations as evidence of His Majesty's indifference to the white colony in Saint-Domingue and, by extension, his disapproval of slavery. By the summer of 1791 the slaves knew "that the power of France was no longer effective in the colony. They seemed, like the French peasants of 1789, to think that the king was on their side."[33] Gene Ogle adds that the slaves' understanding of monarchy may have drawn more on Congolese precedents than Bourbon grandeur, but "the distant king and his white flag served as multivalent symbols to which different groups among the insurgents could attach their own meanings."[34] Such similarities may seem less far-fetched when one realizes the extent to which island-based witnesses drew analogies between events happening in France and its colony.

In angry denunciations of French domination of Saint-Domingue published by colonial émigrés in Paris and London, a long list of analogies reveals the damage wrought to this island by the French. According to one: "The colonists remark that all the great movements of France were repeated in Saint-Domingue; the flight and arrest of Louis XVI was the signal of the burning of the north part of the island, the revolt of the *hommes de couleur*, and the assassination of some colonists who were attached to the Revolution."[35] A certain Monsieur Deraggis seconded this charge, claiming that "the negroes brought devastation and death everywhere, to establish the king on his throne."[36] Presaging the bitter controversies relayed in Victor Hugo's colonial novel *Bug-Jargal* (1826), another brochure sarcastically described the opportunistic royalism of the blacks: "the mulattoes and the negroes, those regenerated citizens of April 4 [decree outlawing slavery] who, in the midst of their regeneration, have never stopped wearing the white cockade and fighting for Louis XVI and Louis XVII, have been covered with honors and rewards."[37] These critics claim that although the colony as a whole remained loyal to its metropolitan master, the lack of military presence on the island proved the state's indifference to the plight of white planters. Their point was that Saint-Domingue should thus be freed from French law. The king's treason and his insufficient support for the French planters are just two of the betrayals that drove the colony into enemy hands and that prove that the French no longer deserve ownership of its lucrative possession. The chain of disasters all began with Varennes.

Varennes provided ammunition to royalist reaction in France as well, where it built upon an already-impressive arsenal of anti–Louis XVI propaganda. Louis's preferred model of nurturant, or paternal, rule was skewered mercilessly in the eleven pamphlets entitled *Entretiens des Bourbons* (Conversations of the Bourbons; 1790). In dialogues with ancestors, including Kings Louis IX, Henri IV, Louis XIV, and Louis XV, the husband of Marie-Antoinette is taken to task for his shortcomings, primarily his cowardly submission to his wife and courtly pressure groups and his reluctance to use armed force. Advice rains down upon the monarch as each of the distinguished Bourbons scolds Louis for his "pitiful excuses" and explains how to govern with examples from his own experience; the main advice being: You are king, so stop crying and act like one![38] It will not surprise readers to learn that these titles were considered "incendiary brochures" and hotly pursued by the Paris police in summer–fall 1790.[39] The politics of hard-line legitimism may give pause to those who expect monarchists to support their king, but the *Entretiens* stood primarily for the Bourbon dynasty and the purity of royal blood, not necessarily for King Louis XVI. Scrutiny of the king's legitimacy rekindled new animosities after Charles X's flight in 1830, as analysis of Balzac's *Père Goriot* below will show.

LOYALISTS RESPOND

But loyalists did not suffer criticism of their king without putting up a fight. One year after Varennes a novella entitled *Le Règne du Prince Trop-Bon dans le royaume des fols* (The reign of Prince Too-Good in the Kingdom of Fools; 1792) riposted the hostile criticisms of Varennes pamphlets and the *Entretiens* by presenting a glowing image of Louis XVI with Henri IV firmly behind him. The author of this work, known only as "still a countess" (i.e., not a *ci-devant*, or *former* aristocrat), intended it to complement her frequent contributions to the right-wing newspaper *L'Ami du roi* (The friend of the king). The ploy was sure to win readers: the various newspapers named *L'Ami du roi* enjoyed strong subscription rates (approximately five thousand a year from 1790 to 1792) and inspired a hotly contested rivalry between three competing publications with that name.[40] *Le Règne* covers much of the same territory as the king's own *Déclaration*: Necker's fiscal incompetence, the creation of the National Assembly, and the October Days are symptoms of a contagion that has transformed the once-peaceful kingdom into anarchy. When the king tries to reason with the people and their elected deputies, they shout back vulgarities or babble incoherently. Desperate for a solution, he tries to seek advice from an oracle of the East, but that effort is aborted by armed madmen in an isolated inn. Upon being captured by maniacs, the sad but dignified family rides back to their prison and despairs of finding a cure. But while praying together, an apparition appears of a warrior in a coat of mail whose bright eyes and fine moustache, combined with his hearty exclamation, "Ventre saint-gris," reveal Henri IV to their wondering eyes.[41] Empathizing about their mutual misfortunes, Henri lifts up his armor to show the gaping wound left by his assassin and tells the little group, "August, unfortunate and respectable family, dry your tears; loyal prince, beloved by the God of believers, you have loved your subjects too much for them not to love you in return."[42] Sympathetic to Louis's frustration and unrequited paternal love, Henri takes him by the hand and leads him to a window looking northeast, where a vision emerges on the horizon: "numerous troops of brave, generous, wise, modest, and charming men [enchanteurs] . . . arrive among this people of fools, and with every step they take, they dazzle Prince Too-Good and his family" with an awesome prodigy.[43] With that promise of a magical reconciliation, the tale ends.

La Correspondance littéraire deemed *Le Règne* a "sad pamphlet" for its lack of stylistic refinement, but the fact that a market existed for no fewer than three editions of this text in 1792 is significant.[44] Granted, the redemption fantasy was a quixotic hope in a year that gave evidence of the republican army's increasingly effective efforts to withstand foreign incursions on French soil, notably at the battle of Valmy in September and Jemappes in November. But it served as a marketable wish-fulfillment device nonetheless for a certain segment of readers. The public for *Le Règne*—published in Paris and in four émigré communities abroad—was likely the same public who devoured Galart de Montjoie's reactionary *Histoire de la Révolution de France* (1791–92), whose words form the epigraph: "En 1792, une armée victorieuse entrera dans Paris" (In 1792, a victorious army will enter Paris). This bluster pleased those who still held out hope for a Bourbon restoration and reminds us that the king's destiny was not yet a foregone conclusion. Moreover, in his disparaging stylistic critique, baron de Grimm, the editor of *Correspondance littéraire*, shows that he misunderstood the readers' expectations: fairy-tale language and plot conventions were quite appropriate for a public who wanted to believe in an unbroken lineage from Henri IV to Louis XVI. The primary merit of *Le Règne* lies precisely in the temporal effect created by combining conventions of the *Arabian Nights* with a monarchist dialogue with the dead. In what may be the kindest denouement imagined for the monarchy in 1792, the scene between the troubled Bourbon and his ancestor concludes without conclusion, to be continued.

Although the actors are long dead, today's readers can still feel the passions excited in observers of the Varennes episode by perusing these texts. The implicit dialogue between *Les Entretiens* series and the colonial complaints, on the one hand, and *Le Règne du Prince Trop-Bon* and Louis's *Déclaration*, on the other, pivots on the question of guilt and blame. Where the former hold Louis accountable for all kinds of mistakes, including the loss of France's most lucrative colony in the Antilles, the latter two blame agents beyond his control. Like the king's opening salvo in the *Déclaration*, where he stresses his long-suffering patience, *Le Règne* makes initial appeal to the decent people, or *honnêtes gens*, who are still loyal to him.[45] Its last scene makes an even stronger indictment: through the invocation of a *deus ex machina* which should arrive from the East to save the monarch and his Kingdom of Fools, *Le Règne du Prince Trop-Bon* releases the captive Louis XVI and directs attention toward the émigré troops and foreign sovereigns who are tasked to intervene on his behalf. Where are they and when will they arrive?

This allusion to imminent invasion comes across more pessimistically in the engraving by the constitutionalist G. Texier, *Apparition d'Henri IV à Louis XVI, ou La Vérité découverte* (Vision of Henri IV to Louis XVI, or Truth discovered; ca. 1792; fig. 16); the similarities between text and image are so striking as to suggest an explicit dialogue or retort between artist and writer. Texier's image focuses on Louis XVI in his richly appointed study; heavy drapes frame the room and an ornate carpet lies underfoot. He is seated at his desk and apparently interrupted in a reading of Voltaire's *Henriade*: a not-insignificant detail. That Henri is trying to tell him something is clear in the scene's composition: placing one hand on Louis's arm to get his attention, Henri gestures with the other toward a dazzling sight. It is Truth, a beautiful young woman with long blond hair who exhorts the king to "flee the traitors." Written in Truth's book, whose pages detach as if by magic, the traitors' names are legible to the spectator and pointed at by three putti at Truth's side. A fourth cherub stands by Louis's knee and offers him a sword. The king reels back in his chair, staggered by the revelation that his enemies are none other than his closest advisers, family, and

16. G. Texier, *Vision of Henri IV to Louis XVI, or Truth Discovered* (*Apparition d'Henri IV à Louis XVI, ou La Vérité découverte*). Dedicated to the Nation. Engraving, ca. 1792. Photograph by Jean-Yves Chermeux, Musée national du château de Pau.

friends: the baron de Breteuil, the prince de Condé, the prince de Conti, and his cousin the duc d'Orléans.[46] Unlike most earlier caricatures, which were influenced *by* events rather than aiming to exert influence *on* events, this image expresses an urgent call to the king to rein in counterrevolutionary political energies before they get out of hand.

Texier's caricature thus rebuffs the hard-line monarchism of *Le Règne* and exhorts the king to eschew the dubious contact of émigrés for the well-being of a throne and a nation whose destinies are inextricably linked. The Henrician reference recalls a political tendency noted in the introduction: it underlines hopes for a popular constitutional monarchy (viz., the reference to *La Henriade*) that exemplify Pochet's novel *La Boussole nationale* (1790). Both text and image show Henri IV materializing physically to underline the kind of caring yet hardworking ethos that France needs. Where in *Apparition* Henri literally delivers Truth, in *La Boussole* he is a role model plowing the fields (fig. 1). The important point is Louis XVI's exoneration from guilt. He is neither tyrant nor traitor; rather, he is an appealing and good-intentioned ruler doing his best in trying times. This kind of blameless imagery largely disappeared from view in the months following June 1791, however, until it reemerged cast in dark irony under the pen of Balzac.

The appeals to pity inscribed in these texts produce affective effects that vary according to their intended audiences. The imagined scenes of witnessing (whether they are true or false does not really matter, since these were the most widely circulating versions of Varennes on the market) provide an excellent example of what William Reddy calls "emotives" in action. Similar to linguist J. L. Austin's concept of "performatives," which in speech act theory signify words that accomplish something (e.g., "I do" in a wedding vow), emotives are emotional declarations that have a transformative effect on the self and others and can be used by people to try to get what they want. "Emotives are neither true nor false," Reddy cautions. "But they may also be efficacious or ineffective, depending on whether their effects confirm or disconfirm their claims."[47] Thinking back now on the recognition scene at Sauce's inn, we realize that no matter what the king might have said, his communication was doomed from the beginning by the discrepancy between his apprehension of reality and that of his audience. While Louis was likely worried about his own and his family's well-being—an ordinary reaction in ordinary circumstances—the guards assembled in Sauce's inn were worried about the hostile foreign troops they believed to be massed on the borders and who they suspected were acting on the king's orders. Like the king's official request to the French that they "forget" the events of June 20–21, the suppliant air and appeal for fellow feeling represented by these literary alter egos could not have been less plausible . . . or less welcome.

MARKETING THE KING'S SHAME

After Varennes the king's voice became a fungible asset, used and abused with or without his consent. The once-weighty question of who shall speak to the king became an increasingly trivial affair as more opinions entered the print market and challenged the monarch's authority. This tendency had begun years earlier to be sure. Whereas information was traditionally transmitted by the Crown or the church through its authorized channels (handbills, papal bulls, or the *Gazette de France*), by the mid-1750s the printers and news purveyors had diversified. Roger Chartier has noted how the *cahiers de doléances*, or grievances, assembled in 1788–89 invited the populace to speak to the king in unprecedented ways and raised expectations that the king would respond in kind.[48] But although the content of the *doléances* reveals a population in distress, the tone is respectful of the king's authority. Similarly, in the first two years of the Revolution the *Journal de Paris* and the *Moniteur* frequently printed articles describing the royal family's

charitable activities, their visits to the Gobelins tapestry factory or workshops of the Faubourg Saint-Marceau, transcripts of Louis's speeches to the
assembly, and other respectful accounts of their daily life. After Varennes
that kind of reportage virtually disappeared. Instead, we find the king's generals, his brothers, revolutionary authorities, and ordinary citizens appro-
priating his voice for their own ends. They presented newspaper addresses
to the king and demanded a reply, they sent in articles speaking for the king
without his approval, and they related their own suspicious or derogatory
interpretations of his actions, as if daring him to prove them wrong.[49] This
accumulation of voices and opinions created the impression of a mute and
powerless throne, where the king was simply a pawn in a game that others
controlled. The question-and-answer format of the periodical press and the
multivocal debates on the king's fate over the months of his December 1792
trial emphasized that development.

   These same techniques were employed to redeem the king in novels
of the late 1790s, where the king's voice, letters, and diary entries were
forcefully reinserted into history. But the conflicting perspectives sowed
confusion over the man's motivations and, by extension, over the legitimacy of monarchy as an institution. Although a plethora of novels with
royalist-sounding titles were published in the late 1790s–early 1800s, their
authors' eclectic borrowing from "secret history," newspapers, religious traditions, legal documents, and sentimental, pastoral, or troubadour styles—
commonplace in a corpus that is best described as hybrid—muddied the
political messages that their titles conveyed.

   The most dramatic result of Varennes was the commodification of Louis
XVI as a pig or swine-king. "We hereby warn citizens that a fat pig has fled
the Tuileries; we ask those who find him to bring him back to his home,"
announced Camille Desmoulins's newspaper in June 1791.[50] Ugly caricatures followed, showing the royal family of pigs or the king alone being
led back to the Tuileries in various guises: this merchandise was so common among street vendors and news shops that an official complaint was
lodged against it with the police.[51] One of the most famous versions recast
the dialogue-with-the-dead motif by imagining Henri IV in appalled disbelief before Louis's metamorphosis (fig. 17). "Ventre Saint Gris, where is my
son? What! He is a pig?" exclaims the dapper monarch dressed in his signature cross of Saint Louis and ruff, pointing to a wooden wine barrel marked
"Wine of June 21" in which a pig perches with his stiff legs and black body
propped up in the straw. "It is himself; he is drowning his shame," replies
the pig, whose face alone resembles the monarch. Note that the symbolic
attributes surrounding Louis (wine bottles, chamber pot) point to his drunk-

Ventre Saint Gris ou est Mon fils?
Quoi! C'est un Cochon?

C'est Lui même, il noye Sa honte.

17. "'Ventre Saint Gris, where is my son? What! He is a pig?' 'It is himself; he is drowning his shame.'" (Ventre Saint Gris où est mon fils? Quoi! c'est un cochon? C'est lui même, il noye sa honte.) Engraving, ca. 1791–92. Bibliothèque nationale de France, Paris.

enness and bodily filth and that the once-mighty oak, emblem of the French throne, is reduced to a spindly stick shoved into a bottle holding "wine of Spain." Other wine bottles, tipped over precariously and spilling their contents into the hay, carry equally damning appellations: wine of aristocrats, wine of the Rhine. The only vestige of France's former greatness is Notre Dame Cathedral off in the distance behind Henri IV. Definitively condemned by what DeBaecque calls the "desacralizing" laugh, this Louis XVI is a degenerate king, the end of a line whose degradation Henri IV can only deplore.[52]

The pig was a symbolic reduction of catastrophic dimensions for the once-sacred Bourbons. Not only is the four-footed, hoofed animal considered a "lower" genus than *Homo sapiens*, it is also held to be an unclean creature because of its predilection for mud and slovenly ways. In French, as in English, slang a pig or a swine (*cochon* or *porc*) is a dirty, vulgar, or debauched person. But the pig is also an animal prized among farmers: the annual killing of the pig was and still is a special early-winter event for peasants and rural dwellers, as they gather together to slaughter the animal and butcher the carcass, prepare the meat, the head, the various organs, ears, feet, and tail, all of which are eaten during the hard months ahead.[53] It was thus especially awful to juxtapose the first Bourbon king with a successor who was nothing but peasant fodder. As a ditty from 1791 cleverly points out: "Consider the flight and arrest of that gang of pigs / City, town, and village / Everyone runs to catch / Such big fat lords / . . . / Cruel destiny would have starved us / Bacon was running short / But now we have caught them [and will be hungry no more]."[54] Scholars have often commented on the cannibalism of the sansculottes or *peuple mangeur de rois* in their most brutal forms, as in Gilray's 1792 caricature of monstrous Jacobins devouring hapless aristocrats or the caricature of a Herculean nation casting the king onto a flaming funeral pyre.[55] I think that this little song and the pig caricatures project an equally devastating combination of insult and threat to the king.

Following his execution on January 21, 1793, numerous prints and artifacts commemorated the regicide, the most cruel and provocative being Villeneuve's *Matière à réflection pour les jongleurs couronnées* [sic] (Something to reflect upon for the crowned jugglers; 1793; fig. 18). But if these bloody images proffered fleeting thrills to the populace, they also gave people second thoughts. As Daniel Arasse has explained, the blade of the guillotine severed the French from their past at the same time as it generated a new sense of awe and regret over the now-martyred king.[56] Less macabre and less familiar to today's readers are the celebrations of the king's life that were produced after his death. The relative obscurity of this art may derive from its illegality: in the France of 1793–1814 it was dangerous to reveal loyalist feelings or to purchase or sell books, portraits, or objects that portrayed the royal family in a sympathetic light.[57] Nevertheless, anger and grief ran high not only among the French peasantry in solidly Catholic regions like the Vendée but also among the many loyalists who sought to honor the dead king from abroad. Consider the wildly successful publication in Brussels of the king's first biography in July 1793: Geoffroy de Limon's *Vie et le martyre de Louis XVI* ran through more than thirty editions and was translated into German, Dutch, and Italian. Or consider the immense demand for the king's will and testament, which upon its first publication in February 1793 sold out several editions in just eight days, not to mention all the funeral elegies, epitaphs, letters, and other pseudohistorical works that capitalized on a king whose martyrdom suddenly made him marketable.[58]

The bleak memory of the swine-king lived on as well. During the tumultuous winter of 1797–98, following the coup d'etat of 18 fructidor Year 5 (September 4, 1797), which restored power to a left-wing-dominated Directory government, a brochure hit the streets with a forceful reminder of Louis's infamy. *La Tête ou l'oreille du cochon* (The head or the ear of the

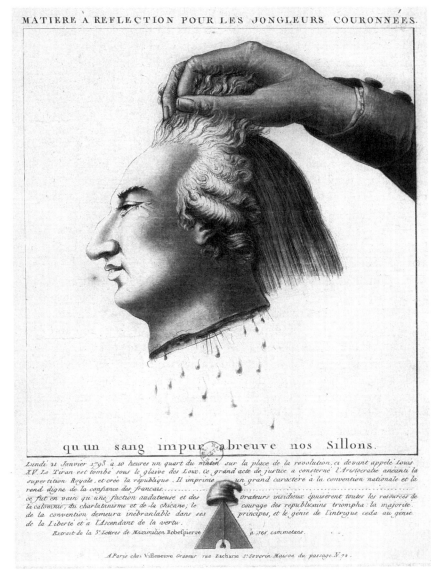

18. Villeneuve, *Something to Reflect upon for the Crowned Jugglers (Matière à réflection pour les jongleurs couronnées* [sic]) (1793). Bibliothèque nationale de France, Paris.

pig; 1798) proposed that new republican festivals be created and specified the food to be served: Bastilles cakes for July 14, a capon for August 10 (in memory of the king who became the "turkey" of his own plot), and a pig roast on January 21. This last event would be the highlight. Each family would kill their pig and put his head on the table to celebrate "the happy day when the head of the treasonous [*parjure*] Louis XVI fell and delivered us from his pitiful presence [*sa triste présence*]." Emphasizing the importance of symbolism, the author declares, "Yes, such are the symbols that we can and must use if we want to keep eternally in our hearts the memory of these great and memorable events."[59] The annual killing of the pig, the mocking display of his severed head, and the consumption of his flesh formed a coherent way to retain republican memories and to keep the Bourbons at bay.

From 1793 to our day, masses have been held in French churches on January 21 to commemorate Louis XVI's death and to honor the Bourbon dynasty. Left-wing celebrants have allegedly commemorated the same day with a banquet featuring a pig's head, which was at some point replaced by a calf's head, *tête de veau*. This delicacy was chosen either because it was more easily accessible to urban dwellers or, to believe Gustave Flaubert, because the French were emulating English regicides and their macabre feasts in honor of the Stuarts' demise.[60] So when French statesmen—such as former presidents Valéry Giscard d'Estaing and Jacques Chirac, both of whom made a point of it—mention their penchant for calf's head, it is not just an allusion to their earthy tastes or fondness for regional cooking (*le terroir*) but also refers to their staunch commitment to republican values inherited from the Revolution.

Apart from this reminder of anti-Bourbon sentiment, most of the commemorative artifacts that have survived convey a sympathetic attitude toward the king. Alongside the many paintings and prints on the themes of Adieux and the "separation of the king from his family" that were produced and marketed in England by émigré artists, and that prompted a cottage industry of Adieux-themed fans and "other suspect objects" seized by the Parisian police in Year 5 (1796–97), are multiple kinds of memorabilia of a more subtle nature.[61] Hints of persecution and censorship create a kind of complicity between the modern reader-observer and these artifacts of another time. Perhaps an emotional response is appropriate, given that private life and political militancy have always remained blurred and never more so than during revolutions.[62] To pretend that remembrance of the king was a purely political matter would deny an important facet of the literature and art created after his death: that is, the artists' effort to establish a feeling of authentic connection with the reader-observer, whether it was the perverse pleasure-in-observing-distress that Burke describes or the shared pathos that the king himself attempted to elicit in his 1791 *Déclaration*. If there were to be any great works of art about this period, authors needed to find a way to speak from and to a sector of human experience for which political partisanship would be neither the primary principle nor the most relevant concept. Although their techniques seem clumsy and their appeal to raw emotion strikes us as maudlin, the artifacts that commemorate Louis XVI's leave-taking provide a fascinating case study on how to rehumanize a public figure.

PART 2: *LES ADIEUX*

CAPTURING THE END OF AN ERA

On the surface, the historiography of the king's good-byes on January 20–21, 1793, seems to contain little of the controversy that characterizes the royal family's flight to Varennes: the main elements of the story remain fairly stable and simple.[63] At 6:00 on the night of January 20, 1793, Minister of Justice Garat came personally to the Temple prison and notified the king of the Convention's verdict. The king's request for a delay was refused, and the death sentence would be carried out in twenty-four hours. The king's request for a confessor was granted, as was his request for a private meeting with his family. Garat assured Louis that the nation, "always great and generous," would take care of his family. When the Irish non-juror confessor[64] Abbé Edgeworth arrived, he found the king surrounded by officials and described him as "gracious, even tranquil." The king dined heartily on a three-course meal with two kinds of wine: a detail judged more or less extravagant, depending on the source. At 8:30 p.m. the king's wife, Marie-Antoinette, his daughter, Marie-Thérèse (fifteen years old), his son, Louis-Charles (nine years old), and his sister, Madame Élisabeth, came down from their third-floor dwellings and joined him in the dining room of his apartment. They shut the door for a meeting that lasted about seventy-five minutes; a glass panel allowed municipal guards and the king's valet Cléry to hear and see what was happening. Many tears were shed. According to Marie-Thérèse's memoirs, the king made his family swear never to avenge his death. At 10:15 p.m., the king rose, and final good-byes, kisses, and hugs were exchanged. He promised to visit them one last time before leaving.

But he did not visit as promised the next morning. Instead, after receiving last rites by Abbé Edgeworth, he walked through the soldiers lined up along his path to the carriage and rode quietly through the foggy, heavily guarded streets with Abbé Edgeworth by his side; together they read psalms and prayers for the dying as they proceeded slowly to the place de la Révolution (now place de la Concorde), where they arrived at 10:10 a.m. The king initially struggled against the executioner when the latter tried to bind his hands, but on the advice of his confessor, he submitted. Some variations exist on his last minutes. Standing on the platform amid a constant drumroll, he demanded silence, and silence fell—or not—so that the crowd of thousands heard him declare—or could not hear—one of three things. He either said, "I die innocent of the crimes charged. I pardon those who are carrying out my death sentence and pray God that the blood that they are spilling will not spread across France." Or he said, "You all know that I am innocent, but if the sacrifice of my life will bring peace to my people, I offer it gladly." Or he may have tried to elicit the people's commiseration.[65] At any rate, when he tried to say more, someone—possibly the chief of the National Guard, Santerre—ordered the drummers to start up again, and they drowned out his voice. As the blade fell, Abbé Edgeworth reportedly cried out, "Son of Saint Louis, rise to the heavens" (Fils de Saint Louis, montez au ciel) or "Go, son of Saint Louis, heaven awaits you" (Allez, fils de Saint-Louis, le ciel vous attend).[66] His decapitated body was taken not to the sacred crypt at Saint-Denis but rather to the nearby Madeleine Cemetery, where it was temporarily buried, with the head between the legs and its hands tied, in an uncovered wooden coffin in a common grave. Quicklime was thrown on top.[67]

The controversy over his last words holds the key to what would follow. Did the king pursue his counterrevolutionary schemes right to the last and ask for the people's empathy, as Santerre implied, so that he might launch a so-called insurrection of pity? Or did the king submit in Christlike resignation to the law and offer his pardon and his life so that France could emerge from the trauma intact? Was he a plotter or a saint? Given the heavy censorship that governed the French press and publishing industry in 1793–94, we have few testimonials to the latter interpretation; most newspapers took a vehemently antiroyalist stance and celebrated the country's liberation from the "tyrant" and his dynasty.

However, a flourishing black market soon emerged for artwork aiming to capitalize on the public's remorse and to wrap a mystical halo around the victim. Imagery of codified mourning whereby profiles of the royal family were superposed on republican monuments was particularly popular during

19. *The Weeping Willow* (*Le Saule pleureur*). Engraving, ca. 1794–99.

the years 1794–99. Scenes of *Le Saule pleureur* (The weeping willow; fig. 19) and *L'Urne mystérieuse* (The mysterious urn; fig. 20) were reproduced not only in black-and-white engravings but also on precious colored porcelain plates and bowls imported from China, and remain highly prized still today among collectors.[68] While Claude Langlois interprets such objects as consoling relics by which royalists could discreetly grieve for the monarch without getting caught by police, my researches have revealed proof of police searches for exactly this kind of "suspect objects."[69] Secret or not, the meaning of these scenes defies straightforward exegesis.

Unlike traditional portraits of the monarch—full body in signature regalia—here the king is freed of conventional accessories. In fact, he has no body at all. His essence dominates the scene nonetheless as an otherworldly shadow, carved into the stone of the royal tomb he never knew. Signs of

20. *The Mysterious Urn (L'Urne mystérieuse)*. Engraving, ca. 1794–99.

age and death (the monarch's plump silhouette, the symbols of time's passing—hourglass, scythe, wings, skull and crossbones) are superposed on symbols of regeneration (Phrygian bonnet, willow tree) to perplexing effect. The
composition itself implies a double meaning: the white-on-black projection
of the king's profile against the funerary objects seems to reverse his mor-
tality and restore his sacred essence, reminding us that he does not exist
in time like ordinary mortals but *above* time like Christ.[70] Nevertheless,
the lack of cross or other Christian symbolism, the prominent imagery of
a hissing snake (emblem of Robespierre), and the classical temples in the
background suggest that these pictures may also be read as tributes to the
Republic's triumph over the now-defunct Bourbon bloodline. The characters that people the scene are equally elusive. Draped over the tombstones,

THE ONCE AND ONLY PITIFUL KING

the sorrowful ladies could be mourning the Bourbons' untimely deaths or awaiting the rebirth of a new, republican lineage, as suggested by the rays of sunlight illuminating the "mysterious urn" (is it sunset or sunrise?) and the weeping willow's association with resurrection. Ronen Steinberg has shown how the stone expiatory monuments erected after the Terror and during the Restoration took on changing styles and meanings in keeping with the different social and personal needs they served.[71] Perhaps this print imagery should be seen in a similarly fluid manner. According to the viewer's circumstances, the urn or willow could have reaffirmed the republican cause, suggested hope for resistance to revolutionary repression, or expiated the Revolution's sins through Bourbon loyalty.

Hidden profiles were also exploited for more obviously polemic ends in images such as *Un Sans-culotte instrument de crimes* (A criminal sansculotte; ca. 1794–96; fig. 21). Here the outline of Louis's face seems to be jammed against the throat of a sansculotte who is brandishing a banner marked "Festival of January 21" and trampling lists of the Revolution's victims underfoot. Since the sansculotte falters and falls back in surprise, he clearly feels the impact but cannot see its agent. If the spectator's eye moves from Louis's head to the left of the image, however, one finds the raised hand of a doleful goddess, Humanity, who is barring the criminal from approaching her cenotaph, apparently with the help of this invisible force from the past. Meanwhile, the nation in the background expires in an orgy of violence and despair.

Unfinished mourning motivates all Adieux narratives, whether they are set in France or in one of many sites where émigrés found refuge abroad. Stories of families torn asunder and emotional accounts of the grief and shock felt by former courtiers and nobility abound in the literature of emigration. This genre is particularly useful in showing how people shared news and commiserated with each other's suffering from afar. The most famous is Gabriel Sénac de Meilhan's *L'Émigré* (1797), which presents a voluminous correspondence between noble friends and family members, all of whom are haunted in one way or another by memories of the dead. News of Louis XVI's execution wreaks havoc on their sensitive nerves; as one character writes: "That horrible image plagues my mind day and night. . . . I am sometimes tempted to hope that the catastrophe is only a terrible dream."[72] This motif of impotent suffering did not necessarily hinge on the principal's innocence. Witness the literature generated in the wake of Robespierre's execution, where one also finds characters reliving the horrors of unholy deaths and disrupted mourning, including that of the Incorruptible himself.

21. "A criminal sansculotte dancing in the midst of the horror outrages Humanity, who
is weeping near a tomb. He thinks he sees the shadow of one of the Revolution's victims
seize his throat. This terrifying vision suffocates him and knocks him down." (Un Sansculotte instrument de crimes dansant au milieu des horreurs, vient outrager l'humanité
pleurante auprès d'un cénotaphe. Il croit voir l'ombre de l'une des victimes de la révolution
qui le saisit à la gorge. Cette effrayante apparition le suffoque et le renverse.) Engraving,
ca. 1794–95. Inv. 84.871, Marque de la collection Soulavie, © Coll. Musée de la Révolution
française / Domaine de Vizille.

THE COMPLEX POLITICS OF EMOTION

The most interesting cultural productions of the transitional period between
Robespierre's death and the rise of Napoleon's Empire oscillate between apprehension over the powerful apparatus of the French state, on the one hand,
and an appreciation for strategies that allowed individuals to transcend, side-
step, or otherwise shrug off its control, on the other. Consider *L'Histoire
d'un poignard française* [sic] (History of a French dagger; 1803), which la-

ments the Terror as a time when "it was forbidden to cry" and declares, "Thus, the tyrants sacrificed those who were the most humane, compassionate, and sensitive. And why? Because those Frenchmen had the courage to cry."[73] According to Reddy, this penchant for weepy emotionalism as a stand-in for political virtue remained strong until Napoleon seized power and the virtues of pragmatism took hold. The writers and statesmen of the First Empire, he claims, disparaged the revolutionaries' public outpourings of feeling and the humanity it was supposed to signify and taught readers to analyze emotional displays dispassionately.[74] This schema may help explain some facets of postrevolutionary material. But things were not quite so simple. For long before Napoleon crowned himself emperor, the literary productions of Thermidor, the Directory, and the Consulate periods were at work on changing people's attitudes toward emotion and its relation to politics. The irony that master writers such as Voltaire and Laclos had wielded with aplomb under the ancien régime was still appreciated as well, as seen by the popularity of authors such as Rétif de la Bretonne and Sade and the ribald humor of *Melchior ardent*. These facts throw a wrench into Reddy's narrative of the "affective registers" that supposedly dictate cultural taste.

It is undeniable that the weepy or sentimental genre, which had enjoyed such fame in the 1760s thanks to the phenomenally popular *Nouvelle Héloïse*, rose in marketability during the late 1790s and early 1800s: one need only recall the brisk sales of works by Sophie Cottin, Valérie de Krüdener, Chateaubriand, and Senancour. But what can the fad tell us about postrevolutionary France? I think that gushy outpourings—whether penned by struggling writers or sure-footed statesmen—require a grain of salt or, more precisely, a longer-term historical context to be appreciated appropriately.

Consider Maximilien Robespierre. His tearfully poignant speeches of 1790–92 have recently been touted as masterpieces of Jacobin earnestness: the man's apparent sincerity did much to increase his party's strength, claim David Andress and William Reddy.[75] But if we look just a few years farther back at Robespierre's prerevolutionary *Éloge de Gresset*, we find that the author adopted a very different position toward public virtue. In 1785 Robespierre defended Gresset (a minor poet of the rococo style) against cynics who did not believe in his repentance and he expressed nostalgia for the decline of witty banter (*badinage*) that had made Gresset's fame. It is unsurprising to find the young lawyer defending Gresset from allegations of immorality (he was forced out of the Jesuits after mocking a convent in his poem *Ver-Vert*): defending underdogs was what Robespierre did best.[76] What is surprising is Robespierre's endorsement of badinage. Did he really like the battle of wits that characterized elite salon culture? Or was his praise of banter motivated by other forces, such as a desire to advance his own stand-ing among those aristocratic arbiters who might give a prize to the *Éloge de Gresset*? Perhaps his political writings were motivated by similarly mixed motives.

A few years after *Éloge de Gresset*, Robespierre forcefully disassociated himself from most court values. Although he never abandoned his some-what old-fashioned manners and mode of dress, he wanted to be taken seri-ously as a lawmaker and adopted the vocabulary of sentimental transpar-ency borrowed from Rousseau to drive that home. However, as chapter 4 shows, some witnesses were taken aback by Robespierre's abrupt changes in the public personas he adopted. The veneer of homely goodness that he used to such effect in 1790–92 was regarded with suspicion by those who had seen him exhibit other façades at other times. Perhaps we too need to inter-pret sentimentalism with a bit of caution. Despite its considerable cachet, the vogue for public displays of emotion was a style, as artificial as pastoral, melodrama, or the *style troubadour*, which also sold well during and after the Revolution. It lasted longer than most styles, but it is an error to think that the reading public was somehow brainwashed into quiescent accep-tance or melancholy by reading or hearing sentimental rhetoric. People's ap-petite for serious political debate and verbal showmanship remained strong, as did their relish for well-wrought irony. What is most interesting to me is not the styles in themselves but how authors used the styles to attain political, commercial, or aesthetic success.

Censorship remained strong in the waning years of the century. The government of the Consulate was by many accounts more repressive and more effective in its persecution of writers than the "terrorists" of 1793–94 or the monarchists who predated them. So clever authors cloaked their political messages in less visible plots and adopted a wittier kind of engage-ment. Most exemplary of this trend is *Le Cimetière de la Madeleine* by a prolific author known as Julius-Junius (J.-J.) Regnault-Warin.[77] This book's influence is seen in the two spin-offs published the same year, the police pursuit discussed below, the publisher's advertisements, and the author's many reminiscences of the travails he suffered because of the *Cimetière*.[78] The novel has garnered no little interest among today's readers too, judg-ing from the lively dialogues running on Internet sites such as http://www.passion-histoire.net/, two new English translations in paperback, and the price that the novel can demand on eBay: a bound copy of the first edition could be bought for 10–40 euros in 2007, whereas in 2011 it sold for 275 euros.[79] Few scholars have studied this work with care. It remains one of the unknown best sellers of the late revolutionary era.

LE *CIMETIÈRE DE LA MADELEINE*: A LITTLE-KNOWN CAUSE
CÉLÈBRE OF THE CONSULATE

At first sight, *Le Cimetière de la Madeleine* (The Madeleine Cemetery)
seems to present an apology for King Louis XVI. Regnault-Warin's narrative
begins where Louis XVI's life left off, in the Madeleine Cemetery. Deliberately juxtaposing the Paris of the present with its recent revolutionary
past, the main character, a sensitive and curious young man, launches the
nine-hundred-page opus when he wanders through the streets of Paris on
a festive evening and revisits various revolutionary sites of memory under
the glare of scarlet fireworks, surrounded by a boisterous and chaotic crowd.
Unmoved by their merriment, he leaves the revelers behind and makes his
way up to the unfinished Madeleine Church, where he solemnly surveys
the tombs of France's departed heroes. While enthralled by visions of hid-
eous, blood-soaked ghosts, he hears strange music and follows it to an el-
derly gentleman who sits in the dark singing a sad song. When approached
by the youth, the old man initially hesitates in fear, taking his unknown
interlocutor for an agent of the secret police, but he stands up to him nonetheless and announces, "your presence in this place at this hour . . . tells me
that I have been discovered. I will go without a fight because I am without
crime. The government will not punish my tears of pity as if they were
conspiratorial regrets" (1:10). This challenge places *Le Cimetière* firmly in
the lineage of Thermidorian writings that dared to tell the truth about the
Revolution's victims and brandished the government's promise of free expression as a metaphorical shield. Once he is reassured by the youth, who
promises him "an inviolate complicity," the elder gestures to the tombs at
their feet and proffers brief homage of his onetime friends and associates
Malesherbes, Lavoisier, and Louis XVI (1:13–15). Since both share nostalgia
over the recent past, they agree to continue the conversation the next night.
It is only then that the narrator realizes that this intriguing elder is none
other than the king's confessor, the Irish non-juror priest Abbé Edgeworth.

A series of twelve conversations, or "Nights," ensues wherein the priest
relates the last years, days, and hours of Louis XVI, Marie-Antoinette, the
dauphin, and royalty itself. The complicity between the old man and the
narrator models a Rousseauian convention of shared feeling and pity, relayed in what has been called a *style à fracas* that combines "the brush of
a Ducray-Duménil with the palette of a Young," that is, a sentimental dip
into the graveyard genre.[80] An early moment in the narration breaks down
when the priest bursts into tears and begs his listener's pardon by explaining: "I saw him in misery; I saw his family in tears; I saw him perish on the

scaffold! . . . history will tell if he was guilty; I owe this debt of tears to his misfortune."[81] The narrator's reaction to this outburst anticipates the reader's response in an echo chamber or mise en abyme of communicative sentiment. He first exclaims over the story's interest ("What a lot of topics of curiosity! What an endless source of reflection!"), then he explains the chain of emotions that the tale has elicited in him by borrowing terms from the physiopsychological terminology of sensationalist philosophy: "The ingenuous heart has a network of fibers that resonate easily and correspond somehow to those of the hearts of fellow beings, [and] when a point of contact is found and analogies are established, the sweetest, most touching harmony can result."[82] Although such purple prose may leave modern readers cold, it was apparently effective among reading publics in 1800. One account indicts the first volumes of *Le Cimetière de la Madeleine* for causing nervous breakdowns among women, impressing the impressionable, and opening old wounds that the government preferred to leave well enough alone.[83]

The casual reader will doubtless assume that *Le Cimetière de la Madeleine* presents an apology for Louis XVI. After all, the narration includes more than twenty *pièces justificatives* (supporting documents) that appear to defend the king as if he were on trial. Inserted into the multiple layers of dialogue that run through this book—the frame dialogue between the young narrator and the old priest and the various dialogues and meetings of the king and different people relayed verbatim by Abbé Edgeworth—one finds raw materials from what could be a legal case. The alternation between romantic narration (as in the opening scene), pseudolegal data, unpublished correspondence, and political documents creates a jarring effect of hybridity but also a powerful sense of immediacy. Among the *pièces justificatives* are documents that could, if they were authentic, be verified to substantiate the foreign affairs related in the book—dated letters from the king to General Dumouriez, to the lawyer Malesherbes, and to the king of Prussia—but also letters of a very personal nature. In the notes exchanged by the king and his wife and their conversations as repeated by Abbé Edgeworth, the author shines light on a complex marriage. In the letters purported to be communicated to the captive king by means of a "concave mirror" (2:83–84, 166–67), we fathom the extent of the conspiracies and plots apparently hatched by royalist friends to save the family from their fate. Eventually we turn the page to the entire (fake) text of Marie-Antoinette's will and testament (4:57–63). The initial effect of this massive evidence is a feeling of verisimilitude: life is confusing, we are invited to reflect; many perspectives assault us every day with conflicting viewpoints and multiple choices. The king's life was even more confusing; as the priest points out: "the facts I am about to tell you are complicated; some of them are known; the most interesting ones are not" (1:19). These details provide *Le Cimetière*'s reason for being.

Inside the echo chamber of sorrowful telling and tearful listening, however, the narration relays certain comments that disrupt the ambiance of royalists in mourning and signal a certain irony over the king's fate. Jean Gillet, one of the few critics to study this novel, admits being "struck . . . by a discreet kind of reserve in the tale."[84] Even Abbé Edgeworth admits a critical edge. Consider his comment that "Louis XVI was never so great as when he ceased to be king" or the scene where he depicts the king regretting his poor judgment and lamenting: "every night, I blame myself for what I did that day."[85] Political asides inserted into the text by various narrators confuse readers trying to pinpoint the novel's ideology. I noted above the old man's anxiety on their first encounter when he suspected the youth of being a police spy, but I could just as easily foreground scenes where the youthful narrator expresses his optimism and confidence in the new regime, which he calls "the friend of free thought and generous action" (1:20). The very composition of the novel proves the government's goodness, as the author notes in opening volume 1: "Since I am allowed to write this book, I feel that freedom is not just a dream" (Depuis qu'il m'est permis de l'écrire, je sens que ma liberté n'est point une chimère; 1:21).

This ironic doubling of perspective is no accident or illusion; it forms an integral part of the author's self-appointed challenge in publishing *Le Cimetière de la Madeleine.* Although legends of the author's imprisonment long circulated in nineteenth-century biographies and in catalogs of rare-book dealers, it was not until recently that my research confirmed such claims. It turns out that *Le Cimetière de la Madeleine* left quite a paper trail and really was the object of a massive police effort of search and seizure that lasted almost two years, from 2 fructidor Year 8 to 29 germinal Year 10 (August 20, 1800, to April 19, 1802). Other novels had come in for some police scrutiny in these years: Madame Grandmaison Van Esbecq's *Adolphe, ou La Famille malheureuse* (ca. 1797) was designated a "dangerous" book by Paris police because it was "beloved by royalists," but the campaign of search and seizure lasted only a couple of weeks, in pluviôse and ventôse, Year 7 (February–March 1799).[86] The pursuit of *Le Cimetière de la Madeleine,* on the contrary, targeted cities all over France: Paris, Orléans, Bordeaux, and Marseille, with particular attention to Avignon, which appears to have been a hotbed of clandestine publishing.

According to documents in the archives of the Paris police, the novel was seized and banned immediately upon its first printing in 1800 and the author was brought before authorities, who warned him to desist. He agreed. And then he set to work producing a second volume (including what are called tomes 3 and 4) and a second edition of the first volume, which were denounced by a spy (apparently the author's landlord), who brought it to the attention of police on 2 vendémiaire Year 9 (September 24, 1800). Although exact details of the timing and quantity of the print runs have yet to be determined, my research has confirmed the wide dissemination of this book and its profitability. Police historian Peuchet notes that "bookshops are pulling in considerable profits despite the clandestine selling," and a letter from a certain Citizen Spiels describes the working conditions in a clandestine print shop during the book's publication. Because of the novel's notoriety and illegal status, workers were held under lock and key until the job was done. The magnitude of this print run was impressive: according to Spiels the printing would take a whole week and produce fifteen thousand copies.[87]

Being hounded by policemen and spies gave Regnault-Warin just the opportunity he sought for some good publicity! In January 1801 he wrote to Prefect of Police Dubois and, presenting himself as an ardent patriot, claimed that his book brought a double advantage to the government by its portrayal of time-honored virtues and by the gratitude and love the judiciary would enjoy (from his readers, one presumes) for allowing the book to be read. After expressing righteous indignation over those who impugned his patriotism, the author declared, "It is my book itself that will resolve these allegations." The letter closes on a solemn and apparently deferential note that nevertheless transmits an equivocal message: "The victory and the will of the people created the Republic. A few tears or flowers tossed with pious feeling onto the tomb of a defunct line will not damage a constitution that promises such happiness. Citizen Prefect, religious men are subject to authority; and *those who cry do not kill.*"[88] According to the police memorialist (who admits appreciating Regnault-Warin's clever reasoning), the pursuit stopped here, although the provocation did not go unnoticed, by either the police or the public: the author shared his letter with many friends and allies and inscribed his mishaps right into the *avertissement* of tome 3 (vol. 2, 1801). Judging that their ongoing attention to this pest would only fan the flames of his acclaim, the Paris police force abandoned the case.

The book hunt nonetheless continued for months outside Paris, and *Le Cimetière* was heaped with all kinds of opprobrium. A Bordeaux commissioner described it as a work "born of partisanship and perverse intentions . . . [product of] the corrupting venom of the Republic's enemies"; another taxed it with being "contrary to laws and good morals"; a Marseillais police officer called it poison; and an Orléanais claimed the author was plotting to "make people regret Louis and his family, whom he presents as being quite interesting." In response, publisher Lepetit protested his innocence, cited with amazement critics who deemed the book "capable of recalling dangerous memories," and demanded his and the author's rights in accordance with the law of July 19, 1793, on copyright. Some other booksellers went on record as well defending the book and its publisher because they operated under the law of the land and thus should be spared such persecution.[89] In short, this novel sparked what was one of the first causes célèbres of the Consulate.

The furor makes sense if one looks closely at the text. In the *avertissement* published at the head of the second volume and throughout the novel as a whole, the author exploits the pull of emotion to incite political reflection. Like the masses of documentation, the narrative's alternation between irony and empathy was calculated to create an effect. (At least one reader, Antoine DeBaecque, was so taken by the author's "research" that he considered *Le Cimetière* a work of authentic testimony!)[90] Regnault-Warin wanted at all cost to elicit interest—whether it was the dangerous interest of the forces of order or the traditional interest of sensitive souls who read novels. A wink, almost a goad, at the police emerges on several occasions in the text, as when the author claims that "this pen . . . is not to be feared" and consequently compares himself to Tacitus, who used his "vengeful pen" to bring down the tyrants (3:iii–iv). Or when he intervenes toward the end of the novel to stress that he only assented to becoming the depository and messenger of this tale because he felt it was "quite proper to pique [the reader's] curiosity, to sustain interest, without causing a public nuisance or troubling the calm and imposing workings of the government" (4:91). At the same time, sincerity and pitiful compassion are crucial themes. The first pages announce: "It will be memorable to see a citizen whose political principles are and have always been . . . far from fanaticism . . . and royalist superstitions . . . trace with a pathetically truthful touch the misfortunes of a *man who was king.*"[91] Religion is enlisted to remind us of the respect we owe to the dead: "How these details will become valuable to your heart if you remember that while you are reading, we will be walking on the ashes [*nous foulons la cendre*] of those whose story they tell!" (2:196). A highly emotional connection between the two narrators—and, by extension, the reader—punctuates the entire book, notably at the ends of the chapters, where they marvel over the interest of their subject before departing for the night. This soulful communion comes to a climax after the execution of Louis XVI when the young man, the old priest, and apparently the author himself join together to explicitly lay out the parameters of whom they foresee as their audience and how that audience will react. A few lines suffice to appreciate the orgy of fine feelings: "Come, sweet, naive girls [and] virtuous young men, come and listen to me! In return for the long nights that I have spent in sadness, may I awaken in your heart a fellow feeling and make your breast heave delicious sighs! May these pages, confidantes of my feelings, be moistened by your tears! What sweeter reward could there be for the friend, the artist of woe [*le peintre du malheur*]" (3:95–96).

Yet after this high point (which is located in the middle of the four tomes), the narrative breaks down. One hundred or so pages earlier Abbé Edgeworth had already prayed for the repose of the king's soul and given up, admitting: "History will judge if this monarch was guilty; for me, I only want to show how unhappy he was" (2:193). While the novel continues for about three hundred more pages, the narration loses its bearings and the narrator's sympathies stray. After winding through a number of subplots that concern Queen Marie-Antoinette, the duc d'Orléans, and an arrogant woman writer who must represent Madame de Genlis,[92] and that end with the queen's death, the book continues by piecing together a cluster of more or less disparate narratives on Louis XVII and then peters out. It ends on an inconclusive note.

This equivocation makes sense when one considers the politics that Regnault-Warin proclaimed in his other writings. Although he was only twenty-six years old when *Le Cimetière* came out, he had already applied himself to an array of literary genres for ten years with little to no success. By 1800 he was the author of several Jacobin pamphlets of a shocking violence, a *Citizen's Library* containing a civic catechism (1791), and a Gothic novel; in 1802 he published a pastoral and an anti-British satire. The immediate and lucrative success enjoyed by Élisabeth Guénard for *Irma* (ca. 1799–1800) doubtless inspired Regnault-Warin to try the royalist-in-mourning genre, a genre he pursued in *Les Prisonniers du Temple* and *L'Ange des prisons* as well. Critics such as Bruno Durruty claim that such opportunism is "rather rare" among authors of the revolutionary period, but my researches have uncovered a good number who operated in a similar fashion as Regnault-Warin.[93] The ironic manipulation of emotion in *Le Cimetière de la Madeleine* corresponds perfectly to that transitional period between the Revolution and Empire. The unstable governments and widespread violence of those years forced people to scrutinize each other's political sympathies. It was not easy to be sure where anyone stood. Just like words of law, individual words of honor lost their power to reassure those who lived under a series of regimes dictated by self-interest, fear, and short-term alliances.

It is thus unsurprising that the politics of *Le Cimetière de la Madeleine* defy easy categorization. The novel begins by underlining the unhappiness of the king and his humanity, but it ends with a scene that lends credence to the Republic. Once the dauphin dies, we are no longer called upon to pity the Bourbon dynasty, which is furthermore qualified as a "lost cause." The narrator justifies this change of perspective by noting: "As much as he pitied and felt attached to the son of the last king, the king's brothers inspired little affection. The cowardly indolence of the one [the comte de Provence] and the guilty idiocy [*les coupables étourderies*] of the other [the comte d'Artois] seemed quite likely to have caused the state's downfall" (4:199). At the end, the new government is represented as neither an enemy to vanquish nor a traitor to denounce. On the contrary, the author seems most desirous to restore public order and maintain the republican regime that seemed to be merging with the Consulate in the first months following Napoleon's coup d'etat in November 1799. The final moral borrowed from the Gospel according to Luke outlines the humility expected of good Christians: "He hath put down the mighty from their seat / and the rich he hath sent empty away" (Desposuit potentes de sede, Et divites dimisit inanes; *Cimetière*, 4:200; Luke 1:52–53). In hindsight, it may seem bizarre to herald the new Napoleonic leadership as emulating Christian humility. But one must recall the sense of hope and renewal that swept the nation in early 1800. According to Chateaubriand, it was commonplace in those days to see émigrés chatting peacefully with the assassins of their parents, while former radicals sold baked apples on street corners.[94] Ever alert to shifting tides of opinion, Regnault-Warin wove this sense of pragmatism right into his parting words and celebrated the peace that once more seemed to be descending on France as an afterthought to the royalist history. The combination was exasperating to police and tantalizing to readers.

HELEN-MARIA WILLIAMS EDITS THE KING

One last example of a work that exploited emotional responses to King Louis XVI is the collection of royal letters edited by an English expatriate known as a "friend of the Revolution": Helen-Maria Williams (1761–1827). As in *Le Cimetière de la Madeleine*, Williams insists on the authenticity of her sources and promises to depict the king's "private life and real feelings." Unlike the French editors of an earlier edition who, according to her, published the same letters in view of preparing the king's apotheosis, Williams offers her own "Observations" wherein insider information emerges for all to see. This kind of guerrilla documentation is necessary, Williams claims, because of the present times. As she explains, "We are living, everyone knows, in a scrutinizing century [*un siècle examinateur*], when the first impressions produced by objects are often displaced by greater scrutiny"; in other words, people's words no longer have the same power as before, and multiple pieces of evidence had to be analyzed before judgments could be made.[95] Williams employs this quasi-scientific method to compare the king's acts, writings, and public speeches with the feelings excavated from his private letters. And the results are shocking. A few examples will reveal how Williams's caustic pen punctured the king's carefully wrought rationale. They also underline the importance of paternal symbolism in the royal imagination; during the nineteen years of letters recorded here (1774–93), he never gave up hope of receiving the people's love.

Before delving into Williams's book, it is necessary to point out two caveats. First, *La Correspondance politique et confidentielle* is widely considered a forgery that was foisted upon the unsuspecting editor by a couple of unscrupulous counterfeiters. It remains unclear how she could have been misled and why she undertook this venture. In some ways, such matters are irrelevant: what counts is that Williams's work was widely considered definitive and the letters were reprinted three more times (1817, 1862, 1864), until the more or less "authoritative" edition of 1864–73 took its place.[96] Second, although this book sold well across the Continent, it was not appreciated by Napoleon and his police force. In fact, it generated a police case not dissimilar to the stormy treatment of *Le Cimetière de la Madeleine* by French detectives. The reader may wonder: why study the forged correspondence of an author vilified by the First Consul? The answer lies in my approach to history through literature. Williams's *Correspondance* merits attention precisely because it was so controversial and wielded such a long-lasting influence on the king's memory. Until 1838 at least, when the forger's confession was published, readers did not have access to the strange story behind these hefty tomes (two volumes in French; three in English).[97] Despite the efforts of monarchists such as Bertrand de Moleville, most readers were unaware of the hoax or, if they consulted one of the later editions by Williams's imitators, assumed that it was exempt from errors.[98] In addition, the book provides an early example—albeit mechanical and often clumsy—of an ironic double-voiced narration that would be made most famous by writers of the great nineteenth-century novels like *Le Père Goriot*. But as the police case and later editions will reveal, even heavy editorializing did not save Williams from charges of monarchist complicity. That ambiguity is the virtue and peril of irony.

Let us consider a couple examples of Williams's editorializing in action. In an exchange between King Louis XVI and his brother the comte d'Artois in September 1789, where the comte reminds him of the courage and resistance he will need to vanquish the factious, Louis replies with words that could have been lifted right out of an earnestly royalist novel (or a sarcastic *Entretien des Bourbons*): "My brother, you are not king! The heavens, in putting me on the throne, gave me a sensitive heart, the sentiments of a good father. All the French are my children; I am the communal father of that great family entrusted to my care. . . . Stop, my brother, stop accusing me . . . that seems like joining my enemies, and breaks my fatherly heart." The editor reads between the lines in her "Observation." Although noting that she was initially moved by indignation and pity for the king ("who did not have the courage to resist this torrent of perversity"), her conclusion casts a cold light on the monarch's judgment. The king claims he had "sacrificed himself for his people," she declares, but "it is difficult to divine what those sacrifices were. If the proofs are supposed to be in this letter, they are all against him." The text boils down to an exercise in self-delusion: "The king, at that time, was used to being fooled, and fooling himself."[99]

The Varennes debacle provides another opportunity to reveal the disjunction between the king's words and deeds. In a letter purportedly written to his brother comte de Provence, on July 23, 1791, the king laments the results of the trip: "this flight, which was so necessary to me, which perhaps was going to make my happiness and that of the people, will prompt terrible accusations. I am threatened. . . . The French people used to love their kings; what have I done to be hated, I who have always carried them in my heart?" The king bares his soul to his brother, who he believes will empathize with his plight, but Williams's editorial asides introduce a different message on Varennes. Her intervention works in two clever ways: by juxtaposition and by annotated commentary. The July 23 letter is juxtaposed in the collection to a letter written by the king to the assembly six weeks earlier, where he exclaimed, "I am penetrated . . . by the justice that the assembly has done to me. If you could read the feelings in my heart, you would only see feelings that justify the nation's confidence. All suspicions would dissipate; we would all be happy."[100] When the reader peruses the first and then turns to the second, the surprise is palpable. One cannot help being taken aback at the king's fickle attitude toward the Constituent Assembly and his frustration with a population alienated by his own acts. The other editorial tactic is annotated commentary, as when Williams comments acidly, "it is impossible to read this letter, without noticing the extreme ease with which the king deludes himself, not only about other people, but also about himself," or "it seems that the king was quite mistaken about the nature of his errors."[101]

The king's writings and other people's views all support the barbed "Observations" of Williams's *Correspondance*. A deputy claimed that the king was "a decent man, but deceived by traitors and enemies of the fatherland": this claim is borne out in a letter penned shortly after the monarchy fell (August 12, 1792), in which Louis laments, "I am an odious sight in the eyes of decent Frenchmen. . . . That is the cruelest thing to suffer. My brother, soon I will be no longer; remember to avenge my memory by letting it be known how much I loved that ungrateful people."[102] Even the nonspecialist would likely be a bit taken aback by this last demand regarding the ungrateful people, given the king's oft-cited love for his subjects and his aversion to vengeance or hatred. But for Williams it proves suitable closure to the collection because it supports her theory of revolution: "The repeated reiteration of these sad forebodings prove that Louis regarded events as inevitable. The wretched system could only lead to catastrophe."[103]

Williams's editorial efforts were not lost on the police, who pursued this book with even more vigor than they did *Le Cimetière de la Madeleine*. Again missing the double-voiced narration that made *La Correspondance* anything but a paean to monarchy, a police report of July 4, 1803, declared, "All the letters of this more than apocryphal correspondence are followed by reflections by the author and notes which tend only to represent Louis XVI as the most virtuous, or even a constitutional, king and as he who brought together the most enlightened political views and the purest sentiments. This work has all the color of the novel *Le Cimetière de la Madeleine*, but in a more serious and methodical genre." Given its documentary status, the book was not allowed the relatively liberal treatment doled out to Regnault-Warin. On the eve of its distribution a raid descended on the print shop and seized two thousand copies of the English edition and three thousand of the French edition. The next day, July 8, Williams wrote to the prefect of police and explained why her editorializing should have saved the book from censorship. But while one agent apparently concurred that she had painted the monarch "in quite a contemptuous, if not odious, light," another retorted that "several of the monarch's letters could renew regrets over the sorrows that many French have felt." Sales were brisk. The English translation arrived as planned in London in August, and although it was widely attacked in the press, a French edition was published there as well. Other counterfeit editions published in Metz, Paris, and Lyons were reportedly destined for émigré markets in Hamburg and Leipzig.[104]

Oddly enough, Williams has come under suspicion again in recent years for her supposed monarchism. In 1997 Jack Fruchtman Jr., editor of Williams's *Eye-Witness Account of the French Revolution*, charged that *La Correspondance politique et confidentielle* "represented Louis as a most virtuous king and a true constitutional monarch."[105] It is true that the later letters and editorial comments in *La Correspondance* depict the man dolefully awaiting his fate, but it is still an exaggeration to describe this corpus as a prop for the Bourbons. The editorializing paints a much more complex picture than that, and one that I think is at least somewhat justified by what Williams would have seen around her: images of King Louis XVI as a weak ruler who harbored outdated notions about his legitimate rule and about the love due to him as father of the French people.

A glance at the "authentic" edition of the king's letters reveals a less emotional and more statesman-like personality. In the multivolume edition published in 1864–73, one finds a letter reputedly sent by the king to the bishop of Boulogne in 1789 wherein he requests the church's assistance in calming the unruly populace but also defends the institution of the National Assembly. The king asks the bishop, "May the people entrust themselves to my protection and my love; when the whole world abandons them, I will watch over them. But there has never been a time when the people had such a broad-based coalition [*un concours général de volontés et d'affections*], from all the orders of society, working on their behalf. Exhort them then, in the name of religion, to show some gratitude and to manifest it by obeying the laws of justice."[106] This collection reveals none of the regret or anxiety about Varennes that were so pronounced in Williams's edition either. Instead, there is a statement issued from the king to the National Assembly on July 7, 1791, in which he forcefully reiterates his claim of intending to set up a satellite government in Montmédy and denies rumors that he had authorized deserters to recruit for the émigré armies. Moreover, he warns those who spread such rumors that legal consequences will follow. The most touching letter in this collection, which was also published in the *Moniteur*, is dated July 25, 1792, and concerns the Brunswick Manifesto, when France was threatened with imminent invasion by foreign powers. Admitting that he did at one time try to leave France, the king vows here to stay in Paris until the danger is over. "Eh! What are personal dangers for a king who is threatened with losing the love of his people! . . . One day perhaps the people will know how much their happiness is dear to me, how it was always my unique concern, and my first need. How many sorrows could be forgotten by the slightest sign of its return!"[107] These letters show a calmer and statelier tone; there is no mention of vengeance or urgency, and recourse to the king's authority remains an option. They also underline the king's abiding wish for public approval and affection. A fatherly longing for an ideal filial relationship was a mainstay of Louis XVI's identity: it stuck with him beyond the grave.

CODA: HOW FATHERHOOD FAILED THE KING, ACCORDING TO BALZAC

Balzac's novel *Le Père Goriot* (1835) may not appear the most likely source for a coda on the pitiful king. Although this novel is set during the Restoration—the action takes place between November 1819 and February 1820—the actual Bourbon king appears only once in the narration and is not even named; the power of his court is felt indirectly. Moreover, the main character, Père Goriot, is, by the time we meet him, a sixty-nine-year-old of humble means who seems to circulate in an orbit far removed from the glittering Faubourg Saint-Germain of the aristocracy. What makes the story of Goriot's last months reminiscent of Louis XVI's final descent is not only their ages (had he survived, Louis would have been sixty-five) and the feeling of imminent crisis but the contrast between their actions and principles as they understood them to be and how they were interpreted by others. Like Louis XVI, Père Goriot strives to exemplify an impossible ideal of fatherhood—at once sacrificial and powerful—and he is stymied by the pain he incurs as a result. We saw above in perusing the king's writings that Louis XVI held fast to the idea of being father of the people. His disappointment over the people's actions was inevitably chalked up to circumstance, error, or factionalism rather than their refusal of him. Similarly, Père Goriot never abandons the pretense of being a beloved patriarch despite his daughters' repeated snubs. This delusion persists until his last breath.

The affinities between kings and fathers in *Père Goriot* are patent—King Lear looms large—yet allusions to French kings are few as are overt references to French politics and history in general.[108] When the novel first appeared in *La Revue de Paris* (in four installments), Balzac did not even wait for it to be complete before assuring correspondents that it was a success. He was right: the first edition sold twelve hundred copies before the official announcement was even made. If criticism was extensive, so were the letters written to the author by his readers.[109] Critics may have argued about the novel's morality and verisimilitude, but readers enthused about their identification with characters. Indeed, Martin Kanes posits that the painful consequences of social life are what keep this book relevant for every generation of readers, a sentiment echoed by Pierre Barbéris: "La politique ne touche que quelques-uns. La vie privée concerne tout le monde" (Politics touches only some people. Private life concerns all of us.).[110] Today's critics interpret *Père Goriot* from a variety of more or less apolitical angles: as a case study in human passions or homoerotic tensions, as a reflection of nineteenth-century mass culture or Parisian topography, or as a bildungsroman of familial change and moral complexity.[111] Politics have been somewhat lost in the shuffle. But the subtle sarcasm that Balzac weaves around the tale of the failed Father Goriot and the royalist melody that accompanies a pivotal moment in the plot reveal that revolutionary politics are not as far away from this world as some might think. By highlighting the parallels between the two father figures as they are narrated here and in the materials studied above, I propose to show how Balzac's tragicomic exploration of paternity, forty years after the Adieux, make this work a fitting endpoint to Louis's story.

Balzac's political views and ambitions have confounded more than one reader.[112] On the one hand, in his first signed novel, *Les Chouans* (1829), the author expressed a certain admiration for republicanism. In the vignettes of brave and principled troops quashing the rebellion of bedraggled, fanatically Catholic and royalist peasants, it is pretty clear which side Balzac is on.[113] On the other hand, when Balzac wrote to friends about his hopes of being elected deputy in 1831, he announced himself as a royalist.[114] He never did join a political party or follow through with these plans. But he did pen a long article entitled *Du Gouvernement moderne* (On modern government), which reveals Balzac's mature political philosophy. The article apparently displeased the editors of the right-wing newspaper where he submitted it in summer 1832, and so it remained unpublished until 1900. This rejection is unsurprising given that the author points out the errors of no less influential people than Minister Polignac (who had "too much honor, fear, or imbecility") and the peers of France ("old men who survived all the regimes . . . fanatic in their pride and selfishness").[115] The pretentious gerontocracy of the Restoration, which Balzac skewers with such wit in *Père Goriot*, is already on display.

Du Gouvernement moderne is noteworthy because it lays out Balzac's sociopolitical ideals: an antidemocratic agenda based on an aristocracy of birth and talent. The lower classes (*la masse pauvre et ignorante*), he declares, should have no hand in elections, no access to arms, and no sovereignty. But those who enjoy middle and elite standing—and who possess all the superiorities created by money, power, and intelligence—are responsible for ensuring the happiness of their inferiors, who "need work and bread."[116] Balzac's platform embraces some facets of counterrevolution as expounded

by Edmund Burke and Joseph de Maistre, and he admires the strong-arm
rule of a Bonaparte, but theological considerations do not enter into the
equation, nor does the hereditary legitimacy of the Bourbons as embraced
by Chateaubriand.[117] Legitimacy, as he saw it, was manifest in the exercise
of power: it belongs to him who, in the historical circumstances in which
he finds himself, is most able to protect the state and combat the forces that
threaten it. The basis for state power and unity was the family, governed by
a strong and lucid father-leader who ensures its equilibrium and provides its
vision. Balzac flatly repudiated the notions of popular sovereignty and con-
sensual government that were a legacy of 1789: the people-children were to
follow the orders of the king-father, not vice versa.

But this insistence on legitimacy leads to a paradox as concerns the
king: his superiority is at the same time a given and something that needs
protection. In a striking passage at the end of *Du Gouvernement moderne*,
Balzac declares, "Royalty, as a principle of power, should be largely defended
and off-limits to discussion. To put it alone in the presence of the masses is
to expose it to succumbing immediately; and nonetheless, the fall of Louis
XVI did not prevent that of Charles X. Singular fatality! Thus, a popular
kingship is not viable; it clashes with its own principles. Legitimacy, as absurd as it may seem, is a principle that one would have to invent if it did not
exist."[118] For a writer who prided himself on systematic logic, this allusion
to legitimacy in the face of human weakness and failure seems illogical. But
that is only if we neglect the human side of Balzac's work, that is, his insatiable curiosity and compassion for human psychology and pathology in its
manifold misery and splendor.

Looking at *Père Goriot*, we will see that legitimacy is the master key
that unlocks its plot. It takes a while to realize this, however, because
the narrator's initial focus is on other places, people, and things, namely
Eugène de Rastignac and his discovery of Paris. Rastignac is a twenty-two-
year-old law student from an impoverished branch of an old noble family
of Angoulême who initially meets Monsieur Goriot at the tawdry boardinghouse where they both rent garret rooms on the fourth floor. They see
each other daily at communal meals with a motley group of lodgers lorded
over by landlady Madame Vauquer. At the beginning of the book, Rastignac
interacts with Goriot as the other boarders do: he eyes with suspicion the
older man's movements around town and the lady visitors he receives, he
voices contempt for the man's shabbiness by referring to him as Père Goriot
(Father or Old Goriot), and he laughs at the many jokes made at Goriot's
expense. Goriot speaks little and rarely defends himself. In passages that are
not bereft of irony, the boarders (*des gens à tête vide*) speculate vacuously

about him and announce that he is an "imbecile," a "fool," a "mollusk."[119] As the narrative zooms in and out from the group's speech to the individual boarders' habits, we have occasion to listen in on Goriot, however, and thus come to realize that his silence is partly due to his preoccupation with two daughters. To ensure his daughters' happiness, he thinks he needs to offer them a constant influx of cash and unconditionally accept their boorish behavior. In other words, he thinks he has to accept the status quo and does all he can to maintain it, as patently unfair as it may be. Nothing can budge this idea from his mind.

What Goriot *thinks* is paramount to his reality. But what he says and does lead others to presume otherwise about his situation. This split between the real and the perceived is what makes *Père Goriot* infinitely fascinating, for Balzac's novel does not so much tell the reader what events mean as prompt the reader to deduce meaning from situational cues. As Kanes reminds us, Balzac "forces the reader to *construct* the fictional world rather than merely observe it."[120] Using that modus operandi as my guide, I propose to reveal how Goriot's plight doubles as a grotesquely bourgeois version of Louis XVI's decline after the October Days. This hypothesis builds on links between Balzac's characters and the imagery of the king noted in chapter 1 and above, where we saw how the king was imagined first as *le boulanger* (the baker) and the good papa of 1789 whose presence was supposed to ensure that the Parisian people would have plenty to eat and later, after Varennes, how the king's image devolved into that of a puppet or mindless pig whose movements were dictated by others. By focusing on the unfair manner in which other people see Goriot and how he allows himself to become their victim, we will recognize his similarity to Louis XVI.

When Goriot first arrived at Madame Vauquer's in 1813, he brought all the trappings one might expect of a prosperous merchant newly retired: fine clothing, silver, and china. Although his speech betrayed humble rank (he said *ormoires* instead of *armoires*), the man comfortably inhabited the most spacious room on the second floor and frequently dined in town. But as time passed, his possessions and fortune disappeared. He began eating in more often than not. He moved up to the third, then the fourth, floor. By November 1819, when the action opens, he is living in a squalid, unheated cell with peeling wallpaper and hand-me-down bedding and paying a meager two louis a month for rent.

Goriot's problem, like the problem with Louis XVI after 1789, is that he wants to think that his diminished status is temporary when actually it is permanent. Both struggle to achieve moral lucidity and fail through lack of will. Just like Louis XVI in the Tuileries palace (1789–92) and then the

Temple prison (1792–93), Goriot in his garret still reckons himself as an authority, even though he must know deep down that it is no longer true. His daughters, like the subjects of Louis XVI in 1789–93, see him quite pragmatically: at best he is a means to their ends; at worst he is a relic of the past. In both cases, moreover, the father figure sins by indulgence. Goriot willingly gives all his assets to his greedy daughters, whereas Louis XVI passively acquiesces. A master of what Hardman calls "constructive inaction," the king refused to thwart his subjects' wishes (at Versailles in October 1789) or to fire on hostile citizens (at Varennes in 1791), even if it meant relinquishing his own power and safety (*sûreté*).[121] Both men operate on the assumption that if they give away their power or refuse to fight for it, they will be loved. In other words, they understand their legitimacy to be grounded in generosity and consensus rather than control. A few months or years later, when they find themselves deprived of money (Goriot) or political identity (Louis XVI, then Citizen Capet), their change in status becomes flagrant. In the eyes of others the man becomes a hindrance, a social liability, a redundant reminder of a now-outdated circumstance.

We have seen the tortured and sometimes-touching logic attributed to Louis XVI in correspondence where he sought to save face and find peace despite a hostile public. As for the taciturn Goriot, he benefits from the unexpected compassion of young Rastignac. The secret behind Goriot's habits is revealed to Rastignac in a chance encounter with two aristocratic ladies: the vicomtesse de Beauséant (a distant cousin of Rastignac's) and her society rival, the duchesse de Langeais, who tells the story of how Goriot rose from humble beginnings to become a flour merchant and noodle maker (*vermicellier*) during the tumult of 1789. From his shop's location near Les Halles aux blés (the Wheat Market), Goriot was well situated to capitalize on opportunities: he accepted the presidency of his district, thus ensuring his safety and falling into cahoots with the Jacobin government. When a wheat shortage starved Paris in 1793, he made a spectacular fortune by selling wheat for ten times what he paid for it and became known as a shrewd and respected businessman. By 1808 he had amassed enough wealth to marry his two daughters above their rank—one to the banker Nucingen and the other to comte de Restaud—and at their insistence he retired from public life in 1813.

Unbeknownst to Goriot, however, a crushing blow befell his daughter Anastasie when rumors of his flour business recirculated at the Restoration court.[122] To legitimize her presence amid the Restauds and their noble clan, Anastasie needed an audience with the king. Unfortunately, the day she was scheduled to meet His Majesty fell on the same day as the audience of a pastry cook's daughter. At the sight of these two women, the king "began laughing, and made some Latin jokes about flour—*Ejusdem farina*"—thereby suggesting that the two women were made "of the same flour."[123] I see the king's conduct here as symbolically rewriting the memory of October 1789 to restore his power over the people. Years before, this man (then comte de Provence) had already acquired a reputation for biting satire, particularly through the anonymous pamphlets he published against his rival Louis XVI. He despised playing second fiddle to a brother he believed unfit to reign. As Chantal Thomas notes, the libels he wrote and disseminated, inspired by spiteful jealousy, played right into the campaign for regicide.[124] Even though he was nearly sixty years old, obese, and hobbled by gout by the time he assumed the kingship in 1814, he accepted the role as if it had been his all along (the interval from 1792 to 1814 and the advent of Napoleon's empire being mere diversions in the rightful scheme of things). This scene in *Père Goriot* makes perfect sense: it allows the king to publicly disavow the revolutionary past and to set one more piece of the record straight. Whereas Louis XVI cowered in front of the angry women marchers from Les Halles and meekly obeyed their demands to return to the capital as a figurative *boulanger*, Louis XVIII triumphs over the plebs with an esoteric joke about flour and publicly snubs them into silence.

This petty act of recrimination has a disastrous effect on the Goriot clan, yet no one seems to care but Rastignac. Once word of the ridicule spreads, doors are closed to Anastasie throughout the haughty Faubourg Saint-Germain. In her shame she turns against her family, and within two years of the Bourbon reascension to the throne, both sisters refuse to acknowledge their father. "They have disowned their father," Rastignac intones, to which the vicomtesse flippantly replies, "They have indeed. Their father, the father, a father . . . a good father." And the duchesse concludes, "Ah! Dear me, yes, it all seems quite dreadful, and yet we see it every day" (68–69). This injustice incites a sentimental outburst by Rastignac, who suddenly perceives Goriot not only as a legitimate member of society and kindly paterfamilias but also as a Christological victim who is martyred by an ungrateful world. "Père Goriot is sublime!" the teary-eyed youth concludes (71).

Awed by what he thinks is paternal love in its purist incarnation and tantalized by the possibility of moving up in the world with the help of Goriot's daughter Delphine, Rastignac becomes Goriot's defender, his lieutenant in the battle against the lodgers. At dinner that night Rastignac issues a challenge to the table: "From now on anyone bothering Père Goriot will be attacking me. . . . He is worth more than the lot of us." He tells Goriot,

"You are a good, decent man [*un brave et digne homme*]" (75–76).[125] Goriot's attitude changes in tandem. Leaving behind the mute resignation of the powerless, he starts expressing hope, then excitement, about an imminent rapprochement with his daughter. Certain rules apply, however. Goriot insists, "My two daughters are both very fond of me. I am happy to be their father." And he requests Rastignac, "I beg you not to talk about me except to say how kind my daughters are to me," as if fearing to hear words that might destroy the illusion (106–7).[126] Goriot's effusive description of what it means to be a father must be one of the most touching—and bizarrely over-the-top—speeches in literature. Lying back on his putrid mattress, Goriot extemporizes like a king on his dais: "Let me tell you something strange. Well, when I became a father I understood God. His presence is everywhere, since all created things come from him. That is how I am with my daughters. Only I love my daughters more than God loves the world, because the world is not as beautiful as God, and my daughters are much more beautiful than I." Reiterating the sacred aura that Rastignac casts around this man, the narrator declares with tongue in cheek, "Père Goriot was sublime" (120–22).[127] This overheated emotionalism runs throughout the novel, such as when, after receiving a gift from Rastignac, Goriot spills a teardrop on his hand and opines, "God is just, you see. . . . So you want to be my dear child too?" (138), or toward the end when the narrator calls Goriot "the suffering Christ of Fatherhood" and shows him hugging Rastignac in a kind of frenzy, exclaiming, "Oh my boy! I'll be more than a father to you, I'll try to be a family. I'd like to be God and cast the whole universe at your feet" (221).[128] Critics are split on the meaning of these passages: some interpret them as a quasi-religious reflection on paternity and its virtues, an instance of the Balzacian sublime, whereas others read them as a sarcastic tableau of a deranged mind.[129] That these scenes elicit such diverse reactions underlines the importance of perception in Balzac's universe and the multiple meanings wired into the irony.

As one now discerns, the narration of Goriot's story shares two key features with Louis XVI's last months as narrated by the commentators discussed above: (1) pathos, as in the weepy genre and its signature tears, the rhetoric of self-sacrifice, and Christological lamentation; and (2) a double-voiced narration which shows both the principals' ability to delude themselves and the narrator's sometimes-delectable revelation of unpleasant facts. Satirical authors such as Voltaire and Jonathan Swift wielded irony well before Balzac or Helen-Maria Williams and used it to establish a kind of in-joke status with initiates or like-minded readers. What is new here is the seemingly deadpan way that the words mock what they say. Characters in *Père Goriot* are constantly being told the truth or forced to see the truth about their situation only to ignore it. Balzac builds on the kind of double-voicing employed by Williams to create a more subtle irony that involves the reader more actively. This explains the power and fascination of *Père Goriot* some 175 years after its publication: depending on the reader's frame of mind, the scenes conjure up radically different responses varying from sorrowful contemplation to a kind of malicious hilarity.

Balzac's narration also features a psychosocial component that we have not witnessed in earlier literature: the significant minutiae of material life. Cleverly indirect commentaries accompany the action in this way. Through description of the physical décor of setting, accents, and word choice and the use of popular legends of science, crime, and entertainment, latent meanings emerge. These details support my hypothesis about the lost chapters of the French Revolution, for they would have been visible to Balzac's audiences even if they have eluded more modern readers since.

A case in point is the mockery of fatherhood-kingship made by the rascally and flamboyant Vautrin during the pivotal scene at the beginning of book 3, "Death-Dodger" (Trompe-la-Mort). Despite his mysterious nocturnal outings and equivocal morality, Vautrin brings a much-needed levity and congeniality to relations at Madame Vauquer's until his arrest by the police later in this chapter. From the beginning, we see him take a particular interest in two of his fellow boarders: the beautiful yet penniless Victorine Taillefer and the handsome young Rastignac: a love match whose fortune he predicts and, through a diabolical scam, in whose profits he plans to share. As the narrator points out repeatedly, Vautrin is the most lucid observer in this universe and he sees with particular acuity into the heart of Rastignac.[130] In the scene in question, Vautrin lets Rastignac in on the impending murder that will ensure Mademoiselle Taillefer's—and thus their own—vault into fabulous wealth. While he is still stunned by that news, Goriot enters the salon, and after secluding the young man in his garret room, he informs Rastignac that his daughter Delphine, baronne de Nucingen, has fallen for him. Not only is she smitten, but she and her father have prepared a sumptuous apartment for him situated in a chic neighborhood near her own house: an arrangement that the older man sees as his ticket out of Vauquer's place too.

The rivalry for Rastignac's favor thus comes to a head and the youth must choose. Which father figure's advice will he heed: Vautrin's or Goriot's? Thanks to the gift of a Bréguet watch and promises of other luxuries to come, Rastignac's loyalties surge in Goriot's favor and a scene of pure pathos ensues: "Yes, my dear Père Goriot, you know very well that I am fond of you," gushes Rastignac, to which Goriot replies, "I can see that at any rate you are not ashamed of me! Let me embrace you" (162).[131] And he hugs the student. Given the close proximity of their rooms and the heated emotions exchanged during this scene, it is likely that Vautrin overheard them. Minutes later Vautrin's voice breaks in from the doorway, where he stands singing lines from "Ô Richard, ô mon roi."

Now, "Ô Richard, ô mon roi" was a song with powerful connotations to readers in Balzac's day. Readers will recall that it was sung at the infamous banquet on the night of October 2, 1789, when loyalist soldiers and Flanders guards drank to the king's health and future of the Bourbon monarchy. Along with the black cockades that they brandished, the song became a symbol of royalist opposition to the revolutionary cause; it is widely considered one of the factors that precipitated the women's march on Versailles. (In his 1837 history, Carlyle included a section on the October Days entitled "O Richard, O My King.") Scholars, translators, and editors of *Père Goriot* routinely note the song's provenance from the opera *Richard Cœur de lion* (Richard the Lionheart) by composer Grétry (libretto by Sedaine; 1784). But they fail to recognize its sociopolitical meaning and importance to the unfolding of this novel.

Despite Vautrin's rollicking rendition and the liberties he takes with the lyrics, this is a slow and solemn song. In the opera it is sung in act 2 to the imprisoned king by his faithful servant Blondel:

Ô Richard! ô mon roi!	O Richard! O my king!
L'univers t'abandonne,	The universe abandons you,
Sur la terre il n'est donc que moi,	In the whole world, there is no one but me,
Qui s'intéresse à ta personne.	Who cares for you.
Moi seul dans l'univers,	I alone, in the universe,
Voudrais briser tes fers,	Would like to break your chains,
Et tout le reste t'abandonne.[132]	And all the rest abandon you.

Laura Mason has documented the importance of this song for the political culture of the revolutionary years when "Ô Richard, ô mon roi" was the veritable anthem of royalist opposition. When the Comédie-Italienne decided to perform *Richard Cœur de lion* in autumn 1790, just weeks after the judicial hearings about the October Days were over, it was a provocation. According to *L'Ami du roi*, the audience expressed noisy admiration for the faithful Blondel, who "had the rare courage to take the part of his king" and shed tears when the king was freed from his imprisonment. A month later, however, a performance was interrupted when shouts from the theater floor fought back against the loud applause from the loges; left-wing newspapers advised against performing an opera that excited such painful memories. In 1791 when the opera was again staged at the Comédie, it took on new connotations, as memories of the king's escape attempt to Varennes were still fresh in people's minds. Royalists who applauded "Ô Richard" were expressing their conviction that the king was being held hostage by the Revolution. Eventually, the ruckus inside the theater—when rival groups would shout out the rebel song "Ça ira" to drown out "Ô Richard"—became an effective form of political expression. As Mason concludes, "it was through such associations that [ordinary citizens'] performances came to signal political opinion with great clarity and force. As revolutionary journalists, pamphleteers, and legislators began to describe these new practices and acknowledge the political import of singing, the gap between practice and representation narrowed."[133]

This expression came to an abrupt halt when the opera was banned in 1791. But when the revival of royalty made the revival of the opera possible, *Richard Cœur de lion* was again staged with enthusiasm in 1806.[134] It may have benefited from the rage for Gothic accoutrements (or the *style troubadour*), which was then at its height, and it surely flattered Emperor Napoleon with its paean to faithfulness and loyalty. Sedaine's libretto reads: "A troubadour / Is all about love / Loyalty, constancy, / And without hope of a reward" (Un troubadour / Est tout amour, / Fidélité, constance, / Et sans espoir de récompense). Significantly, *Richard Cœur de lion* was again banned by the revolutionary regime of 1830, presumably to avoid audiences' emotionalism over King Charles X's exile. So although Vautrin bursts into song on more than one occasion in *Père Goriot*, it is undeniable that the timing and choice of this instance wield a shrewd commentary on the action.

The scene that opens with his song proves to be a turning point in the plot. Given the chivalrous effusions and royalist sentiments that readers would associate with Rastignac by this point (especially in his dealings with nobles of the Faubourg Saint-Germain), one might interpret Vautrin's words as a light-hearted jest.[135] Actually, they are deadly serious. Vautrin sings this ballad of allegiance to an exiled king to alert Rastignac that he has discerned the youth's change of heart and finds it annoying; it disrupts his own well-laid plans. The song is his way of informing Rastignac and Goriot that he knows of their complicity, mocks it, and plans to thwart it. We know that Vautrin's political views tend toward the Left; he explicitly cites his reverence for Jean-Jacques Rousseau and *Le Contrat social* (although as a master criminal in disguise he seems more akin to an anarchist kind of Robin

Hood).[136] Given the hints of Goriot's past as a grain speculator and flour merchant at Les Halles aux blés during the Revolution, one might assume that he too holds liberal convictions. After all, it is thanks to the Revolution that he amassed the huge fortune that allowed his daughters to marry so well. But the sixty-nine-year-old relic of Vauquer's boarding house is a far cry from his youthful avatars that occasionally flick across the fictional screen. Judging from Vautrin's caustic comments and hostile attitude, he, like the other lodgers, judges Goriot to be a failure, shamefully evacuated of whatever power or politics he may have once embraced: a laughable "Goriorama."[137] Vautrin himself wants to be Rastignac's guide to the world, and yet it is Goriot who secures the loyalty of this promising youth.[138] It is most irksome! The song, then, is his mocking tribute to Rastignac's tribute to this "king" of nothing. During the evening that follows, Vautrin takes the lead in launching a boisterous dinner, during which, amid the laughter flowing from bottles of his own fine wine, he sneaks an opiate into the drinks of Rastignac and Goriot and foils their plot to foil his plans. My king, indeed.

If we fast-forward to the end of the novel, the issue of legitimacy comes front and center and casts a glaring light on poor old Goriot's delusions of grandeur. Claustrophobia and solitude cloak the final section, book 4, "The Father's Death" (La Mort du père), in an atmosphere of imminent doom. Lying on his deathbed too weak to get up, Goriot nevertheless issues threat after threat against his daughters' double-dealing husbands, and since he himself cannot rob a bank or broker a deal to get the funds they need, he demands that the law be brought to their assistance. But there is no such law, Delphine reminds him; there is only her reputation at stake. This confusion between legality (law) and legitimacy (esteem and tradition) is telling. His impotence to help her in either regard is articulated plaintively in Goriot's ultimately incorrect lament about this new world: "I protest. The country will perish if fathers are trampled down" (274).[139]

This end eerily echoes the will and testament of Louis XVI. Imprisoned by those "who were [his] subjects," the king expresses amazement over the world-upside-down in which he finds himself and "whose end is impossible to foresee, on account of the passions of men, and for which one can find neither pretext nor means in any existing law." Nevertheless, he, like Goriot, expresses forgiveness to his children-people and asks his son, the dauphin, to "forget all hate and grudge."[140] Though both father figures in these deathbed statements adopt an Olympian attitude toward their children-subjects and try to transcend the sordid details of death in order to forge an inner peace, they are perceived very differently by observers on the outside. The ultimate irony of *Père Goriot* is the delusion with which he dies, believing that the sorrowful figures by his bed are his two daughters rather than the two students whom he happened to meet at the boarding house—chance acquaintances, soon forgotten. The ultimate tragedy of Louis XVI's end is the splintering of the kingship itself: there is no throne for his son to inherit, only a cold and dirty jail cell where the boy will sicken and die.

Louis's words on the scaffold may have been drowned out by a drumroll and his reputation defamed for years, but his final ascent was accompanied by the famous prayer of a distinguished abbot and inspired a martyr cult that continues to our day.[141] Goriot's last moments benefit from no such flourish: the narration of his death is starkly material. Noting the accuracy with which Balzac charts the man's struggle against a growing cerebral impairment and the agonal coma that makes him unable to tell his daughter from the medical student at his side, neurologist Robert April notes, "Death is no longer a transcendental, spiritual issue, attended by religious rites, but a physical state . . . in keeping with the empirical, realistic view of the dead body in the medical dissecting room."[142] The funerals and graves assigned these men also drive home the indignity of their ends. Like the body of Louis XVI, which was thrown into a makeshift resting-place and covered in quicklime, Goriot receives the cheapest funeral money can buy, and his body is laid in a temporary grave.

The description of Goriot's last hours wields emotional impact precisely because of its bluntness. Part of this is due to our modern impatience with the conventions of sentimentalism and our thrill at the morbid shock value of these pages. Part is due to the inescapably human paradox that Goriot exemplifies and that the epigraphs by Machiavelli and Dostoevsky at the beginning of this chapter capture so well. Neither iron-fisted control nor touchy emotionalism can dominate a life, yet our situation requires both to be truly human. The banality with which Balzac surrounds the dead body evokes from the reader sadness for its abandonment and pity for the delusions that the old man clung to in his dying moments. But it makes us think of the solitude that awaits us too. The predictions spoken by Goriot and Vauquer just a few pages earlier prove untrue: this is not the end of the world (la fin du monde); life goes on. With his internal monologue finally silenced and the discussion of his character now discarded by an empty, indifferent boarding house, Goriot's corpse weighs heavy on the reader's imagination. It forces us to recognize the fundamental frailty that we all experience sooner or later. Similar to the feeling imparted by the mean-spirited editorials on Louis XVI by Helen-Maria Williams, upon closing Père Goriot readers may feel a bit ashamed at the laughs we shared with Balzac's mocking narrator. The judgments that we and the other characters harbored against Goriot feel petty and unnecessarily harsh. Perhaps power and legitimacy are not the most important yardsticks for a life well lived after all.

This ending forces us to rethink the legitimacy of Rastignac's heroism too. Although he is frequently described as suffering the plight of "superior young men" or those endowed with "great souls," Rastignac ultimately proves to be a rather small-minded fellow.[143] After summoning all of Paris with a defiant cry—"It's between the two of us now" (À nous deux)—he descends from Goriot's grave at Père Lachaise cemetery . . . and goes to dinner. This seems a rather pitiful start for a modern kind of hero. And that is precisely the point. Just as Goriot and, by extension, Louis XVI were second-rate villains, Rastignac is a second-rate hero for our times.

CHAPTER FOUR

How Literature Ended the Terror

The two days known as "Thermidor" Year 2 (July 27–28, 1794) are often portrayed as the final paroxysm of France's Reign of Terror. But despite the claims of historians such as Louis Saurel, it is not at all obvious that the Terror did end in summer 1794. It depends on how one defines events. If one focuses on the judiciary, it does appear that the French state had reverted to a more equitable form of due process already on 14 thermidor and the Jacobin-led repression was winding down. But if one focuses on the memory of the Terror or its polarizing language, the end date is more difficult to determine.

Perusing the literary traces of this period—and its historiography—one gets the feeling of being manipulated by enemy camps of opinion. During the most crucial months of 1793–94, few were the journalists and pamphleteers to condemn events directly; more passed judgment indirectly or applauded with exaggerated zeal. By summer 1794 journalists started propagating terrorist stereotypes and pinned the worst abuses on identifiable scapegoats, notably Robespierre, his comrades-in-arms, and sanculottes broadly writ. From such writings there emerged a noxious current in nineteenth-century letters: a fascination with the criminality of the "dangerous classes" that justified their segregation from the ruling oligarchy and its values of Law and Order. Newspapers were especially influential: the specter of mob violence that journalists whipped up post-Thermidor allowed statesmen, army generals, and police commissioners of successive generations to make repression a more socially accepted practice to curtail popular incursions into politics. But in the long run it was literature, and the literary sorts of historiography born during the nineteenth century, that dealt the definitive blow to 1793–94 by showing how the Jacobins' ideal of a Justice that might establish a truly egalitarian society was experienced and remembered instead as a tragic fluke, an accident of history gone awry. The story of how historians insinuated their version of facts into the public imaginary has already been brought to light,[1] but the literature of Thermidor and its echoes in the nineteenth century remain unknown.

THE END OF THE TERROR

Most everyone seems to agree that the "tyrant" Robespierre and his one hundred or so partners in crime were due for punishment in July 1794 and that the ten-month phase of state-sponsored repression was best left behind. Rightly or wrongly Robespierre was held responsible for measures adopted by the Convention under his presidency on September 5, 1793, when, faced by a delegation of angry section leaders and members of the Paris Jacobin Club, it took action against grain hoarding and other illegal practices.[2] When on October 10 the government issued a decree declaring itself "revolutionary until the peace," the temporary actions were regularized to put an end to earlier regimes' improvisational tactics of law enforcement. What ensued may well have been alarming to ordinary citizens, at least to the extent that it touched their lives. On top of unannounced home searches, or *visites domiciliaires*, and local interrogations by representatives who spread through the countryside to explain the policies and dispel local opposition to the Republic, a newly invigorated Revolutionary Tribunal was charged with intensifying efforts against enemies of the people. Such measures have been justified by the state of affairs in spring–summer 1793, when army losses and desertions, weak harvests, and a mushrooming black market were forcing France ever deeper into financial chaos, political uncertainty, and popular misery.[3]

Few have attempted to justify the more aggressive turn taken by the Convention a few months later, however. Even the Terror's most sympathetic memorialist admits that the Law of Suspects of 22 prairial (June 10, 1794) was an error and largely due to the poor judgment of Robespierre.[4] A suspect was defined as anyone who was an "enemy of freedom" and whose conduct, social relations, words, or writing demonstrated his or her support for tyranny or federalism; equally suspect was anyone who could not supply a certificate of civism or proof of income and émigrés, their families, or any agents who had not "constantly demonstrated their loyalty to the Revolution." The revolutionary judiciary went awry. No longer acting out of rational concern for the well-being of the state and its citizens, it started targeting internal demons of its own design. This internecine battle had begun earlier with the extermination of the center-right party of the Gironde, the

Catholic and royalist insurgents of the Vendée and Brittany, and the book and newspaper publishers. It now took on a broader scope, as the law effectively eliminated the necessity of evidence against the accused, obviated their recourse to defense or an interrogation, and put an end to deportations. Sentences were reduced to three: acquittal, detention, or death.[5] What followed was a brutal period of rapid judgments and round-the-clock executions (or, in the provinces, drownings, murders, and the leveling of entire regions) known as the Great Terror. Consequently, historians have dated the end of the Terror to the execution of its purported leader, Robespierre.

Those who lived through the period were less sanguine. Their writings give little evidence of consensus on how to keep the repression in the past or how to deal with its memory. That Robespierre was dead was indubitable; that the Convention government was trying to reform the workings of the Revolutionary Tribunal and mitigate the caustic shape, or *formes acerbes*, it had taken following the law of 22 prairial was evident as well.[6] Rumors ran wild, however, about the tyrant's snake-like ability to reproduce himself through remnants left behind: his disembodied head might sprout a new tail and spawn new plots among confederates who had escaped the purge. A flurry of brochures and artwork hit the streets featuring Robespierre's head speaking to his tails and frightened people with hints of ongoing subterfuge and nefarious schemes. It seems that claiming to capture Robespierre or end the Terror was a surefire strategy to ensure publishing success.

HISTORIOGRAPHY OF THE TERROR

As David Andress, Jean-Clément Martin, and Timothy Tackett, authors of multiple works on the topic, have noted, this cottage industry in revolutionary historiography was then and remains today "an industry with a surprisingly ill-defined product" because "no one can assign clear boundaries to 'the Terror.'" Tackett has dubbed the Terror's genesis "an enduring mystery." Andress lamented in 2004 that "trying to understand the social dynamics of this period can lead into an abyss of complexity."[7] The scholar who ventures into this field risks ending up like Flaubert's hapless clerks Bouvard and Pécuchet, the antiheroes of his unfinished novel *Bouvard et Pécuchet* (published posthumously in 1881). Their enthusiasm for history led to a voracious program of readings which provided ample facts for passionately held beliefs: Bouvard first declared himself a Constitutionalist, then a Girondin, and finally a Thermidorian, while his friend Pécuchet brandished the bonnet rouge of a sansculotte and admitted sympathy for the Robespierrists. But at a certain point in the readings, history overwhelmed

them. Confused and confounded by the books' battling interpretations, they
got into a terrible muddle.

The blurry contours of the field derive from the dates and actions that
are included, or not, as part of the Terror. Where a certain tradition ties its
beginning to the September 5, 1793, announcement that "terror is the order
of the day," others claim it began with the September 1792 prison massacres
in Paris, when a group of overzealous patriots took it upon themselves to
purge the prisons of a thousand or so people (mostly clergy and petty criminals) who were allegedly scheming a return to monarchy. Or maybe it began
earlier. Simon Schama declared that the "violence *was* the Revolution
itself" and traced the origins of the Terror to July 1789, when disgruntled
Parisian workers suddenly realized the power of collective, armed action.
Claude Mazauric has argued that the seeds of the Terror were sown in 1762
by Rousseau's *Contrat social,* which spelled out the conditions under which
a state may legitimately defend itself against its own people. Pushing that
orientation to its logical conclusion, Caroline Weber in 2003 interpreted the
entire Terror as a "discursive affair" inspired by Rousseau.[8] However, more
recent scholarship seems to be turning the tide against such approaches and
demanding a more temporally precise narrative of individual action. Scholars now ask what the legislation of 1793–94 meant for those who wrote the
laws and lived under them.

The name "Terror" has long conjured up attacks against tearful holy
men and sad-eyed aristocrats, thanks to paintings such as Charles-Louis
Muller's *Roll Call of the Last Victims of the Reign of Terror* (1850) and
novels like *A Tale of Two Cities* (1859). But as Richard Cobb pointed out
almost forty years ago and more recent researchers such as Alan Forrest
have reminded us since, the repression also punished prostitutes, peasants,
the urban working class, and soldiers—career military men and those who
were mobilized by the draft of 1793. It also left many people untouched.[9]
Indeed, the most thought-provoking recent discussions of the subject build
on Cobbesian doubts about the political coherence assumed for the Terror. Consider Joseph Clarke's *Commemorating the Dead in Revolutionary
France* (2007). Clarke's analysis of the state funerals (Panthéonisation) for
Mirabeau, Voltaire, and Rousseau is illuminating, especially because his
juxtaposition of the three events held in April 1791, July 1791, and October
1794 allows us to see how the Pantheon—and the Republic's founding fathers—underwent a change in meaning during successive regimes but were
still revered even after the Terror when the optimism of '89 had supposedly
evaporated. Or consider Howard Brown, who in *Ending the French Revolution* (2006) debunks assumptions regarding the so-called failure of juries,

magistrates, policemen, and gendarmes who were charged with protecting the French citizenry during the 1790s. Drawing on a database of thousands of criminal proceedings and military tribunals, Brown proves that the judiciary did its job rather well according to the laws under which it operated. After years of a revolutionary historiography driven by left-wing politics that celebrated republican culture in all its brutal and moving naivety, these two books deliver a rude reckoning. Brown alludes to the "bloody reign of virtue" which led to "an even bloodier reign of military prowess"; Clarke claims that the Revolution's primary outcome was the creation of widows and orphans.[10] By exploring little-known documents from the Directory and Consulate periods, this scholarship dredges up a harvest of simmering resentments that is sure to ignite controversy. It proves that the Terror must be understood in the context of a long lineage of political and judicial practices for protecting the state from its enemies and celebrating national heroes.

But neither of those scholars dealt the world a shock equal to Jean-Clément Martin, who has questioned the very concept of the Reign of Terror. In his 2006 book *Violence et Révolution* and follow-up article in *Les Politiques de la Terreur* (2008), Martin argues that it is ridiculous to assign a date to the event because there never was any actual system of Terror adopted by the representative government in 1793–94. Rather, he contends that at its founding moment in fall 1793 there were a variety of militant demonstrations, populist demands, and spectacles of demagoguery that, for all their clamoring for a system of Terror, fell on deaf ears in the Convention. Fulminating against critics who irresponsibly employ the term to vilify the Jacobin-majority legislature, Martin demands that scholars instead define exactly what they mean in studying the particular institutions, popular demands, repressive measures, and the more or less contradictory laws passed in 1793–94. The existence of a judicial system that resorted to violence does not necessarily justify the term. Just as Howard Brown demonstrated that repressive practices were no stranger to the French judiciary well into the 1830s, Martin reminds us that the ancien régime and early constitutional phase of the Revolution were rife with incidents of ghastly torture (used to get confessions from prisoners) and drawn-out, bloody scenes of public execution. Indeed, a cursory glance at the news listed under the *Chronique de Paris* rubric Châtelet for October–November 1790 brings up a gory cluster of results: one thief was sentenced to be whipped and branded, and three other felons were sentenced to be broken publicly on the wheel (*rompu vif en place de Grève*). So offensive were these practices that they generated resistance and even popular violence on occasion by a citizenry that was increasingly revolted by cruelties used against petty criminals. Echoing Ernest Hamel, who in 1867 insisted on correcting misconceptions about Robespierre's semantics—he embraced an ideal of revolutionary "justice" instead of "terror"—Martin argues for more precise terminology.[11] Modern readers may have forgotten that the actual term *terroriste* was not widely used until after Thermidor in August 1794, by agents anxious to disassociate themselves from Robespierre and others killed in the purge.[12]

Warning readers who are fascinated by this recalcitrant period and challenged by the difficulty of making sense out of it with general historical laws, Martin lays out guidelines for the study of 1793–94:

> The performative value inherent in the notion of Terror was thus more real by the threats it carried and the violence it justified than by the juridical reality that it never had. This reality—limited to incantation—does not allow one to conclude the existence of a system. So it is appropriate to refuse anecdotes that claim to explain the functioning of an organization when all that they can reveal are the mistakes of individuals and specific groups . . . excesses committed by numerous individuals who robbed, raped, and killed under the cover of politically terrorist principles.[13]

Terror needs to be understood as much as an aesthetic concept inspired by Burke's 1757 treatise as a coherent political principle; the burden of proof lies on the researcher.

A METHOD FOR A LITERARY HISTORY OF THE TERROR

This chapter accordingly has rather modest aims. To the extent that texts can capture emotions, communicate them, and mold subsequent reader reactions, I seek first to reconstruct what it was like to live through the Terror by studying Parisian print culture generated during and shortly after events. Unlike the other chapters of *The Frankenstein of 1790*, here the focus is on the unfolding of a series of events over time and the biography of one central figure: Robespierre. The materials are somewhat different. Instead of relying on historiography to reconstruct the Terror, I follow the news of the Revolutionary Tribunal day by day as it was reported in the *Journal de Paris national*. The newspapers wielded an enormous power over audiences during the Revolution, likely more than they do today. Taking my lead from Ezra Pound's notion that the man "who believes what he reads in the papers" is the fundament upon which modern democratic societies are built, and Jeremy Popkin's confirmation that audiences in the 1790s were convinced that papers printed true stories, "the result of concrete actions at specific times by identifiable individuals and groups," I present the Terror as it was written for and read by contemporaries.[14] This massive (and possibly overwhelming) exposure to events as they build up to Thermidor seems to me the most powerful way for us to connect with the people who lived during them. It is my hope that this method may help readers appreciate the humdrum continuities of life in 1793–94 as well and begin to understand which literary titles were most valued by readers in the months following Thermidor and why.

Why focus on just one newspaper? Elsewhere in this book, literary representations of revolutionary events have been held up for comparison with commentary from the *Chronique de Paris*, the *Journal de Paris*, the *Moniteur*, and *Révolutions de Paris*. All four papers were well regarded by contemporaries and are respected by scholars still; all four also maintained operations consistently from 1789 to summer 1793.[15] But this method breaks down in 1793. The *Chronique de Paris* folded on August 25, 1793; its subscribers were directed instead to the *Feuille de salut public.* The editor of *Révolutions de Paris* was arrested for *incivisme* and imprisoned in June 1793; its tone became gradually more reserved until it closed in February 1794. The politically agile *Moniteur* continued publishing throughout 1793–94 although it was not exempt from the scrutiny of the Committee of Public Safety or from its demands for corrections of suspect nuances and omissions.[16] The *Moniteur* did survive, however, and we will have frequent recourse to it in the pages ahead. Described as "gigantic" not only because of its folio-size paper stock but also because of its length (typically eight to twelve pages), it aimed at exhaustive reportage of governmental debates: a format that appealed to the most serious and dedicated readers and that explains its ongoing appeal.

In four quarto pages, the *Journal de Paris* (or *Journal de Paris national* as it was known during the Terror) reproduced much of the same news but in a form that was easier to read. Although statistics on subscription rates are spotty, the *Journal de Paris* counted twelve thousand subscribers in 1791, whereas usual newspaper circulation rates ran from two thousand to five thousand.[17] It was known as a moderate or constitutionalist paper in 1789–91 and reemerged as a champion for the Girondins in spring 1795, though the paper's politics faded from view during 1793–94. These subscription figures and the editors' cautious approach to revolutionary partisanship suggest that the *Journal de Paris* had a broad reader base: doubtless a factor that helped it survive and remain intact.[18] Since its trial reportage is virtually identical to that of the *Moniteur* and its subscription rolls were likely comparable, I have adopted the *Journal de Paris national* as a vantage point to discover what an imagined average, politically moderate reader might have learned about events as they were transpiring.

Although the modern reader may be chilled by the sober execution lists printed almost daily from summer 1793 to fall 1794 and struck by the maudlin symbolism used to describe audience reactions to the trials, it is impossible to ignore that life also continued as usual. Witness the many kinds of news, ads, and features that were printed alongside tribunal listings and competed for readers' attention. Book reviews for titles such as *Le Glaive vengeur* (The vengeful blade; 1794), prison memoirs, and biographies of Robespierre reveal a public anxious to punish the villains and grieve for the dead—or perhaps merely to catch up on the latest gossip or experience a surreptitious thrill of schadenfreude. A sense of indignation was clearly expected from readers of the best-selling memoirs penned by Marie-Jeanne Roland and other Girondins and published in spring 1795. The lurid accounts of Robespierre published during the Directory and Godwin's melodramatic *Caleb Williams* (1794) were equally intent on eliciting an emotional response: be it a shudder of horror or sober reflections on how power corrupted the Incorruptible.

All this literature operates on what one might call a classical form of spectacle. Like tales of famous criminals or the gallows speeches of public executions, the villain's actions are dissected under a hard and bright light and form a readily legible cautionary tale. The reader/observer and the punishing authority (the king or the sovereign people) are complicitous: both agree that chastising the villain is the right thing to do, and both expect that the spectacle of his suffering will stop others from following in his steps. By the time that Dickens wrote *A Tale of Two Cities*, however, this moralizing impulse had lost some of its credibility, and anyway, Dickens was loath to make his novel a stance of soap-box polemics. So instead of highlighting the deeds of a famous evildoer, he invented a small cast of nobodies who bump up against some mighty powerful crowds and suffer the results of some long-simmering resentments beyond their control. The scenes of Dr. Manette's reunion with his daughter and his gradual "return to life" in England seem even more pitiful because they are book-ended between violent confrontations of aristocrats and sansculottes; the contrast contributed to the book's appeal to middle-class English audiences of Dickens's day (and its ongoing unpopularity in France). Despite the incongruous martyr scene at the end, there is no spectacle that will correct the criminals of *A Tale*. The tragedy of modern times unfolds with no one in particular running the show.

Flaubert skewers the emotionalism of writers like Godwin and Dickens with droll irony. Historiography becomes a matter of personal enthusiasm for the amateur researchers Bouvard and Pécuchet, who understand the past only as it pertains to folks like them, that is, well-minded petits bourgeois. After their brief enthusiasm with historiography burns out, Revolution takes on the stock meaning in their eyes of a nightmare led by thugs: the recurrence of which is to be avoided at all cost. This explains the fears that run through the pendant to *Bouvard et Pécuchet*, *Le Dictionnaire des idées reçues*, with its multiple entries on the origins of the Revolution, concerns about workers' opposition to "order," and the ever-present specter of "dangerous classes."

Flaubert's view of a complacent bourgeoisie and its preference for navel-gazing over truth-seeking also rings true today, reminding us of the preponderance of sound-bites over learning in our information-saturated age. Although our media are electronic instead of paper, the mechanisms of mass culture that govern received ideas are not so different from those of Flaubert's time. Nor has the public's memory or attention span expanded much. The reduction of the Terror to a banal story of luck, timing, and politics, and its uncertain legacy among a highly distracted public, are two of the most important lessons to be learned from the present chapter. Equally unsettling is the suspicion cast on the few heroes found here. From Lamourette to Loiserolles, everyone seems to be angling for his or her own interests. Solidarity, fraternity, fellow feeling? Caveat lector.

THE REVOLUTIONARY TRIBUNAL

IN THE NEWS

The first revolutionary tribunals were short-lived experiments. Decreed on August 17, 1792, and disbanded on November 29 of that year, the initial one was a hybrid court created in the wake of the August 10 debacle. After it folded, in the absence of a high court to defend the state against political crimes, local tribunals did the job.[19] In January and February 1793, under the rubric Tribunal criminel, the *Journal de Paris national* published a list every week or so that gave the names, ages, crimes, and sentences of the people tried in Paris. Most of the forty-two were counterfeiters. (King Louis XVI was tried and condemned by the Convention itself by votes and decrees passed on January 17–20, 1793.) By March 1793, the Convention enacted an Extraordinary and Revolutionary Criminal Tribunal. In the eyes of many, this and other measures enacted that spring were long-overdue

improvements. Economic controls were desperately needed to rein in inflation, discourage speculation, and avoid food shortages. The results of hoarding and black-market commerce were evident to all those who suffered the
long bread lines that regularly wound their way through the capital. During
the king's winter 1792 trial, it became evident that Bourbon loyalists, former noblemen, and other malcontents were plotting to overthrow the revolutionary government by undermining state finances, assassinating its leaders, or seizing the Convention, as evidenced by the king's own manifesto of
June 20, 1791, and other sources. This tribunal could thus be considered a
much-needed arm of law enforcement.

Because of the urgency associated with crimes against the state, it is
difficult to evaluate if and when the tribunal departed from its original intent. In the decrees passed on March 10 and 11, the Convention ruled out
appeals to lower courts, provincial courts, or the police and effectively gave
this body the authority of a self-sufficient supreme court. From the moment
when the prisoner heard his or her accusation until judgment there were
only forty-eight hours; punishment followed within twenty-four hours of
sentencing. These policies generated alarm in at least one deputy, namely
Maximilien Robespierre. Robespierre spoke out against the vague definition of "plotter" (*conspirateur*) and proposed that more precise guidelines
be written for juries on what kinds of activities should be judged conspiratorial or counterrevolutionary, lest good citizens be victimized by a tribunal
meant to protect them.[20] His proposal did not make it into the law.

TRIALS, EXECUTION LISTS, AND THEIR READERS

The court's functions were strictly defined by Convention orders of March
1793 and thereafter, but judging from the newspaper it appears that other
entities—notably local or national surveillance committees—wielded an
important role and their judgments could be rather arbitrary.[21] Under the
rubric Prisons on April 9, 1793, is a list of five men who were detained, including a water-carrier arrested for seditious speech (*propos séditieux*) and
two others detained for no particular reason (*sans motif énoncé*). The rubric
Tribunal criminel soon disappeared and was replaced by Tribunaux, and the
first trial of the Extraordinary and Revolutionary Criminal Tribunal was
announced. It was the case of a nobleman tried and condemned to death
for service in the émigré armies.[22] The next death sentence by this court
was reported on April 11 against a man accused of "trying to reestablish
royalty in France," followed on April 15 by the case of Philibert-François
Blanchelande, former maréchal-de-camp and lieutenant governor of Saint-

Domingue, who was convicted of misusing authority and conspiring against the state, among other things. By April 30, there was about one trial announced daily under the rubric Tribunaux (which later became Tribunal révolutionnaire), many of which culminated in the death sentence.

It does seem reasonable to announce the trial of a dishonest émigré or a corrupt governmental official, but what are we to make of the irregularity in the length and severity of punishment in other listings? How can one reconcile the news of a fifty-five-year-old maid sent to the guillotine because of "provoking the massacre and dissolution of the Convention" with the report of a twenty-six-year-old laborer who was acquitted for "fanatic and uncivic language"? The oldest person condemned was a ninety-year-old man, who like so many was a victim of bad timing. If he had been condemned just one day later—11 thermidor Year 2—he would likely have survived. The youngest were age seventeen, but there are also several cases of fourteen-year-old girls and boys given twenty-year jail sentences. The sentences seem disproportionate to the crimes, based on an exaggerated assessment of the danger at hand. So do the cases of press-related crimes. Consider Antoine Jean Clinchamp, a Benedictine known as Saint-André who was condemned to death for writing and selling a fourteen-page brochure entitled *Aux Amis de la vérité* "with criminal and counterrevolutionary intentions."[23]

How did readers of the *Journal de Paris national* comprehend this rapidly evolving situation? Because of the political nature of the crimes, public memorials to victims were virtually nonexistent until after Thermidor, as were published complaints about the tribunal. Although complaints were voiced in the Convention even in the midst of the famous deliberations of September 5, 1793, that made "terror the order of the day," without delving into the actual deliberations of the deputies, judges, and juries, which most readers could not have known, such conflicts would have gone unnoticed.[24] One can nevertheless observe a few traces of editorial comment in the *Journal de Paris national*'s description of the tribunal's spectator gallery.

In his classic work on the Parisian sansculottes of Year 2, Albert Soboul claimed that emotions ran high in fall 1793 in the working-class faubourgs, where people were pleased by the rude justice being handed down.[25] But this assertion is subject to caution because of the sources he consulted: Soboul favored Jacobin tracts and speeches and minutes of certain section meetings to make his case. For readers of the *Journal de Paris national* there is not much evidence to go on: only seven incidents of audience reaction were reported from April 1793 to August 1794.[26] Two are highly politicized— the trials of former deputies Georges-Jacques Danton and Jacques Hébert— where the audience reportedly disapproved of the accuseds' undignified behavior and cheered at their condemnation. When Antoine-Joseph Gorsas, another formerly left-wing deputy and journalist, received his condemnation in vendémiaire Year 2, he "protested his innocence, recommended his wife and children to the people, and said that his death would be avenged." This public mention of vengeance is prescient, as is the sign of the cross with which Adrien Lamourette, bishop (juror) and former deputy of the National Assembly, blessed the court on learning of his condemnation in January 1794.[27] How to avenge the dead and salvage the religion of the living emerged as a major quandary after Thermidor.

Most evocative of Soboul's claims about the revolutionary crowd are the populist enthusiasms depicted at the trials of the Dethorre family, Charles Leroux, and widow Maréchal. A full-blown melodrama was brought to readers of the *Journal de Paris national* with the case of Antoine Dethorre, aged sixty-four, and his wife, Françoise, aged fifty-five, charged with unpatriotic language. The assembly "shuddered with horror" (*frémit d'horreur*) upon learning of their innocence. And when Citizen Dethorre pleaded for the four witnesses who had denounced her (who were her neighbors), "a touching scene happened; tears flowed." Rigor gave way to clemency: "the people, who are always just and always good, demanded justice and applauded the tribunal's judgment [of innocence], shouting, '*Vive la République!*'" As for shoemaker Leroux, aged fifty-five, he is portrayed in the arms of a joyful judiciary at his acquittal on January 24, 1794. Moreover, since he was "in the deepest poverty [*misère*]," the judges made a special collection on his behalf and he left the courtroom with 181 livres in hand! This must have been one of the most volatile days at the tribunal. After Leroux's acquittal and a death sentence pronounced against a thirty-three-year-old surgeon, the next item listed is the acquittal of a fifty-one-year-old boardinghouse owner, the widow Maréchal, at which point we read: "the room filled with shouts of '*Vive la République!*' The judges embraced this citizen, whose pupils were taught the purest republicanism. Tears flowed."[28] The nameless schoolteacher who denounced her was not so lucky. He was immediately tried and condemned to death.

The line between impartial reportage, left-wing polemics, and traditional melodrama seems deliberately blurred in these passages where the newspaper transforms ephemeral moments into what Popkin has dubbed symbolic stories that live on for years. With their invocation of a kindly judiciary shedding tears over the Good and summarily punishing the Evil, the reportage of tribunal reactions brings to mind the wooden language of Jacobin tracts published in those days: a style and genre employed by later authors to demonize the working classes.[29] Yet the scenes are not without real pathos. Readers would have known that the Dethorres and Maréchal really did face danger and actually could have been condemned to death; similar cases of seditious speech usually did produce that outcome. Françoise Dethorre's plea on behalf of her accusers could have been interpreted as contempt of court; that her sensitivity was seen as a virtue was merely luck.

A few years later, Directory writers had to reckon with fleeting moments such as these and the symbolic stories that they generated. In the conflicted efforts at social harmony running through the works of now-forgotten novelists such as François Ducray-Duminil and C. A. G. Pigault-Lebrun, I see authors trying to celebrate the effusions of the "little people," punish scapegoats, and protect the state (or an imaginary community standing in for the state) in an inoffensive manner. It is a tall order to be sure, and one that explains some of the moral-political incoherence running through this literature. Consider Ducray-Duminil's *Cœlina, ou L'Enfant du mystère* (Year 7, ca. 1798–99), where the two main evildoers turn out to be distant family members of the heroine. As if admitting that he could not decide how best to punish this duo, the author tries to kill off Truguelin père by what seems to be a magical act of nature after punishing the son in a more pedestrian manner (he is tracked and killed by authorities). Standing on the point of a craggy precipice in the midst of a squall, and tortured by his guilty conscience, the elder Truguelin sees a phantom descending from the clouds with flames shooting out of his eyes and snakes devouring his gaping heart. (These horrors are, alas, not quite captured in the frontispiece; see fig. 22.) "Truguelin," says the vision, "I am condemned to eternal torments and my misery is your handiwork! Your principles, your conduct, your pernicious advice have made your son into a monster such as me. I am waiting for you, I am waiting!"[30] Dizzied by the shock, Truguelin falls—but is not killed until, after committing more dastardly deeds, he finally takes poison and drowns himself. Divine intervention, legal warfare, suicide, or the fires of Hell: the solutions available to dysfunctional families were dire indeed![31]

News of the Extraordinary and Revolutionary Criminal Tribunal was sporadic in summer 1793. Whereas May brought a steady stream of trial news (twenty-seven executions and eight acquittals), and mid-June brought news of the Roüerie case, which sent eleven Bretons to death on June 17, no news followed until the splashy case of Jean-Paul Marat's murderer Charlotte Corday a month later. There appeared only four articles on the court in August (four death sentences, three detentions, one deportation), and in September thirteen more executions (and fifteen acquittals). In October the pace and the rigor picked up considerably. Queen Marie-Antoinette's trial

22. "Truguelin! You will sleep next to me! I am waiting for you, I am waiting for you!˙
(Truguelin! Tu vas dormir près de moi! Je t'attends, je t'attends!) Frontispice of François
Ducray-Duminil, *Cœlina, ou L'Enfant du mystère*, vol. 5 (An 7; 1798–99). Bibliothèque
nationale de France, Paris.

and condemnation were announced to great effect in mid-October, on October 25 the twenty-two Girondin deputies were brought to trial and condemned, and their so-called accomplice Marie-Jeanne Roland perished in early November. The duc d'Orléans (aka Louis-Philippe-Joseph Égalité) and Jean-Sylvain Bailly, former mayor of Paris, were also executed in November. Meanwhile, the prison population was swelling exponentially. There were 283 prisoners listed for the Parisian prisons on June 22, 1793; by August 2 of that year there were 1,511 prisoners; by September 27, the total number was 2,488; and just six months later the total announced was 7,351.[32]

In a horrifying yet logical reaction to the overcrowding in the prisons, coupled with the legislation of the Convention government, tribunal listings accelerate markedly in the next six months. Between the November 1, 1793, and March 31, 1794, listings in the *Journal de Paris national*, 377 people were condemned and 196 acquitted. Between April 1 and July 31, 1794, 2,229 condemnations were reported and only 480 acquittals. It is during this period that the journal assumed its most sinister affect and presented a roll call of the condemned on a near-daily basis. The news given under the Tribunal révolutionnaire rubric increased. On some days it covered as many as four columns with up to thirty-four names per column (fig. 23). As the weeks went by, under the pressure of numbers, the newspaper abandoned all discussion of the trials and noted only people's names, ages, hometowns, and sentences. The multiparagraph discussion of alleged crimes is reduced to a sketchy trace: for instance, "convicted for conspiring against the freedom and sovereignty of the French people, etc." Details for some people, such as Th. André and M. Toupin from the Finistère region, whose condemnation was reported on June 25, 1794, were altogether lacking. This simplified format remained the norm until fructidor Year 2 (August 1794). Most famous of course is the listing of 11 thermidor that begins with "Maximilien Robespierre, age 35."

It is important to recall that the *Journal de Paris national*'s Tribunaux section did not stand alone. It was situated after international news briefs and a section that provided transcripts of governmental actions: speeches, debates, and decrees passed by the Convention. The Tribunaux section was situated alongside news of the Paris Commune, a list of people confined or released by Paris prisons, and miscellaneous news on accidents, armies, and even astronomy. It was sometimes followed by advertisements for books, classes, music, and art (portraits of Marat were especially in demand), poems, and theater listings. (The two- to eight-page *Suppléments*, which allowed people to pay to place grievances and lost-and-found notes or advertise real estate, books, and spectacles, appeared sporadically until

G. *Henry*, âgée de 25 ans, née & demeurant à Verdun, fille dudit *Henry*, Préfident;

Barbe *Henry*, âgée de 17 ans, fille dudit *Henry*;

M. A. *Lagirofière*, âgée de 18 ans, native de Bonze, demeurant à Verdun, fille de *Lagirofière*, Prévôt des Campagnes;

G. E. *Dauphin*, âgée de 56 ans, née & demeurant à Verdun, veuve *Brigaud*, Capitaine des Grenadiers de France;

Anne *Vatrin*, âgée de 25 ans, native d'Etain, demeurant à Verdun, fille de défunt *Vatrin*, Militaire;

H. *Vatrin*, âgée de 23 ans, native d'Etain, demeurant à Verdun;

H, *Vatrin*, âgée de 22 ans, née à Etain, demeurant à Verdun, filles de *Vatrin*;

Marguerite *Croute*, âgée de 48 ans, née à Verdun, Horlogère;

N. *Milly*, âgé de 31 ans, natif de Verdun, Gendarme;

J. *Petit*, âgé de 50 ans, né & demeurant à Verdun, Vigneron;

Convaincus d'être auteurs ou complices de manœuvres & intelligences tendantes à livrer aux ennemis la place de Verdun, à favorifer les progrès de leurs armes fur le territoire françois, à détruire la liberté, à diffoudre la Repréfentation nationale & à rétablir le defpotifme, ont été condamnés à la peine de mort.

En vertu de l'art. III du titre V de la première partie du Code pénal, la peine de mort prononcée contre Claire Tabouillon fille, & Barbe Henry fille, a été commuée en 20 ans de détention.

J. E. *Bertault*, âgée de 48 ans, native de Pithiviers dans le ci-devant Gâtinois, rue de Bièvre, n° 4;

F. *Bonin*, âgé de 47 ans, natif de Souchamp, Département de l'Eure, Imprimeur, rue Zacharie, n° 68;

M. *Schweryer*, âgé de 40 ans, natif de Munzengen en Brifgaw, Cordonnier, rue de la Harpe, n° 135;

J. *Pomméraye*, âgé de 40 ans, natif d'Orléans, ci-devant Perruquier, actuellement Canonnier, cazerné à Popincourt;

J. F. *Noël*, âgé de 34 ans, natif de Verneuil, Potier d'étaim, demeurant à Meaux;

Convaincus d'une confpiration qui a exifté contre la liberté & la fûreté du Peuple, contre l'unité & l'indivifibilité de la République, &c.

Bertault, eft compofant, écrivant & colportant une lettre fuppofée écrite par Fouquier-Tinville, au Citoyen Robefpierre, laquelle lettre fuppofoit un plan de confpiration de ce Repréfentant du Peuple pour rétablir la Royauté en France, en mettant fur le trône le fils du tyran Capet, & en lui donnant un Régent;

Bonin, en qualifiant, dans un lieu public, Robefpierre de confpirateur & en prétendant qu'il ne tarderoit pas d'être puni, en infultant la Convention Nationale & en provoquant les Citoyens contr'elle;

Schweyer, en affichant dans plufieurs endroits publics, des placards par lui compofés, écrits qui avoient pour but d'exciter le maffacre de plufieurs Députés & l'anéantiffement de la Conftitution Républicaine;

Pomméray, en entretenant à l'Abbaye où il étoit détenu, des propos contre révolutionnaires, en chantant des chanfons tendantes à provoquer le rétabliffement de la Royauté, en cherchant à foulever fes co detenus, en criant à plufieurs repifes *vive le Roi*;

Noël, en infultant à la cérémonie civique faite à Meaux lors de l acceptation de la Conftitution Républicaine, en traitant cette cérémonie de bétife & de cochonnerie; en infultant les Citoyens de garde dans leur pofte; en déclarant qu'il fe moquoit de l'ordre & de la Nation, ont été condamnés à la peine de mort.

Adam *Feintzel*, âgé de 43 ans, natif de Pemberg, en Artiche, Facteur de Clavecin, rue de Bufly, N° 411, accufé d'être complice de cette confpiration en participant à l'affiche ou placard fufdit, & à tous les crimes commis par Schweyer;

A. *Coftrejean*, âgé de 42 ans, natif de Patis, Imprimeur en Taille douce, rue des Carmes, N° 8, accufé de cette confpiration, en excitant du trouble dans la falle du Tribunal criminel du Département de Paris, en provoquant le rétabliffement de la royauté, & en criant: *vive le Roi*.

J. *Gelis* dit *Pelliffier*, âgé de 43 ans, natif de Verfailles, ancien Commis des vivres de la Marine, rue Traverfière, accufé d'être complice de cette confpiration, en difant, dans un Caffé de la rue Traverfière, que la Convention nationale n'étoit compofée que de fcélérats, qu'il fe moquoit des décrets qu'elle rendoit, &c.;

J. B. *Philippe*, âgé de 42 ans, natif de Reims, Poftillon des Relais militaires, demeurant à Meaux, accufé de cette confpiration, en tenant, lorfque les Citoyens de Meaux plantoient l'arbre de la Liberté, des propos contre-révolutionnaires, &c., ont été acquittés.

N° 81. SUPPLÉMENT.

spring 1795, when they became a regular feature again.)[33] Finally, a small box at the end of this four-page newspaper listed births, deaths, marriages, divorces, and winning lottery numbers; that feature disappeared in 1794. With just eight columns to cover all those topics, space was at a premium.

Some errors made their way into the paper. The first name under Tribunaux on December 4, 1793, was that of Jean Vincenot of Gondrecourt, who was accused of participating in the Lyons conspiracy and "condamné à la même peine." Same as what? On October 5, five condemned men are listed merely as "soldiers." Some apparently ordinary listings would later be revealed as signaling dramas of superhuman sacrifice made tragic by timing, such as the mention on 10 thermidor of "S. Loiserolles père, 61 ans," to whom I return below. Even the accurate listings typically appeared one or two days after the trial, and the delay could last up to four days. Life-and-death mistakes were subject to a certain kind of black humor following Thermidor; witness the novel entitled *Les Contre-temps, ou La Femme crue veuve* (Inopportune incidents, or The woman thought to be a widow; 1794).

How Did the Terror Affect Readers?

My point in combing through these trials and sentences in such detail, and in describing how they were presented in print, is not only to demonstrate the imperfect proceedings and the increasingly rapid pace of criminal justice starting in April 1793 but also to suggest the impact that these notices might have had on readers of the paper or writers of the literature that followed in its wake. The Terror as I see it not only was a set of state-sponsored policies to control financial abuses such as hoarding and counterfeiting and political abuses such as treason but must also have created a particular mental condition in people, marked by anxiety and stress or at least a bit of nervous irritability. But from our vantage point almost 220 years later, how can we distinguish emotional reality from political maneuvering? The right-wing émigré novel, for instance, made gazette-reading a commonplace. When the newspaper arrives in one of the small communities where émigrés gather, it is invariably a moment of imminent tragedy, as the discovery of an execution or trial prompts devastating reactions (usually in the form of crying jags, madness, or suicide). Or the afflicted newspaper reader may be spurred to join the counterrevolutionary insurgency to avenge the murder of a loved one.[34] The graveyard genre discussed in chapter 3 provides countless tales of survivors whose lives are wrecked by painful memories of executions, hallucinations of cadavers swimming in blood, and so forth (see *Le Cimetière de la Madeleine*, 3:47). In *A Tale of Two Cities* Charles Dickens stresses the callousness of Paris jailors by depicting their black humor: it was a standard joke to announce the roll call of the condemned with the teasing refrain "Come out and listen to the Evening Paper, you inside there!"[35] Period correspondences and prison memoirs confirm the enormous impact that the news of the tribunal wielded over people's lives and minds as well. A London-based newspaper issued a discreet apology to its émigré readership in July 1794 and noted that the psychic stress that it dealt to readers was a necessary evil for remaining up-to-date on French politics. "We saw in the last number the list of 97 victims felled by the guillotine's blade. We could not avoid afflicting the unfortunate relatives of those victims who have gathered around us here, but we hasten to calm fears of émigrés from Nantes," the editor wrote, concluding with the good news that a rumored mass execution was not held as planned.[36] Anxiety-provoking lists like this were not only a European phenomenon; multiple issues of the Saint-Domingue-based *Affiches américaines* in July 1793 featured lists of people who were authorized or forced to leave the island "by the first boat that will arrive." It is hard to know how much credence to lend to the traumatic scenarios of list reading in memoirs and fiction, given that they were penned by right-wing partisans, writers under terrible duress, and hacks seeking sensationalism. Lists may have also elicited satisfaction, as in the left-wing *Affiches américaines*, whose readers may have been relieved to see wealthy planters leaving the island.

One tantalizing hint of a causal relation between political news and its psychological impact emerges in a new kind of medical speculation. A certain doctor, Gachet, argued in 1790 that since July 12, 1789, France was in a most pitiable situation because "terror has caused all kinds of illnesses," including eight hundred more cases of insanity than usual.[37] The ailments listed include nervous ills—nightmares and irrational fears—and physical defects imprinted on the fetuses of pregnant women who happened upon cadavers or bloody heads being paraded about in the streets. The fact that this writer cited the debilitating effects of terror well before 1793 is interesting and suggests that Jean-Clément Martin's warning about the free-floating signifier is justified. Similarly, a post-Thermidor treatise on public hygiene declared, "During the disastrous era of [the economist and banker John] Law, London hospitals filled with madmen and maniacs. In our own day . . . when the ferocious Robespierre covered the country with scaffolds, blood, and grief, the famous doctor Desault noted that aneurisms have mounted precipitously at the Hôpital-Dieu in Paris." Opinion on this topic was di-

vided, however. Many witnesses, including Desault himself, noted symptoms of renewed physical vigor among the population in 1789 and claimed
that events had cured some citizens of once-prevalent ills (especially hypo-
chondria, apathy, and nervous disorders).[38] The lack of what we would consider a properly scientific vocabulary does not justify dismissing such concerns out of hand. Rather, they complement accounts of journalists and
novelists and help us appreciate the assumptions that contemporaries made
about their experience of 1793–94.

The increasing availability of civil statistics in the Republic and especially in the Napoleonic state allowed doctors and bureaucrats to make
quantitative correlations between social ills and individual disorders, and
the ravages caused by the Revolution were a prime target. "Who is more sui-
cidal, Londoners or Parisians?" asked an 1815 article in a British journal. The
answer, Parisians, triggered a fierce cross-Channel quarrel because it tied
the Revolution's suppression of Catholicism to people's tendency to despair.
Such debates were not new. The fact that the number of suicides saw a sharp
spike during 1793–95 and touched aristocrats and sansculottes alike was
credited with political connotations that covered the gamut of opinion.[39]

Some scholars might raise an eyebrow over my claims of cause-and-
effect relations between political events, their dissemination in the news,
and the emotional impact on the public. They might retort with evidence
of a population that remained impervious to what was going on. Richard
Cobb once declared that "for many, it was possible almost to live outside
the Revolution, to opt out of collective commitment altogether, and . . . for
a few, it was even possible to ignore it."[40] Cobb drew this conclusion from
analysis of archival documents on the "little people" (menu peuple), and he
was doubtless right about the ignorance of the urban poor and rural tran-
sients, who then, as now, have little time or means to read papers and keep
up with events, given their day-to-day struggles to survive. Regional differences come into play as well. Despite its ambitious title, the Journal de
Paris national did not adequately capture the impact of the Terror outside
Paris, where the ravages could be much greater, as in Lyons, where 1,800
people were condemned by April 1794, or hardly noticeable, as in the center
of the country.[41]

In addition, David Andress has argued that we can never know how
touched or untouched people were by the Revolution. How much more unsettling could the events of 1793–94 have been, he asks, than the precarious
lifestyle that most people already experienced under the ancien régime? The
point is a good one and so I reprint it in its entirety:

How traumatic must it have been to be challenged to a duel, or to learn that one's cousins were plotting against your throne? How traumatic to face battle in an age of bayonet-charges and sabers, as young noblemen did from their early teens? Or how traumatic to have half your children die in infancy? To be thrown out of your home for debts and see every face in the village turned against you? To go bankrupt? To be forced into prostitution? The potentially "traumatic" episodes of premodern life are almost limitless. Going too far down the road of attributing responses to particular episodes of "trauma" suggests both that the rest of life was easier than it in fact was, and that we have better access than I think we do to the real mental processes of long-dead folk.[42]

Andress is correct to emphasize the relative nature of stress caused by the Terror as opposed to the ordinary stressors of daily life in these years. But he overlooks a key tool to such analysis, and that is the written documents left behind or purporting to be left behind by folks long dead, especially those that address the memory of emotions. Some documents attest to people's attitudes during these years, and whether one calls it "trauma," "heartbreak," or "a case of nerves," a heightened emotionalism does accompany the Revolution's written remains.

Consider the last-letter genre. Most of the people whose names were printed on execution lists had no opportunity to speak publicly, to leave a published trace of their defense, or to pass a message to loved ones before dying. The letters they wrote while awaiting execution most often went unread, as the prison guards systematically confiscated them. When Public Accuser Fouquier-Tinville was himself executed in 1794, hundreds of these letters were shipped off to the archives and forgotten until Olivier Blanc reprinted a sampling in 1984. If the response to the hundred or so letters gathered in Blanc's collection is any indication, these messages from beyond the grave are profoundly affecting to readers even now. Modern-day reviewers cited the painful sensations conjured up by reading them and the feeling of emptiness left in their wake.[43]

Other documents written during the tribunal's busiest season were designed to inspire strong feelings too, but of a less sympathetic nature. Book reviews were rare in winter 1794—only ten were published in the *Journal de Paris national* from January 1 to March 31, including one for an edition of Shakespeare's *Othello*—and so it is doubly striking to find a review of a book by an unknown author singled out for praise, H. G. Dulac's *Le Glaive vengeur de la République française* (The vengeful blade of the French Republic; 1794). Lauded as an "interesting collection" enriched by "patriotic

reflections," the book review fills up half of a column.[44] Whether deliberate
or not, the timing was ironic. The review appeared just five days before the
tribunal condemned the legendary *Père Duchesne* author Jacques Hébert,
who was known for the radical invective of a newspaper that sounds much
like this book. Where *Le Père Duchesne* exhorted his sansculottes readers
to slay their enemies or at least hang them from their thumbs, *Le Glaive
vengeur* surveys those same enemies at the moment of death, shedding a
tear over the occasional shopgirl gone astray and vilifying traitors broadly
writ. A catalog of calamity, *Le Glaive vengeur* complements the facts one
could get from the news media with apparently insider information on the
last words and acts transmitted from inside the courtroom and next to the
guillotine up to February 8, 1794. We learn that Blanchelande, for instance,
"died furious; he replied by gnashing his teeth to the booing and indignant
shouts of the immense crowd," and that the tribunal was not sympathetic
to Gorsas's claims of innocence either. Indeed, "[Gorsas] inspired nothing
but indignation and contempt. He had the opportunity to judge that himself
on the way to the scaffold." *Le Glaive vengeur* relates Lamourette's bless-
ing of the tribunal mentioned in the *Journal de Paris national* but reminds
readers that the bishop's hands were "still stained with the blood of virtuous Chalier" and that a "public confession of repentance for his crimes
would have doubtless been worthier in the eyes of the divinity than that
vain monkey business [*singerie*] which no longer demands any respect here
on earth."[45]

It is interesting to see how Dulac used the noise of the crowd in the
courtroom—that same crowd of sansculottes and *tricoteuses* which would
terrify readers of Carlyle and Dickens—to sway his readers' opinion in a
positive way. When a shop-owner of rue Poissonnière (second arrondissement) lamented, "I die innocent," after his condemnation for uncivil language, we read that the huge crowd "must have calmed the conscience of
the jurors by its applause and the unanimous shouts of '*vive la République*';
that is the people's sanction." Faced with the pale and aged appearance of
another alleged conspirator, a sixty-year-old boardinghouse manager in the
third arrondissement, the author notes that "the people might have demanded a pardon for him if in similar circumstances, they had not felt that
even pity must be silenced for the great work of national vengeance." The
spectators' insults and involvement cast an approving regard on the tribunal and its duties: the two cooperate in an ancient form of justice. Just as in
olden days, the vengeance of the people is called upon here to assist in the
vengeance of the sovereign—only now the sovereign is a tribunal instead
of a king.[46]

Lest readers suspect that the "vengeful blade" cut along class lines, it is important to point out that the most outstanding victim cited in this collection is Marie-Jeanne Roland. Wife of the former minister of the interior, Roland frequented the highest ranks of politicos during the early years of the Revolution: she went to jail for consorting with enemies of the Republic in secret meetings at her home. No mention is made of the fairness of her sentence or trial in *Le Glaive vengeur*, but a lengthy description draws out the pathos of her last moments: "it is difficult in such a moment, when riding to a certain death, to wear a countenance more free or serene than we saw on Madame Roland." Also moving was the solicitude she showed toward a comrade in sorrow, which Dulac admits was "without example."[47]

Admitting that readers likely need a break after this gallery of the dead, the editor intervenes at the end of the 124-page list with a chapter entitled "A Moment." But where one might expect a word of compassion for the deceased, this text lashes out in terms that recall Saint-Just's warning against "false pity": "Far from our mind, however, is any kind of personal feeling for those monsters, sworn enemies of the commonweal." He saves his emotion for the nation under attack and intones, "What citizen will not shudder at the sight of the innumerable plots against the Republic? Who will not feel proud of its victories, its strength, and energy? Who will not bless its defenders?"[48] With its diehard Jacobinism and defense of the government, *Le Glaive vengeur* proffers a rare and unusual glimpse into "terrorist" logic as it was propagated in popular print culture. Editor Dulac categorically praises the abstract virtue of sacrifice to the nation and ridicules visceral feelings such as fear or anger. No matter how lowly or elevated the person's rank, whoever embraces that morality finds a certain dignity here by the words allocated to his or her memory. The "vengeful blade" may be heartless, but it is at least egalitarian (fig. 24). The book's frontispiece—of an unmanned guillotine standing in an empty landscape where it awaits the next opportunity to serve—conveys that sense of single-minded rigor.

The silence in the *Journal de Paris national* surrounding the government's relentless rigor and the accelerating pace of executions in 1793–94 is practically complete. Although some prisoners were judged in groups in trials that lasted over several days, each day's condemnations appear ex nihilo in the journal. There is no mention of any lasting beneficial effects on the nation's vulnerability to attack or impact on the nation's reputation. In fact, the disparity between the events and the lack of any emotional trace concerning them in the paper, like the paper's nonreportage of the disparity between the nation's need for force and its use of force, may have been

Traîtres regardez et tremblez elle ne perdra son
activité que quand vous aurés tous perdu la vie.

24. "Traitors, look at this and tremble. She [the guillotine] will not stop her
work until you are all dead." (Traîtres, regardez et tremblez, elle ne perdra son
activité que quand vous aurez tous perdu la vie.) Frontispiece of H. G. Dulac,
Le Glaive vengeur de la République française (An 2; 1794). Beinecke Rare
Book and Manuscript Library, Yale University.

a quiet and cautiously wielded editorial tactic. Those more partisan newspapers such as *Le Vieux Cordelier* that did not hesitate to point out the
declining logic behind the government's policies may well have regretted
their boldness: Camille Desmoulins, editor of *Le Vieux Cordelier*, was executed in April 1794. It was nevertheless impossible for readers to ignore
that the nation was gaining an upper hand against her enemies. They had
ample news of triumphs coming in from Toulon (December 18–19, 1793),
the Vendée (December 1793), and especially Fleurus (June 26, 1794), making
it less obvious why the Convention and its committees needed to maintain
a police state. But such concerns would not be voiced directly in the *Journal
de Paris national* until after Thermidor.

AFTER THERMIDOR

After Thermidor Year 2, the *Journal de Paris national* gradually took on a
different format, with a greater emphasis on light features such as poetry,
more emotional accounts of trials, and a less-frequent listing of people in
the section Tribunal révolutionnaire (the heading disappeared in May 1795
and was replaced by new rubrics such as Commission militaire). In September 1794 one entire column, out of a total of eight in the paper, was
devoted to a patriotic poem every week, and this feature recurred on and off
through March 1795. In poems and vaudeville songs such as "The Return
of Decency," "The Pleasures of Fraternity," "Patriotic Gaiety," and "The
Oath of Peaceful Citizens," authors stressed the nation's deliverance from
the recent tyranny, thanked government officials for liberating them from
prison, and celebrated the joys of family life.[49] The paper also published
more book reviews. Like the choice to devote precious print space to maudlin poetry, the choice of books promoted post-Thermidor in the *Journal de
Paris* and the *Moniteur* reveals the newspaper editors attempting to forge
new memories and scapegoat those people now known as terrorists.

The news in October–December 1794 was dominated by reports from
the trial of General Jean-Baptiste Carrier and the troops who annihilated
the resistance of the Catholic and royalist forces of Vendéens and Chouans
in Nantes and western France. Both the *Journal de Paris national* and the
Moniteur dedicated the bulk of their issues to relaying the grisly details
of the executions, the drownings, and the massacres of women, children,
and peasants in the west. Profiting from this opportunity to turn attention
away from Paris, the Convention—with the apparent support of the newspapers—whipped up the people's fervor with rhetoric borrowed from the
ancien régime court case or cause célèbre and a tinge of Gothic gore. As a

representative of Nantes harangued the assembly to much applause on 30 nivôse:

> We cannot, alas, bring life back to the livid and bloody ghosts who throng the desolate banks of the Loire, those monsters took it away from them; [but] we would at least like to give them an honorable burial, we would like to honor the memory of the 20,000 victims tossed into the pits next to our walls, we would like to dry the tears of their desperate families, who have no other hope than your sensitive souls; we would like to tell them, sharing their tears: your husbands, children, and friends have perished under the sword of those bloodthirsty wretches [*ces hommes de sang*], but the Convention will protect you . . . and humanity will be avenged.[50]

This rhetoric was employed so frequently and the awful details were reprinted so often that readers may have justifiably cried, "Enough!" The news of "terrorist" carnage was not to end any time soon, however. Despite new waves of popular violence being committed in the provinces in what is now known as the White Terror, and by the "gilded youth" (*jeunesse dorée*) of Paris, the focus remained on bringing terrorists to court. There were many representatives-on-mission who had to be brought to trial, people such as Joseph Lebon (1765–95), who had led a rigorous repression against counter-revolutionaries in the northern department of Pas-de-Calais, Gabriel-Jérôme Sénar (1760–96), who was a member of the Committee of General Security under Robespierre and notorious for the harsh justice he dealt to folks living in his hometown of Tours, and Deputy Joseph Fouché (1759–1820), the so-called Butcher of Lyons. Newspaper reports of delegations from these and other regions around France, requesting justice from the Convention and demanding vengeance, form a veritable litany of outrage starting in August 1794 and continuing through spring 1795. The gory details and acts of inhumanity were dutifully relayed to readers of the papers.

Some of these details made their way into fiction too, as in Joseph de Rosny's novel *Les Infortunes de Mr. de La Galetierre pendant le Régime décemviral* (The misfortunes of Mr. de La Galetierre during the Rule of Ten; Year 5 [1796–97]). This novel was extensively revised and amplified to make an even stronger anti-Jacobin statement in Year 7, when the author inserted explicit links between how the Terror was experienced in western France and in Saint-Domingue (by white planters and settlers). The *decimvir*, or Rule of Ten, in the title refers to the revolutionary committees (the Committee of Public Safety and the Committee of General Security) that virtually dictated government action during the Terror, and the foremost villain of the novel is onetime committee member and representative-on-mission Sénar. His cruel and drunken misdeeds are recounted in detail, and the author gives the names of more than eighty people who allegedly died by his orders in Tours. One of the ways that Rosny claims to try and bring events to a close is by announcing the ignominious death of Sénar ("qui fut aussi misérable que sa vie avait été odieuse") and noting that his memory is now execrated by all.[51] The accumulated violence and cruelties related in *Les Infortunes* belie Rosny's purported pacifism; after reading this tableau of heartbreak (including the drawn-out deaths of La Galetierre's wife and infant son on a desert island), it is hard to believe that the author really wanted to elicit reactions other than vengeance and regret. Perhaps Rosny's novel can be best appreciated as contributing to what Olwen Hufton has called the "squaring of the record" that ran through regions where revolutionary repression was most devastating. As Hufton notes, "without this act of revenge for loved ones lost or families severed by the revolutionary record, normality could not be achieved."[52]

One reader pleaded for respite in the *Journal de Paris national* in January 1795 and in so doing announced a new literary market on the horizon. In an unsigned letter printed on 9 nivôse, the author thanks the editors of the paper for political news: "in presenting to our eyes the long script of counterrevolutionary atrocities committed by Carrier and his confederates, you have well served the Republic: publishing crimes prevents their return." But he admits that a certain compassion fatigue has set in, noting that "our souls are weary of so many horrors and we need softer emotions for relief. Nothing refreshes the blood of a decent man [*un honnête home*] . . . like the tale of a good deed." The letter ends by producing "that happy effect on your readers" with the example of a generous shopkeeper in a lower-class neighborhood known for its left-wing militarism.[53] His shop is located on la rue de la Chanvrerie (first arrondissement), future setting of the barricade and the battle that took so many lives in Victor Hugo's *Les Misérables* (1862). This valorization of the worthy workingman would launch a major publishing industry in mid-nineteenth-century France.

Also notable is the fanfare surrounding feats of sacrificial heroism. The death of Loiserolles on 8 thermidor, for instance, is revealed in January 1795 to be an instance of a citizen who defied Jacobin authorities in the name of a higher order, family. The son's testimonial in Parisian newspapers laid out the father's glory, which then circulated in the form of popular poetry and song (*romance*) and left an indelible trace on the visual arts in the famous *Collection complète des tableaux historiques de la Révolution française*

25. "Loiserolles devotes himself to his son unto death" (Loiserolles se dévoue à la mort pour son fils), July 26, 1794 (8 thermidor An 2). *Collection complète des Tableaux historiques de la Révolution française composée de cent treize numéros en trois volumes*, vol. 2 (An 13; 1804). Reproduced from the original held by the Department of Special Collections of the Hesburgh Libraries of the University of Notre Dame.

(1804; fig. 25) and its imitators.[54] While republicans might have balked at the disobedience implied in this image—the father's raised right hand making a mockery of the civic oath—it has gone down in history as a legend of Christian selflessness.[55] Dickens was inspired by such feats to imagine the surprise ending of *A Tale of Two Cities,* in which the ne'er-do-well Sydney Carton sacrifices his life to save his erstwhile rival Charles Darnay and thus ensures the survival of the Manette-Darnay clan for posterity. But first, France had to escape the grasp of the "terrorists." How did print media help?

For one thing, some of France's most outspoken journalists returned to the public eye. One of the leading plotters against Robespierre, Louis-Stanislas Fréron (1754–1802), began publishing *L'Orateur du peuple* in September 1794 and was soon coordinating what historian William Doyle calls a "private street army" of gilded youth who made it their business to harass Jacobins, disrupt the meetings of left-wing political clubs, and break up public occasions of which they did not approve.[56] A whole range of right-wing papers mushroomed at this time and launched heated debate with the Convention regarding press freedom. By winter, Pierre Louis Roederer (1754–1835) joined the fray. Roederer had been forced into hiding after learning of a warrant for his arrest in the roundup of the Girondins in October 1793, but in January 1795 he bought half-ownership of the *Journal de Paris national* and came back to work. Under his leadership the paper resumed its old name, engaged new writers, and adopted a more pointed approach to the news. Under the rubric Esprit public editors kept up a running commentary on the political scene and animated forums on controversial topics such as the restoration of Catholic worship. To pave the way for these changes Roederer published a clever exchange of letters between himself and the editors, all of which were penned by him. He blasted the paper's poor political analysis, exclaiming, "Say, citizens, why is your newspaper so deplorable and why has it been that way for such a long time? What news of the Convention! . . . What vassal of Robespierre was in charge of that section?" This jibe allowed the editors to cast a look back on publishing practices during the Terror: "We must admit, it was perhaps not possible for [the former reporter on the Convention] to be impartial; under the tyranny writers were not free to write their conscience; they were not even free not to write. You will recall that, in those days, some men were suspected, accused, and punished even for their silence, and that the closure of a print shop would have prompted a death sentence for the printer."[57] But all that was changing now, at least for a while.

PRISONERS' TALES

Prisoners in the News

Although not exactly designed to produce happy effects on the reader, prison memoirs were suddenly the rage in 1795, judging from numerous book reviews, a flurry of letters to the editor, and advertisements published in the papers between March and November 1795.[58] In large part, this trend simply put a new twist on a genre that had fascinated readers since the taking of the Bastille. After all, Prudhomme's *Révolutions de Paris* had been in the practice of reproducing verbatim "Papers of the Bastille" since 1789, and some of them sound pretty horrendous, such as the May 1790 reprint of *Copie d'une lettre écrite au cachot sur du linge avec du sang, par un prisonnier détenu 26 ans à la Bastille* (Copy of a letter written in blood on clothing by a prisoner held for 26 years in the Bastille). Compared with these accounts, the memoirs touted post-Thermidor may seem somewhat tame. But the editors' politics are not irrelevant. Where Prudhomme brandished his left-wing credentials in plain sight, the editors of the *Journal de Paris* were less explicit. The book reviews said it for them.

The first evidence of literary alliance building in spring 1795 is a review linking the memoirs of Bordeaux lawyer Honoré Jean Riouffe and Deputy Jean-Baptiste Louvet, formerly de Couvray. Both these books and Madame Roland's memoirs were published by Louvet's print shop, a fact not unrelated to the Girondin politics that were shared by these authors and the editors of the *Journal de Paris*. Heralded as two parts of the same story—the May 31, 1793, arrest of the Girondin deputies—both books were acclaimed for the way that they weaved the author's personal plight into a critique of the Terror. Louvet was already a well-known author by 1795, beloved for his rocambolesque tales of the philosopher-adventurer Faublas, but the titillating style that made *Une Année de la vie du chevalier de Faublas* a best seller in 1787 and sustained sales of *Faublas* sequels in 1788 and 1789 apparently disappointed in this rather more serious genre. Riouffe's memoirs, on the other hand, promised to "enrich the history of the human heart."[59] While Robespierre's biographer Hamel would later label Riouffe's memoirs a pack of lies, the *Journal de Paris* heralds it as a model of remembrance.[60]

The *Journal de Paris* also praised the personal approach to history in the memoirs by Deputy Henri Maximin Isnard, another controversial figure who, despite his forceful support for the Girondin platform, escaped arrest in 1793 and reemerged as a leader of the anti-Jacobin reaction when his party was allowed back into the Convention in February 1795. The editor avoids all mention of the author's public role. Rather, his portrait of a tortured mind in solitude is declared a great service to humanity:

> Those unfortunates who, like Isnard, can observe the states of their soul in the diverse situations that they experienced will be more useful to *l'art social* [i.e., psychology] than the most faithful narrators of historical events, [because] they will be the first to help us understand mankind. What novel phenomena—the human mind in the midst of such new and diverse circumstances! O you, who give us the history of prisons, give us especially the history of your emotions [*affections*]. Rest assured that the insights into your soul will not be less interesting to us than the portrait of your jail cell; and that we will identify more easily with you among your thoughts and feelings than with your cellmates.[61]

Here and elsewhere in the *Journal de Paris* the careful reader notes a sustained attack on Jacobins and a hagiographical rendition of the Girondins, who appear to be not only innocent victims but also thoughtful and gifted writers. In a clever move to avoid openly addressing political recriminations, the editors promoted individual memoirs as the best means to remember the nation's past. The best memoirists just happened to be Girondins.

A Psychological Approach to Loss: Riouffe's *Mémoires d'un détenu* (1795)

Riouffe's *Mémoires d'un détenu* (Memoirs of a prisoner) went through two editions in 1795 and remained a major reference for the next eighty years at least.[62] It is to Riouffe that Thomas Carlyle, a notorious critic of parliamentary democracy, turned for details of the Terror in his *French Revolution* (1837), which in turn informed Dickens's *Tale of Two Cities*.[63] The book recalls earlier works in the genre yet captures a certain modern sensitivity as well. In some ways, all prison memoirs resemble each other. Like the Renaissance outlaw François Villon's *Ballades des pendus* (1489), the Russian dissident Aleksandr Solzhenitsyn's *Gulag Archipelago* (1973), and the American felon Kenneth Hartman's *Mother California* (2009), Riouffe reprises the common bitterness against imprisonment and the inhumane conditions of his cell, along with a haunting awareness of death and of time passing. Riouffe too denounces the cruelties he suffered at the hands of prison guards. He heaps particular venom on a gendarme, formerly a cook in Agen, who shackled him to an eighty-pound cannon ball to show off to his pals while the convoy passed that town on the way to Paris.[64] The lyricism of *Mémoires d'un détenu* is also noteworthy; the reviewer for *Le Moniteur* exclaimed, "One cannot read it without crying in pain and shame [but] one cannot finish it without wanting to read it again."[65] Part of that appeal is the awful juxtaposition of the refined, intelligent Riouffe alongside filthy cellmates who represent criminality in its repugnant guises: the mutilated assassin, the weasel-like counterfeiter, and the cunning bandits, all of whom speak a slangy language particular to their trades. Of course, Riouffe was not a common criminal but a political detainee, and the conflicts he witnessed and the portraits he produced—of the Girondin deputies, Danton, and Madame Roland—made this work the subject of no little controversy. Like the author of *Le Glaive vengeur* but with a more sympathetic intention, Riouffe fills in the gaps left out of the historical record. He records a song that he and his fellow cellmates sang to pass the time and bolster each other's courage, for instance, and his second edition even has an appendix where one can find the last letters and unheard defense speeches written by cellmates.

But there are two things that set Riouffe apart from his predecessors and make this book modern: his solidarity with other political prisoners and his sense of survivor's guilt. Riouffe's appreciation of human suffering comes out best in the passage where he describes the Spaniard who was arrested at the same time as him: "Relating my misfortunes, is telling about his; our persecution had the same causes, the same irons enchained us, the same dungeons held us, and the same blade was to end both our lives." While witnessing another prisoner's torture by revolutionary troops, he notes a similar sense of kinship: "I felt like I saw all the French people being humiliated in his person."[66] Most remarkable for our current sensibilities is the survivor guilt he admits at the end: "What had I done? What crime marked my birth, so that I had to see so much blood spilled so close to me? The poisoned dart of despair has pierced my soul; I will carry it always, and if my executioners' fury is not assuaged by 14 months of hard captivity, and if they do not sign off on an honorable condemnation, I will succumb under so many awful memories, and die of shame for having been born a man." This admission is articulated even more baldly in a letter to a friend in the appendix: "If I have survived, at least one cannot accuse me of having tried to do so."[67] Although born into the ranks of the elite, Riouffe claims the status of Everyman here, reproaches himself for his earlier indifference, and indicts an unnecessarily cruel penal system. The author's plans to help change that system are left unspoken. The reader is not expected to judge him or the lessons he learned in prison but to sympathize with his suffering and to remember the horrors of 1793–94.

FIGHTING FOR A VOICE:
ROLAND'S *APPEL À L'IMPARTIALE POSTÉRITÉ* (1795)

If Riouffe's memoirs are unknown today, that is likely because they were overshadowed by another tome appearing that spring, *L'Appel à l'impartiale postérité* (Appeal to impartial posterity). This book was published posthumously by the same publisher as *Mémoires d'un détenu* and on behalf of a woman whom Riouffe himself commemorated: Marie-Jeanne Roland. Judging from the *Journal de Paris*, the *Moniteur*, and other publication data, it is safe to say that of all the titles hitting the streets that spring, Madame Roland's *Appel* made the greatest impact.[68] The author was killed on November 8, 1793, and her husband—the former minister of the interior and leading Girondin Jean-Marie Roland de la Platière—committed suicide shortly thereafter, so their goods were sequestered by the state. The profits from this posthumous book of reflections went to her young daughter; buying it was a way to get a good book and do a good deed, as *Le Journal de Paris* pointed out in one of seven reviews published between April and June 1795.

Roland's flattering portrait of Robespierre is one of the most surprising discoveries in the *Appel*. Even though her imprisonment was arguably the result of policies dictated by Robespierre, Roland paints a nuanced image of the man in an early section of part 1 and initially chalks up his errors to a zeal and enthusiasm for liberty—both of which she shared. She notes being pained by his abrupt mannerisms and poor speaking style but attributes them to shyness and declares, "He maintained principles with warmth and perseverance; and there was some courage in continuing to do this, at a time when the defenders of the cause of the people were infinitely diminished in number. The court detested and calumniated them; to support and encourage them, therefore, was the duty of the patriots. I esteemed Robespierre on this account, I told him so . . . he occasionally came to dine with me."[69] Granted, her portrait of the man in the days following the king's flight to Varennes is unflattering. He appeared terrified, she writes, and when Deputies Brissot and Pétion spoke of preparing the people for a republic, Robespierre, "with his usual sneer and biting his nails, asked, 'What is a republic!'"[70] But the general thrust of Roland's comments in this passage focuses on the psychological effervescence that Robespierre felt and how it impacted events. Like many others who were swept up in the excitement, he did not and could not foresee the consequences of his acts.

Later in her memoirs, Roland admits feeling differently toward Robespierre, and she uses blunt language to make her point. In a passage dated October 3, 1793, she writes, "That Robespierre, whom I once thought an honest man, is a very atrocious being. How he lies to his own conscience! How he delights in blood!"[71] As time goes by and her situation does not improve, Roland finally resorts to a direct address to the deputy in person. Recalling their earlier acquaintance, she writes to the deputy: "Robespierre, if I deceive myself, I put it into your power to convince me, that I am wrong."[72] Following that are five pages (in-octavos) wherein the author defends the actions of her husband and recalls her own quiet lifestyle, modesty, and enthusiastic admiration of the Revolution as traits that baffle her from her present position behind bars. "Whence, then, arises this animosity? I cannot conceive."[73] Finally she closes with a veiled reproach to this erstwhile friend of the family: "I know, and you cannot but feel, that a person who has known me, cannot persecute me without remorse."[74] Despite being justified, the ploy did not work. The timing doomed it to failure. By October

1793 Robespierre's loyalties lay elsewhere; his self-imposed obligation to model an impeccable public virtue was at its peak.

Nonetheless, there is no little irony in considering Marie-Jeanne Roland as a victim of the Republic because she comes across as a model republican or, more precisely, a *républicaine.* Describing herself as a "friend of liberty," she recalls, "I beheld the revolution with delight, persuaded that it was destined to put an end to the arbitrary power which I detested, and to the abuses I had so often lamented, when reflecting with pity upon the fate of the indigent classes of society. I observed the progress of the revolution with interest and I spoke with warmth about public affairs; but I did not out-step the bounds prescribed by my sex."[75] Like a Roman lady of lore, she goes willingly to her fate. Or she would go willingly if only she could be heard first. What ultimately strikes us in reading this book is the disappointment that emerges toward the end of part 2, when the author's belief in the Revolution and her confidence in the fairness of its processes give way to frustration over the silence surrounding her plight.

An awareness of the peculiar quality of revolutionary time and the individual's vulnerability to history-in-progress run through this text. Time sometimes appears open-ended and expansive; at other times it feels unpleasantly compressed. Remembering her first weeks in prison, when she was confident that the tribunal would sooner or later realize the error of her arrest, Roland anticipated the future: "I flattered myself that I should contribute to my husband's glory, and help enlighten the public, if brought to trial."[76] A regular reader of the newspapers, which she had delivered to her cell, Roland could not help but realize the decline of public debate during the months of her confinement—June to November 1793—which as noted above were the same months when the Revolutionary Tribunal adopted a more rigorous stance toward suspects and accelerated the pace of judgments. By October, however, she had concluded glumly: "Two months ago, I aspired to the honour of ascending the scaffold; the victim was then allowed to speak and the energy of a courageous mind might have been serviceable to the cause of truth: now all is lost."[77] For the benefit of the reader studying these pages in a future time, much as she foresaw her eleven-year-old daughter doing, Roland nevertheless claims to defy her captors. One can only imagine the bitter glee she must have taken in penning these impudent lines on her interview with Public Accuser Fouquier-Tinville: "'How I pity you,' said I calmly. 'I forgive you even the disagreeable things you say to me: you think you have a great criminal before you, and you are impatient to convict her. How unfortunate is the man who entertains such prejudices! You may send me to the scaffold; but you cannot deprive me of the satisfaction I derive from a good conscience, nor of the persuasion that posterity will revenge Roland and myself, by devoting his persecutors to infamy."[78] But Roland did not delude herself. As one who pored over the execution lists published daily and noted with pain the gag order imposed on Deputy Gorsas among others, she expected that her case would get short shrift. And so she prepared her own judgment, execution, and afterlife in these pages. In one uncanny passage after her interrogation was cut short, she reports telling the court what to think of her, and what is more, she uses a refined version of the Jacobins' own *langue de bois* to do so, announcing, "It is a rule with tyranny to sacrifice those whom it has grievously oppressed, and to annihilate the very witnesses of its misdeeds. I have this double claim to death at your hands, and I expect it."[79]

Roland's suspicions about the silence that awaited her in court and the press turned out to be well founded. She never did get called by the tribunal to present the speech she wrote in her defense (and which is printed in this book). On the day after her execution, the *Journal de Paris national* published a perfunctory notice listing her name, age, hometown, and sentence. Even more infuriating is the way that the *Moniteur* framed Roland's death alongside some of the vilest misogyny to be found in its pages. This too may have been a quirk of fate. Early November 1793 was not a propitious moment to commemorate the life of a feisty and politically active woman because, judging from the news from the Commune and the Convention, female politicking was less welcome than ever in their quarters. The Convention had declared all women's political societies illegal on October 30, 1793. And when a delegation of concerned *citoyennes* showed up at the Paris Commune on November 17, they were greeted with shouts of "À bas le bonnet rouge des femmes!" (Down with red-bonnet-wearing women!). Anaxagoras Chaumette, prosecutor of the Commune, protested for the record that "it is awful, contrary to all laws of nature, that a woman should make herself into a man," before launching into a bitter tirade against Madame Roland, "who thought herself fit to govern the Republic," and Olympe de Gouges, whose head fell by the law's "vengeful blade."[80] His speech and the final motion banning all women from speaking to the Commune, at present or in the future, were "frequently interrupted by enthusiastic applause and adopted unanimously."[81]

Worse yet is the diatribe entitled "Aux républicaines" (To women republicans), which was published alongside this news item just nine days after Roland's execution. In a mean-spirited eulogy of three recently executed women, this text briefly evokes the errors of Queen Marie-Antoinette (bad mother, debauched wife) and Olympe de Gouges (madwoman who forgot her femininity) but saves the brunt of its attack for Madame Roland. "A monster in all respects," Roland is scolded for vainglorious learning, her contempt of the people's court, and the "ironic gaiety" that she brought to the guillotine—which are held as proof of her lack of remorse and indifference to motherhood. Echoing Chaumette's repugnance for this woman, who "wanted to rise above herself," the article concludes with a stirring apostrophe to readers: "Women! Do you want to be republican? Love, follow, and teach the laws that remind your husbands and children of their rights; take pride in their actions on behalf of the fatherland, because they reflect well on you . . . and never attend popular gatherings with the hopes of speaking there."[82] It seems somehow appropriate for this Jacobin source to scold Madame Roland for her voice after the tribunal had already silenced it forever.

Nevertheless, by releasing her memoirs into print strategically after the splashy arrival of three other related works on the Terror in spring 1795, Roland's friends and admirers launched her into literary immortality. Contemporary reviewers took issue with a few aspects of the book, but they unanimously applauded the author's style and strength and stressed her femininity. The *Journal de Paris* declared the author was "a good mother and an excellent woman who was enthused about liberty and the well-being of her country." The *Moniteur* also exhorted its readers to pick up her book: "It is in the book that one must learn to know this extraordinary woman, who, under the tranquil shelter of her father's roof, was happy from the cradle to be surrounded by flowers and books, just as she was at the end of her life, in the narrow confines of a prison, in the midst of hardships imposed by the most revolting tyranny; she forgot men's injustice, their crimes, and evils, among books and flowers."[83] Although the author might have bristled at this portrait of herself as a dreamer lost in pastoral contemplation, Madame Roland would certainly have approved of the portrait of her last moments rendered in *A Tale of Two Cities*, where her heroic good humor and strength of character are lent to character Sydney Carton on his ascent to martyrdom. She would likely have been pleased as well by the reprint of the *Moniteur* that appeared a year later. Echoing the admiration of Carlyle and Dickens, the 1860 editor of the *Moniteur* added a long footnote to the newspaper of November 8, 1793, wherein he apologizes for the brevity of the original execution notice, cites other sources for more information on her appearance at court, and presents Madame Roland's last gesture of kindness, when she allowed another prisoner to mount the scaffold before her, as an example of supernatural courage under fire.[84] Roland's *Appel* and correspondence are today among the most well-known works about the revolutionary era, and her prison memoir has become a must-read on the Terror.

Did Roland get the last word after all? Maybe. In Flaubert's *Dictionnaire des idées reçues* her famous last words constitute the entry for "Freedom": "How many crimes are committed in its name!" (Liberté: Combien de crimes on commet en son nom!). But then again, almost the same words are listed for "Law and Order."[85] In the strangely resonant but mindless echo chamber sending readers back and forth from one entry to the other, Flaubert slyly undermines the hagiography surrounding this most famous victim of the Terror. The duplication reminds us that sometimes a slogan is just a slogan, politics are just politics, and no one remembers where they all came from or what exactly they are supposed to mean.

CRIME NARRATIVES

CRIME IN THE NEWS

Following Thermidor, the *Journal de Paris national* began printing more of what we would now call human-interest stories from the judicial register and police beat. This trend became more marked by the spring of Year 8 (1800), when under the rubric Mélanges editors placed small headlines on items, such as "Advice to Police," "Impudent Thief," and "Tragic Sensitivity." But already in fall 1794 crime stories and domestic dramas began inching their way into national media and back into the public eye.[86] In an attempt to keep the recent horrors in citizens' minds or to make up for their cowardice under Jacobin rule, the papers first highlighted victims of state power. For months, the *Journal de Paris* and the *Moniteur* devoted entire pages to nothing but eyewitness accounts of trials for crimes committed during the Jacobin-led repression and peppered such news with hints of audience reactions, such as the "shudder of horror" (frémissement d'horreur) that swept through the courtroom in an October 1794 Nantes trial, or the March 1795 reading of allegations brought against some representatives-on-mission in Strasbourg when "the entire assembly shuddered with horror." Most alarming were accounts of criminals who were still at large. Under the rubric Crime atroce (Atrocious crime) in June 1795, we find the report of a certain Denelle, suspected Robespierrist and resident of Faubourg Antoine, who after poisoning his wife and four children apparently found their dying too slow and so bludgeoned them all with a hammer before escaping into the city streets. "May his cross-eye and wild and sinister manner make him

noticed; and may his punishment soon serve as an example to other criminals," the report warns.[87]

This admonition twists the spectacle-logic of public executions that
dominated the early-modern judiciary in a particularly Thermidorian manner. The causality that linked publishing crimes to the likelihood of avoiding their return runs predictably through publications of 1795–99 like a
reassuring refrain. Just as the harsh light shone on the events leading up
to 9 thermidor was believed to bring down the reign of the tyrant, the publicity shone on crimes committed by his agents near or far was believed
to prevent their spread. But how? The Atrocious Crime story noted above
gives one method: in its emphasis on the "wild and sinister" look of the
felon it suggests profiling based on appearance, a precursor of the pseudoscience of phrenology or cranial analysis that flourished in the 1800s. (It is not
for nothing that the entry for "Convict [*Forçat*]" in Flaubert's *Dictionnaire
des idées reçues* declares that they "always have sinister faces [*une figure
patibulaire*]. They wear their crimes on their faces.")[88] The narratives of
Robespierre's crimes used that tool and provided others as well, including
an early form of psychological profiling that sought answers in the subject's
childhood and family dynamic. Whatever the method, the anxieties over
understanding the criminal mind and preventing its influence, return, or
spread are palpable. What is less obvious is how they were politically and
literarily aligned to keep the Jacobins and their allies among the working
people forever vilified in the eyes of "law and order."

The public's appetite for tales of famous political crimes and criminals
apparently grew after Thermidor; witness the sudden profusion of titles
such as *Les Noyades, ou Carrier au Tribunal révolutionnaire*, *Les Crimes
de Marat et des autres égorgeurs*, *Les Crimes des terroristes*, and so forth.
Some were based on colonial fears, such as *Crimes des noirs* (ca. 1796),
which purported to recount the horrors occasioned by slave leader Toussaint Louverture, or *Pitt à Saint-Domingue, ou Les Crimes de l'ancien
comité de Salut-public*, in which a soldier stationed in Saint-Domingue
reveals how the Committee of Public Safety let the colony fall into English hands.[89] Some were based on villains of international disrepute and
were not dissimilar to the popular "black histories" of Marie-Antoinette
and Louis XVI that had gone through multiple printings since 1788 and
that were themselves indebted to a well-worn tradition of leaders gone bad.
However, the bad monarch genre had been irrevocably changed since 1788,
according to Carla Hesse, with the arrival of Louise de Kéralio-Robert's
Crimes des reines de France in 1791. This version effectively knocked the

queen off her throne and put the black history to the truly radical purposes of removing the woman and the monarchy from sight instead of merely re-forming their ways.[90] One might view the black legends of Robespierre-the-criminal as attempting a similar deflation of purpose: its authors attempted to end the Terror not only by arguing that the notion of a repressive repub-lic was an oxymoron but also by reducing it to the flesh and blood of its flawed leader.

   The traditional crime legend, such as the lives of the eighteenth-century bandits Cartouche and Mandrin or their successor Moneuse (captain of the *chauffeurs du Nord*) that circulated in broadsides or in chapbook form, de-scribed the criminal as a kind of man-from-nowhere, a master at disguise and self-fashioning, who regularly put his life on the line and excelled at creating and sustaining fear.[91] It may culminate in a gallows speech, where he admits repentance, but the thrust of the tale lies in the villain's superhu-man awfulness. The handbill invented by Caleb Williams's enemies is not atypical of the genre. William Godwin, the author of the novel, describes the handbill as "the most wonderful and surprising history, and miraculous ad-ventures of Caleb Williams," in which he escapes from prison "in the most wonderful and uncredible manner," he wears "various disguises," and he joins "a most desperate and daring gang of thieves."[92] The most influential Robespierre biographies of the 1790s refuse him this dimension. And the tactic was just as damning to the leader of the Jacobins as Kéralio-Robert's was to the subject of her work: where the latter wrote Marie-Antoinette and the absolute monarchy out of history, the former denied Robespierre and his reign the mantle of "greatness." The ploy apparently worked, at least until Ernest Hamel took up the cause in the 1860s. Looking back on this period in 1800 Pierre Roussel claimed that "the confederates of Cartouche, and the greatest brigands, did not commit worse crimes [than Robespierre et al.], and the former had this advantage, in that they risked their lives in taking those of the people they robbed."[93] In other words, the Jacobins were cowards as well as criminals.

ROBESPIERRE: THE FIRST MODERN CRIMINAL?

A Career Abruptly Ended

Considering the vast amount of ink spilled by Robespierre observers before and since his demise, the account of his arrest and execution on 9–10 ther-midor in the *Journal de Paris national* is astonishingly concise. For years beforehand, he had commanded glowing reviews for his ideas and speeches made at the Jacobin Club and the Convention. As author of a book on the National Guard, Robespierre was celebrated in the *Chronique de Paris* (1791) as "one of the most decent citizens [*les plus honnêtes*] and who is known to have no other party than the Revolution, no other goal but the common good."[94] Even the efforts of talented Deputy Louvet could not tarnish his reputation. Louvet launched a forceful indictment of Robespierre before the Convention in October 1792, accusing him of power-mongering and criminal agitation following August 10, when he joined the provisional Paris Commune government. But Robespierre demolished Louvet's proofs point by point and impressed the assembly and a crowd of spectators during his November 5 rebuttal. Most effective was the question he posed: "Citizens, did you want a revolution without revolution?"[95] By putting the urgency of national reform on the table in this way and suggesting that the Girondins were plotting against the common good by proposing a campaign of ruinous foreign wars, Robespierre used Louvet's charges to undermine the Gironde party's legitimacy. Although his opposition to the war effort was eventually overruled, a year later Robespierre's star was clearly ascendant. The motions he proposed on December 5, 1793 (regarding a declaration to send to the foreign kings in league against the Republic), and December 25, 1793 (on the principles of revolutionary government), were both reported as "interrupted by much applause" and "adopted unanimously." His speech of May 7, 1794, in which he proposed a cult of the Supreme Being met thunderous applause throughout and was stopped midway by a group of teary-eyed children who stood up and shouted, *"Vive la République!"*[96] Although not lacking in controversy, Robespierre was a key player, if not *the* key player, behind the "regeneration" of the French, and he incarnated the hopes of many for the Republic's future, facts duly noted by the *Journal de Paris*. But his fall came fast. In the paper of Saturday, July 26 (8 thermidor), Robespierre's signature is listed alongside that of Bertrand Barère de Vieuzac and other members of the Committee of Public Safety on an anodyne decree regarding agricultural labor for the upcoming harvest. The next day, he is reported to have given a long speech wherein he refuted accusations of his supposedly dictatorial ambitions, which, despite drawing "loud" discussion and "rather long debate," was authorized for print and distribution to the Convention. The newspaper mentions in passing a speech by Barère celebrating the victories of the republican armies and the "enthusiastic applause" it received, before closing with elaborate details on the festival to be celebrated in honor of the martyrs championed by Robespierre: Joseph Barra (killed at age fifteen) and Agricola Viala (shot by federalists at thirteen) upon their imminent entry into the Pantheon.

In what seems to be a baffling reversal of fortune, on Tuesday, the eleventh, readers of the *Journal de Paris national* learned that things had turned sour. It appears that Barère had denounced Robespierre for secretly plotting to restore the monarchy in France and called for his arrest. Surely, this insinuation would have come as a surprise to Robespierre's colleagues in the Jacobin Club, not to mention the population at large! Nevertheless, Barère claims to have seen a fleur-de-lys stamp in Robespierre's proximity, and the report mentions that several other deputies "shouted that they had seen it too."[97] Since it is only Barère's damning words that receive attention here—published in installments over four days in the *Journal de Paris national*—and since Robespierre's rebuttal is not quoted at all, readers are led to believe such allegations. Five years later this rumor became legend when a novelist embellished it in what became a best seller of the early 1800s, *Irma*.

Similarly astonishing is the report of Robespierre's last attempt to speak to the Convention on the night of Sunday, 9 thermidor: "Robespierre is announced at the door. [Deputy] Thuriot asks that he not be introduced, because a tyrant's body is only permissible in the vicinity of a king's."[98] Again, no commentary marks the outrageous disrespect of these words that were spoken among peers. The facts of Robespierre's "outlaw" status, the Luxembourg prison's refusal to house him, his return to the Hôtel de Ville and his impending execution are summed up together, and his surname is replaced by the insulting nickname "the modern Catilina." Moreover, the notice of his execution conforms strictly to those listed under the rubric Tribunal révolutionnaire: the once-powerful man is described merely as "Maximilien *Robespierre*, 35 years old, born at Arras, deputy of the National Convention." He heads up the list of twenty-two people executed on 10 thermidor, all of whom are said to be "declared outlaws . . . and upon identification by witnesses, were delivered to the executioner to be put to death in 24 hours." The following day a similar list appeared with seventy-one more names on it, on 13 thermidor twelve more names were listed, and the purge of conspirators appears to conclude with the announcement of Pierre-André Coffinhal's execution in the newspaper of 19 thermidor. In total, 106 men aged twenty-six to sixty-two years old, whose professions included wigmaker, wood seller, ex-deputy, ex-president of the Jacobin Club, shoemaker, pastry cook, painter, and farmer, were condemned and their executions reported along with Robespierre's over these four days.

It is not until Sunday, 16 thermidor (August 3), that readers were finally provided with a play-by-play account of the events but still with no trace of Robespierre's own words. The crisis—as bewildering as it was to readers accustomed to Robespierre's prominence in the public eye—seemed to be past.[99] Or was it? In the next section we depart from a day-to-day focus on news reportage to show how the stunning implications of Robespierre's rise and fall were felt and immortalized in the following few years. This section underlines the capital accrued by authors and publishers who made terror into a literary commodity and probes the political motivations behind the pseudoscientific genre of "terrorist" biography.

The Immortality of Robespierre:
Early Pamphlets, Biographies, and Popular Art

That tensions continued to run high about the tyrant's power is evidenced by a flurry of pamphlets that hit Parisian streets immediately following Thermidor. Frustrated by what appeared to be disingenuous actions by the Convention, rumors started circulating that the Terror lived on. Observers now claimed that Robespierre was a symptom, not the cause, and cited as proof his threat to return from the dead. "You can cut off my head," he reportedly warned, "but I have left you my tail" (Vous pouvez couper ma tête, mais je vous ai laissé ma queue).[100] This fear-inducing thought spread like wildfire thanks to a pamphlet entitled *La Queue de Robespierre* (Robespierre's tail) dated 9 fructidor Year 2 (August 26, 1794), which was printed in several tens of thousands of copies and elicited almost a dozen equally frenetic replies. Given that the thrust of *La Queue* was to unveil the evil maneuvers of Convention deputies such as Collot d'Herbois and Barère himself, who were allegedly trying to restrict the freedom of the press and reinstate the Terror, it is unsurprising that the bulk of pamphlets denounced or defended various parties and policies then operative in the government. In typical pamphlet style they appeal directly to readers by declaring, "People, read and tremble!" Or they accuse the people of already forgetting Robespierre's infamy. Or they urge the people to fight for their freedom of speech or simply to fight for "freedom until death!"[101]

In unearthing this little-known anecdote of Thermidorian France in his 1989 book, Bronislaw Baczko filled in one gap of the history. Robespierre's reference to a rear-guard action that would outlive him was a chillingly prescient warning of what was to come five years later when the ineffectual Directory government was overthrown by a new kind of martial law ushered in by General Napoléon Bonaparte on 18 brumaire Year 8 (November 9, 1799). But the popularity of these brochures was not only due to vague worries about a dictator waiting in the wings. They also deliberately sought to stoke fears of the dangerous classes: first understood as the sansculottes and then broadened to signify anyone identified with the working class or the poor, who were seen as a bloc that became involved in public life for the first time in 1789–93 and needed to be kept out of politics going forward. Whether these sorts of people were actually part of any organized political movement or not is debatable. The point is that belief in the connection between lower economic status, left-wing politics, and criminality became second nature, to the point that the unpredictability and potential radicalism of working men were listed as commonplaces in Flaubert's *Dictionnaire* ("Worker: Always honest, when he is not rioting").[102]

The sansculottes or inhabitants of the impoverished faubourgs were not the only bugbears after the state's repression was lifted: new groups of vigilantes and bandits stepped in to enforce their own notions of justice and punishment. Along with rumors (sometimes praising) of the right-wing gilded youth who broke into Jacobin clubs and straightened out former radicals, the *Journal de Paris national* reported violence wrought by rural gangs (such as the Compagnons de Jéhu in the south), the *chauffeurs de pieds* (who burned their victims' feet until they got their way), and individual outlaws such as Eugène François Vidocq. This fear-inducing reportage exploited what Howard Brown calls a "banditry psychosis," meaning that the slightest hint of danger became quickly blown out of proportion as people fostered suspicions about criminal networks operating across a whole province and beyond.[103] Why else would rumors about the tyrant's tail stay around so long? Readers could see that the Convention was not infringing on their freedoms of speech in the many right-wing papers now for sale and the well-publicized trials of former terrorists that took place in 1794–95. Yet the fear of Robespierre's minions and others brigands lived on and remained steadily in the public eye.

The most spectacular response to *La Queue de Robespierre* emerged in a 1796 pamphlet entitled *L'Ombre de Robespierre* (The shadow of Robespierre, by Rondot), which relates a melodramatic struggle of good versus evil that has less to do with protecting free speech than with drumming up panic about left-wing militants. Cast upon a cadaver-strewn place de la Révolution, the narrator is dragged by a gang of thugs to the foot of the guillotine. Rushing to implore pity from the shadowy figure orchestrating the carnage, he realizes with horror that it is the dead Robespierre himself surrounded by sansculottes. The phantom blames the crowd for nourishing his plots and scolds them for allowing his name to be dragged in the mud: "Avenge my ignoble death!" Robespierre demands.[104] But just as the crowd takes a vow to pursue vengeance, lightning strikes, a volcano explodes, the earth breaks open, and they all fall into the breach. Awakening with a start, the narrator

26. Satirical allegory of a descent into Hell, ca. 1794. Ancien fonds, Inv. p. 805, Musée Carnavalet, Paris. Reproduced by permission of The Image Works, Inc.

exclaims an oath to the constitution of Year 3 and vows to support the legislature. The titanic clash is what makes this brochure stand out from the
others. This larger-than-life Robespierre threatens the populace with a vast
and secret plot and must be stopped by something more powerful. Whether
it is an earthquake and a constitution, as here, or a newly emboldened bourgeoisie, as in other responses, a solution was always found for the "tail of
Robespierre" as for the other forces that supposedly threatened the Republic's future. And in the years following Thermidor, such solutions usually
involved quashing the incipient radicalism of the people.

The fear-inspiring specter of a snaky immortal marked the visual arts
as well. Consider the allegorical painting of a "descent into Hell" (fig. 26),
where Robespierre and his confederates are depicted as serpents slither-
ing down a barren mountain. The unhappy nation, symbolized as a flag-
bedecked carriage/house with most of its riders jammed onto the third floor,
is pursued by the snakes while heading into Hell. Snake imagery winds
through the trompe l'oeil mourning pieces such as the *Le Saule pleureur*
(fig. 19) and *L'Urne mystérieuse* (fig. 20) too. Note the sly presence hissing in the foreground of both prints and the deliberate way that the ser-
pent is held at bay by the sorrowful ladies shadowed by royal silhouettes. A

conflation of the tyrant's head with the Medusa myth of eternal ignominy marks the frontispiece of Robespierre's earliest biography, L. Duperron's *Vie secrette, politique, et curieuse de M. J. Maximilien Robespierre* (fig. 27). The open eyes and snaky-looking gore dripping from this disembodied head endow it with a mythic air that is underlined by the epigraph on the title page: "There exist crimes that a wrathful heaven never forgives." It is a vengeful god who speaks these words to Oedipus; it is a vengeful people who repeat them to the specter of Robespierre.[105]

Like Duperron's frontispiece, the first texts to exploit the "crimes of Robespierre" genre exemplify what one might call the Gothic Robespierre: nowhere is the man depicted in a more brutally sensationalized fashion. From cannibalism, torture, and intimidation to petty criminality, this Robespierre incarnates the awful. The archvillain Hannibal Lecter, who stitched together a shirt from the skin of his victims in the grisly horror film *Silence of the Lambs* (1991; directed by Jonathan Demme), has nothing on the Robespierre of Abbé Proyart's *La Vie et les crimes de Robespierre* (1795). The latter merely puts an ironically utilitarian spin on the gore by ordering that the guillotine's victims be skinned and their hides reused as shoe leather, thus "making the dead useful to the living."[106] Since Paris workshops provided shoes for the army, Proyart speculates that some republican soldiers likely tread on the skin of their own dead parents! Stressing Robespierre's livid hue, sunken eyes, and mocking smile, Proyart declares this physique "revealed all the peevishness of a bilious nature" (67). Moreover, he insinuates that the man's powers were somehow inscrutable, thereby exploiting the fear-mongering potential of the crime narrative to keep his readers on the edge of their seats:

> Since nothing is incredible, in the atrocious genre [*genre atroce*] on the part of Robespierre, a tyrant of whom it is notoriously said that his confederates, on September 2 [1792], drank human blood in glasses, tried to eat the still-beating heart of Princess de Lamballe, and actually did eat the roasted flesh of priests and the Countess of Pérignan, on place-Dauphine, we will relay a fact that we cannot guarantee like the others, given the silence of discretion or uncertainty that the Convention government has wrapped around the affair. (279)

This description of the *genre atroce* captures its perverse appeal: through graphic rendition of physical and mental suffering, one relives the political anxieties and terrifying circumstances in which they were witnessed. Crucial is the role played by Robespierre: whether portrayed as a villain of

27. "I deceived the French and the divinity. . . . I am dying on the scaffold and I've earned it well." (J'ai joui les Français et la divinité. . . . Je meurs sur l'échafaud, je l'ai bien mérité.) Frontispiece of L. Duperron, *Vie secrette, politique, et curieuse de M. J. Maximilien Robespierre* (An 2; ca. 1794). Bibliothèque nationale de France, Paris.

Greco-Roman myth, melodrama, or the fantastic, the Artesian deputy choreographs the killing and thus stars in a thrilling, politically legible tale of crime, punishment, and vengeance. As with the other sensational materials noted above, however, Proyart's influence was short-lived. Translated into German, English, and Italian shortly after publication in 1795, Proyart's biography was reprinted only once, in Arras (1850). It fell to more serious biographers to try and fix the man's relation to the history of the Republic.

Vestiges of the *genre atroce* are necessarily present to some degree in every Robespierre biography—except Ernest Hamel's perhaps, and the apologists of the Third Republic discussed below—and in every account of 1793–94. Two of the most reputable chroniclers of the 1790s are not exempt, yet their works give evidence of an effort to desensationalize the man's life and to develop the beginnings of a dispassionate, psychological approach to the criminal mind. In *Histoire de la conjuration de Maximilien Robespierre* (History of the conspiracy of Maximilien Robespierre; 1795) by Galart de Montjoie and in *Crimes de Robespierre* (1797; slightly revised and republished the same year as *Précis historique de la vie, des crimes, et du supplice de Robespierre*) by Nicolas LeMoyne Desessarts, one finds a more balanced character study and a genealogy harkening back to the deputy's childhood in Arras. Both of these accounts admit that Robespierre was not always as mean-spirited as he seemed to become in 1794, and that a strange metamorphosis must have overtaken him in winter 1792–93. The trick was explaining how that change came about so that all charges could still be pinned on him.

Desessarts (1744–1810) was a lawyer and man of letters who claims to have known Robespierre fairly well, at least early in his career. By 1797 Desessarts was author of a number of publications, including the monumental *Les Causes célèbres*, a 196-volume periodical that was published from 1773 until 1790, and *Procès fameux* (Famous trials; 1786–98), both of which were praised for eschewing sensationalist treatment in favor of a psychological approach to trial reportage.[107] The author's reputation as an impartial chronicler of judicial facts thus preceded him, although it seems hard to jibe with the rather frantic tone of his *Crimes de Robespierre*. A fundamental schizophrenia runs through Desessarts's rendition, and I think it is related to the turnabout noted earlier (chap. 3) in our discussion of Robespierre's *Éloge de Gresset* of 1785. The man was simply impossible to pin down: first a nervous nobody, then a coldly calculating evil genius—he seems to be two different men depending on when one observes him. The Robespierre of 1789–91 visibly suffered his public role; as the author notes, "At the Constituent Assembly, Robespierre was a timid deputy who took the floor with

28. *Maximilien Robespierre*, from *Collection complète des tableaux historiques de la Révolution française composée de cent treize numéros en trois volumes*, vol. 3 (An 13; 1804). Reproduced from the original held by the Department of Special Collections of the Hesburgh Libraries of the University of Notre Dame.

trepidation, who spoke in broken sentences that revealed his ignorance and bad taste, and who almost always stepped down from the bar amid laughs elicited by his own stupidity [*idiotisme*]." Even partisans smiled slyly at his humiliation. His voice is described as "shrill and disagreeable," his regard "unsure," and his countenance "convulsive." The portraits of Robespierre that survive to our day, such as in the *Collection complète des tableaux historiques de la Révolution française* (fig. 28), do not capture these unpleasant features; he looks well-dressed in the aristocratic fashion and poised if rather severe. It must have been in his speech and movements that Robespierre elicited this weird repugnance. Or perhaps it was a figment of the observers' imagination, made legend by repetition.[108]

Over time it seems that the young deputy acquired new powers. Desessarts provides quotations from the speeches and writings of people such as Marat, Hébert, Danton, and especially Louvet, in which he shows them attacking Robespierre for his cold-hearted support of the September massacres, among other misdeeds. But the wily villain parries the blows with ease, as when refuting Louvet's charge of dictatorial ambitions in 1792, he intones, "if my death can soothe the terrible divisions between political parties, dash the hopes of our enemies, and cement our nation's happiness, I am ready to surrender myself and will put my head beneath the blade."[109] As readers would have known, this tactic of setting virtue against calumny served Robespierre well; he outlived most of his detractors. Although the author tries to lay all the blame for the repression on Robespierre, his ascent to power in February 1793 implicitly suggests the impact on the man of larger political trends, namely the radicalization of the Revolution in response to the declaration of war against Great Britain, the Dutch Republic, and Spain (February–March 1793) and the government's increasingly fraught pursuit of political enemies among its own populace (as in the Federalist uprising in Marseilles in April 1793). It also implies, *pace* Duperron and *L'Ombre de Robespierre*, that Robespierre was not alone in clamping down on national security, and that it was the common people and sansculottes who, in their hero worship, pushed him and the committees to take overly aggressive action against hoarders and other enemies of the Republic. Apropos, *Les Crimes de Robespierre* includes numerous examples of the praise that Robespierre received in letters from all around France, where he was idolized as a model Spartan, an Athenian, or a latter-day Messiah. Some even baptized their children with his name. The people's idolatry was not unrelated to the nation's undoing.[110]

Les Crimes de Robespierre had a longer-lasting impact on the European literary market than any other biography, judging from publication and translation data, but it was to Galart de Montjoie that readers of the *Journal de Paris* were forcefully directed.[111] Announced in a grandiloquent book review in October 1795, *Histoire de la conjuration de Maximilien Robespierre* is cited as *the* answer to readers' lingering questions about the recent past: Galart de Montjoie's argument leaves "not a shadow of a doubt"; moreover, "his book is perfectly written."[112] What distinguishes the two is the effort by the latter to pinpoint the psychological roots of Robespierre's ambitions; as his translator commented, "In developing the true character and aim of Robespierre and his adherents, the author appears to have displayed much knowledge of the human heart."[113] Galart de Montjoie's portrait of the young Robespierre is bland; he notes merely that the boy "had not to blush for his birth" and that he was "peaceable," manifesting "no spark of strong passion" (8, 11). In fact, his instructors saw no indication that young Robespierre "would not remain in the multitude of obscure men" (11). But brilliant academic results led him to dream of a better life, and after a couple

of public humiliations dashed such hopes and wounded his pride, he grew
bitter and vindictive. A heavy dose of Roman history imbibed at college
combined with a natural vehemence and lack of social graces predisposed
Robespierre to join the extreme left wing of the assembly. His awkwardness
remained a liability; according to Galart de Montjoie, he had "few means to
make himself followed even by the rabble" (55).

External signs pointed to an unbalanced psyche within the man, according to this portraitist, whose rendition lived on for years: "He had in his
hands, shoulders, neck, and eyes a convulsive motion. His physiognomy,
his look was without expression. He carried on his livid countenance, on
his brow, which he often wrinkled, the traces of a choleric disposition. His
manners were brutal, his gait at once abrupt and heavy. The harsh inflec-
tions of his voice struck the ear disagreeably" (55).[114] Judging from Robespierre's pallor at morn, Galart de Montjoie speculates that "his sleep was
disturbed, painful, and tormented by frightful images. Those, at least, who
surprised him rising from his bed, declared that his eyes were very dull, his
lips much discolored, his face sodden, his manner reserved, and his look
more gloomy than in the course of the day" (232).[115] If this dichotomous portrait of an anxious and withdrawn man by day and a gloomy, tortured man
by night sounds familiar, it may be because later authors picked up on it to
evoke the physical traces left by evils lurking within the psyche, as seen, for
example, in *The Picture of Dorian Gray* (1890) and *The Strange Case of Dr.
Jekyll and Mr. Hyde* (1886).[116]

Like those invented villains, Robespierre was apparently a loner. In
what one might read as sociopathic tendencies today, he is said to have "not
a single friend," being "mistrustful to excess." His cold heart was notorious:
when informed that some state prisoners were perishing before they could
even attend their trial, he allegedly retorted, "Very well, why do such people
need to live?"[117] In short, he was "a nasty fellow, whom no one would have
sought, but all would have avoided" (231–32). Nevertheless, the conundrum
exists that he apparently managed to dominate an entire country, and Galart
de Montjoie, like others, seems stymied by that. He cites Robespierre's vanity, oversize ambition, and obstinate perseverance to explain how he became elected, respected, and eventually a leader among the Jacobins and the
Convention government. He admits that the man's hypocrisy—symbolized
by his habit of wearing spectacles à la Ben Franklin despite having perfect
vision—served him well (60–61). But when confronted with the cruelties of
the nation-wide repression and its *genre atroce*, he comes up short. Explanations rotate between the traditional religious one ("Some demon, hostile

to the human race, was possessed of his soul"; 166) and the more modern, pseudoscientific invocation of situational madness ("vanity had absolutely deranged his mind"; 166).

A certain sadistic satisfaction can be detected at the end of these books when readers are reminded that the scourge was after all a mere mortal like the rest of us. Both biographers detail Robespierre's last hours when he lay bleeding on the table of the Committee of Public Safety, mocked and spit upon by spectators. Legend has it that while riding in the tumbrel to his death, a woman climbed up the side and shouted a forceful indictment of his crimes right in his face, condemning him in the name of all the wives and mothers. "These painful words must have penetrated into his soul," comments Desessarts approvingly; "the moral torture may have been too weak to expiate his enormous crimes, but it was satisfying for sensitive souls to know that the monster suffered, and that she helped heighten the horrors of his demise."[118] Robespierre's screaming pain on the scaffold when the executioner ripped off the bandage and, with it, his lower jaw is the ultimate stroke in this litany of punishment. Divine justice comes to mind. Lest his final humiliation be unclear to readers, we should remember that Robespierre's disembodied head was visually represented (fig. 27) in 1794 as a mirror image of Villeneuve's ghastly death mask of Louis XVI (fig. 18), which was printed in 1793 over some menacing words by Robespierre himself. Here the modern Catilina is framed by instruments of killing—a revolver, a guillotine blade, and icons of the Terror—and admits, "I deceived the French and the divinity. . . . I am dying on the scaffold, and I've earned it well."

This fictional gallows speech could have been overheard only by the executioner on the scaffold, and it could be interpreted as lending a note of pity to the grotesque. The motif of confessions passed along by the hangman reemerged a generation later in Victor Hugo's stunning diary of a prisoner on death row (*Dernier jour d'un condamné*; 1829) and Honoré de Balzac's memoirs of Sanson the executioner (1830) to make a penetrating criticism of capital punishment even for the most deserving. The decapitated head that relives his death or relays secrets from beyond the grave blossomed into the curiously fertile *genre frénétique* of the 1830s as well, when authors such as Charles Nodier and Alexandre Dumas married their gifts for the supernatural with a similar politics.[119] In this instance, however, the scene is more reminiscent of a mythical injunction—with a modern-day Perseus warning all those who still regret the tyrant—or a Sadean torture exhibit such as those on display in the *120 Journées de Sodom* (1785), played out in excruciating detail to give readers a vicarious sense of power over the dead.[120] The man's life ends with no political epiphany or spiritual reckoning but rather with a sickening thud, as his mangled skull lands in the blood-soaked basket. The villain remains as inexplicable in death as he was in life.

Modern Biographies

Sympathetic details of Robespierre's suffering as scapegoat for the Terror are minor notes in the biographies published in the 1790s–1820s; it would not be until after the Bourbon restoration was forcefully ended and Robespierre became a hero of the Socialists that this theme developed into a full-fledged counterdefense. When Socialist Albert Laponneraye edited the memoirs of Robespierre's sister Charlotte and then published a collection of famous speeches, he initiated scholarship on what David Jordan has called "the ideologue, the man whose deeds were verbal, whose ideas explained and enflamed."[121] Ernest Hamel continued in that vein in the 1860s, scrutinizing all his speeches and writings and the articles about him in the *Moniteur* to produce what he announced was the first positivist history of the fallen of Thermidor. According to Hamel, the facts provide overwhelming evidence of the man's unerring devotion to the people with the one exception of the law of 22 prairial. Hamel argues that Robespierre was scapegoated in July 1794 by colleagues seeking to save their own skins, who falsified public records and commissioned the kinds of materials discussed above to protect their fragile standing among the French people. He points to the body count post-Thermidor to prove his point, comparing the number of known Jacobins who survived and served under the Directory and successive governments (i.e., none) with their many adversaries who switched politics with every new regime. The reader of Hamel's *Histoire de Robespierre* is left with a portrait of a dedicated public servant who remained just as firm in his loyalty to the "real people" (*le vrai peuple*) during his short-lived political career as the "real people" remained loyal to him even after death. The pinnacle of his argument lies in the words of a peasant woman who, upon hearing the news of Robespierre's death, was so shocked and distraught that she dropped the child she was holding and, lifting her hands and eyes to heaven, cried out in her dialect, "Oh! The happiness of the poor people is finished. They killed him that we loved so much" (O qu'os nes finit pol bounheur des paouré pople. On a tuat o quel que l'aimabo tant).[122]

French scholars writing on Robespierre in the 1920s–1950s seconded Hamel's opinions and sought other scapegoats to replace Robespierre in the public eye. Led by Albert Mathiez, Georges Lefebvre, and the Société des études Robespierristes, this school of thought casts blame mainly on Robespierre's friend-become-rival Deputy Georges-Jacques Danton, whom they portray as a self-serving turncoat and traitor to the Jacobin cause. Mathiez erects the legend of Robespierre as "ideological strategist" who formed an alliance with the common people to force France into social revolution; Mathiez's pupil Marc Bouloiseau embroidered on this portrait to depict an "expiatory victim" beloved by the humble. In an interesting combination of left-wing partisanship and his own experience living in occupied France, where he was devastated by his brother's execution by the Nazis for involvement with the underground, Lefebvre cast Robespierre as the "incorruptible head of the revolutionary Resistance."[123] This group of Marxist intellectuals also produced important scholarship on the Thermidorian period more broadly defined and reignited interest in the age-old motif of the scapegoat, a figure whose contemporary significance was illuminated by René Girard. Whether their sympathy for Robespierre was due to archival discoveries, as they claimed, or to their single-minded devotion to Socialist dogma, as critics have charged more recently, this flurry of biographies featuring Robespierre-the-unhappy-statesman has been overshadowed by a less overtly partisan revisionist historiography in more recent years.

Psychological methods guided most biographies of the late twentieth century. Paternal abandonment holds the key to Robespierre's strange destiny, according to Max Gallo (1968). Based on evidence of Robespierre Sr.'s multiple failings—bankruptcy and paternal irresponsibility chief among them—Gallo speculates that at age six the lad was pushed to assume control over his three younger siblings, tried to give them the father figure they needed, and from this early trauma developed an inflexible vision of duty: "Maximilien must have felt this wound, this original and crushing shame, and bore within him the guilt for a father whose very memory he wanted to rub out, and whom he had to renounce in adopting a radically opposed attitude." Others blame the man's shortcomings on his sense of class inferiority or the pain of maternal neglect. John Hardman (1999) sees in Robespierre's humble beginnings the source of an insecurity about climbing the social ladder. The fanatical sense of propriety and devotion to the state that he exhibited in 1793–94 was his way of repaying the debt of gratitude; he "came to believe that those to whom the Revolution had given most must give back most." Patrice Gueniffey (2000) argues that Robespierre's tearful speeches give him away: they prove that he did not see himself as part of a collective whole but rather sought the special superiority that comes from being *the* representative of the people or *the* Martyr of the Nation. This vainglorious striving for incorruptibility is what made him a terrorist, Gueniffey concludes. In insisting on his own purity and singularity, the man refused to admit the basic principles of democracy as a mechanism that allows unity to emerge from a consensus of the group. Just like other dictators of more recent history, Robespierre made speeches to the people that were relevant only in that they aimed to save him from reprisal. And like his notorious successors Mao, Hitler, and Stalin, he too failed. David Jordan (1985) also notes Robespierre's resemblance to later revolutionaries of ill repute, but instead of labeling the man's unbudging resistance to ideology a hypocrisy, he signals its unique value. For Jordan, Robespierre is "the first to attempt to describe the unconditional giving of self to the revolution"; he is the consummate, sincerely engaged political actor, the prototypical revolutionary who believed his own moral integrity would ensure the success of the movement.[124]

Others take a more tender approach to the Incorruptible's psychology. Jean Artarit (2003) delves into the man's infancy and speculates that his mother's embarrassment over being pregnant with Maximilien at the time of her marriage to his father and her fears of being abandoned by this less-than-exemplary husband soured the relation between mother and son. Given that his mother died shortly after giving birth to a fourth child, it is plausible that the boy held his father responsible for her death and sought to act as if he never existed. "That is the secret motor behind his acts," writes Artarit; from this willful forgetting derives "his obsession with his own image, and his desperate narcissism." Robespierre's latest biography, Ruth Scurr's *Fatal Purity* (2006) adopts a more light-handed psychologism that tends to explain by recourse to common sense rather than Freudian theory. "It is reasonable to assume," Scurr comments, "that Robespierre grew up with a vague but persistent sense of familial shame."[125] It also appears reasonable that, as a lawyer in Arras, Robespierre would adopt a mind-set like that of his hero Rousseau: he "identified with the victims of injustice—those misunderstood, isolated, denied or despised" (26); and "he was excited by the idea of intervening in the lives of criminals and sick people—making a difference for the better" (39). In an updated gloss on the sensational physical portraits provided by earlier witnesses, Scurr notes a servant's claim that "every night he bathed his pillow in blood" and explains: "Perhaps Robespierre had nosebleeds (people with high blood pressure and fiery tempers often do). These certainly would have left him anemic and contributed to the unusual pallor of his skin that many contemporaries noted" (112). No physical or psychological mechanisms can explain the rapid changes in the man's attitude with the coming of the Revolution, however, and Scurr admits that in 1789, "there was already something unnervingly vehement" about Robespierre's principles (112). That these traits—unnatural pallor, a

strangely vehement devotion to study, and antisocial tendencies—seem familiar should come as no surprise: any number of modern criminals (real
and imagined) share them.

Of course, readers of the 1790s lacked the tools of modern-day criminol-
ogy and the psychology of deviance. They had to invent their own methods.
But where Proyart merely titillated readers with a horror show, Desessarts and Galart de Montjoie claimed to draw lessons from Robespierre's
political crimes to prevent their recurrence in the future. *Les Crimes de
Robespierre* and *Histoire de la conjuration de Maximilien Robespierre* may
strike modern readers more like crime thrillers than careful life-writing, but
they were not interpreted that way by contemporaries. Reviewers believed
that Galart de Montjoie's book in particular was psychologically useful and
promoted it as such. Looking at how the criminal mind was understood in
other popular literature allows us to bridge this conceptual leap, at least
in part. In the nineteenth century, an appreciation of mankind's complex
psychology and an effort to probe the links between criminality and socioeconomic stress became increasingly important in both politically ori-
ented fiction that promoted social reforms or criticized social problems and
an aesthetically decadent movement whose imagined scenarios tested the
power of mind over matter.

THE IMMORTALITY OF ROBESPIERRE:
TWO NOVELS AND A SPECTACLE

Novels featuring a character named or symbolizing Robespierre prove no
better at explaining this enigmatic man, but they do build on his inspiration
in more psychologically complex ways than we have seen in the genres of
brochure, early biography, and popular art. Some novelists abstracted from
the Terror's cold-hearted justice an emotional energy, such as infuses the
villain Falkland of Godwin's *Caleb Williams*, the diabolical policeman Javert in *Les Misérables*, and other tragedies of ambition run amok. Others
elaborated upon his rumored misdeeds with "secret histories" of the Terror. All were anchored in political currents of their own day, however, and
as time passed the Convention's concern to protect the French Republic
from its enemies and the victims' demand for a memorial to the Terror
started to feel less urgent, even quaint. In the analyses that follow, I shuttle
between interpretation of each work's impact at the time of its publication
and broader-ranging consideration of its significance for the literary afterlife
of the Revolution.

The Pathology of Guilt: Godwin's *Caleb Williams* (1794)

Written during 1793–94 by a prominent British man of letters and Jacobin sympathizer, *The Adventures of Caleb Williams, or Things as They
Are* (1794) is one of the first novels to build an entire plot around the psychopathology of guilt, remorse, and terror. Like the British press, which
warmly embraced it in 1794, French reviewers in the *Journal de Paris* and
the *Moniteur* were enthralled with this book when the translation appeared
in 1796; both praised its larger-than-life dimensions and the startling crimes
it portrays: "Everything is big, everything is terrible in this novel" (Tout est
grand, tout est terrible dans ce roman), enthused one reviewer.[126] The plot
revolves around a young secretary (Caleb Williams) and his suspicion that
his employer, the prominent landowner Ferdinando Falkland, murdered one
of his neighbors some years previously. More precisely, it revolves around
Williams's insatiable curiosity about Falkland's past and his will to force a
reckoning. Just as determined as the servant, however, is the master, who
devises an elaborate network of connections in the underworld and the judiciary to keep the young man under surveillance, imprisoned, or otherwise
powerless against him.

William Godwin does not explicitly pass judgment on Robespierre in
the novel, in which the phrase "Terror was the order of the day" apparently refers to the English treason trials rather than the Jacobin repression.[127] Indeed, in his *Enquiry concerning Political Justice* (1793), Godwin
boldly defended a Robespierrian kind of public morality by demanding that
the people's dedication to the well-being of the nation should prevail over
private concerns. In an oft-cited passage, he argued that if a fire broke out
and only one person could be saved, either Archbishop Fénelon or his valet,
it should be Fénelon. This is because the life of the author of the "immortal
Telemachus" (1699), a book that benefited "thousands who have been cured
by the perusal of that work, of some error, vice, and consequent unhappiness," is "really preferable" to the life of his valet.[128] Even if the valet was
one's brother, father, or benefactor, Godwin claimed that one should let
him die. (Unsurprisingly, the author was roundly attacked for this and other
such inflammatory ideas from *Political Justice* in postrevolutionary Britain.)[129] Williams's portrayal of the ravages wrought by a guilty conscience in
Caleb Williams serves the philosophy of *Political Justice* and critiques the
double standard of private versus public virtue. But it also shows that virtue
can be taken to undue extremes. And this, I think, is why it was embraced
by French readers of the Thermidorian period.

In their descriptions of the villain Falkland's maniacal defense of his reputation, the French reviews made a striking parallel to Robespierre and the moral inflexibility that sustained the Reign of Terror. They describe *Caleb Williams* as a compelling read because it portrays a passion as terrible as love, one that led a man "to a degree of exaltation such that he went from the greatest virtues to the vilest crimes; in whose thrall he became capable of conceiving and executing the most awful excesses; where all other considerations fell beneath the object of his passion; where he would immolate human victims to his idol."[130] These terms echo Desessarts's description of Robespierre's idée fixe: "When one sees men in all countries and ages seduced by ambition, who aspire with all their might to achieve arbitrary power and spare no crime to obtain it . . . one is baffled by the charms that tyranny holds for them, and what pleasures they find in this pursuit, given the crimes that one must necessarily commit to succeed."[131] Also of interest are Godwin's allusions to his villain's "principles of inflexible integrity" and his mode of living, which is described as being "in the utmost degree recluse and solitary." Like the austere Robespierre, "he had no inclination to scenes of revelry and mirth" and "appeared a total stranger to every thing which usually bears the appellation of pleasure" (6–7). The parallels are patent.

A certain schizophrenia plagues Godwin's villain. Although initially benevolent, he occasionally falls prey to a mysterious nervousness: "Sometimes he was hasty, peevish, and tyrannical . . . he would strike his forehead, his brows become knit, his features distorted, and his teeth ground one against the other. When he felt the approach of these symptoms, he would suddenly rise, and leaving the occupation, whatever it was, in which he was engaged, hasten into a solitude upon which no person dared to intrude" (6–7). When Falkland discovers Williams snooping in his secret documents, this situation only grows worse; he eventually launches an obsessive campaign against his former protégé. But things did not need to go so awry. As Williams comments in despair after suffering months of unremitting persecution: "his own interest required that he should purchase my kindness; but he preferred to govern me by terror, and watch me with unceasing anxiety" (167). Like Robespierre toward the end of his life, Falkland seems aware that this infernal pas de deux would end badly for one or the other, but he is at a loss to stop its unfolding. In a rare moment of candor, he admits the paradox: "I began life with the best intentions and the most fervid philanthropy; and here I am—miserable—miserable beyond expression or endurance" (136).

Falkland devolves into a walking corpse, "sunk and debilitated," by the

end of *Caleb Williams*. In the trial scene when he hears the bruising indictment against him, Falkland accepts his guilt and tells the magistrate: "I am
prepared to suffer all the vengeance of the law. You cannot inflict on me
more than I deserve. You cannot hate me more than I hate myself. I am the
most execrable of all villains" (376). After throwing himself into the arms of
his stunned accuser, the felon dies three days later. But his specter lives on
in visions that plague the hero and make his life a hell. Guilt, persecution,
and remorse turn out to be indelibly bound to each other: no one wins in the
race to expose the truth. Godwin thus ultimately dismisses reputation, like
Robespierrian virtue, as a false and fantastic honor that is woefully unfit for
the morally complex modern world.

A Puzzling Legacy

The fall of the real Incorruptible is just as puzzling as this fictional demise. In his last speech to the Convention, Robespierre seemed to sense
that the tide was turning against him. Yet instead of admitting that he may
have been at fault or proposing a new course for governance, he resorted to
the same wooden, declamatory style that had sustained the repression for
months and warned of nameless enemies lurking in their midst. He pegged
his hopes on the listeners' pity, exclaiming, "Who am I that I should be accused? A slave of liberty, a living martyr of the Republic. . . . If you take
away my [good] conscience, I am the most unfortunate of citizens; I do not
even have any rights."[132] Robespierre's self-portrait as a law-abiding citizen
caught in the snares of factional strife is hard to square with the other information that was circulating, including his rumored condemnation of his
own sister Charlotte. Perhaps that is why his proxy comes in for such rough
treatment in fiction: readers wanted to see him punished.

As one would expect, Robespierre appears in numerous novels published
during the regimes of the Directory (1795–99) and the Consulate (1799–
1804) following Thermidor. He is a shadowy presence forcing others into
peril in Pigault-Lebrun's burlesque *L'Enfant du carnaval* (1796), and he mas-
terminds the campaign of repression enacted by Sénar in Rosny's *Les Infortunes de Mr. de La Galetierre*. The events of 8–10 thermidor provide the
dramatic dénouement to many a melodrama of émigré suffering, such as
Bruno's *Lioncel, ou L'Émigré* (1800) and LeBastier's *Dorbeuil et Céliane de
Valran: Leurs Amours et leurs malheurs pendant la tyrannie de Robespierre*
(1795).[133] So-called secret histories of the Terror, such as Roussel's *Histoire
secrète du Tribunal révolutionnaire* (written 1800; published 1815), depict
Robespierre and his colleagues as a type that would dominate in certain

nineteenth-century fictional works, that is, the misanthropist whose low opinion of mankind justifies any number of crimes.

There are more forgiving approaches to his career as well. The dialogue between Catherine de Médicis and Robespierre in Balzac's study of 1828 (*Sur Catherine de Médicis*) is arresting because it expiates their faults by insisting on the legitimacy of their intentions—a legitimacy that can be perceived only by taking a long-term perspective on events. In a dream sequence set in 1786, the Renaissance queen appears to the young man and explains how she tried to quell the Protestant opposition to the Valois throne before it got out of hand, that is, through what is now known as the Saint Bartholomew's Day massacre. He is startled when she announces that he too will be implicated in a struggle over the country's future, and that he too will be martyred for his efforts.[134] Both leaders are doomed, as prophets of unpopular causes in an unforgiving world.

In countless tales from the nineteenth century up to the present, Robespierre is found at meetings of the Committee of Public Safety, the tribunal, and other sites of awful memory. The best stories aim at capturing the enigma instead of reducing him to a morality tale run amuck. Like the trompe l'oeil painting in Pierre Michon's novel *Les Onze* (The eleven; 2009), his eyes seem to follow the reader, now with a spiteful impatience for human frailty, then with the cool calm of the just.[135] But if we had to pick one example of Robespierre legendry to exemplify the instability of the late 1790s, it would have to be *Irma, ou L'Orpheline malheureuse; Histoire indienne*, published in Year 8 (Irma, or the Unfortunate orphan: An Indian story; 1799–1800) by Élisabeth Guénard ("la C.ᵉ G.ᵈ" on the book's title page; otherwise known as baronne Brossin de Méré).

Robespierre the Graveyard Ghoul: Guénard's *Irma* (1799–1800)

The choice of *Irma* as a "must read" of Robespierrian myth may come as a surprise because Guénard's novel is little known today and the few critical opinions published on it disagree somewhat. On the one hand, some depict *Irma* rather dismissively as a sentimental novel in the Oriental mode like others of its ilk. On the other hand, one critic applauds Guénard's courage in defending the monarchy through the story of the Bourbon princess Irma just months after Napoleon carried off his November 1799 coup d'etat. Indeed, some copies of the novel were seized along with *Le Cimetière de la Madeleine* by the Bordeaux police in prairial Year 9 (June 1801), cited as being "as opposed to the government" as Regnault-Warin's work.[136] But by that time the novel was already heading into its third edition, and the second edition had been openly advertised for sale (at the author's home) in the *Journal de Paris* (floréal Year 8; April 1800). This was shortly after the Consulate launched a rigorous police campaign against publishers of monarchist, anarchist, or other politically suspect materials. How are we to explain this sequence of events?

The literary and political climate in which *Irma* was first published requires a more nuanced appreciation. It is true that the Consulate government breathed new life into the policing of art and culture after the coup d'etat of 18 brumaire. A section entitled Ministère de la police générale shows up in the *Journal de Paris* on 21 brumaire Year 8 and soon becomes a standard fixture. Based on the articles published there in Years 8 and 9, the police were launching a serious effort to warn citizens about the dangers of seditious speech and writing and did crack down as promised on publishers, writers, and sellers of materials that could "compromise the public order," as in the case of *Le Cimetière de la Madeleine*. Plots to restore the Bourbon pretender to the throne of France, particularly in Brittany and Normandy with the help of the English, continued to be a source of concern. Royalist conspirators such as a certain widow Mercier (executed in June 1800) were hotly pursued: such charges were taken very seriously. But one must not overestimate the government's fears of literature; these measures were primarily aimed at journalism and the political press. As explained in chapter 3, Regnault-Warin's persecution was to a certain extent a kind of media event that he brought on himself to sell books. He deliberately—and successfully—marketed his novel as a politically dangerous commodity by weaving duplicitous asides about the new government right into the plot and speaking explicitly to readers about his problems with the Parisian police. It was not illegal to speak about the monarchy, however, or to poke fun at republicans, provided one did so in a way that appeared innocuous. Moreover, some claimed that the events of 1789–94 were already ancient history.[137]

Like Regnault-Warin, Guénard exaggerated the illicit nature of her work to draw readers in. The tenth edition (1816) includes a preface explaining how she tore the story of *Irma* away from the revolutionary genius that governed "India" in those days and delivered the manuscript to the printer "in the shade of mystery and with the urgency of fear."[138] But she does not mention that so-called secret histories of the Bourbons and their friends were meanwhile generating a cottage industry in French-language publishing circles. In 1796 a little book called *Les Adieux de Marie-Thérèse-Charlotte de Bourbon* appeared (by Michaud), containing within it the story of the two royal children Souli (anagram for the dauphin Louis) and Erima (anagram for Marie). In summer 1800 a certain L. C. R. published *Correspondance de Louis-Philippe-Joseph d'Orléans* to critical acclaim, followed a year later by Guénard's edited memoirs of the Princess de Lamballe, favorite lady-in-waiting of Queen Marie-Antoinette, which was also praised by the *Journal de Paris*.[139] *Irma* was Guénard's biggest seller and most long-lasting hit. She revised it several times and added four volumes to the original two so that the novel eventually achieved some one thousand pages (in the tiny sextodecimo format of the tenth edition, 1816), before culminating in a three-volume sequel, *Le Triomphe d'une auguste princesse* (1825). This was hardly a clandestine affair.

The most potent rendition of the Robespierre legend emerges in the first edition of *Irma*, published in volatile Year 8, and it is found about three-quarters through the story after Irma has lost all her family members and is finally alone in prison. The narrative reads like an epistolary novel à la Madame de Graffigny's *Lettres d'une Péruvienne* (1747). Thrust into a world that she does not understand, the heroine pines for her distant beloved (her cousin, the duc d'Angoulême). She describes being confined in a horrible fortress when, suddenly and inexplicably, her fortune improves. The guard's wife offers her a bath and a light repast and nurses her back to health. One day, she dresses Irma with particular care, sets two places at her table, and puts flowers around the room but never explains why. The suspense mounts as Irma hears the heavy bars being pushed back down below, and suddenly before our eyes is a pale, smallish, and well-dressed man whose forehead is prematurely wrinkled "not from age but from fury" and who suffers from nervous tics that pull his arms and shoulders into spastic shrugs.[140] "But nothing disturbed me as disagreeably as his voice," Irma recalls; "it was shrill; he seemed to scream instead of to speak." After reminding her of the good tidings he brings, he tries to get the frightened young woman to sit and eat with him. "You are wrong to be afraid of me; I wish you no harm," he coaxes. Avoiding her repeated calls of "who are you?" he offers to let her brother out of prison if only she will give him her hand in marriage. When that offer proves ineffective, he departs with this chilling reminder: "I will return in several days; think about what I told you, and prepare yourself to submit blindly to my will. Your fate and that of your brother depend upon it" (2:94).

The preparations for their second meeting are even more elaborate. "You must be very pretty today; my master is coming. . . . Do not play the proud girl like last time," warns the servant, as she weaves pearls into the girl's hair; "there is nothing so kindly and good as my master, but if you make him angry he will wreak vengeance, not only on you but also on your brother" (2:96–97). Observing the elegant feast laid out in her room, Irma makes an uncharacteristically plebeian comment: she compares this meal to the royal larder, sighing, "poor people . . . you will always be victim of those who govern you" (2:99). Although she allows him to feed her dainty delicacies, when the clumsy suitor makes a cavalier comparison between her and the loose women he usually frequents, she retreats in repugnance. Finally, he divulges his name—Ximacelem (anagram for Maximilien)—in a litany of self-aggrandizing bravado. When she still does not relent, he orders her and her brother into solitary confinement, in a gesture reminiscent of other anecdotes of Robespierre the thwarted suitor.[141]

Irma then languishes in the dark for three months until one evening Ximacelem reappears, jubilant about the great event planned for the morn, when he will become "sovereign pontiff" of the kingdom and proclaim the existence of a God of his own devising (2:113). After his eloquence wins over the people, he explains, she will take his hand on the stage, and they will join their clans to rule the Indians. She is once again dressed in sumptuous robes and adorned with fine gems but silently agonizes over the impossible choice: either she must murder this regicide monster or commit suicide by his side. But what about her brother? Just as suddenly as the festivities were announced, however, the plans are called off, her fancy garb is taken away, and she is left alone. It is only later, she writes, that she learned what happened: Ximacelem's speech was too long and the Indians got bored. For the first time in months, complaints were spoken and calls for divine justice were heard. The marriage was postponed. Many more months pass until one day after hearing sounds of fighting and angry voices, her solitude is broken by a servant who announces the end of Ximacelem's reign.

True, depicting Robespierre as the would-be suitor of the Bourbon princess is unoriginal; it merely embroiders upon Barère's accusation from the fateful night of 8 thermidor. Also conventional is the causality running through the marriage plot which explains Robespierre's disgrace as resulting from his arrogance at the Festival of the Supreme Being. (It is inaccurate too. In the first days following the June 8, 1794, event, the deputy enjoyed spectacularly positive reviews.)[142] But the vaguely Oriental fairy-tale atmosphere that Guénard weaves around this courtship is a clever touch in that it magnifies the malignancy of the villain and places the whole story in the realm of the impossible.

The last section of *Irma* changes gears: the political views imparted by a new companion add a wrinkle to the supposed royalism of Guénard's work. In a series of exchanges between Irma and her new lady-in-waiting, she learns that the Terror was but a freakish phenomenon; like a monster in

the natural order, it should never recur. Instead of looking back, Rantchêne
(anagram for Catherine?) dispels Irma's anxieties by evoking a peaceful and
cosmopolitan new nation, bound in friendship and commerce to other nations around the world. "Despite the prejudices of my upbringing, I could
not help but share her enthusiasm!" the heroine muses. "I wished I had not
been born to reign . . . so that I too might perhaps vow, like her, for universal freedom."[143] As the months go by, this friend provides other useful
lessons. On the anniversary of the Bourbons' ascension to the throne, Irma
dresses for a state ceremony only to wait in vain. Noticing her disappointment, Rantchêne explains, "Remember, dear Irma, that we must obey the
laws of our land; they do not prohibit warm feelings of friendship . . . but
it would be a glaring error if [the republicans] celebrated, or even permit-
ted the celebration, of a king's apotheosis. . . . No one is more worthy of
homage than your father; but it is to historians that we must allow honors
to be bestowed; it is not the place of a free people." In reply to this stirring
defense of republicanism, Irma thinks, "I could not help but agree that her
ideas were right."[144]

Significantly, this political commentary extends to more recent regimes
as well. When Irma meets a representative of the new government who announces her imminent departure in a prisoner exchange, she admits that
"there was no rapport between the present administration and the arbitrary
laws of that tyrant" (2:164–65). In the end, it is the monarch of her new
home who thwarts Irma's fondest hope, of bringing Rantchêne with her. As
the servant once again explains to her mistress, "People accuse republicans
of insensitivity," but the icy pride of courtiers is harder to move. "Republicans, in a fervor that may partake of fanaticism, sometimes forgo natural
bonds in the name of the nation, but [royalists] sacrifice everything to self-
interest and absurd prejudices."[145] Irma finally is allowed out of prison and
joins her mother's relatives in a foreign land ("Tybet").

It is strange that Huguette Krief's interpretation of the novel misses this
important political subtext and its meaning for the book. Irma does not
refuse her seducer; she merely benefits from his demise. The royal lineage
does not "triumph necessarily over the terrorist tyranny"; rather, it enters
into a sympathetic dialogue with a more enlightened republicanism before
leaving France at the end.[146] Like William Reddy, Krief seems rather too
hasty to label cultural products of this transitional period with a simple
political moniker, when the realities are more complex.

It is in "Tybet," while wandering around the palace gardens one night,
that Guénard's heroine espies the villain in his afterlife and that *Irma* deals

the most bizarre thrills to the reader. Stumbling upon a cenotaph engraved with her parents' names, Irma suddenly finds her fiancé and falls into his arms. But when they join hands to renew their vows over the king's tomb, the marriage plot stalls yet again. Putting an ironic turn on the vogue for oath-taking that marked the France of the Federation (1789–90), this gesture runs through many Thermidorian fictions. In prison tales and other accounts of suffering under the Montagnards, one finds victims whispering oaths to each other to nourish the flame of freedom while awaiting better days to come.[147] The subject of their oath is no longer the king or the constitution of 1791 but rather the basic ideals of 1789—*liberté, égalité, fraternité*—that were obfuscated by the Terrorist state. (The awful Jacobins of *L'Ombre de Robespierre* as we saw above prompted a terrified bystander to take an oath to the constitution of Year 3.) An oppositional kind of oath-taking punctuates dramatic moments in royalist fiction too, as here, where family ties reemerge with special poignancy. That the gesture was significant to readers can be verified by the evidence of the book's production: the frontispiece of *Irma* celebrates this vow-taking scene with a special verve, since the hidden profile of a furious-looking Robespierre juts out of the folds of Irma's gown (fig. 29)!

But before Irma and her lover have a chance to finish the oath, lightning strikes and breaks the urn, and the heroine is suddenly transported back to the capital city at midnight and into its gloomy catacombs. She is trying to gather up the bones of her father when a ghost comes into view, covered with bloody rags and cut with a deep wound. "What do you want with me?" he asks in an awful voice. "Who has sent you to this terrible place?" His eyes are cruel, as he guards the royal tomb. "In vain you hope to steal away your father's remains," he growls; "since I have been vomited back on earth by a frightened devil [*tatare*] who had no punishment fit for my crimes, I will haunt this lugubrious place, I will devour my victims' bodies!!! Never will they return to dust" (2:203). Watching an awful grimace crease his lips, she realizes (finally!) that she is face-to-face with a spectral Ximacelem. Startled by the thought, Irma awakens, and the novel ends with a promise of a sequel shortly to come.

This invocation of Robespierre in the catacombs, suddenly appearing after pages of prorepublican exegesis and a culminating moment of Bourbon lovemaking, strikes me as a clever tactic to protect the work's exchange value in the volatile political climate that was France around the beginning of the Consulate, when fears were running high of an imminent dictatorship or a Bourbon restoration. The monstrous Incorruptible may be immortal,

Je te Jure par l'ombre Sacrée de ton Père;
Que je n'existerai jamais que pour toi,
Elle répète le même Serment.

29. "I swear to you on the sacred remains of your Father. That I will never exist but for you. She repeats the same vow." (Je te jure par l'ombre sacrée de ton Père. Que je n'existerai jamais que pour toi. Elle répète le même serment.) Frontispiece of Élisabeth Guénard, *Irma, ou Les Malheurs d'une jeune orpheline; Histoire indienne*, vol. 1 (An 8; ca. 1799–1800). Reproduced from the original held by the Department of Special Collections of the Hesburgh Libraries of the University of Notre Dame.

but he exists far from the lofty Pantheon of national memory: his eternity is confined to an underground limbo. By extension, the Jacobins are rendered as powerless to hurt the Bourbon princess's hopes for the future as they are to threaten the new republic and its ambitions. The graveyard ghoul thereby brings closure to the legend of Robespierre's tail. But it leaves the future of the real French state wide open and thus nicely serves the equivocal politics of a transitional moment.

Robespierre in Phantasmagoria

Guénard's image of a spectral Robespierre haunting dark catacombs may not have seemed as incongruous to her readers as it does to us. Why? Three reasons: (1) melodramatic sequences were commonplace in turn-of-the-century drama and fiction; (2) visits to Paris cemeteries and catacombs were rapidly becoming a tourist destination for the intrepid; and (3) images of the ghostly Jacobin were actually a well-known feature of the phantasmagoria shows that enlivened boulevard theaters in Guénard's day. These shows were advertised in the same venues as Guénard's books and appealed to the same kinds of literate, well-heeled audiences.[148] In the memoirs of the premier purveyor of phantasmagoria, E. G. Robertson, we find a description of a spectacle that sounds familiar:

> The sky opened, and lightning struck. . . . the ghosts seemed to come out of a subterranean vault. . . . Sad, severe, silly, gracious, fantastic scenes all mixed in together, until some current event made up the key attraction. "Robespierre," said the *Courrier des spectacles* (4 ventôse Year 8), "comes out of his tomb and wants to get up . . . lightning strikes him and reduces him to dust. . . . Such are the effects of optics, that each person thinks he can touch the objects with his own hand."[149]

Other popular spectacles included an allegory of Napoleon's coup d'etat of 18 brumaire (the Peacemaker offers an olive branch to Minerva, who makes it into a crown and places it on his head), David meeting Goliath, and Macbeth confronting Banquo's ghost. The only attraction banned by the French censors, claims Robertson, was a spectral Louis XVI. In reply to the provocateur (*chouan*) who called for a sighting of the deceased at a show in 1798, Robertson allegedly replied, "I used to have a formula for that . . . but I will probably never find it again, and it will never again be possible to make kings come back to France."[150] Never was the line so fine between politics and popular entertainment.

CODA: HOW LITERATURE ENDED THE TERROR

The years that followed brought new glories and tragic developments to both France and England as Napoleon launched wars of conquest and dragged the Republic into an age of brilliant and repressive military rule, before Louis's brothers returned in a triumphant but ultimately rather dismal period of Bourbon restoration. The country then embarked on an era of capitalist success, booming industrialization, and colonial expansion, which nevertheless was lamented by critics as a moment of intellectual and artistic poverty known as the Second Empire, or what is equivalent to the Victorian period in England. In what follows, I cast my sights on two writers who aimed to portray the Terror as it was remembered in those days, when the politics of 1789 were far removed in time and yet had left lasting traces in the imagination.

THE MEMOIRS OF A RELUCTANT REPUBLICAN: *A TALE OF TWO CITIES* (1859)

More than any other title in the English language, Charles Dickens's *A Tale of Two Cities* is used to document the Terror for today's audiences. Adolescents throughout the United States regularly read the novel in high school, and even the least attentive invariably recall the powerful opening and its evocation of the best of times that were simultaneously the worst of times. Yet the power wielded by *A Tale of Two Cities* to relay historical truth is paradoxical, because the novel offers no straightforward presentation of facts, nor does it follow a linear development that is easy to follow. The historical orientation of *A Tale of Two Cities* is chaotic. Dickens called his novel a "chronicle," which means a short, chronological record of events, and he divided it into three books dated 1775, 1780, and 1792. The book chapters and subtitles emphasize the primacy of linear movement over time, but its temporal structure is anything but linear. The books are of wildly unequal length and each includes multiple crosscuts, foreshadowings, and flashbacks.[151] Placid scenes of intimate domesticity are described for pages on end, while breath-taking dramas of worldwide impact are evoked in a line or two. Describing Paris in January–October 1793, for instance, the narrator declares, "There was no pause, no pity, no peace, no interval of relenting rest, no measurement of time. . . . And yet, observing the strange law of contradiction which obtains in all such cases, the time was long, while it flamed by so fast" (3.4.283). The reasons behind the history are equally unclear; even the four famous monarchs who open the tale remain nameless, known only by their fair faces or large jaws.

Nevertheless, it works. The reason that *A Tale* works is the focus on the individual minutiae of daily life. By watching through the magnified perspective of just a few sets of eyes and telling gestures, the reader can imagine how the tensions that erupt into the Revolution might have built up for members of three families over the course of forty or so years. This prods us to identify with them more powerfully than we would with a famous person

and to hesitate lest we judge them too hastily. The force of historical contingency is also felt strongly. The ten or so primary characters are frequently
dwarfed by mob scenes in which throngs of rowdy sansculottes or noisy
bystanders burst from the pages in deafening, impolite, and vulgar reactions
against British or French authorities. Allegorical names—The Vengeance,
Jacques One, Jacques Two, Jacques Three, the Crunchers—and period des-
ignations such as Brutus and Monseigneur further foster the alienation
between the anonymous masses, the powerful, and the little group of protagonists. Not one leader of the French Revolution is named; the Revolutionary Tribunal itself is portrayed only as a cluster of feathered hats.

The experiences of Dr. Alexandre Manette breathe life into the Terror
with more evocative power than any other book I know. The novel tells
how one individual suffered mightily at the hands of the French judiciary
until he became, for a short while during the worst months of the Terror, a
hero. That is, until he himself was consumed by the wrath of the Republic.
The chronology of *A Tale* may seem chaotic or uneven, but it is extremely
effective for revealing the dilemma of this one man's life. Because if there
is one lesson to be learned from Dr. Manette, it is about the individual's
impotence to change the course of history or to control the influence of his
own words. Even the words he commits to writing betray him in the end.

The chronology involved in Manette's memoirs—the original composition and its delayed reception—is intriguing for what it reveals about the
changes in French mores from 1767 to 1789 to 1793. When he pens the
memoirs in 1767, Manette is portrayed as justifiably bitter about the decade
he has already spent in solitary confinement. He thinks he has been forgotten by the aristocratic Evrémondes and the Bourbon judiciary in a "living
grave" from which the text will never be found or read, at least not during
his lifetime (3.10.331–44). The dire prophecy against the Evrémonde family,
spoken first by the peasant boy whose life he tries in vain to save and which
he records in his memoirs, captures that feeling. By adding to the denun-
ciation a temporal precision, "to the times when all these things shall be
answered for," Dickens weaves in an intriguing hint of millennialism. In
1767 this would have referred to Judgment Day, as is implied in the text
("I denounce them to Heaven and to earth"). Such grandiloquent rhetoric
was the appropriate register for a solitary man on what he thought was his
deathbed and would have been accepted as such.

Melodrama, millenarian denunciations, and death threats, however,
took on new connotations in the political climate of 1789, when Ernest
Defarge discovers the text in the wall of the Bastille and reads it for the first
time. One small detail signals this change. Manette's account describes the

dying peasant boy raising his right hand to take God as his witness in damning the Evrémonde clan to ignominy. In the context of 1789, however, the act of raising one's right hand was most common in political arenas, where it symbolized loyalty to the French nation or National Assembly, as in the Tennis Court Oath. The meaning of the gesture was already being altered by its political circumstances. This is driven home by the fact that the only other person to take such an oath in *A Tale* is Madame Defarge, who prophesies about the workers' vengeance against the nobility (2.16.185).

Like a shrewd media manager, Monsieur Defarge rolls out Manette's memoirs for general consumption at the most opportune moment: that is why the public does not discover this book's existence until four years later (book 3, chap. 10, five chapters before the end). And it is not revealed by Manette himself but rather by nameless Jacobin forces in the tribunal. What we then realize is that the Defarges' choice to hold back this knowledge was part of a long-term cross-generational strategic plan. As they had hoped, it unfurls with diabolical political effect at the trial of young Darnay (né Evrémonde), when "all these things [were] answered for." The young man is condemned to the guillotine and his father-in-law finds the corridors of power closed to him forever.

The psychological payoff of this scene may disappoint readers of *A Tale*. The climactic finale strikes many as incongruous, and the principals' reactions—the son-in-law's Christian piety, the daughter's filial devotion, and the father's long-suffering silence—are typical of the most conventional melodrama. Indeed, critical assessments of Dickens's talents as a psychologist are often scathing. Although the earliest review, which appeared after only a few chapters of *A Tale* had been published in serial form, praised the author's "extraordinary command over our emotions as a pathetic narrator," claiming to have read the novel "through our tears," others were not so generous. In the *Fortnightly Review* of 1872 George Henry Lewes put things crudely, if humorously, describing the Dickensian effect: "one is reminded of the frogs whose brains have been taken out for physiological purposes." On a slightly more charitable note, George Gissing noted in 1898: "Of psychology—a word unknown to Dickens—we, of course, have nothing. To ask for it is out of place." Or consider George Orwell, who in 1946 claimed that "Dickens's characters have no mental life." Assessment of Dickens's gifts for psychological analysis has radically changed in recent years. Critics are much more willing to appreciate the psychologism of Dickens's work, to the point that the narrative of Dr. Manette's intermittent psychic distress in *A Tale* has recently been cited as "an early case report of posttraumatic stress disorder" and the novel itself is deemed worthy of psychoanalysis![152] Just as the earlier criticisms were unfairly dismissive, these recent attempts to celebrate the psychic density of Dickens's novel strike me as exaggerated. I find more interesting his ability to *show* emotion through spectacles of pain and pathos. These spectacles may tell us more about the message of *A Tale* than the words themselves.

The concept of showing runs through the text. Ernest Defarge only "shows" the convalescent Dr. Manette in his attic room "to a chosen few . . . to whom the sight is likely to do some good" (1.1.34, 40). When Defarge later agrees to take the workman nicknamed Jacques Five on an outing to Versailles, he explains his cunning to Madame Defarge by noting: "Judiciously show a cat, milk, if you wish her to thirst for it. Judiciously show a dog his natural prey, if you would wish him to bring it down one day" (2.15.179). Showing has to suffice until the day comes to tell the awful truth and mobilize the people. Showing—and hearing—Manette's weirdness allows readers to sense the awful devastation that his long years of solitary confinement have dealt to him as well.

The most spectacular symptom of Manette's sorrowful mania is the tap-tap-tapping sound generated by his hammer on a cobbler's bench as he fashions and sews the same lady's shoe, over and over again, for years on end. This tapping sound punctuates the narrative regularly through each of the three books. It accompanies our first sight of him in Defarge's attic in the chapter entitled "The Shoemaker" (1.6); it recurs in the "low hammering sound" that follows his meeting with Lucie's suitor Darnay (2.10); and it dominates the tense atmosphere of the explosive chapter entitled "Nine Days," where the "low sound of knocking" haunts the Manette household nonstop until his friends forcefully intervene to make him stop (2.18). It also continues after the supposed talking cure has been effected, in the next chapter ("An Opinion," 2.19), and it is heard again in the eerie forebodings brought by a knock at the door ("A Knock at the Door," 3.7). Moreover, the novelist's remarkable descriptions of the doctor's hands, "busily working" or patterning a lady's shoe or bringing relief to prisoners in Parisian infirmaries, make his feelings palpable and visible to the reader.

Nothing prepares the reader for the shock of seeing Darnay denounced by his own father-in-law at the second trial. Imagining the words of Manette's memoirs being read aloud by the president of the tribunal, one cringes at how their meaning is skewed to conform to the Jacobin credo. What was once a private witnessing from a man to his God here becomes an inexorable death sentence passed on an unknown and possibly innocent victim. What was written for the divine is immortalized by a politico aiming to eradicate the aristocracy. Worse yet, the motivating causality between

the original trauma and its agent seems to be nonexistent. We get no sense
of Manette's ongoing resentment against the Evrémonde family or anger at
their treatment of the boy who died in his arms back in 1757. Now as then,
Manette is merely a pawn of larger forces, caught in the wrong place at the
wrong time.

Like most moderates who embraced the Revolution in its early days,
Dr. Manette is initially depicted as a hardworking, progressive, professional
man. Despite the hardships caused by his long-term imprisonment, by 1780
he is again known as an innovative scientist and devoted public servant
with a broad client base in London, his adoptive home, and a sterling reputation. When he comes back to Paris in 1792, he is seen to "use his personal
influence so wisely" that he is soon employed as the inspecting physician
of three prisons. While the monarchy falls, his fortune rises. "Among these
terrors, and the brood belonging to them," the narrator notes, "the Doctor
walked with a steady head . . . using his art equally among assassins and
victims, he was a man apart. In the exercise of his skill, the appearance and
the story of the Bastille Captive removed him from all other men" (3.4.284).
His political loyalties and personal integrity are irreproachable. Operating
on the principle of "judiciously show," Dickens does not voice Manette's
political thoughts explicitly. But to judge from his actions in the Paris prisons during the ten months of Darnay's confinement, and the warm response
he receives among the revolutionaries, we see him embracing Jacobin principles. He is, after all, employed by the Convention government and thus
presumably conforms to the norms and dictates set up therein.

Perhaps reluctantly, Dr. Manette becomes a republican. In a scene that
echoes the melodramatic trial reportage of the *Journal de Paris national*,
Manette wins over a crowd of sansculottes at Darnay's first trial and incites
the spectator gallery to shed tears of joy over his innocence and to shout,
"Long live the Republic!" (3.6.295–96). But when Manette's private memoirs are made public that night and his own name as signatory is used to
denounce the Evrémonde-Darnay family, there is nothing he can do. He
ends up being victimized by the very values he had helped propagate just
months before.

With its conflicted emotional resonances, the Thermidorian slogan "to
forgive is not to forget" (pardonner n'est pas oublier) applies especially to
life-writing such as Manette's prison memoirs.[153] But even its most compassionate scribe could not satisfactorily efface the pain of the unfinished story.
When at the end of *A Tale* the hero returns to England, he is once again
reduced to a catatonic state and described as "this helpless, inarticulately
murmuring, wandering old man" (3.13.369). Manette's loyalty to the nation

was destroyed by its opposition to family love at the tribunal, so he no longer can consider himself a citizen-hero of the sansculottes. Manette's cobbler's bench was destroyed as well and with it the cathartic obsession that gave life meaning, so he can no longer work with his hands and thereby express his feelings. Of course, the novel does not end with Dr. Manette's return to England but rather with the mawkish scene of Sydney Carton mounting the guillotine and pronouncing his own reconciliation with the Republic.

Yet the final scene effects no harmony. When Carton explains why his death will do more for humanity—by serving future generations of Manettes—than anything he could have done on earth, Dickens presents a repugnant message about the differential value of human lives that he himself refutes in this novel and in many of his other novels too. It is implied that Carton can be eliminated because he adds no value to respectable society, being ill-dressed, drunken, single, and childless, despite the fact that his brilliant intellect has saved many an innocent from the London gallows. As scores of readers have complained since the book was first published, Carton is neither a convincing nor an acceptable choice for revolutionary redemption. When biographer Jane Smiley recently dismissed this issue in the name of the Christian transfiguration at the end of *A Tale*, she too missed the point.[154] The gushing embrace of Christianity that marks Carton's death scene does not resolve the tensions running through this book; its very incongruity should warn us that something else is afoot. Mainly, I think, it warns us that there is no easy redemption for this world.

Dickens wrote countless novels about "these times," portrayed neither as the best nor as the worst of times but rather as a heartless present. Despite their grim situation, in most of these books the characters attain a certain wisdom by the end that augurs some optimism for the future. Consider *Hard Times: For These Times* (1854), where a sweet and indefatigable circus performer's daughter guides her adoptive father (and, by extension, us readers) out of our pitiless and one-dimensional attitude toward the working poor. In *A Tale of Two Cities*, on the contrary, the characters give no evidence of evolving toward wisdom; and there are no easy answers to the social problems that led to the outbreak of revolution and that still exist at the end. Even if the French government could emerge from this mess intact, there are no suggestions for how the people might restart their lives. Where *Hard Times* leaves the social order largely untouched, as here, at least the characters have learned something from the buoyant presence of Sissy Jupe; even dour Mr. Gradgrind gives proof of compassion by the end. By the end of *A Tale*, the reader has gained some wisdom and some cynicism as well. We realize, for instance, that Manette's fame was not due to any bravery or intelligence; his only virtue was surviving. Similarly, the tragic ending of Manette revolves around the dumb force of historical contingency. Nor does the fate of Manette's son-in-law Darnay—his presumed successor—reveal any inherent heroism or larger truths coming to fruition. He was just lucky.

Through their minute focus on the individual will, Robespierre's biographers and William Godwin transformed the Terror into an easily legible parable of ambition run amuck. Through his creation of exemplary nobodies who are superposed on a vast, moving, and unpredictable historical canvas, Dickens cast off the reflex of blaming somebody for the Terror and made it into a different kind of spectacle. The Dickensian spectacle of *A Tale* is characterized more as a whirlwind of unfortunate encounters rather than a tableau of causal determinism. In his theory of spectatorship, Guy Debord contended that an important cultural moment may be assimilated into the mainstream in two opposite ways: it may be integrated in "a totalizing historical moment" or it may be remade into a "dead object, to be gazed upon as a spectacle."[155] The former makes the cultural moment into a force wielding the power to critique society, while the latter merely defends the status quo of class power. I think that the choices that Dickens made in *A Tale*—to avoid depicting actual people; to stretch the revolutionary period out from 1757 to 1793; to put characters into the hands of a nameless crowd; to rewrite individual identity as static allegory; to offer up a victim who is not worthy of martyrdom and a victor who has not done much to deserve surviving—prove that he wanted to elicit questioning rather than resolution regarding the revolutionary spirit. Precisely because the end of *A Tale of Two Cities* does not deliver a satisfying catharsis, its political urgency remains alive. It is not a dead object of vacuous spectacle but rather a dynamic force to be dealt with, for each reader in each age, on his or her own terms.

Leaving interpretation of the Terror up to individual judgment, however, can be a dangerous move. The ideal democracy presupposes an intellectually schooled and discerning reading public seeking detailed information on all aspects of any argument. This was not the case in Dickens's day, nor is it ever likely to be. The hilarious results of that exasperating fact are brought home by Flaubert.

FLAUBERT'S CHRONICLE OF BANALITY

When Flaubert's erstwhile researchers in *Bouvard et Pécuchet* decide to take on revolutionary history, they proceed in much the same way as they had with their other enthusiasms, such as archeology and agriculture. They pore over books and consult all kinds of expert opinions until the mixture turns their heads: "The more they discussed it, the more passionate they grew." In the random anecdotes and conspiracies they cull from their readings, one sees revolutionary historiography reduced to sensational soundbites that recall the Thermidorian pamphletry discussed above. They argue about Charlotte Robespierre's royal pension, for instance, and Bouvard contends that "'Rise to Heaven, son of Louis!', the virgins of Verdun, and breeches made of human skin were incontrovertible facts." (Flaubert's readers would have smirked over the dubious truth-value of these claims, which were all common currency in counterrevolutionary propaganda. The pious exclamation "Rise to Heaven, son of Louis!" was attributed to Abbé Edgeworth upon witnessing Louis XVI's death on the scaffold. The "virgins of Verdun" were a group of French women who, after offering food to Prussian troops upon their defeat at Verdun in 1792, were executed for treason during the Terror. The "breeches made of human skin" alludes to Robespierre's reported desecration of his victims' remains such as was noted in Proyart's biography.) Pécuchet for his part sympathizes with Robespierre. He approves the king's execution and the cult of the Supreme Being, suspects Danton's wrongdoing, and blames all the crimes on aristocratic plotting and foreign gold.[156] But both men hit an impasse when they discover the frustrating reality of historical contingency. They are dumbfounded, that is, by the fact that there was no preordained force behind the Revolution's unfolding. When they ponder what might have happened without the flight to Varennes, or if Robespierre had escaped on the eve of Thermidor, all the high-flown theories and expertise of the experts are revealed to be for naught. So they give up.

Nonetheless, their belief in truth remains, as does their hope that truth will emerge from a combination of scholarly theory and assiduous study. So they decide to continue their work, eagerly moving from topic to topic and book to book—until the fateful day in 1851 when they learn of Louis Napoleon's bloody repression of the Republic, and their principles are put to the test. This is where Flaubert's wry cynicism comes to the fore. For all his declarations of sansculottes sympathy, when the risk of violence comes home to Pécuchet he pronounces a firm belief in the police state and exclaims, "Let him gag the people, crush them underfoot, exterminate them—it will serve them right."[157] Bouvard emphatically agrees. Exhausted and disheartened by this upsetting experience, both men then abandon the search for truth and retire from public life (in other words, they cease to seek out chats with neighbors or dinners hosted by the local nobleman). At last sight, they are setting up a new double-size desk in their cozy home and preparing to resume the job that they were made for: copying the words of others.

Their lives appear to be unwinding in perpetual calm (if not bliss), as they mindlessly copy on without a thought in their heads.

Bouvard et Pécuchet was meant to form part of a trilogy with the *Dictionnaire des idées reçues* and a third volume that would document all the platitudes copied by the copyists.[158] So it is not surprising to find in the fragments that make up the *Dictionnaire* the disembodied voices of these two characters swapping findings from their research with other unqualified opinion makers and enthusiasts. The pat analogies—Louis XVI is "that unfortunate monarch"; a thief is always a "Republican"; a mob is always "vile"; and a Girondin is "to pity more than to blame"—remind one of their superficial knowledge and facile conservatism. So do the claims about phenomena designated as "sources of" or "terrible in times of" revolution: applied to butchers, the duc d'Orléans, faubourgs, Figaro, Freemasonry, Jesuits, and workers. A short or faulty memory runs through entries on even the most abhorrent events: the Terror exists alongside other significant moments, all of which are trivialized in ironic one-liners. (The September 1792 prison massacres are recalled by an apocryphal glass of blood, and the 1572 Saint Bartholomew's Day massacre of Protestants is dubbed an "old wives' tale," or *vieille blague*).

The causality of historical action is robbed of its sacred aura. For "Concession," one reads: "Never make any. They were Louis XVI's downfall." A scaffold is described as a place "to pronounce some eloquent phrases before dying." And of conspirators ("Conjurés"), we learn that "they are crazy about seeing their names on lists." History thus loses any sense of organic coherence or divine meaning such as the romantic historians of the Victorian age assumed for it, and the events of 1789–94 are reduced to cautionary aphorisms. What is worse, Flaubert sometimes throws a monkey wrench into the works and inserts two opposing versions of truth into the same entry. What can we make of the mob, for instance, which, although vile, "always has good instincts"? And if caring for the poor "makes up for every other virtue," why is one instructed to "always guard against pity"?[159] In this way, Flaubert mocks the middle-brow appetite for predigested knowledge that was popular in his day and realizes his goal of creating a book whose readers will never know whether or not he is pulling their leg.[160] Furthermore, where Bouvard and Pécuchet admit their limitations, the *Dictionnaire* affects an authoritative air. The bullying yet nonsensical refrains such as "thunder against" (*tonner contre*), "scoff at it" (*blaguer*), and "We're not sure what it is" (*on ignore en quoi ça consiste*) emphasize that knowledge is not necessary to declaim one's opinion. They also underline the predetermined nature of any opinion: "thunder against" represents the agreed-upon necessity of defending family, property, and law and order against attack from bugbears such as revolution, aristocrats, and workers.

I close, then, with this dispirited yet realistic evocation of a society in which people's acts do not reflect their principles, nor does anyone trust in principles anyway. For in the final analysis the Revolution of 1789 did not end with the paroxysm of July 1794. It collapsed in very different circumstances in the following years amid all the clamoring over what went wrong. Purported explanations of the Terror frequently veiled other intents, notably fear-mongering and demagoguery. Where Madame Guénard's novel *Irma* and its vampirish Robespierre satisfied thrill-seeking readers under the Consulate, the most unnerving portraits of Robespierre-the-criminal to my mind adopted a subtler approach to identifying the evils lurking in the human psyche. That is, they suggested that ordinary characteristics shared by many of us—pallor and seriousness, for instance—may cloak hidden malevolence. The killers in tales such as *Caleb Williams* and numerous later villains—think of Dr. Jekyll/Mr. Hyde or Dorian Gray—feature a somewhat Robespierre-like mentality and a physique that matches it. While such similarities may be chalked up to a satanic duplicity that lies latent in all people, I suspect that these traits—nervous tics, a penchant for solitude, and a kind of intransigent intellectualism—have become distinctive features of a modern villainy that originated in 1793–94.

Nonetheless, there is something uniquely awful about Robespierre. The villains of the early-modern age and the Enlightenment, such as Edmund in *King Lear* and Valmont in *Les Liaisons dangereuses,* operated within their own social milieu or sought to bring down the mighty. Robespierre is the first who sought ostensibly to serve the people and yet caused widespread suffering. This discovery is unnerving for the Left. Why? Because it shows how a man who aimed to reform a corrupt system through policies beloved by the Left (transparent governance and an egalitarian judiciary) could go down in history as a mass murderer. True, Robespierre and other members of the Convention committed heinous errors in their devotion to an abstract ideal of justice. But the hard-edged egalitarianism that dictated the legislation of 1793–94 also did much good. That legislation liberated France from the death grip of aristocratic privilege, gave birth to a free and public system of national education, established the foundations of social welfare, promoted a forward-looking spirit of commercial republicanism, and made possible the rise of a true meritocracy.[161] Little of that progress meets the eye. Instead, the literature explored in this chapter fed the reactionary backlash of the late 1790s to restore the power of a tenaciously conservative, anti-intellectual bloc that has battled the Republic ever since.

This book is about how the French Revolution was picked up, processed, and repurposed by authors and artists working in various forms: immediately through the newspapers and prints of 1789–94, a bit later through novels published in 1790–1803, and finally in fiction published during the nineteenth and early twentieth centuries. The concentric circles of my method steadily widen the chronology and offer different approaches to the issue of time and its meaning. While I have argued that the shaping of the revolutionary legacy has key moments from 1789 to 1794, I hope that it is equally clear that this legacy is ongoing: I have tried to shine some light on both the long-term and the short-term processes. A tension nevertheless runs through this shuttling back and forth between past and present. On the one hand, each chapter is based on highly contextualized historical analyses that constitute up to two-thirds of the text. On the other hand, my goal has been to provide readers with tools to develop their own skills for revolutionary reading so that they might identify other analogies going forward. The codas accomplish this to some extent. The examples below venture further afield from the 1790s to provide up-to-date instances on how the contradictions and potential inherent in the revolutionary spirit remain alive in the twenty-first century.

The decision to adopt this dialectic model was driven by many factors, not the least being the open-ended, if not to say bewildered, attitude toward time that characterizes writings from the 1790s. Lynn Hunt has identified some manifestations of this befuddlement in *Measuring Time, Making History* (2008), and Robert Darnton's 1989 article remains a favorite for capturing the excitement felt by revolutionaries in restarting the clock and redesigning the Gregorian calendar. But the most striking revelation to me was a little note in a 1791 newspaper regarding the difficulties of writing the Revolution's history. In one of many such prospectuses published in the *Journal de Paris*, a certain Monsieur Jullien describes with great enthusiasm and abundant detail his projected twelve-volume history of the National Assembly. He concludes, however, by admitting that completing the project is not yet possible. It is too soon and he himself is too implicated in events. He will have to wait ten to fifteen years from 1789, he says, and detach himself from the scene, before the book can be done. (It never was finished.) This sense of frustrated anticipation, of being born too soon, knowing too little or too much, runs through the corpus analyzed in *The Frankenstein of 1790*. Most notorious is Robespierre's rumored intolerance for inherited traditions. In reply to a question about how to end the counterrevolution definitively, Robespierre allegedly replied, "The generation who saw the ancien régime will always regret it. Everyone who was more than 15 years old in 1789 must be eliminated [*égorgé*]; it is the only way to consolidate the Revolution."[1] This chilling measure was never put into law, of course, but its echoes made future plans for civic regeneration look bleak.

Nailing down a proper perspective for capturing the Revolution's work is tricky. My tightly focused contextualization of materials from the years 1789–1803 has sought to combat the teleological tendency that runs through some works on the "causes of the Revolution." But who is to say that it may not fall prey to a similar anachronism? The "results of the Revolution" are equally subject to debate. Many witnesses deplored the campaign of dechristianization that whittled away the ties between Catholicism and Frenchness during 1790–94. When in 1801 the Concordat signed by Consul Napoleon and Pope Pius VII solidified the role of the Roman Catholic Church in France and brought back most of its civil status, a new lament was heard among parish priests. Their melancholy was not over the souls lost to the Terror, however. Rather, priests waxed poetic over the vivifying effect that the Terror had once imparted to their parishioners and that was no longer to be found. "Never were so many good masses celebrated as under the Terror," wrote one clergyman. "The ignorant may believe and complain that Robespierre killed religion in France [but actually] he saved it, by filling the Heavens with souls and purifying our faith." Another echoed these sentiments, explaining, "Oh, the beautiful midnight masses we celebrated then [in 1794]! . . . How strong was our fervor! Like the first Christians, we were always under the executioner's axe, like them, we drew from it an invincible courage."[2] These unexpected effects are just as important to note as the more mainstream results of the Terror; together, the puzzle of Robespierre's legacy makes more sense.

As we move farther in time from the dates 1789–1803, another question arises: how can one gauge the impact of political discourse (or imagery or music) when it is divorced from a relevant context? Consider a music video that is currently available on YouTube: Lady Gaga's "The French Revolution." Created by the Honolulu-based educators known as the History Teachers, this video features an odd juxtaposition of techno-pop music, rap-style lyrics, and a chronology of the major events of 1789–94. While the music of Lady Gaga (aka Stefani Germanotta, 1986–) will likely be forgotten long before this book goes out of print, the lesson taught through her image by the History Teachers holds lasting value for educators seeking a novel way to explain (in a Marxist sort of causality) the links between the Estates General and Thermidor. The fact that the video does so in less than five minutes is an added plus. Yet what is revolutionary about it? Certainly not the form: Lady Gaga's music is neither artistically interesting nor innovative. It is simply a humorous conduit by which a rather traditional rendition of historical events can be transmitted to today's youth audience.

The point is that there is nothing particularly "revolutionary" about many cultural constructs associated with the French Revolution, and to expect it to be otherwise would be unrealistic. Denis Diderot's lament over the stifling influence that peace and prosperity had on talent in 1758 seems to gesture toward a revolutionary poetics:

> Poetry requires something enormous, barbaric, and savage. When the fury of civil war or fanaticism puts a knife in man's hand, when blood flows in streams upon the earth, then Apollo's laurels flourish. They want to be irrigated. . . . When shall we see the birth of poets? It will be after a time of disaster and great misfortune, when the beleaguered people will draw a breath. Then the imagination, shaken by those terrible spectacles, will depict things unknown to those who have not seen them.[3]

Diderot drew this causal connection with respect to the flourishing arts that emerged from the traumatic wars of religion, but his statement could also be read as prophesying the renaissance that might accompany or follow the Revolution. The problem is that most works of literature produced immediately after the events were neither masterpieces nor improvements upon existing genres. Jullien's assessment of the ten or so years needed for the dust to settle, that is, until ca. 1799–1804, has been justified by the materials studied here. Apart from Godwin's *Caleb Williams*, the most literarily interesting texts were not published *during* the events but afterward, in 1799–1801, 1803, 1818, 1829–35, 1859, 1862, 1874, and into the 1900s. A Revolution does not a Renaissance make.

Similarly tenuous connections may be discerned between "revolutionary" words and concepts. Consider the entries for "Liberty" and "Order" in Flaubert's *Dictionnaire des idées reçues*: both include the exact same words in the exact same order! The use of "counterrevolutionary" signifiers does not determine a message's outcome either. Take the term *aristocrate*. Multiple anecdotes from the Revolution tell of servants who criticized their mistresses for unseemly conduct. In contrast to the nobility, whose anger and sobs evince their weakened state, the servants remain silent, observe protocol, or lash out in frustration: "At least *I* act like an aristocrat." In this idiolect, *aristocrate* designates a status unrelated to wealth or standing: it is a proud stoicism, nobility of mien. A planter living in Saint-Domingue also used the term to describe himself in 1795, but his interpretation drew on another meaning. As he wrote, "Less attached perhaps by inclination and by pride to colonial prejudices than most inhabitants, I believed them necessary to the prosperity and safety of the colony, and at the same time my heart was filled with the sentiment that exalted all the French. In a word, I was a *patriote* in France and an *aristocrate* in Saint-Domingue."[4] Or consider the term *ci-devant*, usually used as a pejorative term for a former aristocrat. By 1797, the term had broadened, at least in the mind of one writer, to encompass all the French: "No one is what he used to be in 1789, or what he, in retrospect, expected to be in 1796. . . . We are all former [*des ci-devant*], some former rich people, others former paupers: some former noblemen, others former commoners. . . . The reason is that at present we are all out of place [*déplacés*]."[5] Clearly, one must beware of misinterpreting signs of ideology, social identity, or emotion from the past.

Yet there are some positive ties between a person's idiolect, expectations, hopes, and fears and the era in which she lives. Call it a generation, a mind-set, or a field of cultural production, but a certain consciousness often does unite citizens of a given time and place. Some historians stress the temporal over all other identity markers. In Robert Gildea's *Children of the Revolution* (2008), great writers of the nineteenth century are categorized according to the year in which they were born and the events they lived through. Life is understood as a political entity. This method has some appeal: whether it is the linkage between JFK, Vietnam, 9/11, and Obama, as in my generation of Americans, or *les trente glorieuses* for a French friend who is in her eighties, we are all in some way a product of our time and place; we have absorbed values from the cultural domains within which we have circulated. The reduction of an individual to her generation is nonetheless debatable. Other identity markers, such as class or socioeconomics, may trump temporal considerations. While today's youth culture appears to be media saturated, to a teenager growing up in poverty and without access to a computer, the world looks rather different. It is pretty much the same world her mother grew up in thirty or so years earlier. The conflicting pull of religious teachings versus the ambient sexuality of television, the demands of troubled siblings and friends, care of the babies and toddlers in her midst, money worries, and sporadic neighborhood violence likely demand more of her attention than the latest YouTube video or Facebook posting— let alone the job opportunities, the potential for research, or the creativity that lie on the World Wide Web. Possibilities are muted. Life feels more like a finite cycle than a progression into an unknown and better future.

The revolutionaries' hopes for the printing press and its potential to educate the masses (as seen, for example, in Nogaret's *Miroir*) were just as short-sighted as today's policy-makers' claims about the Internet's ability to empower the poor. Time, education, and money are still stumbling blocks. Laying the groundwork for a different future cannot be accomplished by one person alone; it needs constant cultivation, renewal, and hope. It also needs numbers: numbers of people who realize the moral obligations they owe to their kin and their local community. Perhaps this book may remind readers of our unfinished work on that front. Wherever you live, the dreams of universal human rights and social equality are likely still out of reach for many of your countrymen, perhaps even your neighbors. Nevertheless, the most interesting thing about human life is not how we live our culture's determinism but rather how we are infused with its possibilities. As columnist Leonard Pitts wrote in a commemoration of the fiftieth anniversary of President John F. Kennedy's inauguration, "the lesson wasn't about what we could do, or how we could do, but 'that' we could do, that transformation lived within our hands."[6] Looking back at the modern democracies that gradually emerged from the rubble of 1795 should infuse us with a similar hope.

∽

It is difficult to conclude the questioning that gave rise to this book, for who knows how the stories of the women's march on Versailles or the royal family's flight to Varennes will be reappropriated or repurposed in the books, artwork, and films of the future? While the pitiful paternity of King Louis XVI was captured rather accurately in Chantal Thomas's 2002 novel, *Les Adieux à la Reine*, judging from the American cultural landscape of today the dreams (and ethical responsibilities) of constitutional democracy born in 1789–90 are less appealing than other aspects of the era. Judging from recent popular culture, the Revolution's greatest appeal seems to lie in the vices of a naughty bunch of courtiers that the viewer/shopper may emulate for a modest price.

Consider a Juicy Couture print advertisement of 2010 (fig. 30). A Marie-Antoinette look-alike with an enormous pink hairdo stares out at viewers dolefully. She is cradling, with one hand, a huge bottle of perfume that has a bird perched on top, and gesturing suggestively, with her other hand, to her nether parts. This portrait's subtle repurposing of the Greuze painting *Jeune Fille qui pleure son oiseau mort* (1765) or the eighteenth-century motif of a girl lamenting her pet bird's demise or escape (read her lost virginity) makes a provocative commentary on the queen's rumored promiscuity while inviting consumers to try it on for themselves. Or consider the bizarrely menacing "Napoleonic" ad campaign for Dolce and Gabbana clothing launched in 2006, one of whose advertisements showed two men in dapper period fashions threatening a third in a chair while another lay on the floor bleeding from a head wound. The melancholy for a racier, more dangerous time is tangible. Lest one judge these ads too harshly, it is essential to recall that their delivery systems, that is, high-end fashion magazines, predetermine the cultural values they can be expected to impart. The visual shock provided by sexual provocation and allusions to sadism and torture are attractive commodities among sixteen- to twenty-five-year-olds. It is unreasonable to expect messages of moral restraint and civic responsibility to be reproduced in a genre and product designed to market luxury to the young; elitism, power, and exclusivity sell better. Nevertheless, the slavish admiration of privilege that runs through these images gives pause: why should we citizens of modern democracies mourn this version of the past?

More intriguing and politically useful is the campaign for Motorola's SkyTel pager launched around 2000. In a teasing tone, this ad shows the queen's pager—the cutting edge technology of the time—trying to give her a message: "Marie-Antoinette—Peasants are restless. Do not mention 'cake.' Trust me" (fig. 31). The caption brings home the lesson in a way that resonates with anxious professionals: "If your paging service isn't guaranteed, you could be missing some important messages." Although the apocryphal cake reference has long been disproved, the ad's emphasis on the crucial role played by timing in revolutionary events, and the highly charged semantics of royal speech, are well supported by historical evidence. The message also reminds viewers of the queen's fundamental disregard for other people's opinions. Whether it was her adoptive countrymen back in the 1790s or her electronic messenger, as here, she ignores warnings that might have saved lives.

30. Advertisement for Juicy Couture perfume, 2010.

31. "'Marie-Antoinette—Peasants are restless. Do not mention "cake." Trust me.' If your paging service isn't guaranteed, you could be missing some important messages." Advertisement for Motorola SkyTel pager, ca. 2001.

Sofia Coppola's 2006 film, *Marie-Antoinette*, makes a fitting endpoint to the fate of Louis XVI's court because it also captures the Bourbons' ill-conceived sense of superiority. What seems bizarre about Coppola's film on first sight, however, is how the director tried to make this hide-worn sense of aristocratic privilege into something that would appeal to a young, American audience. In a controversial move, Coppola disrupted the sense of historical accuracy by focusing on the queen's teen years when she first came to France and mixing in icons of American youth culture of the twenty-first century (i.e., Converse shoes and punk rock music). In a further twist, she layered that hip aesthetic on to a conventionally antidemocratic message. Viewers looking for avatars supporting a revolutionary politics may disapprove. But the queen's indifference is actually quite appropriate: it provides a slyly dark commentary on the distance between the Bourbon court's mentality and our American expectations for democracy.

One of the most captivating shots in *Marie-Antoinette* occurs during the opening credits. It appears to be something of an homage to Jean-Luc Godard, who in *À Bout de souffle* (Breathless; 1960) shot a similar frontal dialogue with the camera.[7] In Godard's film that gesture became an iconic breakthrough for avant-garde cinema. While navigating up a country road with one hand on the wheel, Godard's hero, a doomed playboy named Michel (played by Jean-Paul Belmondo), lists the places he plans to go: Milan, Genoa, Rome. Recklessly weaving through traffic, he endangers every car on the road. And then, turning to face the viewer straight on, he launches a challenge to us: "If you don't like the sea, if you don't like mountains, if you don't like cities, then get stuffed!" (Si vous n'aimez pas la mer, si vous n'aimez pas la montagne, si vous n'aimez pas la ville, allez vous faire foutre!) There is no room for dissension; the hero's massive ego fills the screen. But what is striking is how we ride along with Michel and implicitly share his views. We are next to him, in the passenger seat; we too are cool and fast-moving. And, although it should feel offensive, Michel's devil-may-care attitude is seductive.

As for Coppola, she deliberately keeps the viewer out of the scene. In her remake, the queen, played by actress Kirsten Dunst, looks directly at the camera while having her toenails painted by a maid. At first glance, she seems to imitate Jean-Paul Belmondo's attitude while driving through the French countryside in À Bout de souffle. Unlike Godard's character, the queen's glance of recognition does not last. Her head languidly drifts to the side. Instead of sharing a joke with spectators and making us her partners-in-crime, as Belmondo did, she sneaks in a private grin, relishing the fact that we will never be anything but her subjects. The lyrics of the Gang of Four's sour punk anthem "Natural's Not in It," with their cynical take on pleasure ("this heaven gives me migraine"), trivializes her status as trophy wife. The flick of her chin, however, shows us that she does not need our approval. The gesture of looking through the third wall between cinéma and vérité never returns: the filmic world becomes ever more solipsistic and self-absorbed the longer we watch.

This is perhaps the most historically accurate and useful detail of Marie-Antoinette. As readers will have understood by now, the Bourbons did not really want a democratic leveling. They did not believe in republican reforms. So why should we expect it from them or their ilk today? This kind of jarring detail helps keep the emotional resonance of the Revolution alive. By irritating spectators with its lavish spectacles of a spoiled and self-centered monarch who snubs the public, Coppola's film reminds us of why France needed a Revolution. By extension it goads us into remembering why we should continue the fight against privilege.

But what about the social unity and optimism of the early revolution? Surely the combination of egalitarian politics and the user-friendly technologies of the 2010s might be combined to produce more uplifting effects? Indeed, much has been written about the role being played by technologies such as Twitter and Facebook in subverting the traditional mechanisms of state censorship and ushering in the Arab Spring of 2011. The crude imagery of "Mubarak's Ministry of Pigs" posted on the Internet may have accelerated the ouster of Egypt's president Hosni Mubarak in February: this makes an intriguing parallel to the "swine king" Louis XVI and his 1791 disgrace. Other similarities may be seen in the diction of antigovernment opposition: the exasperation expressed by an angry, long-oppressed Us against an all-powerful Them. In his 1789 pamphlet *Qu'est-ce que le tiers-état?* (What is the Third Estate?), the left-wing Abbé Sieyès argued, "What is the Third Estate? Everything. What has it been hitherto in the political order? Nothing. What does it desire to be? Something." A recent song inspired by Egyptian poet Ahmen Fouad Negm sounds a similar refrain: "Who are they, and who are we? / They are the authority, the sultans. / They are the rich, and the government is on their side. / We are the poor, the governed. / Think about it, use your head. / See which one of us rules the other."[8] Other news from Egypt, however, points to less promising results and recalls less glorious aspects of French revolutionary culture.

The most striking images of spring and summer 2011 have been of Arab women in all their diversity: black-robed and angry marching in the capitals of North Africa and the Syrian hinterland, standing before thousands delivering speeches in Cairo, driving cars in Saudi Arabia, or treating the injured in Tunisia. Yet many of these brave protesters have met a chilly response from their countrymen. A celebration of International Women's Day in Cairo ended in an ugly confrontation that prompted some to run for their lives. An April 2011 exposé revealed abuse region-wide and threw down the gauntlet to reformers by declaring, "Women may have sustained the Arab spring, but it remains to be seen if the Arab spring will sustain women." There are no references to equality in the Egyptian constitution passed in March 2011, and a propaganda campaign has sprung up saying, "Now is not the time for women's rights." Furthermore, hundreds of women, throughout the Middle East, have been harassed, beaten, or even raped into silence and submission. Scores have been detained or disappeared.[9] Whether such hostility was prompted by misogyny, religion, or a reactionary anxiety over gender roles does not really matter: the point is that events do not bode well for women's or basic human rights in the so-called new post-Mubarak Egypt and the post-totalitarian Middle East. In fact, this appalling news strongly suggests that there is nothing "new" about the new regimes. It brings to mind the cowardly Convention government of October 1793, which forcibly suppressed women's political clubs. The misogynistic language of anti-feminist protests in Egypt sounds uncannily similar to that of the odious article "Aux Républicaines," which was published shortly after the executions of Marie-Antoinette, Olympe de Gouges, and Madame Roland and heaped insult on injury. Let us hope that those men seeking to construct constitutional democracies in the Middle East will demand an immediate end to the barbarity and start exemplifying the morality that is incumbent upon citizens of a free nation—notably by doing right by their partners, kin, and neighbors: the women who also call those countries their home. The months and years ahead will doubtless reveal further parallels between the complex missteps and triumphs that marked early efforts at liberation in France and the mass movements that are currently sweeping the Middle East. One thing is sure: the revolutionary spirit is still going strong.[10]

The republican calendar was adopted by the Convention government in October 1793 and postdated to refer back to the founding of the French Republic on September 22, 1792. The calendar was thus launched in and dated Year 2. However, other schemes to signal the newness of the revolutionary era were employed as early as 1789, such as, for example, "third year of the Freedom," which dates events relative to 1789. Instead of the Gregorian calendar's traditional start in January, the republican calendar year began at the autumn equinox. In an effort to make timekeeping more rational, the twelve months of thirty days each received new names based on nature, principally having to do with the prevailing weather in and around Paris. Because of the calendar's ties to the equinox, there is a certain slippage in dates; thus, 1 vendémiaire could be either September 22, 23, or 24, depending on the year. Five extra days—six in leap years—were national holidays at the end of every year. These were originally known as *les sans-culottides* (after "sansculottes"), but after Year 3 (1795) they were known as *les jours complémentaires.*

Due to the confusion that predated this decision and ensued in its wake, the dates of period newspapers underwent a series of changes. On October 7, 1793, the *Journal de Paris national* carried a hybrid date: "October 7, 2nd Year of the Republic." The next day is listed as "the 17th day of the 1st month, 2nd Republican Year." Five days later, the formula became "22nd day of first month of Year 2 of the French Republic one and indivisible (Sunday October 13, 1793, old style)."

The French government employed the republican calendar from October 24, 1793, until December 31, 1805 (Year 14), and for eighteen days during the Paris Commune in 1871.

In the notes and bibliography, I give both the republican date and the

Gregorian date unless the text has only the Gregorian date in the original. When a republican date is given but the Gregorian date is lacking from the text, it is designated thus: Year 2 (1793–94) in English or An 2 (1793–94) in French. When no date is present and the Gregorian date is inferred from textual clues only, it is designated thus: [1793?]. When no date is present and the Gregorian date is documented in archival records or other print sources, it is designated thus: ca. 1793.

ABBREVIATIONS

AA   *Actes des apôtres*

AM   *L'Ancien Moniteur, ou La Gazette nationale: Réimpression de L'Ancien Moniteur*, 32 vols. (Paris: Henri Plon, 1858–70); references to *AM* include volume number in this edition

AN   Archives nationales, Paris

ANOM   Archives nationales d'Outre-Mer, Aix-en-Provence

AP   Archives de la Police, Archives de la Préfecture de Paris

CP   *Chronique de Paris*

JP   *Journal de Paris*

JPN   *Journal de Paris national*

MIOM   Call number of microfilm holdings at ANOM

RP   *Révolutions de Paris*

NOTES

INTRODUCTION

1. Nogaret, *Dialogue*, 6.

2. Newspaper reading provided a crucial basis for this project. As Jeremy Popkin points out, "It was the press that molded the dispersed and fragmentary events that made up the era of the revolutionary journées into intelligible form, labeled them, and validated the results as presenting them as public manifestations of the people's will"; *Revolutionary News*, 5.

3. Fish, "Normal Circumstances," 1203.

4. "De 1789 à l'époque du Directoire le roman fut peu cultivé, et chose remarquable, aucun de ceux qui parurent ne se ressentirent directement de l'influence des temps où ils furent conçus"; Duval, *Histoire*, 147. This contention is hard to understand, given the statistics below, unless perhaps Duval used different criteria for defining *roman* and "influence." A note on translations: throughout this book I include the original French from citations for two reasons: (1) to allow readers to test my claims against the originals, as here, and (2) to allow readers access to texts that are important to revolutionary history but whose rarity makes them difficult to access.

5. Sainte-Beuve's comments are more complex than this generalization permits; although he dismisses Condorcet, he appreciates the work of Madame Roland, Madame de Staël, and André Chénier. But his general attitude toward the Revolution is one of melancholy nostalgia for what French letters might have become without it: "Mais la Révolution vint; dix années, fin de l'époque, s'écoulèrent brusquement avec ce qu'elles promettaient, et abîmèrent les projets et les hommes"; Sainte-Beuve, *La Littérature*, 7:99, and see also individual articles on authors. Goncourt and Goncourt, *Histoire*, 1–17, 175–79.

6. DeJean, review of *The Other Enlightenment*, 960.

7. According to Martin, Mylne, and Frautschi, *Bibliographie du genre romanesque français*, about 800 novels (including translations) were published in French between 1789 and 1799. Of that total, approximately 236 were new titles by French authors and explicitly tied to French politics—my focus in this book. To double-check this data and to extend my reach to 1803, I also had recourse to Monglond, *La France*; Hesse, *Publish-*

ing, 177, 205; and the bibliography in Hesse, *The Other Enlightenment*. For bibliographies of theater and song, see Hyslop, "The Theater during a Crisis"; Brécy, "La Chanson révolutionnaire"; and Mason, *Singing*.

8. See Douthwaite, "On *Candide*, Catholics, and Freemasonry."

9. Emmet Kennedy, *Cultural History*, 35–39.

10. Roger Chartier and Daniel Roche coin this concept ("l'usage public de leur raison par des personnes privées") and explain its debt to the groundbreaking work of Jürgen Habermas in "Introduction: Les Livres ont-ils fait la Révolution?" 14.

11. On the network of Jacobin clubs and their role in educating rural populations, see Michael Kennedy, "Les Clubs"; Ozouf, *Varennes*, 354; and Parent, "De nouvelles pratiques."

12. The *Journal de la ville* declared in 1789 that "literature makes us yawn; poetry is tiresome" (la littérature fait bâiller; les vers fatiguent); cited by Rétat, "L'Ebranlement," 22.

13. It appears that fiction was read aloud at political clubs; see *Entretien du citoyen S.B.*, 57. See also *Triomphe de la saine philosophie* (ca. 1795) by Madame Booser, which was supported by the Convention government by decree of November 1794, published in large numbers, and distributed throughout the Republic. These practices bear more research.

14. There exists little biographical information on Pochet. He was once director of the École gymnastique of the Military School in St. Petersburg, and was the author of a proposed festival for Louis XVI on the occasion of his signing the Constitution in September 1791; see his *L'Héroïsme uni à l'espérance*; and Cioranescu, *Bibliographie*, 2:1407. The timing of Pochet's proposed festival doomed it, of course; by September 1791 the tide had already turned against Louis XVI.

15. "Nous bornons nos vœux pour qu'à l'imitation de nos Concitoyens qui forment des Sociétés des Amis de la Constitution, établies dans les villes municipales de Besançon et Strasbourg, MM. les chefs de districts villageois, les curés de campagne, les chefs de régiment et de manufactures, établissent des Sociétés de lecture, qu'on y lise les aventures survenues aux inconséquens parens du descendant du frère de lait de notre bon roi Henri, [et] que cette histoire soit pour eux l'œil du maître, avec lequel ils acquerront les lumières nécessaires à tout bon citoyen"; Pochet, *La Boussole*, 1:n.p. All translations from the French are my own unless otherwise noted.

16. "Les lecteurs trouveront dans ces anecdotes le tableau fidèle et animé du bonheur que l'on goûte en France, et des maux que rencontrent dans les pays étrangers les imprudents qui trahissent leur pays par de coupables émigrations"; *AM* 283 (October 10, 1791): 10:74. See also the reviews in *JP* (June 1791) and *CP* (September 1791) reprinted in *Feuille de correspondance du libraire* (3:61, 10:237–38). News of the royal family's failed escape attempt launched a massive exodus of the wealthy, and these emigrations of nobles robbed the nation of its financial and military might. The characters in *La Boussole*, however, emigrated for religious reasons. But the author's warning against emigration may explain its appeal to readers in the post-Varennes days of autumn 1791. See Boffa, "Émigrés."

17. Ligou, "Franc-maçonnerie," 479.

18. These measures were also used by contemporaries to judge a book's quality; as a book review in the *Chronique de Paris* announced: "La rapidité avec laquelle s'épuise,

dans ces temps-ci, la première édition d'un ouvrage qui n'est point un ouvrage de parti, est une preuve suffisante de son mérite"; *CP* 59 (February 28, 1791): 233.

19. Raymond Williams, *Culture*, 323.

20. Somers, *Genealogies*, 173, 194; see also Somers's useful overview of recent work on the political culture of the French Revolution, 193–201.

21. Casanova, *The World Republic*, 350.

22. "Aussi la vérité de l'histoire, sur ce point comme en tant d'autres, ne sera probablement pas ce qui a eu lieu, mais seulement ce qui sera raconté." Cited by Jacob, *Robespierre*, epigraph.

CHAPTER ONE

1. Price, *The Road*, 101–383; Rudé, *The Crowd*, 61–79; Mathiez, "Étude critique," "Étude critique, suite," and "Étude critique, suite et fin."

2. For more on the political turmoil prompted by food shortages, see Kaplan, *Provisioning*; Tilly, "Food Riot"; Hufton, "Social Conflict"; and Bouton, "Gendered Behavior."

3. Mathiez, "Étude critique, suite," 293.

4. On November 9, 1789, the National Assembly moved to the Salle du Manège, on the grounds of the Tuileries palace. Despite its poor acoustics and awkward design (the building was ten times as long as it was wide), the Salle du Manège housed the Convention government and the Council of 500 of the Directory as well. The Directory finally moved to the Palais-Bourbon in 1798.

5. Thanks to Paul Friedland for sharing this tripartite categorization (email of January 8, 2008). Feminist interpretations include Duhet, *Les Femmes*, 45–50; Godineau, *Citoyennes*; Levy and Applewhite, "Responses"; Melzer and Rabine, *Rebel Daughters*; Landes, *Women*, 109–12. Although colored by a more misogynistic interpretation, female politicking features prominently in J. B. Morton, *The Bastille*, 26–46.

6. A bailiff's clerk named Stanislas Maillard (1763–94) played a leading role in this version. See Rudé, *The Crowd*; Mathiez, "Étude critique"; and Jean-Clément Martin, *Violence*, 72–78.

7. An inquiry was conducted by the judiciary and published in 1790 after 388 witnesses had been heard. Antoine Rivarol proffers a passionate indictment of the duc d'Orléans and his faction in *Mémoires*, 262–325. The one-sided trial aimed to expose a plot by the duc d'Orléans and the comte de Mireabeau, both of whom were deputies and thus benefited from a legal technicality; see Petitfils in Louis XVI, *Testaments*, 50n1. The jury remains out, according to Shapiro, *Revolutionary Justice*, 84–123; Gottschalk and Maddox, *Lafayette*; and Mathiez, "Étude critique, suite et fin," 47–56.

8. Becker, *The Denial*, 35–36.

9. Tocqueville, *L'Ancien Régime*, 43. Tocqueville nevertheless dedicates his efforts at proving that this monumental effort at self-fashioning was less successful than the revolutionaries liked to admit and that most reforms undertaken in 1789–93 built upon existing frameworks.

10. McMillan, *France and Women*, 92–93, 132–35. See also Gullickson, *Unruly Women*, chap. 5.

11. *RP* 13 (October 3–10, 1789): 9–20; *CP* 44 (October 6, 1789): 174; *CP* 45 (October 7, 1789) : 178.

12. *RP* 13 (October 3–10, 1789): 29–31; *CP* 46 (October 8, 1789): 182. On Olympe de Gouges, see McMillan, *France and Women,* 18–19; Blanc, *Olympe de Gouges*; and Levy, Applewhite, and Johnson, *Women*, 87–96.

13. On the Mazarinade literature, see Ronzeaud, "De la Harangère," 739–53. On women in traditional social protests, see Hufton, *Limits of Citizenship*, chaps. 2–3; and Desan, "Crowds."

14. Evidence of women riding astride cannons emerges in the *Procédure du Châtelet* (1790) cited in Mathiez, "Étude critique, suite," 293; and *Les Révolutions de Paris*, 13. Duhet (*Les Femmes*, 48–50) professes surprise over the "innocent" depiction of cannon-riding women in *RP*. On the Jacobins' appropriation of the pose in revolutionary ceremony, see Schama, *Citizens*, 469.

15. *Soirées amoureuses*, 4.

16. Carlyle, *French Revolution*, 1:209.

17. "J'offre mes services à la nation en qualité de guerrière s'écrie Pétronille Mache-fer, digne émule du père Duchêne, au premier coup de tambour, je prends les armes, je lève un escadron d'amazones, je me mets à leur tête, et le sabre à la main, j'enfonce les bataillons ennemis comme du beurre" (*Lettres b . . . patriotiques de la mère Duchêne*, cited in Cerati, *Le Club*, 11).

18. Confirmation of Théroigne de Méricourt's supposed leadership of the female crowd is still up in the air. Roudinesco (*Théroigne de Méricourt*, 26–31) claims that it is a myth created by the ultraconservative newspaper *Les Actes des apôtres*. However, McMillan (*France and Women*, 20) describes her as "an advocate of arming women and forming them into a legion of Amazons, or women warriors."

19. Langlois, "Counterrevolutionary Iconography," 45.

20. "La décoration est celle du dernier acte de Panurge," "Explication de l'estampe destinée à servir de frontispice au volume second des Actes des Apôtres," *AA* 2 (November 10, 1789): 1.

21. The opening citation, "Est modus in rebus / Sunt certi denique fines," is from Horace's *Satires* 1.1.106; a second quotation, "At medias inter caedes exsultat Amazon," and a third, "At non in Venerem segnes nocturnaque bella," are from *Aeneid* 11.648. A pun translates Méricourt's military prowess into an opéra-bouffe: "Tant d'exploits et de si glorieux mouvements lui avaient accaparé toutes les voix pour mettre la bande joyeuse en mesure"; *AA* 2 (November 10, 1789): 3.

22. Schlegel, cited in Kayser, *The Grotesque*, 53.

23. A. P. Moore, "*Genre Poissard*"; Marion, "'Dames'"; Frantz, "Travestis." On the *poissard* motif in Mazarinades, see Carrier, *Mazarinades*, 1:397–98.

24. Seth, *Marie-Antoinette*, 138.

25. Godechot, "La Presse française." The vulgar title of this newspaper, *Lettres bougrement patriotiques du véritable Père Duchêne*, could be translated as "Damned [or fucking] good patriotic letters by the real Père Duchêne."

26. *RP*, February 12, 1791, cited in McMillan, *France and Women*, 28. *RP*, January 19–26, 1793, cited in Desan, "'Constitutional Amazons.'" On Prudhomme's critique of Kéralio, see Landes, *Visualizing*, 91–93.

27. *Considérations politiques des notables de la Halle de Paris sur les affaires présentes* (1791), cited in d'Orliac, *Dames*, 126–27.

28. Landes, *Visualizing*, 62–63. See also Weinbaum, *Islands;* Pastre, *Les Amazones;* and Davis, "Women on Top."

29. "Autrefois les femmes n'étoient qu'aimables, et leur devoir étoit de savoir plaire. Elles ont abandonné ce petit genre-là, et savent maintenant faire du bruit, s'agiter, motionner en politique, en finance, en législation. Mais où elles sont le plus brillant, c'est dans les révolutions; elles s'élèvent jusqu'aux grands moyens, quand le plan exige de la vigueur, du sang, des exécutions. . . . Nous avons supprimé toutes les distinctions, il nous reste à supprimer les sexes"; *Anecdote historique traduite du turc*, 23.

30. The queen's words reveal her secret knowledge of Lafayette's disheveled appearance after making love, as she exclaims, "Sire, que vous est-il donc arrivé? Comme vous êtes pâle et défait! Cependant ce n'est pas moi qui . . . car je ne vous ai pas . . . mais c'est incroyable: vous avez, Dieu me pardonne, pris la figure de notre Général." *Histoire véritable de Gingigolo*, 10–11.

31. Ibid., 12.

32. Necker described his proposed Bureau général des dépenses de la maison du roi as "composé de cinq commissaires généraux versés dans cette manutention, et qui, en réunissant différentes connaissances pourront conduire dans un même esprit le détail entier des dépenses de notre maison"; Necker, *Œuvres complètes*, 3:211–12. I thank Danny Rosas-Alvarez for this insight.

33. "La Femme porte le Fuzi / Le mari porte l'enfant sur ses Genoux. / Le chasseur chase sur la mer et le poison vollé en l'air [sic]"; figure labeled "Women and Fish on Top" in Hesse, *Other Enlightenment*, 23; this title makes homage to the work of Natalie Zemon Davis.

34. Hesse, *The Other Enlightenment*, 22; Davis, "Women on Top," 142. The postcard entitled "Is Your Wife a Suffragette?" is reproduced in Tickner, *Spectacle*, 34. Tickner's analysis of the humor in role reversals is linked to another satirical cartoon, entitled "The Suffragette Not at Home," where a husband scalds the cat while trying to fill a teapot and an unhappy baby looks on in mute wonder. See *Spectacle*, 52.

35. James Fraser, "History and Mystery."

36. Fanchon describes the passerby as a "vilain morciau d'contrebande, il a ma foi bon air t'avec ses mollets ni pu ni moins qu'des échalats plantés dans des bottes pour qu'on ne voie pas ses jambes tortues, et pis ses culottes qui l'y montent z'au menton ? N'diroit-on pas un magot dans un sac?" The client lamely riposdes in an accent resembling the foppish Incroyable lisp that was fashionable during the years of the Directory, "En véité on voit bien que vous êtes de la canaille," before concluding, "Vous êtes de bonnes zens" and promising to stop ogling the women of the marketplace. Vadé, *Œuvres choisies*, 17–19; also reproduced in *Poissardiana*.

37. Marion, "*Dames*," 310–14; Hesse, *Other Enlightenment*, 18. "Si les Grands troublent encore / Que le diable les confonde / Et puisqu'ils aiment tant l'Or / Que dans leur gueule on en fonde / Voilà les sincères vœux / Qu'les Harengères font pour eux"; cited in Schama, *Citizens*, 457.

38. *Lettre du ministre de la maison du Roi, à M. Bailly, le priant de s'opposer à la venue des femmes du marché Saint-Martin à Versailles, pour éviter les manifestations*

populaires, le Roi ne voulant recevoir que les dames de la Halle, August 20, 1789, AN 01 500, fol. 440. Hesse claims that the dissolution of the Confraternity of St. Louis represented the rupture of formal ties between the monarchy and the market women, and connects this institutional change to the emergence of a fear of women's speech, conflating the *Mère Duchene* newspaper with *poissard* literature to project an image of menacing female radicalism; see Hesse, *Other Enlightenment*, 20–27.

39. On the craze for Madame Angot, see A. P. Moore, *"Genre Poissard,"* 268–83; and *Au Temps des Merveilleuses*, 128, 237.

40. "On désigne toujours par le nom de *poissardes* les femmes qui sont allées de Paris à Versailles. C'est un malheur pour celles qui débitent les poissons et les fruits dans les rues et dans les halles; la vérité veut qu'on dise que, loin de se mêler aux fausses poissardes qui vinrent pour les recruter et les mener à Versailles, elles demandèrent mainforte au corps-de-garde de la pointe Sainte-Eustache, pour les repousser"; Rivarol, *Mémoires*, 263.

41. "Les femmes de la halle se faisaient surtout remarquer par l'ardeur de leur loyalisme. La presse joint ses acclamations à celle du populaire"; Mathiez, "Étude critique, suite et fin," 53–56. Marie-Antoinette wrote, "je parle au peuple: milices, poissardes, tous me tendent la main. Je le leur donne"; cited in Mathiez, "Étude critique, suite et fin," 54.

42. Cited in d'Orliac, *Dames*, 143.

43. Mathiez, "Étude critique, suite et fin," 51–52.

44. *RP* 64 (September 25–October 2, 1790): 596–97. On Audu/Audru's arrest and testimony at trial, see *CP* 268 (September 25, 1790): 1071; *CP* 280 (October 7, 1790): 1119.

45. Granier, *Femme criminelle*, 350–51.

46. English novelists were "quick to employ very similar synecdoches to those of Burke" in scenes showing a French mob surrounding a defenseless heroine, according to Grenby, *Anti-Jacobin Novel*, 38–39.

47. For Edmund Burke's original description, see *Reflections*, 165. Wollstonecraft, *A Vindication of the Rights of Man*, 29–30. On Wollstonecraft's changed allegiance in her *Historical and Moral View of the Origin and Progress of the French Revolution* (1794), see Blakemore, *Crisis*, 133–38.

48. "Rapporter ce qui n'est point ou peu connu . . . voilà mon intention"; Roussel, *Château*, 1:62.

49. According to a 1988 source, Louise Reine Audu was a fruit seller in Les Halles, a leader of the march on Versailles, and a participant in the violence of August 10, 1792, when she "fought like a man" and killed some Swiss guards. "Sa force, sa beauté et son audace lui avaient valu le surnom de 'Reine des Halles'"; Caratini, *Dictionnaire*, 46.

50. The best source on the *femme forte* tradition remains MacLean, *Woman Triumphant*, 76–87.

51. "Depuis la célèbre *Debore*, qui succéda à Moïse et Josué, jusqu'aux deux sœurs *Freis*, qui combattent si vaillamment dans nos armées républicaines, il ne s'est pas passé un siècle qui n'ait produit une femme guerrière. . . . Sans qu'il soit besoin de vous citer les noms particuliers des courageuses guerrières, qui ne serviroient qu'à faire ressortir davantage la timidité de notre sexe, par des exemples rares de la valeur de quelques-unes, je vous rappellerai la mâle et guerrière vigueur de cette colonie d'Amazones dont la jalousie des femmes a fait douter de l'existence; je vous dirai que le danger n'effraya pas ces nouvelles Romaines qui se précipitèrent au milieu du tranchant des armes . . . enfin,

je vous montrerai les citoyennes de Lille, qui, dans ce moment, bravent la rage des assail-
lans, et étouffent en riant les bombes qu'ils lancent dans la ville. Que prouvent tous ces
exemples, sinon que les femmes peuvent former des bataillons, commander des armées,
combattre et vaincre aussi-bien que les hommes?" Roussel, *Château*, 2:36–38.

52. On mockery against women's petitions, see Abray, "Feminism," 46–49. References to Roussel's novel as historical document include Levy, Applewhite, and Johnson,
Women, 166. These authors date the scene to autumn 1793, whereas Roussel's narrative closes in December 1792. They may have been misled by Cerati in *Le Club*, 49–51;
however, Cerati mentions that *Le Château* was "sujet à caution, Proussinalle étant
fort hostile à ce groupement, et la présence d'Olympe de Gouges assez déconcertante."
Others who cite Roussel's novel as documentary evidence include Abray, "Feminism,"
52; Godineau, *Citoyennes*, 376; Landes, *Visualizing*, 96–98, 211n46; and Censer and
Hunt, "Liberty," under Account of a Session of the Society of Revolutionary Republican
Women.

53. Gower, *Dispatches*, 289; Ferrières, *Correspondance*, 385; Hatin, *Bibliographie*,
95; Vigny, *Stello*, 149. Laughter was exploited as a political tool by patriots as well; see
DeBaecque, *Caricature*, 13.

54. "Avouez, me dit l'Anglais, que ces extravagances sont bien amusantes.—Je
l'avoue; mais, en y réfléchissant, le délire de ces femmes me fait naître des craintes. Si
leurs têtes s'échauffent, vous connoissez l'entêtement de ce sexe, elles sont capables de se
porter à quelques excès.—Votre nation possède le remède: l'arme du ridicule et du persif-
flage qu'elle sait si bien manier, détruira ces comiques prétentions"; Roussel, *Château*,
2:44.

55. Cuddon, *Dictionary*, 599.

56. The "bumbling chronicler" label was coined by David Eick (presentation at conference of American Society for Eighteenth-Century Studies, March 29, 2008) and builds
upon the taxonomy of Voltairean techniques in Gay, introduction to *The Philosophical
Dictionary*.

57. As the Discours préliminaire announces: "jeunes élégans, que le poids d'un léger
volume ne vous effraye pas; vous serez bien dédommagés de la fatigue qu'il vous aura
causé, s'il amène le sourire de la gaité sur les lèvres de l'aimable enchanteresse à qui vous
en ferez la lecture . . . puissai-je seulement ramener en France le goût de la plaisanterie si
familière aux Français; et si au lieu de vous effrayer, je parviens à vous faire rire, mon but
sera rempli"; Madame S*** [Suremain], *Melchior*, n.p.

58. "L'auteur annonce du merveilleux, mais d'un genre neuf et gai; il tient parole.
Pour s'en convaincre, il suffit de savoir que presque toute l'action se passe dans l'île
Feminensis, où les amours et les plaisirs ne connaissent ni les diables, ni les spectres";
[Une Société de gens de lettres], *Nouvelle Bibliothèque universelle des romans* (Paris:
Maradan, An 9, 1800), 4:195. "L'auteur voyant que le merveilleux est si fort à la mode
aujourd'hui, commence par faire naître son incroyable par le gosier de sa mère; ensuite,
après quelques aventures, il le fait aborder dans une île, où les femmes tuent tout le sexe
masculin, vivent avec des singes, où l'on se salue en tirant la langue hors la bouche, et
où il y a un arbre dont les facultés réproductives fécondent toutes celles et tous ceux qui
en approchent, et par les vertus duquel notre incroyable devient enceinte, etc."; *Journal
général de la littérature* 3 (vendémiaire An 9): 310.

59. "Palper mes habits, me retourner dans tous les sens, me dépouiller de mes vête-mens, fût l'ouvrage dont elles s'acquitèrent [sic] très-promptement et avec une parfaite dex-térité; ma personne fixoit toute leur attention. L'examen ne pouvait pas m'être défavorable, et je le soutins, non-seulement sans murmure, mais encore avec plaisir"; *Melchior*, 41.

60. Bellhouse, "Candide Shoots."

61. "Quelles fonctions ces singes pouvoient-ils remplir auprès de ces dames? Étoit-ce des maris ou des esclaves? allois-je avoir des maîtres ou des concurrens?"; *Melchior*, 43.

62. Didier, *Ecrire la Révolution*, 217–43.

63. "Un homme est parmi nous! Un homme est associé au pouvoir de notre reine! Oh malheur! Déjà on croyoit, ou l'on vouloit faire croire que l'île ne tarderoit pas à être engloutie, puisque parjure aux engagemens communs, la souveraine transgressoit si formellement les lois antiques du pays"; *Melchior*, 71.

64. "Peut-être ne s'en plaignirent-elles pas; mais qui peut lire dans l'intérieur de la pensée d'une femme?"; ibid., 75.

65. On Deputy Target's pregnancy and delivery, see Cameron, "Political Exposures," 97–100; and Landes, *Visualizing*, 63–64.

66. "Si quelques vieilles édentées, craignant de ne pas être pourvues, osèrent encore murmurer, la désapprobation générale et la crainte d'être soumises aux singes, les rédui-sirent bientôt au silence"; *Melchior*, 77.

67. Daut, "Sciences," 13–29.

68. Pellegrin, *Vêtements*, 182–84.

69. Representative titles include Devaines, *Lettres de la comtesse de . . . au cheva-lier; Le Réveil des dames;* and *Les Chevalières errantes*. Secret female societies feature in Lesuire, *Charmansage*, 1:109–18; and Révéroni Saint-Cyr, *Sabina d'Herfeld*, 1:18–31, 37–39.

70. Letter of August 11, 1795, from Edmund Burke to Mrs. Crewe, cited in Norris, "Counter-revolutionary Imagination," 217.

71. AN F7/6152, *plaquette* no. 2, nos. 93–100; and AN F7/7807, nos. 1–3. It is alleged that some women were "disguised as men" while others were dressed in military garb. (It is interesting to note that these complaints are lodged alongside other reports of women wearing see-through clothing; a very different matter for public morals!) In prai-rial Year 7, two police agents reported, "J'ai observé une jolie femme qui étoit déguisée en homme tenant une autre femme par le bras, elle se faisoit suivre et remarquer de tout le monde" and "On remarque, dans les promenades, des femmes travesties en homme, dont quelques unes portent une espèce d'uniforme militaire, ce qui donne lieu à diverses réflexions" (AN F7/6152, nos. 94 and 93). Nevertheless, it is impossible to know exactly what articles of men's clothing were deemed a "travesty," because this episode has eluded costume history as far as I can tell. The challenge to the minister's order is in F7/6152, no. 95. For the folio-size poster of the new law, see F7/7807, no. 3.

72. Rendall, *Modern Feminism*, 291–307.

73. Bidelman, *Pariahs*, 65.

74. Tickner, *Spectacle*, 128; Atkinson, *Suffragettes*, 112–19. Somerville (1780–1872) was a scientist and advocate of women's suffrage after whom Somerville College, Oxford, is named. I use the term "suffragist" instead of "suffragette" because the latter was

coined as a pejorative, "feminized" diminutive, while the former, which was preferred in the United States, applies to both men and women suffrage supporters.

75. Hannam, Auchterlonie, and Holden, *International Encyclopedia*, 104–6 (s.v. "France," "French Revolution"). Abigail Adams's letter notes: "In the new code of laws which I suppose it will be necessary for you to make, I desire you would remember the ladies, and be more generous and favorable to them than your ancestors. . . . Remember, all men would be tyrants if they could. If particular care and attention are not paid to the ladies, we are determined to foment a rebellion, and will not hold ourselves bound to obey any laws in which we have no voice or representation"; cited in Stanton, Anthony, and Gage, *Woman Suffrage*, 1:32. American women won the right to vote in 1920.

76. On the embarrassment of the signers of the Seneca Falls Declaration when faced by public ridicule, see document 5 (Seneca Falls Convention, 1848) in Buhle and Buhle, *Concise History*, 97.

77. Cited in Stanton, Anthony, and Gage, *Woman Suffrage,,* 1:234–37.

78. Buhle and Buhle, *Concise History*, 8; Raylyn Moore, *Wonderful Wizard*, 50. Gage singles out two French women in the first chapter of Stanton, Anthony, and Gage, *Woman Suffrage*, namely Madame Roland and Charlotte Corday.

79. Baum cited in Koupal's introduction to Baum, *Our Landlady*, 12 (see also 6–7); Rogers, *Baum*, 25–44, 63–64. The NAWSA was the National American Woman Suffrage Association, launched by Susan B. Anthony. Gage was a prominent speaker and leader of the NAWSA.

80. Frantz, "Travestis," 18–20; Koupal, introduction to Baum, *Our Landlady*, 8–9.

81. Rogers, *Baum*, 36.

82. "Pour la vertu faut z'être libre; / L'choix qu'on fait soi-même est le bon. . . . Avec l'divorce, mon chien d'homme / N'me f'ra put ant son embarrass; / Il saura que j'peux l'planter là, / Et ça seul le corrigera"; "Le Divorce," in *Poissardiana*, cited in A. P. Moore, "*Genre Poissard*," 343–44.

83. Raylyn Moore, *Wonderful Wizard*, 128; Nye, "Appreciation," 12.

84. Baum, *Marvelous Land*, 88.

85. Rogers, *Baum*, 125–26; Wagenknecht, "Utopia Americana," 155.

CHAPTER TWO

1. "Devant la vogue extraordinaire des automates au XVIIIe siècle, on pourrait s'étonner de ne trouver, à la même époque, aucune exploitation littéraire du thème de la création artificielle"; Amartin-Serin, *Création*, 28.

2. Krief argues that *Le Miroir* is one among several texts in which "l'imaginaire révolutionnaire modèle des créatures dont les expressions du visage et les attitudes du corps permettent de rendre visible ce qui est signifié politiquement . . . la Nation"; Krief, "Écriture," 119.

3. The initial meeting of the humans and the mechanized flautist invented by Frankénsteïn is described as follows: "L'un et l'autre s'approchèrent de la statue, qui s'inclina en leur présence, & les étonna si fort par ce début, tenant du phenomène de l'économie animale, qu'ils réculèrent deux pas; ils la crurent organisée par une main

divine; &, comme s'il y eût quelque chose à craindre de s'assurer du contraire par le tact, ils se rassirent, éloignés d'elle d'une certaine distance"; Nogaret, *Miroir*, 42–43.

4. Shelley, "Introduction to *Frankenstein*, Third Edition (1831)," in *Frankenstein*, ed. Hunter, 172. All citations from *Frankenstein* refer to this edition unless otherwise indicated.

5. Daumas claims that the best definition of "machine" (before Ampère offered his definition in 1830) was penned in 1724: it speaks of an "artificial disposition" that effects movement "with economy of time and energy, which would not be possible by other means"; cited in Daumas, *Histoire générale*, 92. Note the lack of concern for predictable results or interchangeable components, let alone the potential for mass manufacturing, in this concept of mechanics.

6. Gillispie, *Science*, 195–99.

7. Archives parlementaires 30 (séance du 9 septembre 1791): 401; cited in Gillispie, *Science*, 199. A government prize for inventors dated September 18, 1790, is also found in Favier, *Chronicle of the French Revolution*, 172. This sensational move escaped mention in the major Parisian newspapers, however.

8. "Respectueuse pétition des artistes inventeurs," Archives parlementaires 24 (séance jeudi 7 avril 1791), 641–44; cited in Gillispie, *Science*, 195.

9. Gillispie, *Science*, 196.

10. On Boufflers's biography, see Houssaye, *Galerie*, 4:205–25; and Deborah Kennedy, *Helen Maria Williams*, 182–84, 204.

11. *Rapport fait à l'Assemblée Nationale au nom du Comité d'Agriculture et de Commerce . . . sur la propriété des auteurs de nouvelles découvertes et inventions en tout genre d'industrie* (1791); cited in Gillispie, *Science*, 196. Pochet expresses concern over losing French industrial talent abroad in *La Boussole*, 2:316. See also *Réflexions sur le commerce*, which describes French manufacturing as "découragé par le défaut de protection & d'avance pour l'établissement des machines, écrasé par le mépris que les Grands versoient sur ces hommes utiles, [et] gêné par le prix excessif de l'intérêt" (n.p.).

12. *RP* 78 (January 1–8, 1791): 716–19; *RP* 84 (February 12–19, 1791): 266–27, 354.

13. *CP* 36 (February 5, 1791):144.

14. Gillispie, *Science*, 196–99; Hilaire-Pérez, *L'Invention*, 286–87.

15. Daumas, *Histoire générale*, 3:1–12; *Dictionnaire chronologique*, 1:60; Alder, *Engineering*, 127–291.

16. On the comet discovered by Caroline Herschel (or Herschell), see *AM* 22 (January 22, 1790): 3:176–77; and *AM* 30 (January 30, 1790): 3:240 (article by M. de la Lande of the Académie des sciences). Chemistry lessons at the Lycée with M. de Fourcroy are promoted in *AM* 41 (February 10, 1790): 3:327. For advertisements of scientific instruments and other courses, see *AM* 113 (April 23, 1790): 4:258; and *AM* 113 (June 12, 1790): 5:608.

17. Tissandier, *Histoire des ballons*; Delon and Goulemot, *Ballons*. See also the 1785 satirical print "Moyens infaillibles d'enlever les ballons," which shows an aeronaut suspended from a balloon that is about twenty feet in the air and being pulled by a man on horseback (in *L'Art de l'estampe*, 32).

18. This was a pretty expensive outing for most people; for workers' wages in different trades, see Godineau, *Citoyennes*, 363. For balloon ads, see *AM* 194 (July 13, 1790): 5:112; and *JP* 194 (July 13, 1790): n.p. See also *JP* 185 (July 4, 1790): supp. 2; and *JP* 243

(August 31, 1790): n.p., in which the balloonist announces he will be accompanied by M. de la Lande.

19. Shares in the Compagnie aéronautique are advertised in *JP* 119 (April 29, 1790): supp. 2.

20. The *aéro-clavicorde* is advertised in *JP* 111 (April 21, 1790): supp. n.p.; the hydraulic machine is in *JP* 247 (September 4, 1790): supp. iv; the mechanical mills are found in *JP* 42 (February 11, 1790): supp. iv; and *JP* 198 (July 17, 1790): supp. n.p.

21. The method of coded writing—"l'art de rendre le secret de sa correspondance inviolable" (which one can master in five minutes!)—is advertised in *JP* 248 (October 5, 1790): supp. n.p. On the "autographe mécanique," see *Dictionnaire chronologique*, 1:487–88.

22. The ad for French razors is in *JP* 101 (April 11, 1790): supp. iii.

23. Altick, *Shows*, 67–72.

24. Burney, *Evelina*, 65.

25. Under the rubric "Spectacles," Perrin's automaton shows ("Amusemens physiques") are advertised in *JP* 94 (April 4, 1790): supp. iii; *JP* 96 (April 6, 1790): supp. n.p.; *JP* 100 (April 10, 1790): supp. n.p. Virtually identical ads are reproduced in *AM* 87 (March 28, 1790): 3:720, and every day thereafter from April 1 to April 10, 1790 (nos. 91–111). For evidence of crowd reactions, consider this note from the editor of the *Moniteur*: "Nous avons été témoins mercredi dernier de l'adresse de M. Perrin, et nous avons vu avec plaisir le petit Calchas, la tour magique, l'encrier et la colombe. Mais ce qui nous a paru extrêmement étrange, c'est le soin que prenaient quelques spectateurs d'intriguer et de déconcerter M. Perrin. Ils voulaient sûrement prouver au reste du public que celui qui s'annonce simplement comme un physicien-mécanicien n'était pas sorcier." *AM* 100 (April 10, 1790): 4:80.

26. Altick, *Shows*, 63.

27. On the machinery that made these devices run, the best source is still Chapuis and Gélis, *Le Monde*.

28. Nogaret, *Miroir*, 42–43; Hoffmann, *Sandman*, 302.

29. Challenges to the mechanical mode feature prominently in works such as *L'Encyclopédie* and Diderot's *Rêve de d'Alembert*. See Vila, *Enlightenment*, 152–81; Cottom, "Work of Art," 65; Riskin, *Age of Sensibility*, 83–84; and Kang, *Sublime Dreams*, 146–84.

30. Douthwaite, *Wild Girl*, 70–133.

31. Voskuhl, "Motions."

32. Cited in Altick, *Shows*, 66.

33. Review of Antoine de la Salle, *La Méchanique* [sic] *morale, ou Essai sur l'art de perfectionner et d'employer ses organes propres*, in *CP* 212 (July 31, 1790): 845.

34. Rivarol celebrates Mical's machine as a technical tour de force and object of French national pride: "Il y a dans la rue du Temple, au Marais, un ouvrage de mécanique qui attire à lui la foule des connaisseurs, et qu'on va bientôt livrer à la curiosité publique. Ce sont deux têtes d'airain qui parlent et qui prononcent nettement des phrases entières. Elles sont colossales, et leur voix est sur-humaine. . . . Ce n'est point là, comme vous le sentez, l'ouvrage du moment et du hasard; c'est le fruit du travail et du génie"; Rivarol, "Lettre à M. le Président de ***."

35. "1ere tête: 'Le Roi donne la paix à l'Europe.' 2e tête: 'La Paix couronne le Roi de gloire.' 1ere tête: 'Et la Paix fait le bonheur des peuples.' 1ere tête: 'O Roi adorable, Père de vos peuples, leur bonheur fait voir à l'Europe la gloire de votre trône.'" Cited in Chapuis and Gélis, *Le Monde*, 2:204.

36. See also Langlois, *Caricature contre-révolutionnaire*, 123.

37. Johnson, *The Rambler* 83 (January 1, 1751), in *Yale Edition*, 4:73.

38. Darnton, *Mesmerism*; and Baker, *Condorcet*, 76–77.

39. On Marat, see Hahn, *Anatomy*, 223ff.; and Lemaire, "Dr Jean-Paul Marat." On skepticism regarding scientific spectacles, see Stafford, *Artful Science*, 96.

40. Rétif de la Bretonne, *Découverte australe*, 1:24.

41. Gouges, "Trois urnes."

42. DesBordes, "Notice"; Napo, *Index*, fiches 1:788, 1:302–16.

43. The manifesto for this new appreciation of minor authors is Deleuze and Guattari, *Kafka*.

44. "Citoyen miné par l'âge, je fais ce que je puis: ma plume me tient lieu de sabre et de mousquet"; Nogaret, *À la nation*, 1.

45. See Nogaret's letter of March 8, 1783, to Benjamin Franklin, published in *Benjamin Franklin Papers*. On the Masonic morality in Nogaret's play, *Le Réveil d'Adam* (1804), see Janet Burke, "Leaving," 259.

46. Nogaret writes: "Un Jacobin de Paris a dit à la tribune, le 25 nivôse: *il est temps d'exciter l'indignation des Peuples.* Un Jacobin de Versailles, ce jour même, cédait à l'inspiration de promulguer la même idée. La motion de l'un et l'ouvrage de l'autre ont paru en même temps"; *L'Appel*, 1. The author denies his work's link to politics in *L'Aristénète français*, declaring, "Moi, philosophe! Ah! Je voudrais bien l'être. . . . Je fais des Contes pour rire"; Nogaret, "Avis de l'auteur," in *L'Aristénète*, n.p.

47. This dedication emphasizes the integrity of Nogaret's book by aligning it with a man whose name is not found in any accounts of royal bribes or privileges and by asking for his paternal care for the book/orphan: "Mon ami, Soyez le patron de la belle Orpheline dont est question cette Historiette *érotico-politico-patriotique* . . . l'honneur vous ayant toujours servi de guide, c'est justice que je vous préfère à tant d'autres qui ne l'ont jamais connu"; *Miroir*, v–vi. This conception of the book's political utility marks the opening scene, a dream where the author meets the Greek legislator Solon, who encourages him to finish this "instructive bagatelle" (xi).

48. "Elle lui demanda gaiment s'il ne verrait pas avec plaisir tous ces grands faiseurs de machines, depuis si long-tems dans l'inaction, prendre enfin l'essor, & laisser à Syracuse quelque monument de leur savoir?"; ibid., 2–3.

49. I thank Margaret Doody for this etymology and intriguing suggestion.

50. This episode makes reference to Abraham Trembley's discoveries about freshwater polyps from the 1740s, which were popularized by LaMettrie in *L'Homme-Machine* (1748).

51. Signifying "cruel and powerful beast," according to a note, this name combines the noble titles duc de Broglie and prince de Lambesc and other sly puns to make "Lycaon-agrios-kai tyrannos akeirotos-kai-apenès-kai-polé-mios-Brogli-Lam-Besen-Mail-aristos."

52. According to the German legend, a certain Konrad Dippel of Frankenstein was known for his alchemical work; see Florescu, *In Search*, 65–93.

53. Edmund Burke, *Philosophical Enquiry*, 44.

54. Nicator is described as "doué . . . d'une perception à laquelle il était difficile que rien n'échappât, en sorte qu'après avoir mûrement réfléchi, il avait réellement sçu joindre l'agréable à l'utile"; Nogaret, *Miroir*, 45. On Necker's career as finance minister, see Gauchet, "Necker."

55. Shields, *Reality Hunger*, 209; see also Randy Kennedy, "Free-Appropriation Writer."

56. Three copies exist in France: at the Bibliothèque nationale de France, the Bibliothèque municipale de Versailles, and the Bibliothèque historique de la ville de Paris. The one copy in North America, at Princeton University, was declared missing in July 2011.

57. "Aglaonice, ou La Belle au concours" is printed in *Contes et historiettes*, 2:16–123. It is found between "L'Enfant de sa mère," a story of an adulteress who tricks her husband into letting her keep an illegitimate child, and "Le Réveil du dieu de Lampsaque," a rewriting of an ancient fable of Aristenete. A second reprint is in Nogaret, *L'Antipode de Marmontel*.

58. Nogaret, *Contes et historiettes*, 2:116n2.

59. Ibid., 120.

60. Nogaret, *L'Âme de Timoléon*, 3.

61. In *Le Falot*, the fishwives request the help of the public scribe to understand current events, and he replies, "Rien de plus facile que de vous l'apprendre, mesdames, & cela d'après tous les papiers publics"; [Bellanger], *Le Falot*, 13. The young writer of Henriquez's story "tâchait de se rendre utile à ses concitoyens," in *Aventures de Jérôme Lecocq*, 59. Amin's writing is explicitly tied to political involvement; like Rousseau, he speaks truth to the people: "Amin sentit la nécessité de ranimer en lui le feu divin qui l'enflamma si longtemps, et de lui montrer dans son vrai jour le tableau de sa situation"; *Amin, ou Ces derniers temps*, 122–23.

62. On violence and instability during the Directory, see Brown, *Ending*, 29–65.

63. For more on the changing styles of writing during these years, see Hunt, *Family Romance*, 160–91; and Mercier, *Paris*, 1:329–32, 410. On the generation of 1830, see Vaillant, *Crise*, 18–20.

64. Sage, "Diderot," 58–59. Passages where the people are celebrated for eschewing a formerly automaton-like existence are in *Philo*, 51; and [Pochet], *La Boussole*, 3:71. "Vous présentez une mécanique à peine commencée à celui qui doit en tourner la manivelle, & vous lui dites, que la constitution de cette mécanique exige qu'il en tourne sur le champ la manivelle, quoique la mécanique ne soit pas à moitié faite. Qu'arrive-t-il? Qu'il la tourne [cette manivelle], & qu'alors il ne manque pas de déranger & d'altérer les premiers rouages"; Carra, in *Courrier politique et littéraire du Cap-français* 1 (January 6, 1791): 1–8.

65. Condorcet, "Lettre," 240, 241.

66. According to Mercier, the duc d'Orléans was "le mannequin le plus automate qui ait figuré dans aucune histoire. Après avoir été le jouet du cabinet britannique, il le fut de tous les factieux"; Mercier, *Paris*, 1:108. Louis XVI is described as "une pièce mécanique inutile à l'action du gouvernement" (1:138). As for Robespierre, "c'était un automate sorti des enfers pour punir les humains" (1:183).

67. [Doppet], *Commissionnaire*, 73–74. Doppet held many positions in the republican

army before receiving an honorable discharge in 1794. He wrote works of history, fiction, and journalism; see Napo, *Index*, fiches 1:325, 1:20–40.

68. On the practice of keeping life-size dolls, see Antonia Fraser, *Dolls*; and Foulke, *Fourteenth Blue Book*. Thanks to Orley Marron for these connections. See also *Charmansage*, where the love-struck hero paints a plaster head with a likeness of his beloved, puts it on a life-size dummy (*mannequin à ressorts*), dresses the dummy, and makes it "dans un état si singulièrement vrai, que tout le monde croyoit voir une personne vivante"; Lesuire, *Charmansage*, 1:76.

69. Castle, *Female Thermometer*, 11.

70. Castein, "'Zerrbilder des Lebens.'"

71. For an interpretation of this scene's critique of the bourgeois and their "cold, rational" attitude toward art and love, see Röder, *Study*, 61.

72. Freud, "The Uncanny"; for a challenge to Freud on *The Sandman*, see Cherry, "Machines," 12–13.

73. Castein, "'Zerrbilder des Lebens,'" 47.

74. Foucault, *Order of Things*, 309.

75. These approaches are found, respectively, in Michel, "Lesbian Panic"; Spivak, *Critique*; Timothy Morton, *Shelley and the Revolution in Taste*; and Bewell, "An Issue." For more interpretations, see Timothy Morton, *Mary Shelley's "Frankenstein."*

76. Clemit, "*Frankenstein*," 30; Paulson, *Representations of Revolution*, 241–44.

77. Thanks to Greg Kucich and Anne Mellor for insights into the family gender dynamics in *Frankenstein*. Mellor, *Mary Shelley*, 38–69. The assimilation of the Arabian Safie into the bosom of the De Lacey family nevertheless symbolizes a reunion of the like-minded, thanks to their long-term friendship.

78. Furet and Richet christened 1790 "l'année heureuse" in chapter 4 of their *Révolution française*.

79. Consider his decision to travel around Europe for two years instead of marrying Elizabeth immediately (vol. 3, chap. 1) and his decision to "quit Geneva for ever" (vol. 3, chap. 7).

80. Florescu, *In Search*, 65–93; Butler, "*Frankenstein* and Radical Science."

81. Lawrence, *Lectures*, 313–14.

82. For the text of these alterations between the 1818 and 1831 editions, see Shelley, *Frankenstein*, ed. Reiger, 42, 241.

83. Mellor, "Choosing," 165.

84. On this motif, see Ozouf, *L'Homme régénéré*.

85. Shelley, *Mary Shelley's Journals*, 12.

86. Henig, "Real Transformers," 55.

87. Godwin, *Caleb Williams*, 360. Shelley dedicated *Frankenstein* to her father, William Godwin.

88. Huet, "Living Images," 76.

CHAPTER THREE

1. Edmund Burke, *Philosophical Enquiry*, 45–46.

2. Ibid., 46.

3. Louis XVI, *Déclaration du Roi*, 73–76, 81, 48.

4. The other days elicited equally laconic entries in this journal; the fateful turning point of June 21 is mentioned only as "Départ à minuit de Paris. Arrivé et arrêté à Varennes en Argonnes à 11 heures du soir"; cited in Petitfils, *Louis XVI*, 804.

5. Castelot, *Varennes*, 50, 69–72; Ancelon, *La Vérité*, 34–35; Lenotre, *The Flight*, 41–42.

6. Ancelon, *La Vérité*, 34; Tackett, *When the King Took Flight*, 48.

7. Ancelon, *La Vérité*, 37; Lenotre, *The Flight*, 50–51; Tackett, *When the King Took Flight*, 67.

8. Tackett, *When the King Took Flight*, 67. The royal governess carried a passport as a Russian noblewoman named Baroness de Korff. The rest of the group was supposed to be her two daughters, the dauphin being dressed as a girl, and their servants; the king was disguised as the intendant and the queen as the governess.

9. See the testimonials gathered in *Mémoires sur l'Affaire de Varennes*.

10. Castelot charges Choiseul and Bouillé with the greatest crimes in *Varennes*, 95–110, 133–52; Ancelon blames all three officers in *La Vérité*, 87–135; Loomis blames Fersen in *The Fatal Friendship*, 150–198.

11. Petitfils, *Louis XVI*, 806–7.

12. Hardman, *Louis XVI*, 130–31.

13. Viguerie, *Louis XVI*, 310.

14. Hardman, *Louis XVI*, 126.

15. Ozouf, *Varennes*, 25, 114.

16. Hardman, *French Revolution Sourcebook*, 122.

17. The Christological references of Louis's declaration echo two brochures published in 1790 (*Passion de 1790*; *Résurrection de Louis XVI*). Describing the public temperament in the days following the 1789 march on Versailles, Louis writes, "plus le Roi a fait de sacrifices pour le bonheur de ses peuples, plus les factieux ont travaillé pour en faire méconnaître le prix"; referring to his family's aborted trip to Saint-Cloud in April 1791, he claims that "il fallait que le Roi bût le calice jusqu'à la lie"; Louis XVI, *Déclaration du Roi*, esp. 53, 81.

18. "Tant que le Roi a pu espérer voir renaître l'ordre et le bonheur de Royaume . . . aucun *sacrifice* personnel ne lui a coûté" (47); "Mais aujourd'hui que la seule récompense de tant de *sacrifices* est de voir la destruction de la Royauté" (47–48); "il aima mieux se *sacrifier* personnellement" (49); "fidèle au système de *sacrifice* que S.M. s'était fait pour procurer la tranquillité publique" (50); "Mais un *sacrifice* plus pénible était réservé au cœur de S.M" (51); "plus le Roi a fait de *sacrifices* pour le bonheur de ses peuples (53); "tous les *sacrifices* qu'il a faits à ses peuples dans la séance du 23 juin" (53); Louis XVI, *Déclaration du Roi*, my emphasis.

19. Hardman, *French Revolution Sourcebook*, 123. Describing his visit to Paris in the days after the storming of the Bastille, the king notes that "le Roi, fort de sa conscience et de la droiture de ses intentions, n'a pas craint de venir seul parmi les citoyens armés de la Capitale"; describing the scene at Versailles on October 5–6, 1789, he conjures up a battle of Good (the royal guards) versus Evil (the misguided mob): "deux [gardes] avaient péri . . . plusieurs autres avaient été blessés grièvement en exécutant strictement les ordres du Roi qui leur avait défendu de tirer sur la multitude égarée"; Louis XVI, *Déclaration du Roi*,

49, 51. NB: The use of *égaré* is another biblical reference, as in *les brébis égarées*, "the lost lambs of the Lord."

20. "Le Roi ne pense pas qu'il soit possible de gouverner un Royaume d'une si grande étendue et d'une si grande importance que la France par les moyens établis par l'Assemblée Nationale tels qu'ils existent à présent. S.M., en accordant à tous les décrets indistinctement une sanction . . . y a été déterminée par le désir d'éviter toute discussion que l'expérience lui avait appris être au moins inutile"; Louis XVI, *Déclaration du Roi*, 69–70.

21. "Français, est-ce là ce que vous attendiez en envoyant vos représentants à l'Assemblée Nationale, désiriez-vous que l'anarchie et le despotisme des Clubs remplaçassent le Gouvernement Monarchique sous lequel la Nation a prospéré pendant quatorze cent ans? Désiriez-vous voir votre Roi comblé d'outrages et privé de sa liberté pendant qu'il ne s'occupait que d'établir la vôtre? L'amour pour ses Rois est une des vertus du Français, et S.M. en a reçu personnellement des marques trop touchantes pour pouvoir jamais les oublier. Les factieux sentaient bien que, tant que cet amour subsisterait, leur ouvrage ne pourrait jamais s'achever; ils sentirent également que, pour l'affaiblir, il fallait, s'il était possible, anéantir le respect qui l'a toujours accompagné; et c'est la source de tous les outrages que le Roi a reçus depuis deux ans"; ibid., 72–73.

22. "Quel plaisir n'aura-t-il pas à oublier toutes ses injures personnelles, et de se revoir au milieu de vous, lorsqu'une constitution qu'il aura acceptée librement fera que notre Sainte Religion sera respectée, que le Gouvernement sera établi sur un pied stable et utile par son action, que les biens de l'état de chacun ne seront plus troublés"; ibid., 83.

23. "Revenez à votre Roi; il sera toujours votre père, votre meilleur ami"; ibid.

24. For news of the king's "kidnapping," see *AM* 173 (June 21, 1791); and *AM* 175 (June 24, 1791). For the letter from Louis XVI to Condé, see *AM* 177 (June 26, 1791): 8:754. *JP* also employs the term *enlèvement* (kidnapping) for several days, as in *JP* 173 (June 22, 1791): 698; and *JP* 177 (June 26, 1791): 709.

25. "Quel regret pourroit nous inspirer un prince qui abdique volontairement, qui, pour ressaisir les usurpations de la couronne, ne craint pas de livrer 25 millions d'hommes à toutes les horreurs de la guerre"; *CP* 173 (June 22, 1791): 691–92. This reference to 25 million men, in a country of 26 million people, effectively accuses the king of vaulting his entire country into war.

26. Reinhard, *La Chute*, 30–56.

27. *JP* 175 (June 24, 1791): 702.

28. Hardman points out that the *Déclaration* did wield some positive results: "The constitutional committee did try to incorporate some of the king's demands in the finished document and, arguably, paved the way by the repression of popular dissent on the Champ de Mars"; *French Revolution Sourcebook*, 123–24.

29. A letter from the municipality of Paris of September 1791 notes that "le Roi a demandé l'oubli de tout ce qui s'est passé, et que l'assemblée nationale a décrété d'annuler toutes les procédures qui y sont relatives"; AP: "Estampes injurieuses sur le retour du roi," *AA* 86, no. 53 (September 16, 1791).

30. [Femme Honoré], *Lettres*, 6–7.

31. *Grand Jugement*, 2.

32. The comparison with Henri IV emerges in a satirical song to the melody of "Vive

Henri IV": "Vive la France / Mais non son foible roi; / L'infâme engeance / Est indigne de foi; / Notre espérance / N'est plus que dans la Loi"; ibid., 5. For the history of the song, see Mason, *Singing*, 55–57.

33. Curtin, "The Declaration," 173.

34. Ogle, "The Trans-Atlantic King," 91.

35. *Conspirations, trahisons*, 20. See also Ghachem, "'The Colonial Vendée.'"

36. Deraggis, *Adresse au peuple*, 6. The violence committed by blacks was described as "revolutionary, atheist and regicide" in the London-based *Correspondance française* 108 (July 10, 1794): 446.

37. *Extrait d'une lettre sur les malheurs*, 9; Hugo, *Bug-Jargal*, chap. 16.

38. Henri IV reduces Louis XVI to tears in *Henri IV et Louis XIV au petit coucher de Louis XVI*, 2. In the ninth dialogue, Louis XIV advises Louis XVI: "Gouverne par toi-même, et sache dire quelquefois: *je veux*"; *Louis XIV à Saint Cloud*, 7. See also Duprat, "Louis XVI morigéné," 328–29.

39. AP: letter 81, no. 203 (August 18, 1790), and letter 81, no. 232 (October 25, 1790), in *Procès-verbaux des Commissaires de Paris*, 1789–90.

40. Bellanger et al., *Histoire générale de la presse*, 1:485.

41. "Ventre saint-gris" is a corruption of "By the belly of Christ" (Ventre Saint-Christ). Legend has it that as a child, Henri IV swore "Ventre Saint-Christ" and was corrected by his tutors to say "saint-gris" instead. (Some historians speculate that the reference to gray may be a pejorative comment on the Franciscans and their gray robes.) The expression is associated with Henri IV still today.

42. "Famille auguste, infortunée, respectable, séchez vos pleurs; prince loyal, cher au Dieu des croyans, tu as trop aimé tes sujets, pour que tes sujets ne t'aiment pas"; *Le Règne*, 60.

43. "Figurez-vous une nombreuse troupe d'enchanteurs braves, généreux, savans, modestes, qui arrivent chez ce peuple de fols, & qui à chaque pas qu'ils font, donnent au prince Trop-Bon & à sa famille, le spectacle d'un prodige qui surpasse tous ceux du grand prophète"; ibid., 64.

44. *Correspondance littéraire* 16 (June 1792): 157.

45. The *Déclaration du Roi* begins: "Tant que le Roi a pu espérer voir renaître l'ordre et le bonheur du Royaume par les moyens employés par l'Assemblée Nationale, et par sa résidence auprès de cette Assemblée dans la capitale du Royaume, aucun sacrifice personnel ne lui a coûté" (47). The dedication to *Le Règne* reads: "On est sûr d'être bien accueilli du public sage et éclairé, quand on a pour amis les amis d'un roi qui n'est aimé que par d'honnêtes gens" (n.p.).

46. *Voltaire et Henri IV*, 75. See also Kimberly Jones, "L'Iconographie henricéenne."

47. Reddy, *Navigation of Feeling*, 108.

48. Chartier, *Les Origines*, 161.

49. See *AM* from July 2 to July 25, 1791, where citizens relay the repercussions of Varennes in their home provinces; September 23, 1791, where the king's brothers speak for him; and November 29, where rumors are printed of a second flight attempt.

50. Cited in DeBaecque, *Caricature*, 184.

51. "On voit . . . en étalage, chez tous les marchands d'estampes, des gravures qui rappellent le moment du retour du Roi, et des estampes bien plus injurieuses à sa personne,

sous différentes allégories"; AP: "Estampes injurieuses sur le retour du roi," *AA* 86, no. 53 (September 16, 1791). See also Reichardt and Kohle, *Visualizing*, 72; DeBaecque, *Caricature*, 37, 173–77.

52. DeBaecque, *Caricature*, 185.

53. Hernardinquer, "Le Porc familier."

54. "Considérez la fuite et l'arrestation de cette bande de cochons / Ville, bourg, et village / Tout s'empresse à courir / Après de si gros sires / . . . / Par un destin criminelle [*sic*] / Le lard allait nous manquer / Mais on les a rattrapés"; cited in DeBaecque, *Caricature*, 185.

55. James Gillray, "Un petit souper à la parisienne; or, A Family of Sans-culottes Refreshing after the Fatigues of the Day," discussed and reproduced in Reichardt and Kohle, *Visualizing*, 194–95. On "Le Peuple mangeur de rois" caricature, see Duprat, *Les Rois de papier*, 28–30.

56. Arasse, *La Guillotine*, 65–93; and Reichardt and Kohle, *Visualizing*, 82–84.

57. AP: *AA* 245, no. 358 (22 thermidor An 8); *AA* 169, no. 128 (16 vendémiaire An 9); "Procès-verbaux, Section de Paris, Pont Neuf," *AA* 218, nos. 137, 139–40 (3–12 germinal An 10); "Procès-verbaux, Sections de Paris, Cité," *AA* 132, nos. 26–27 (28–29 fructidor An 5).

58. Petitfils, *Louis XVI*, 961–64.

59. Romeau, *La Tête*, 3.

60. Flaubert describes a banquet of 1848 in *L'Éducation sentimentale* (1869); see *Œuvres*, 3:609.

61. On the vogue for Adieux prints, see Langlois, *Les Sept Morts*, 6–33. See also AP: "Éventails transparents représentant les adieux de Louis XVI à sa famille," in "Procès ver-baux, Sections de Paris, Cité," *AA* 132, nos. 26–27 (28 fructidor An 5).

62. Clarke, *Commemorating the Dead*, 6.

63. Accounts by Jacques Necker and Louis-Sébastien Mercier report that the dauphin ran down the stairs upon being separated from his father and screamed, "Je veux parler au peuple. . . . Je veux le suppléer de ne pas faire mourir papa roi"; cited in André, *Examen impartial*, 383. Otherwise, the basic narrative remains consistent in sources such as Jordan, *The King's Trial*, 208–21; Viguerie, *Louis XVI*, 402–7; and Petitfils, *Louis XVI*, 935–51.

64. "Non-juror" (also *non-jureur, non-assermenté*, or *réfractaire*) in this context designates ongoing loyalty to the Catholic Church. Despite the July 1790 Civil Constitu-tion of the Clergy, which required all members of the clergy to swear a loyalty oath to the nation, some priests refused to take the vow. They were prosecuted in numerous decrees that followed (deportation, banishment, execution). See Bianchi, "Clergé/Prêtres." Louis's choice of a non-juror priest is symbolic of his devout Catholicism and defiance of the revolutionary government's disrespect for tradition.

65. According to the legal record (*procès verbal*), Louis's last words were "Je meurs innocent des crimes qu'on m'impute. Je pardonne aux auteurs de ma mort, et je prie Dieu que le sang que vous allez répandre ne retombe jamais sur la France." According to the executioner, Sanson, he said, "Vous savez tous que je suis innocent, mais si le sacrifice de ma vie peut être utile au repos de mon peuple, je le fais volontiers." According to San-

terre, "Louis Capet a voulu parler de commisération au peuple, mais je l'en ai empêché pour que la loi reçût son exécution." See Viguerie, *Louis XVI*, 406–7.

66. Hardman, *French Revolution Sourcebook*, 177.

67. Petitfils, *Louis XVI*, 950.

68. A pair of "urne mystérieuse" and a plate were sold for $10,350 by Christie's in New York, and a similar pair of urns was sold by Christie's in London in May 1995. See http://www.christies.com/LotFinder/lot_details.aspx?intObjectID=1710089 (accessed March 3, 2009).

69. Langlois, *Les Sept Morts*, 13; AP: "Éventails transparents représentant les adieux de Louis XVI à sa famille," in "Procès-verbaux, Sections de Paris, Cité," *AA* 132, nos. 26–27 (28–29 fructidor An 5).

70. Outram, *The Body*, 159–60.

71. Steinberg, "The Afterlives," 30–45.

72. Sénac de Meilhan, *L'Émigré*, 153.

73. "Aussi les tyrans ont-ils sacrifié la plupart des Français humains, compatissans, et sensibles. Eh pourquoi! . . . parce que ces Français ont eu le courage de pleurer"; *Histoire d'un poignard*, 1:180.

74. Reddy, *Navigation of Feeling*, 182–202.

75. Ibid.; Andress, "Living the Revolutionary Melodrama."

76. Scurr, *Fatal Purity*, 49–51.

77. On Regnault-Warin, see Quérard, *La France*, 7:33–35; Boursin and Challamel, *Dictionnaire*, 698; Ménégault and Piquenard, *Martyrologe littéraire*, 317. I thank Sonja Stojanovic for research help on Regnault-Warin.

78. See the two cemetery titles by Villemain d'Abancourt published in 1800–1801. For an account of the author's travails, see Regnault-Warin, *L'Ange des prisons*, v–vii. Publisher Lepetit calls this work "trop célèbre pour avoir besoin d'apologie" and explains that "plusieurs brochures et romans ont usurpé ce titre qui, au défaut du talent, leur garantissait des succès" in *Extrait du catalogue du cit. Lepetit, libraire*, in Regnault-Warin, *Le Cimetière de la Madeleine*, 4:201. The first edition of this book was published in four duodecimo tomes bound in two volumes; the pagination starts anew in each tome, whence my method of citation. All citations from *Le Cimetière de la Madeleine* refer to the 1800–1801 edition by Lepetit held at the University of Notre Dame library: this is the only edition I have found that contains the tome 3 "avertissement" at the beginning of volume 2.

79. Recent editions include Regnault-Warin, *The Magdalen Churchyard* (2008) and *The Magdalen Churchyard* (2010).

80. "C'était le pinceau de Ducray-Duménil sur la palette de l'anglais Young"; Peuchet, *Mémoires tirés des Archives*, 3:246.

81. "Je l'ai vu malheureux; j'ai vu sa famille dans les larmes; je l'ai vu expirer sur l'échafaud ! . . . l'histoire dira s'il fut coupable; pour moi, je dois mes pleurs à l'infortune"; *Cimetière*, 1:15.

82. "Il est, dans un cœur ingénu, de certaines fibres faciles à émouvoir, et qui correspondent, en quelque sorte, à celles des cœurs qui lui ressemblent lorsque les rapports d'analogie sont établis, quand le point de contact est trouvé, il en résulte le plus doux, le

plus touchant accord"; ibid., 16–17. For more on the sensationalist theories from which this discourse is borrowed, see Douthwaite, *The Wild Girl*, 70–92.

83. "Les femmes, toujours sensibles, en avaient des attaques de nerfs. On voulut suspendre ces spasmes monarchiques. En les frappant d'interdit, on les propagea. [Le ministère] avait manifesté son intention [à Regnault-Warin] de ne point voir terminer cet ouvrage qui rouvrait les plaies et exaltait les têtes. Loin d'obtempérer à un pareil ordre, l'auteur s'est obstiné"; Peuchet, *Mémoires tirés des Archives*, 3:246–47.

84. Gillet, "Les Grands cimetières," 660.

85. "Jamais Louis XVI ne fut grand que quand il cessa d'être roi," and "tous les soirs, je me blâme de ce que j'ai fait pendant la journée"; *Cimetière*, 1:35, 37. Huguette Krief comments on this first passage as well, but in attributing it to the author instead of the king's confessor, she misses the narrative's ironic tension. See Krief, "Parole topique," 636.

86. AN F7/6193/A, no. 2569, reports from the Ministère de la Police générale de la République, (21 pluviôse, 30 pluviôse, 4 ventôse, 8 ventôse An 7).

87. Peuchet, *Mémoires tirés des Archives*, 3:246–47; letter from Citoien Spiels to the Citoien Ministre de la Police générale (21 germinal An 10), in AN, Police générale, Affaires politiques, F7/6263, no. 5272, no. 4.

88. Regnault-Warin's letter of 5 pluviôse An 9 (January 25, 1801) reads: "C'est mon livre lui-même que je charge de répondre à ces inculpations. . . . Quelques larmes ou quelques fleurs jetées par un pieux attendrissement sur les tombeaux d'une famille éteinte, n'altéreront pas une constitution qui promet la félicité. Citoyen préfet, les hommes religieux sont soumis à l'autorité; et *ceux qui pleurent n'assassinent pas*"; cited in Peuchet, *Mémoires tirés des Archives*, 3:251. Peuchet notes that the prefect did not deign to reply, but that the last line of this letter was a provocation: "La lettre fit fortune dans un public d'amis, surtout à cause de la phrase absurde qui la termine: *Ceux qui pleurent n'assassinent pas!* Pathos à la mode chez les partis qui n'ont pas le pouvoir pour le moment, mais qui ne nous font jamais rien perdre pour attendre" (3:252).

89. AN, Police générale, Affaires politiques, F7/6263, no. 5272, nos. 3–37.

90. DeBaecque, *Glory and Terror*, 69.

91. "Il sera mémorable de voir un citoyen dont les principes politiques sont et ont toujours été . . . éloignés du fanatisme . . . et des superstitions royales; il sera, dis-je, mémorable de le voir tracer d'une touche pathétiquement véridique, les malheurs d'*un homme qui fut roi*"; *Cimetière*, 1:21, my emphasis.

92. This subplot regards a haughty "célèbre madame de ✱✱✱" who tries to sway the widowed queen to accept the duc d'Orléans as husband and regent (ibid., 3:153–64). Hostility toward Madame de Genlis runs through much of the fiction published from 1789 to 1810 and emerges in later masterpieces such as *War and Peace* and *Les Misérables* as well.

93. Durruty, "Les Auteurs de catéchismes," 15. The most famous case is that of Jean-François de LaHarpe, whose persona metamorphosed from a liberal-minded friend of the philosophes to an intransigent and conservative Catholic.

94. Chateaubriand, *Mémoires d'outre-tombe*, 2:228–29. See also the description of "a rainbow emerging from the storm clouds" (un arc-en-ciel au travers des nuages chargés de foudre et de grêle) from *Mercure britannique* (1799); cited in Bessand-Massenet, *La France*, 264.

95. [Hélène-Marie Williams], *Correspondance*, 1:vii, ix.

96. The editions that reprint Williams's letters include Jean-Baptiste Pujoulx, *Louis XVI peint par lui-même* (1817), *Lettres de Louis XVI, correspondance inédite*, ed. Barnabé Chauvelot (1862), and *Lettres de Louis XVI et preuves de leur authenticité*, ed. B. Chauvelot, 2nd ed. (1864). Controversy continues to surround the issue of which if any of these letters are authentic. Lionel Woodward cites the mid-nineteenth-century edition by Feuillet de Conches as the conclusive edition in *Hélène-Maria Williams*, 238. Feuillet de Conches was director of protocol at the Quai d'Orsay and apparently did research in archives all around Europe, especially in Vienna. Nevertheless, Petitfils claims that all these sources contain forgeries. He recommends that readers consult various archival sources and the memoirs of notables such as Abbé Jean-Louis Giraud, dit Soulavie, *Mémoires historiques et politiques du règne de Louis XVI* (1801). See Petitfils, *Louis XVI*, 13–14.

97. Babié de Bercenay, letter of October 10, 1822, *Bulletin du bibliophile* (1838); cited in its entirety in Woodward, *Hélène-Maria Williams*, 234–35.

98. Bertrand de Moleville denounced Helen Maria Williams's *Correspondance* in *A Refutation of the Libel on the Memory of the Late King of France* (1804).

99. Letter 21, the king to comte d'Artois, September 7, 1789; in [Williams], *Correspondance*, 1:151, 153; and "Observations" to letter 21, in ibid., 157.

100. Letter 43, to Monsieur, July 23, 1791, in ibid., 334; "Observations" to letter 43, in ibid., 322.

101. "Observations" to letters 33 and 41, in ibid., 265, 327.

102. [Williams], *Correspondance*, 2:106–7; letter 69, to Monsieur, August 12, 1792, in ibid., 140.

103. "Observations" to letter 69, in ibid., 143.

104. AN F7/3831, AN F7/3704, cited in Aulard, *Paris sous le Consulat*, 220, 224–25; Woodward, *Hélène-Maria Williams*, 156, 162–63, 215.

105. Helen-Maria Williams, *An Eye-Witness Account*, 11.

106. Letter 465, to Monsieur F. J. de Partz de Pressy, évêque de Boulogne, September 3, 1789, cited in Feuillet de Conches, *Louis XVI*, 3:194.

107. Feuillet de Conches, *Louis XVI*, 3:391, 6:248.

108. On *King Lear* and *Père Goriot*, see Brunel, "Sublime"; and Besser, "Lear and Goriot."

109. On the original publishing and reception of *Le Père Goriot*, see Kanes, *Père Goriot*, 12–15; Lyons, *Reading Culture*, 33; and Lyon-Caen, *La Lecture*, 120–47.

110. Kanes, *Père Goriot*, 54; Barbéris, *Balzac et le mal*, 2:1092.

111. For an interpretation from the perspective of human passions, see Bardèche, *Balzac romancier*, 331–72. From the perspective of homoerotic tensions, see Lucey, "Kinship"; and Miller, "1839: Body Bildung." Mass culture: De la Motte, "Balzacorama." Parisian topography: Marcus, *Apartment Stories*; and Barbéris, *Le Monde*. Bildungsroman: Beizer, *Family Plots*; and Moretti, *The Way of the World*.

112. For an overview of these debates, see Guyon, *La Pensée politique*, 693.

113. Guyon highlights the political dimension of *Les Chouans* in *La Pensée politique*, 249–73. See also Rey's preface to Balzac, *Les Chouans*, 11.

114. Balzac considered running for a post as deputy in Cambrai, Fougères, or Tours in

the summer 1831 elections; Guyon, *La Pensée politique*, 417–30. On his "royalist conversion," see ibid., 201.

115. For publication details, see Notice in Balzac, *Du Gouvernement moderne*, 2:1732–34. See also ibid., 1078, 1082.

116. "Ni fusils aux mains du peuple, ni pouvoir aucun . . . sa souveraineté est une farce tragique"; ibid., 1075, 1076.

117. Courteix, *Balzac et la Révolution*, 138–39.

118. Balzac, *Du Gouvernement moderne*, 2:2082.

119. Irony runs through observations such as Madame Vauquer's "Peut-être l'insouciante générosité que mit à se laisser attraper le père Goriot . . . le fit-elle considérer comme un imbécile," or the spiteful summing up of the comtesse de l'Ambermesnil after having her own advances thwarted, "c'est un grippe-sou, une bête, un sot, qui ne vous causera que du désagrément"; Balzac, *Le Père Goriot*, 41, 46. When he is deep in thought, the other boarders merely see an absent-minded geezer: "Jamais il n'avait semblé plus stupide et plus absorbé qu'il était en ce moment"; ibid., 73. On the political subtexts behind Goriot's nicknames, see Petrey, *Realism and Revolution*, 83–93.

120. Kanes, *Père Goriot*, 23.

121. Hardman, *Louis XVI*, 130–31.

122. Although Balzac does not specify, this would be the court of Louis XVIII (1755–1824), formerly comte de Provence, brother of Louis XVI, who left France when the royal family fled Paris on June 20, 1791. He was restored to the throne in 1814, went into exile again at Napoleon's return during the 100 Days, and was restored again after Napoleon's exile in 1815, at the age of sixty.

123. Balzac, *Père Goriot*, trans. Krailsheimer, 69; all translations refer to this edition.

124. Chantal Thomas, *La Reine scélérate*, 64–68.

125. Balzac, *Le Père Goriot*, ed. Marceau, 119–21.

126. Ibid., 164–65.

127. Ibid., 182.

128. Ibid., 204, 312.

129. See Bardèche, *Balzac romancier*, 345–48; Brunel, "Sublime," 36; Chen, "Le Père Goriot, autodestructeur"; and Krailsheimer's introduction to *Père Goriot*, xv–xvii.

130. "Comme un juge sévère, son œil semblait aller au fond de toutes les questions, de toutes les consciences, de tous les sentiments"; Balzac, *Le Père Goriot*, 38. Rastignac responds accordingly: "il lui semblait que ce singulier personnage pénétrait ses passions et lisait dans son cœur"; ibid., 142.

131. The emotions are stronger in the French original: "'Oui, mon bon père Goriot, vous savez bien que je vous aime. . . .' 'Je le vois, vous n'avez pas honte de moi, vous! Laissez-moi vous embrasser'"; ibid., 236.

132. Sedaine, *Richard Cœur de lion*, 6.

133. Mason, *Singing*, 216; see also 45–48, 51–52, 215–16.

134. Boyle, *Troubadour's Song*, 292–95.

135. Rastignac employs chivalrous formulas in his first meeting with Madame de Beauséant, when he offers to die or kill for her and makes her shed a tear; Balzac, *Le Père Goriot*, ed. Marceau, 105, 117. Royalist leanings may be deduced from the account of his grandfather's dedication to Louis XVI told to the comte de Restaud; ibid., 91–92.

136. "Un forçat de la trempe de Collin, ici présent, est un homme moins lâche que les autres, et qui proteste contre les profondes déceptions du contrat social, comme dit Jean-Jacques, dont je me glorifie d'être l'élève"; ibid., 267.

137. Consider the mean-spirited exchange between the two in book 1, "Une Pension bourgeoise," where Vautrin hits Goriot on the head so hard that his hat slides over his eyes and makes him miss his soup bowl with his spoon (to the delight of everyone else): an incident that elicits impotent fury from the older man; ibid., 83.

138. The links of paternity between Vautrin and Rastignac are well developed: at dinner one night he regards Rastignac "d'un air paternel" (119) and he whispers to Rastignac in his drugged sleep: "Mon petit gars, nous ne sommes pas assez rusé pour lutter avec notre papa Vautrin"; ibid., 241.

139. "Je proteste. La patrie périra si les pères sont foulés aux pieds"; ibid., 345–46. See also Amossy, "Fathers and Sons."

140. "Étant depuis plus de quatre mois enfermé . . . par ceux qui étaient mes sujets . . . impliqué dans un Procès dont il est impossible de prévoir l'issue à cause des passions des hommes, et dont on ne trouve aucun prétexte ni moyen dans aucune Loi existante"; "Je recommande à mon fils . . . de songer qu'il se doit tout entier au bonheur de ses Concitoyens, qu'il doit oublier toute haine et tout ressentiment"; *Testament*, in Louis XVI, *Testaments*, 93, 98.

141. See, e.g., the entry "Louis XVI" in Gobry, *Dictionnaire des martyrs*, 264.

142. April, "Representations of the Dead Body," 79–80.

143. References to Rastignac's superiority emerge in comparisons with *jeunes gens supérieurs* (Balzac, *Le Père Goriot*, 56), *les âmes grandes* (57), and *un homme supérieur* (153).

CHAPTER FOUR

1. Particularly influential were the histories of the Revolution published by Tocqueville, Lamartine, Michelet, Blanc, Quinet, and Thiers, many of whom were also statesmen. See Orr, *Headless History*; Furet, *Interpreting*; Gérard, *La Révolution*; Guilhaumou, *La Langue politique*; and Mellon, *The Political Uses*.

2. According to Robespierre's most sympathetic biographer, these actions were taken more or less despite Robespierre, as he was exhausted by the end of the marathon session and barely had strength to wield the gavel. Hamel, *Histoire de Robespierre*, 3:124–25.

3. Jean-Clément Martin, *Violence*, 147–50.

4. Hamel, *Histoire de Robespierre*, 3:547.

5. Mazauric, "Terreur"; Eude, "Loi de Prairial." For the text of the law, I consulted "Le Droit criminel," http://ledroitcriminel.free.fr/index.htm, on January 6, 2011.

6. *Formes acerbes* was a loaded term: it referred to the speech presented by Bertrand Barère on July 9, 1794, in which he glossed over the unusually high number of arrests and condemnations, and to the many prints produced to satirize this callousness. See Eude, "Loi de Prairial," 557; and for the artwork, see Reichardt and Kohle, *Visualizing*, 200–201.

7. Andress, "Living the Revolutionary Melodrama," 104; Jean-Clément Martin, "Violences et justice," 132; Tackett, "Interpreting," 569; Andress, *The French Revolution*, 200.

8. Schama, *Citizens*, xv; Mazauric, "Terreur," 1020; Weber, *Terror*.

9. Cobb, *The French*; Forrest, "L'armée." Executions of peasants and the working class comprised 89 percent of the deaths in the Vendée, according to Greer, *Incidence*, 164.

10. Brown, *Ending*, 3; Clarke, *Commemorating the Dead*, 273.

11. "Ce n'était pas que Robespierre désapprouvait les mesures sévères décrétées par la Convention; seulement il voulait qu'on les appliquât avec discernement, que rien ne fût livré à l'arbitraire, et que, dans la répression des crimes révolutionnaires, on ne confondît pas l'erreur avec le crime, ceux qui n'étaient qu'égarés avec les coupables. TERREUR était un mot impropre à ses yeux; l'idéal, c'était JUSTICE"; Hamel, *Histoire de Robespierre*, 3:131–32.

12. The first usage of *terroriste* in French is attributed to Gracchus Babeuf, *Journal de la liberté de la presse*, no. 4, according to the *Trésor de la langue française*, http://www.cnrtl.fr/ (accessed on December 20, 2010). It may have been coined earlier according to Van den Heuvel, "Terreur."

13. Jean-Clément Martin, "Violences et justice," 139; see also Cobb's warning for students of the "recalcitrant" Revolution in *The French*, 344.

14. Ezra Pound in *Le Mercure de France* (1922), cited by Trilling in his introduction to *Bouvard et Pécuchet* by Flaubert, ix; Popkin, *Revolutionary News*, 128.

15. For detailed analysis of revolutionary newspapers, see Hatin, *Histoire politique*. For *Journal de Paris*, see 5:126–223; for *Chronique de Paris*, see 5:224–73; for *Moniteur*, see 5:110–25; for *Les Révolutions de Paris*, see 6:317–64.

16. Gough, *Newspaper Press*, 99.

17. Gilchrist and Murray, *The Press*, 9.

18. As the only daily newspaper (other than the court-oriented *Gazette de France*) in existence at the opening of the Estates General, the *Journal de Paris* became by default the official newspaper of the National Assembly in 1789. In the days following the August 10, 1792, defeat of the monarchy, the paper's offices were attacked, the presses broken, and the editors forced to go into hiding. After a six-week-long hiatus, it resumed printing and took the name *Le Journal de Paris national*; it would be retitled *Le Journal de Paris* in February 1795. Hatin, *Histoire politique*, 5:127–88.

19. Clère, "Haute cour," 533; Clère, "Tribunaux"; Pertué, "Tribunal."

20. "Il est important de bien définir ce que vous entendez par *conspirateurs*; autrement les meilleurs citoyens risqueroient d'être victimes d'un tribunal institué pour les protéger contre les entreprises des contre-révolutionnaires"; Maximilien Robespierre, speech at the Convention on March 11, 1793, cited by Hamel, *Histoire de Robespierre*, 2:638. For the text of the final decree accepted by the Convention, see Hatin, *Histoire politique*, 2:639.

21. Matharan, "Suspects."

22. *JPN* 97 (April 7, 1793): 350.

23. *JPN* 101, 107, 108, 110, 111, 362 (April 11, 17, 18, 20, 21, and December 28, 1793): 406, 425–26, 434, 442, 446, 1460. According to the catalog of the Bibliothèque nationale de France, Clinchamp was a prior of La Trinité Church at Clisson, author of only this one book. A more famous case of free speech suppressed by this court is the trial and condemnation of Olympe de Gouges, listed as "Femme de lettres, âgée de 38 ans, native

de Montauban, convaincue d'être l'auteur d'écrits tendans à l'établissement d'un pouvoir attentatoire à la souveraineté du people"; *JPN* 307 (13 brumaire An 2; November 3, 1793): 1236. The oldest person tried was P. L. Foassier, aged ninety; *JPN* 574 (10 thermidor An 2; July 28, 1794): 2318; one of the fourteen-year-olds sent to jail for twenty years was Jean Fournier, whose mother was condemned for plotting to free Marie-Antoinette from the Conciergerie; *JPN* 382 (28 nivôse An 2; January 17, 1794): 1543.

24. Jean-Clément Martin, "Violences et justice," 133.

25. Soboul, *Les Sans-culottes*, 254.

26. Such affect became more prevalent in September 1794; spectacles of "joyous fraternity among sensitive souls" became standard fare in tribunal proceedings printed in fall–winter 1794. See *JPN* 611 (17 fructidor An 2; September 1, 1794); *JPN* 623 (29 fructidor An 2; September 15, 1794).

27. For the trial of the Dantonists, see *JPN* 461 (17 germinal An 2; April 6, 1794): 1863–64. For Hébert's trial, see *JPN* 451 (7 germinal An 2; March 27, 1794): 1823. For Gorsas, see *JPN* 282 (18 vendémiaire An 2; October 9, 1793): 1130. For Lamourette, see *JPN* 377 (23 nivôse An 2; January 12, 1794): 1524. See also the report on a certain Renaud de Beauvoir, who cried out: "C'est inique. Puisque nous sommes condamnés à mort, qu'on ne nous sépare pas, c'est la grâce que nous demandons." There is no mention of the response. See *JPN* 125 (May 5, 1793): 502.

28. On the Dethorres, see *JPN* 317 (23 brumaire An 2; November 13, 1793): 1176. Charles Leroux and the widow Maréchal are in *JPN* 389 (5 pluviôse An 2; January 24, 1794): 1572.

29. On the declining fortune of Jacobin prose between 1789 and 1793, when it lost its power to capture an exciting sense of political immediacy and instead became associated with a wooden or stilted style, see Higonnet, *Goodness*, 222–23; Baczko, *Comment sortir*, 67.

30. Ducray-Duminil, *Cœlina*, 5:212–13.

31. On metaphors of dysfunctional families in period literature, see Hunt, *Family Romance*, 86–87, 176–78.

32. For Marie-Antoinette and the Girondins, see *JPN* 281, 282, 505 (17, 18, 19 vendémiaire An 2; 11 brumaire An 2; October 8–10 and November 1, 1793): 1130, 1132, 1138, 1218. For news of prison populations, see *JPN* 173 (June 22, 1793): 693; *JPN* 218 (August 6, 1793): 877; *JPN* 272 (September 29, 1793): 1054; *JPN* 79 (25 germinal An 2; April 14, 1794): 1896.

33. The *Supplément* was an excellent source of revenue (eighteen livres for one column, three livres for an article under ten lines) for the paper and allowed a good breadth of opinion to be aired. On the controversies that marked its pages, see Hatin, *Histoire politique*, 5:167–69.

34. The characters of *L'Émigré* spend their days in dread of the newspaper and its execution list. See Sénac de Meilhan, *L'Émigré*, 153ff. See also Lafrance, *Qui perd gagne*, 96–101. The more militant response is found in A.-J. Dumaniant, *Les Amours et aventures d'un émigré*, reprinted in Genand, *Romans de l'émigration*, 102–3.

35. Dickens, *Tale*, 3.6.291. All citations from *A Tale of Two Cities* include the book and chapter numbers, followed by the page number of the Maxwell edition.

36. *Correspondance française* (London) 108 (July 10, 1794): 445. Shortly after being imprisoned, Madame Roland wrote, "j'attendois le journal du soir . . . avec une avidité inexprimable"; *Appel*, 1ere partie, 27. See also Helen-Maria Williams, *Memoirs*, 41, 147.

37. Cited in "Mélanges," *AM* 16 (January 16, 1790): 3:129–30.

38. Desault is cited in Alibert, *De l'influence*, 302–3. See also *Gazette de santé*, no. 46, cited in *AM* 16 (January 16, 1790); Ozouf, *L'Homme régénéré*; DeBaecque, "L'Homme nouveau."

39. Hacking, *Taming of Chance*, 64–65; Alex Martin, *Enlightened Metropolis*, chap. 8; Cobb, *The French*, 352–53, 203–4, 162.

40. Cobb, *The French*, 350.

41. Doyle, *Oxford History*, 252–60.

42. David Andress, email of June 17, 2010. For more on the challenges of identifying trauma in history, see Shapiro, *Traumatic Politics*.

43. See reviews by Pierre Chaunu (*Le Figaro*) and Arlette Farge (*Le Matin*) in Blanc, *Dernière Lettre*, 310–14.

44. The notice on *Le Glaive vengeur* reads: "Ce recueil intéressant se trouve à Paris, chez Galleti. . . . *Nota*: Il est essentiel d'observer que cet ouvrage diffère en tout de la liste qu'on a citée dans les rues de Paris. L'auteur, qui l'a calqué sur les registres mêmes du Tribunal révolutionnaire, l'a enrichi de réflexions patriotiques"; *JPN* 443 (29 ventôse An 2; March 19, 1794): 1792.

45. One of Hébert's famous remarks is "Quiconque frappe du glaive, sera du glaive frappé"; cited in Desmoulins, *Le Vieux Cordelier*, 127. On Blanchelande, Gorsas, and Lamourette, see Dulac, *Glaive vengeur*, 71, 114, 176.

46. Dulac, *Glaive vengeur*, 142–43. On the collaboration between the king and the people in premodern punishments, see Foucault, *Discipline and Punish*, 59.

47. Dulac, *Glaive vengeur*, 131–32.

48. Ibid., 195. On the Jacobin concepts of pity and "false pity," see Reddy, *Navigation*, 173–210.

49. "Le Retour de la pudeur," *JPN* 620 (26 fructidor An 2; September 12, 1794): 2502; "Les Plaisirs de la fraternité," *JPN* 626 (2nd *sans-culottide* An 2; September 18, 1794): 2526; "Gaîté patriotique," *JPN* 40 (10 brumaire An 3; October 31, 1794): 166; "Le Vœu des citoyens paisibles" (20 pluviôse An 3; February 8, 1795): 566. Poems in honor of the Committee of Public Safety and the Committee of General Security appear in *JPN* 579 (21 thermidor An 2; August 8, 1794): 2362; *JPN* 23 (23 vendémiaire An 2; October 14, 1794): 92.

50. *AM* 123 (3 pluviôse An 3; January 22, 1795): 23:259.

51. Rosny, *Les Infortunes de Mr. de La Galetierre* (An 5), 60n. The first edition lists the names of eighty-six deceased persons of Tours (23); the second edition lists eighty-nine names, followed by "etc., etc." (28).

52. Hufton, *Women*, 130. I thank Brigid Mangano for bringing this phenomenon to my attention.

53. *JPN* 129 (9 pluviôse An 3; January 28, 1795): 401.

54. See the letter to the editor from Loiserolles fils and Jauffret's poem "Loiserolles, ou Le Triomphe de l'amour paternal," in *JPN* (25 nivôse An 3; January 14, 1795): 465–66.

55. Loiserolle's story has become a favorite among Evangelical Christians in the United States, who interpret him as playing a Christlike role, giving his life two times for

his son and ensuring a future for his family with his own death. The anecdote is cited by Harold Vaughn, editor of the newsletter *Christ Life Ministries Report* (Vinton, VA); see Vaughn, "Hell's Desperate Cry!"

56. Doyle, *Oxford History*, 283.

57. *JPN* 151 (1 ventôse An 3; February 19, 1795): 609; *JPN* 153 (3 ventôse An 3; February 22, 1795): 617.

58. A real-life referent similar to the manuscript in Dickens's book may be found in the advertisement for a prison memoir, *Défense de Charles Eléonore Dufriche Valanzé*, found in the wall of the victim's cell and advertised in the June 7 and August 7, 1795, issues of *JPN*. See also *Les Souvenirs d'un jeune prisonnier; Angoisses de la mort; Atrocités exercées envers les citoyens d'Arras*; Bourbon, *Mémoire de Stéphanie-Louise de Bourbon*.

59. On the *Faublas* cycle and Louvet de Couvray (or Couvrai), see Norberg, "'Love and Patriotism.'" "Litterature," *JPN* 163 (13 ventôse An 3; March 3, 1795): 655. The review is signed R. (i.e., Roederer).

60. "Que d'*Histoires de la Révolution* n'ont pas défrayé, par exemple, les historiettes de Riouffe, *un des plus effrontés menteurs qu'on puisse imaginer*"; Hamel, *Histoire de Robespierre*, 3:159.

61. Book review of *Proscription d'Isnard* (An 3) in *JPN* 165 (15 ventôse An 3; March 5, 1795): 665–66.

62. Baron Riouffe (1764–1813) was a lawyer and writer under the ancien régime and a statesman during the Consulate and Empire. He was imprisoned on October 4, 1793, with the Girondins, whose political views he shared, and was liberated on 9 thermidor An 2 (July 27, 1794).

63. Carlyle, *French Revolution*, 2:308–9.

64. Riouffe, *Mémoires d'un détenu*, 31–32.

65. *AM* 202 (22 germinal An 3; April 11, 1795), 24:169. See also *JPN* 24 (22 germinal An 3; April 11, 1795), 817–18.

66. "Raconter mes malheurs, c'est raconteur les siens; notre persécution avait les mêmes causes, les mêmes fers nous ont enchaînés, les mêmes cachots nous ont reçus, et le même coup devait finir notre vie"; "Il me sembla voir tout le peuple français outragé dans sa personne"; Riouffe, *Mémoires d'un détenu*, 18, 19.

67. Ibid., 132, 170.

68. The 1795 version sold twelve thousand copies in two rapidly released printings. A second edition followed in 1799, two more in 1827, followed by multiple reprints and translations up to the present day. On the first editions, see Berville and Barrière, "Avertissement placé en tête de la première édition," xiv–xv.

69. Roland, *Appeal*, pt. 1, 56–57. "Mais il défendoit les principes avec chaleur et opiniâtreté; il y avoit du courage à continuer de le faire au tems où le nombre des défenseurs du peuple s'étoit prodigieusement réduit. La cour les haïssait et les faisoit calomnier, les patriotes devoient donc les soutenir et les encourager. J'estimois Robespierre sous ce rapport, je le lui témoignois . . . il venoit de tems en tems me demander à dîner"; Roland, *Appel*, 1ère partie, 63.

70. Roland, *Appeal*, pt. 1, 58. "Robespierre, ricanant à son ordinaire et se mangeant les ongles, demandoit ce que c'étoit qu'une république!"; Roland, *Appel*, 1ère partie, 64.

71. Roland, *Appeal*, pt. 2, 180. "Ce Robespierre, qu'un tems je crus honnête homme, est un être bien atroce! Comme il ment à sa conscience! comme il aime le sang!"; Roland, *Appel*, 2ᵉ partie, 198.

72. Roland, *Appeal*, pt. 2, 181. "Robespierre, si je me trompe, je vous mets à même de me le prouver"; Roland, *Appel*, 2ᵉ partie, 199.

73. Roland, *Appeal*, pt. 2, 184. "D'où vient donc cette animosité?—C'est ce que je ne puis concevoir"; Roland, *Appel*, 2ᵉ partie, 202.

74. Roland, *Appeal*, pt. 2, 187. "Dans tous les cas, Robespierre, je le sais, et vous ne pouvez éviter de le sentir; quiconque m'a connu, ne sauroit me persécuter sans remords"; Roland, *Appel*, 2ᵉ partie, 205.

75. Roland, *Appeal*, pt. 2, 259. "Amie de la liberté . . . j'ai vu la révolution avec transport, persuadée que c'étoit l'époque du renversement de l'arbitraire que je hais, de la réforme d'abus dont j'ai souvent gémi en m'attendrissant sur le sort de la classe malheureuse. J'ai suivi les progrès de la révolution avec intérêt, je m'entretenois de la chose publique avec chaleur; mais je n'ai point dépassé les bornes qui m'étoient imposées par mon sexe "; Roland, *Appel*, 2ᵉ partie, 150. This is one of the many passages where Roland insists upon her dutiful domesticity as spouse and mother and thus tries to forestall critics' claims that she struggled for power over her husband. See Walker, *Mother's Love*, 85–94.

76. Roland, *Appeal*, pt. 2, 239–40. "Lorsque j'ai été mise en arrestation, je me suis flattée de servir la gloire de mon mari, et de concourir à éclairer le public, si l'on m'intentoit un procès quelconque"; Roland, *Appel*, 2ᵉ partie, 123.

77. Roland, *Appeal*, pt. 2, 240. "J'ambitionnois, il y a deux mois, l'honneur d'aller à l'échafaud; on pouvoit parler encore, et l'énergie d'un grand courage auroit servi la vérité: maintenant tout est perdu"; Roland, *Appel*, 2ᵉ partie, 124.

78. Roland, *Appeal*, pt. 2, 256–57. "Que je vous plains! lui dis-je avec sérénité. Je vous pardonne même ce que vous me dites de désobligeant: vous croyez tenir un grand coupable, vous êtes impatient de le convaincre; mais qu'on est malheureux avec de telles précautions! Vous pouvez m'envoyer à l'échafaud; vous ne sauriez m'ôter la joie que donne une bonne conscience, et la persuasion que la postérité vengera Roland et moi, en vouant à l'infamie ses persécuteurs"; Roland, *Appel*, 2ᵉ partie, 146.

79. Roland, *Appeal*, pt. 2, 262. "Il est dans les principes de la tyrannie de sacrifier ceux qu'elle a violemment opprimés, et d'anéantir jusqu'aux témoins de ses excès. A ce double titre, vous me devez la mort, et je l'attends"; Roland, *Appel*, 2ᵉ partie, 154.

80. "Commune de Paris," *AM* 59 (29 brumaire An 2; November 17, 1793): 18:450. For more on the closing of women's clubs, see McMillan, *France and Women*, 24–25.

81. "Commune de Paris," *AM* 59 (29 brumaire An 2; November 17, 1793): 18:451.

82. [*La Feuille de Salut public*], "Aux Républicaines," *AM* 59 (29 brumaire An 2; November 17, 1793): 18:450.

83. *JP* 250 (10 prairial An 3; May 29, 1795): 1011; *AM* (20 prairial An 3; June 18, 1795): 24:702.

84. "Quelle époque que celle où une femme s'exprimait ainsi en face du bourreau! Quelle époque surnaturelle"; *AM* 50 (21 brumaire An 2; November 10, 1793): 18:374.

85. For the entry "Liberté," see Flaubert, *Dictionnaire*, in *Bouvard et Pécuchet*, 537; "Ordre: Que de crimes on commet en ton nom!"; ibid., 544.

86. On crime narratives before the Revolution, see Jean-Clément Martin, *Violence*, 15–50; and Maza, *Private Lives*.

87. *JP* 260 (20 prairial An 3; June 8, 1795): 1051. On Denelle, see also Cobb, *The French*, 203–4.

88. Flaubert, *Dictionnaire*, in *Bouvard et Pécuchet*, 518.

89. *Les Crimes des noirs* is cited in *Histoire de Toussaint-Louverture*, 22; see also *Pitt à Saint-Domingue*.

90. As Carla Hesse reminds us, the black history was typically a reformist narrative. Louise de Kéralio-Robert's *Crimes des reines de France* (1791), however, critiqued the institution of queenship itself. See Hesse, *The Other Enlightenment*, 94–98.

91. These feats were widely disseminated in the popular Bibliothèque bleue series sold by peddlers in rural areas and contributed to the "banditry psychosis" discussed by Howard Brown (see below). See also Gordon, *Thème de Mandrin*; Ellenberger, *Cartouche*; and Gallez, *Brigand Moneuse*.

92. Godwin, *Caleb Williams*, 311–12.

93. Roussel, *Histoire secrète*, 2:176.

94. Review of Robespierre, *Discours sur l'organisation des gardes nationales*, in *CP* 46 (February 15, 1791): 181.

95. "Citoyens, vouliez-vous une révolution sans révolution?"; Maximilien Robespierre, *Œuvres*, 9:89.

96. "Ici beaucoup d'enfans, qui assistoient à la séance, frappés du pathétique de ce passage, se sont levés spontanément, ont crié: *vive la République*; & des applaudissemens réitérés ont répondu à cet élan sublime de reconnoissance & de sensibilité"; *JPN* 494 (20 floréal An 2; May 9, 1794): 1995. For the text of the speech, see Maximilien Robespierre, *Œuvres*, 10:442–65.

97. *JPN* 575 (11 thermidor An 2; July 29, 1794): 2320–21.

98. Ibid., 2320.

99. As the *Courrier français* (Philadelphia) commented in 1794, "Quel a été enfin le crime de cet homme dont la voix s'était tant de fois fait entendre au sein de la Convention, dont l'éloquence faisait la gloire de cette Assemblée, et dont l'énergie avait contribué au salut de la République? Ce sont autant de questions que se fait l'ami de son pays que cet événement extraordinaire jette dans la stupeur"; cited in Jacob, *Robespierre*, 180.

100. Cited in Baczko, *Comment sortir*, 83.

101. Citations are drawn from, respectively, Rouy, *Assassinats*, 1; Saintomer, *Jugement*, 1, 16; and Méhée de la Touche, *La Queue de Robespierre*, 1.

102. Cobb, *The French*, 238–43. Flaubert, *Dictionnaire*, in *Bouvard et Pécuchet*, 545.

103. Brown, *Ending*, 46–65. Vidocq's combination of courage, cruelty, and intelligence later made him the lead detective of the Parisian police: an astonishing destiny that inspired Balzac's character Vautrin and whose traits can be seen in both the former convict Jean Valjean and the police inspector Javert of *Les Misérables*.

104. Robespierre scolds his followers: "votre coupable zèle, quelquefois commettait des forfaits que ma bouche n'avait point commandé, et que j'étais même loin de concevoir: c'est vous enfin, vils complices, c'est vous qui après avoir servi ma lâche complaisance, avez été les premiers à demander ma mort: lors du 9 thermidor, vous fîtes tomber ma tête"; Rondot, *L'Ombre de Robespierre*, 6.

105. "Il est donc des forfaits / que le courroux du ciel ne pardonne jamais" is from Voltaire's tragedy *Œdipe,* in *Œuvres,* 3:387; cited by Duperron, *Vie secrette,* title page. Strangely enough, these exact words are also found in an account of Saint-Domingue where they are aimed at Toussaint Louverture, who is portrayed as a traitor to the French cause and leader of a murderous army of ruffians. See Perrin, *Incendie du Cap,* 155.

106. Proyart, *La Vie et les crimes,* 279. Hannibal Lecter's "first principles" and penchant for the memoirs of Marcus Aurelius also connect these villains of film and politics.

107. Sgard, *Dictionnaire,* 2:622–24. Desessarts's massive *Causes célèbres, curieuses et intéressantes, de toutes les cours souveraines de royaume, avec les jugemens qui les ont décidées* (1773–90) was followed by *Procès fameux: Contenant les anecdotes piquantes & les jugemens fameux des tribunaux de tous les temps & de toutes les nations* (published in sixteen volumes, from 1786 to 1798).

108. Citations are from Desessarts, *Crimes,* 1:8–9. See also "Portraits of Robespierre" in Jordan, *Revolutionary Career,* 249–56.

109. "Si ma mort peut calmer l'aigreur funeste des partis, faire évanouir les espérances des ennemis de l'état, cimenter le bonheur de ma patrie, je suis prêt à m'accuser moi-même, et à porter ma tête sous le glaive"; Desessarts, *Précis,* 1:38.

110. Desessarts, *Crimes,* 1:59–62. Duperron employs the same reasoning in his closing salvo: "Peuples! Que cet exemple te guérisse enfin d'une maladie cruelle qui feroit ton malheur; l'idolâtrie pour les individus; ne jurons plus au nom de tel et tel citoyen, ne jurons qu'au nom de la liberté et de la patrie"; *Vie secrette,* 36.

111. Desessart's biography was issued three times in 1797 and six more times by 1823 and was translated into Dutch and German (1798). Galart de Montjoie was also a nobleman and lawyer under the ancien régime, editor of *L'Année littéraire* (1790), then founder of *L'Ami du roi.* His biography went into four editions in Paris, another in Switzerland, and three translations: English (1796), German (1795), and Spanish (1802). Much of Galart de Montjoie's biography was copied verbatim by Desessarts.

112. *JP* 9 (9 vendémiaire An 4; October 1, 1795): 34–36.

113. "Advertisement," in Galart de Montjoye, *History,* 1. Quotations in the text are to this edition.

114. I cite the French original to show the similarity with later portraits: "Il avoit dans les mains, dans les épaules, dans le col, dans les yeux, un mouvement convulsif; sa physionomie, son regard, étoient sans expression; il portoit sur son visage livide, sur son front qu'il ridoit fréquemment, les marques d'un tempérament bilieux; ses manières étoient brutales; sa démarche étoit tout-à-la-fois brusque et pesante: les inflexions aigres de sa voix frappoient désagréablement l'oreille; il crioit plutôt qu'il ne parloit"; Galart de Montjoie, *Histoire,* 59.

115. Ibid., 233–34.

116. The physical changes wrought on man by the evils he commits constitute a theme of both later books. The confrontation between Dorian Gray and his picture, shortly after he prompts the suicide of Sibyl Vane, is legend: "the face appeared to him to be a little changed. The expression looked different. One would have said that there was a touch of cruelty in the mouth. . . . The bright dawn flooded the room, and swept the fantastic shadows into dusty corners, where they lay shuddering. But the strange

expression that he had noticed in the face of the portrait seemed to linger there, to be more intensified even. The quivering, ardent sunlight showed him the lines of cruelty round the mouth as clearly as if he had been looking into a mirror after he had done some dreadful thing"; Wilde, *Picture*, 94. Or consider the portrait of Dr. Jekyll on the day after Hyde's murder of Sir Danvers Carew: "there, close up to the warmth, sat Dr. Jekyll, looking deadly sick. He did not rise to meet his visitor, but held out a cold hand, and bade him welcome in a changed voice"; Stevenson, *Strange Case*, 19.

117. "Eh bien, quelle nécessité y a-t-il que ces gens-là vivent?" Galart de Montjoie, *Histoire*, 156. This notorious comment is repeated in Desessarts, *Crimes*, 1:75.

118. Desessarts, *Crimes*, 1:124.

119. Hugo's entire novel could be considered a gallows speech; Balzac's novel delegitimized the death penalty through the eyes of a horrified executioner and his family members. Robert LeSieur, introduction to *Souvenirs d'un paria*, by Balzac, i–iv. On the *genre frénétique*, see Daniel Sangsue's beautifully illustrated essay "De quelques têtes coupées."

120. On the Perseus-Medusa theme that runs through portraits of guillotine victims, see Arasse, *La Guillotine*, 144, 168–72. On Sade's minute focus in *120 Journées de Sodom* on the pleasure derived from watching other people suffer, see Steintrager, *First Sexual Revolution*. The rapprochement with Sade is not irrelevant; members of the Committee of Public Safety were rumored to reread favorite passages of *Justine* during breaks from committee meetings and to return to work with their appetites newly whetted for killing.

121. See *Œuvres de Maximilien Robespierre*; *Mémoires de Charlotte Robespierre*; Jordan, *Revolutionary Career*, 19–20.

122. In response to the rumor of the woman who shouted at Robespierre while he was riding to the guillotine, Hamel notes: "Qu'importait à Maximilien ces lâches et stupides anathèmes? Il savait bien que le vrai peuple n'était pas mêlé à cette écume bouillante . . . le vrai peuple se tenait à l'écart, consterné"; Hamel, *Histoire de Robespierre*, 3:802. The anecdote of the peasant woman is on 3:805.

123. Mathiez, *Robespierre terroriste* (1921); Bouloiseau, *Robespierre* (1957). On Mathiez, see Darnton, *The Kiss*, 46; on Bouloiseau, see Crouzet, "French Historians and Robespierre." Lefebvre's family history is cited in Crouzet, "French Historians and Robespierre." See also Friguglietti, "Rehabilitating Robespierre." Lefebvre's quotation is found in Georges Lefebvre, "Remarks on Robespierre," 10.

124. Gallo, *L'Homme Robespierre*, 29; Hardman, *Robespierre*, 6; Gueniffey, *La Politique*, 328–39; Jordan, *Revolutionary Career*, 10–11.

125. Artarit, *Robespierre*, 16, 18; Scurr, *Fatal Purity*, 21.

126. *JP* 187 (7 germinal An 4; March 27, 1796): 717–18. In *AM*, the critic exclaimed: "Godwin a le talent de dessiner avec force, avec énergie les caractères, de tirer un grand but moral des événements qu'il varie avec un art inifini; enfin, d'avoir attaqué, avec la massue du genie, cette tyrannie chevaleresque, source de tant de désordres dans la société humaine"; *AM* 187 (7 germinal An 4; March 27, 1796): 28:57. The years 1793–94 mark the zenith of Godwin's short-lived fame.

127. The April 1831 preface cites the 1795 preface: "This novel was first published in May 1794, thirty-seven years ago, 'in the same month in which the sanguinary plot broke

out against the liberties of Englishmen, which was happily terminated by the acquittal of its first intended victims [Thomas Hardy, John Horne Tooke, Thomas Holcroft, &c.] in the close of that year'"; Godwin, *Caleb Williams*, xxiv.

128. Godwin, *Political Justice*, 70–71.

129. Prompted by news coming from France, British reactions grew against this rigorous kind of public morality, and as the author refused to abandon his principles, he became increasingly vilified by friends and foes alike. Godwin's fame waned under a torrent of abuse; he descended gradually into poverty and oblivion and died in 1836. See Carter's introduction to Godwin, *Political Justice*, xi–xxxv.

130. "Voici en littérature une nouveauté intéressante; un roman sans amour; une passion aussi terrible que l'amour. Une passion portant un homme à un degré d'exaltation où il passa des plus grandes vertus aux plus grands crimes; où il devient capable de concevoir et d'exécuter, pour la satisfaire, les plus énormes excès . . . où il immole à son idole des victimes humaines." Review of *Les Aventures de Caleb Williams* in *JP* 187 (7 germinal An 4; March 27, 1796): 717. See also *AM* 187 (7 germinal An 4; March 27, 1796): 28:54–57. Four years later, a reviewer voiced less enthusiasm, writing, "Ce roman n'est qu'un manifeste très-violent contre la société & la civilization actuelle," but admitted that Williams was nevertheless "le premier romancier britannique qui ait fait une sorte de sensation parmi nous depuis la révolution." This changed perspective may be due to the mitigated interest in Robespierre and issues of public morality in the Consulate period. *JP* 322 (22 thermidor An 8; August 10, 1800): 2586–87.

131. Desessarts, *Précis*, 1:1.

132. "Qui suis-je, moi qu'on accuse? Un esclave de la liberté, un martyr vivant de la République, la victime autant que l'ennemi du crime. . . . Ôtez-moi ma conscience, je suis le plus malheureux de tous les hommes; je ne jouis même pas des droits du citoyen"; Maximilien Robespierre, "Séance du 8 thermidor An 2," in *Œuvres*, 10:556.

133. *Dorbeuil et Céliane* ends on a typically jubilant note: "Heureusement le 9 thermidor vint tout réparer. Jour cent fois heureux! Tu vis rompre les fers pesans de toute la France gémissante; tu vis arrêter les flots de sang innocent qui l'inondoient de toutes parts. O le plus beau de tous les jours!"; LeBastier, *Dorbeuil et Céliane*, 2:176.

134. Balzac, *Sur Catherine de Médicis*, 292–94.

135. Nineteenth-century examples include Regnault-Warin, *Les Prisonniers du Temple* (1800); Vigny, *Stello* (1832); and Hugo, *Quatrevingt-treize* (1874). See also Andrzej Wadja's film *Danton* (1982); Hillary Mantel, *A Place of Greater Safety* (1992); and Matt Sherman, *The French Revolution, a Novel* (2010). Some of this material is discussed in Cook, "Robespierre in French Fiction."

136. The former critical claim is put forth by Krief, *Vivre libre*, 284; and Sol, "Trials." On the latter claim, consider Pigoreau, who wrote: "Elle a fait Irma, c'est-à-dire que dans un temps où l'on ne pouvait sans danger, parler de l'infortuné Louis XVI, elle a eu le courage de nous raconter les malheurs de la jeune orpheline de nos rois"; *Petite Bibliographie*, http://www.textesrares.com/irma/irmoo.htm. On the confiscation by the police, see AN, F7/6263, Police générale, no. 5272, no. 18, 2.

137. On the changing fortunes of royalists and republicans in popular culture, consider the satirical poem "L'Intelligence bien prouvée": "Un Républicain disputoit / Hier avec un Royaliste, / Et celui-ci lui répétoit: / Tais-toi, tu n'es qu'un Anarchiste; / Tu fis

périr notre bon Roi / Pour ta chienne de République: / Mais je ris bien quand je te voi / Encore plus détesté que moi"; *JP* (12 brumaire An 8, November 3, 1799): 200. On the short memory of the French, consider the work of Roland's editors. Already in 1799 her second editor, Champagneux, felt it necessary to provide more explanations. As Berville and Barrière note, "Déjà l'époque était reculée, les souvenirs étaient moins présens." Comparing Roland's era to their own time (1827), the editors comment, "Les temps dont il s'agit sont déjà loin de nous. . . . Où chercherait-on la vérité de nos jours, s'il ne lui était permis de trouver un refuge dans l'histoire?"; Berville and Barrière, "Avertissement placé en tête de la première édition," xv, xviii.

138. "Lorsque je recueillis les feuilles éparses du récit d'Irma, je les avais en quelque sorte arrachées au génie révolutionnaire qui gouvernait l'Inde à cette déplorable époque. Ce fut dans l'ombre du mystère, et avec la précipitation qui accompagne toujours la crainte, que je les livrai à l'impression"; Guénard, "Avant propos," in *Irma* (1816), 1:v. Guénard does not mention the 1801 seizure; she claims that the ninth edition was prohibited in 1809, after which the princess herself was restored to France, which was good news for the book: "Neuf éditions passèrent ainsi, et la dernière fut proscrite. Alors je crus que l'ouvrage intitulé *Irma* ne reparaîtrait plus, et que les Indiens l'oublieraient, comme ils paraissaient avoir oublié celle dont il retrace les vertus et les malheurs; quand tout à coup l'auguste orpheline fut rendue à l'Inde. Alors les restes de la neuvième édition furent remis en vente et enlevés assez promptement"; ibid., vi–vii.

139. Her busy pen did not stop there: in that same year Guénard published a sentimental novel (*La Malédiction paternelle*) and, under the name M. de Faverolles (one of her many pseudonyms), a Gothic thriller entitled *Les Capucins, ou Le Secret du cabinet noir*. Reviews of *Les Mémoires de Marie-Thérèse Louise de Carignan, princesse de Lamballe* and *La Malédiction paternelle* are in *JP* 272 (2 messidor An 9; June 21, 1801) and *JP* 262 (22 prairial An 9; June 11, 1801). Biographical information is from Quérard, *La France*, 3:503.

140. Guénard, *Irma* (An 8), 2:92. All subsequent references are also to this edition of *Irma*.

141. Consider, for example, the case of Madame de Sainte-Amaranthe, owner of a gambling establishment who was allegedly condemned to death by Robespierre, along with her son and pretty young daughter, because the girl refused his advances. See Blanc, *Dernière lettre*, 53–54.

142. For details on the cult of the Supreme Being and Robespierre's treatment by the media following this event held on Pentecost 1794, see Edelstein, *Terror of Natural Right*, 232–56.

143. "La paix rendra le calme à notre patrie; alors le monde entier, devenu une grande famille, n'aura d'autre ambition que d'étendre le cercle des connaissances humaines. La navigation libre raviveroit toutes les parties du globe; par-tout on trouveroit des amis, comme la nature a mis par-tout des frères. . . . Je ne pouvois me défendre de partager son enthousiasme! j'aurois voulu n'être pas née dans le rang suprême . . . ne fut pas un obstacle aux vœux que j'aurois peut-être formés comme elle, pour l'affranchissement de l'univers"; *Irma* (An 8), 2:132–33.

144. "Songez, ma chère Irma, que nous sommes obligées de nous conformer aux lois de notre pays; il n'y en a point qui puissent interdire les doux témoignages de l'amitié, et le républicain fier, mais sensible, cultivera toujours des fleurs pour en parer l'innocence; mais

il y auroit une inconséquence marquée, s'il célébroit ou laissoit même célébrer l'apothéose d'un roi. . . . Personne ne fut plus digne de cet hommage, que le chef de votre famille, mais c'est à l'histoire à marquer sa place parmi les grands hommes, et non à un peuple libre . . .—Je ne pus m'empêcher de convenir que ses idées étoient justes"; ibid., 162.

145. "On accuse les républicains d'insensibilité, comme si l'orgueil des cours ne gla-çoit pas encore davantage le coeur de ceux qui les habitant. Les premiers, dans un enthou-siasme qui tient peut-être au fanatisme, immolent les plus doux sentimens de la nature à l'amour de la patrie; mais les autres sacrifient tout à leur intérêt personnel, aux préjugés souvent les plus absurdes"; ibid., 172.

146. Krief, *Vivre libre*, 284–86; the same analysis is also in her *Entre terreur et vertu*, 110.

147. This scenario is replayed several times in Rosny, *Les Infortunes de La Gale-tierre*, 2nd ed., vi, 60, 70–71. On satires of oath-taking, see Douthwaite, "On *Candide*, Catholics, and Freemasonry."

148. Advertisements for "Fantasmagorie de Robertson, cour des Capucines, place Vendôme," are found in *JP* 181 Supplément (1 germinal An 8; March 22, 1800) and there-after every few days for several weeks that summer. Robertson had rivals: a spectacle called "Fantasma-Parastasie" promised "Apparition des Fantômes & Evocation des ombres, tells que se les figurant les Illuminés" [sic] in *JP* 182 (2 germinal An 8; March 23, 1800) and every two days thereafter that summer. Perrin announced his "Récréations de physique amus-ante" on 5 germinal (March 26, 1800) and thereafter as well; see, e.g., *JP* 204 (24 germinal An 8; April 14, 1800): supp. n.p. A more intimate commerce with the dead, sort of a combi-nation Mesmerist session and séance, features in Verne, *Voyageur sentimental*, 299–314.

149. Robertson, *Mémoires récréatifs*, 1:282–83.

150. This famous quotation is from an article by Poultier (*L'Ami des lois*; March 1798), cited in Robertson, *Mémoires récréatifs*, 1:220.

151. For the designation "chronicle," see Dickens, *Tale*, 7. All references to *Tale* are to Maxwell's edition, cited by book, chapter, and page. For evidence of the historical scope, consider book 3, "The Track of a Storm" and chapter headings "The Period" (1.1) and "Five Years Later" (2.1).

152. "Charles Dickens's New Work: *A Tale of Two Cities*, nos. I, II, and III" (1859), reprinted in Glancy, *Dickens's "A Tale,"* 60–61. Lewes, Gissing (*Charles Dickens*; 1898), and Orwell (*Dickens, Dali, and Others*; 1946) are cited in Withers, "Dickens and the Psychology of Dreams," 1001, 984, 1001, respectively. Huber and te Wildt, "Charles Dickens's *A Tale*," 334; Dever, "Psychoanalyzing."

153. Roussel, *Histoire secrète*, epigraph.

154. Smiley, *Charles Dickens*, 161–62.

155. "La fin de l'histoire de la culture se manifeste par deux côtés opposés: le pro-jet de son dépassement dans l'histoire totale, et l'organisation de son maintien en tant qu'objet mort, dans la contemplation spectaculaire. L'un de ces mouvements a lié son sort à la critique sociale, et l'autre à la défense du pouvoir de classe"; Debord, *Société de spec-tacle*, 143.

156. "Dans l'esprit de Bouvard, montez-au-ciel-fils-de-saint-Louis, les vierges de Verdun et les culottes en peau humaine étaient indiscutables"; Flaubert, *Bouvard et Pécuchet*, 187; on Pécuchet's politics, see 186–87.

157. "Qu'il le [le Peuple] baillonne, le foule et l'extermine! Ce ne sera jamais trop"; ibid., 258.

158. On the connections between the two books, see Ton-That, *Lectures*, 35–36, 80–82, 105–6; and Herschberg-Pierrot, *Dictionnaire*, 34–53, 128–29.

159. "Concession: N'en jamais faire, elles ont perdu Louis XVI"; "Échafaud: S'arranger quand on y monte, pour prononcer quelques paroles éloquentes avant de mourir"; "Conjuré: Les conjurés ont toujours la manie de s'inscrire sur une liste"; Flaubert, *Dictionnaire*, in *Bouvard et Pécuchet*, 500, 510, 501. "Louis XVI: Toujours dire: 'Cet infortuné monarque'"; "Républicain: Les républicains ne sont pas tous des voleurs, mais tous les voleurs sont républicains"; "Foule: 'La vile populace' (Thiers)"; "Girondins: Plus à plaindre qu'à blâmer"; ibid., 537, 549, 519, 523. "Foule: A toujours de bons instincts"; "Pauvre: S'occuper d'eux tient lieu de toutes les vertus"; "Pitié: Toujours s'en garder"; ibid., 519, 546, 547.

160. In a letter of September 1850 to a friend, Flaubert explained that the *Dictionnaire* would be written "de telle manière que le lecteur ne sache pas si on se fout de lui, oui ou non"; cited by Herschberg-Pierrot, *Dictionnaire*, 5.

161. For more on the positive consequences of Jacobin legislation in the short and long run, see Livesey, *Making Democracy*; Higonnet, *Goodness*; Woloch, *Jacobin Legacy*; and Desan, "Reconstituting the Social."

IN GUISE OF A CONCLUSION

1. Jullien: "Il faudra peut-être se reporter à 10 ou 15 ans de l'étonnante année 1789, pour juger sainement les faits, apprécier sans indulgence comme sans prévention les personnes, & fixer avec certitude l'influence des uns & des autres"; *JP* 59 (February 28, 1791): Supplément 26, ii–iv. Apart from the eight-page prospectus (1791), Jullien's *Tableau historique & philosophique des discussions importantes de la première Assemblée nationale de France* was never published. On Robespierre's alleged remark, see Desessarts, *Crimes*, 79.

2. Chanoine Claude-Joseph Duchastanier (aka *Le Pape de la petite église*) and Saint Marie-Madeleine Postel, both cited in Hufton, "The Reconstruction of a Church," 52.

3. Denis Diderot, *De la poésie dramatique*, cited in Russo, *Styles of Enlightenment*, 200.

4. For anecdotes of servants who act more nobly than their masters, see Thomas, *Adieux*, 181, 191–92. *Histoire des désastres de Saint-Domingue* (Paris, 1795), cited in Curtin, "The Declaration," 175.

5. M. Thébenien, review of *De la situation intérieure de la République*, *JP* (March 4, 1797), cited in Wagner, "Fête et dissolution," 528.

6. Pitts, "Young."

7. I thank Jim Collins for this reference and its connection with *Marie-Antoinette*.

8. Sieyès, *Qu'est-ce que le tiers-état?*, 1; Negm cited in Creswell, "Egypt."

9. Younis, "Egypt's Revolution"; Rice et al., "Women."

10. For an exciting glimpse of how the spirit lives on, see Martial Poirson, ed., *Mythologies révolutionnaires: La Revolution française dans les cultures et imaginaires populaires aujourd'hui* (forthcoming).

BIBLIOGRAPHY

PRIMARY SOURCES

À bout de souffle (Breathless). Directed by Jean-Luc Godard. 1960. DVD. New York: Wellspring Media, 2005.

Affiches américaines. Multiple numbers. ANOM: 87 MIOM 15.

Alibert, J. L. *De l'influence des causes politiques sur les maladies et la constitution physique de l'homme.* N.p., n.d., ca. 1795–96. ANOM: 87 MIOM 17.

Amin, ou Ces derniers temps. Paris: De l'Imprimerie, rue Meslée, An 6 (1797–98).

André, J. F. *Examen impartial de la vie publique et privée de Louis XVI.* Paris and Hambourg: n.p., 1797.

Anecdote historique traduite du turc. Constantinople: Dans le Palais du Sultan, 1790.

Angoisses de la mort, ou Idées des horreurs des prisons d'Arras. N.p., n.d., ca. 1795.

Atrocités exercées envers les citoyens d'Arras dans la maison d'arrêt dite La Providence. N.p., n.d., ca. 1795.

Babeuf, [Gracchus] Citoyen. *Le Journal de la liberté de la presse* 4 (1794).

Balzac, Honoré de. *Les Chouans, ou La Bretagne en 1799.* Edited by Pierre-Louis Rey. Paris: Pocket, 1990. Originally published in 1829.

——. *Du Gouvernement moderne.* In *Œuvres diverses,* vol. 2, edited by Pierre-Georges Castex, Roland Chollet, René Guise, and Christiane Guise, 1066–84. Paris: Gallimard, Pléiade, 1996. Written in 1832; published posthumously in 1900.

——. *Le Père Goriot.* Edited by Félicien Marceau. Paris: Gallimard, 1971. Originally published in 1834–35 in serial form and in 1835 as a book.

——. *Père Goriot.* Translated by A. J. Krailsheimer. Oxford: Oxford University Press, 1991.

——. *Souvenirs d'un paria: Les Mémoires de Sanson.* Edited by Robert LeSieur. Paris: Nouvelle société d'édition, 1944. Originally published in 1830.

——. *Sur Catherine de Médicis.* In *La Comédie humaine,* vol. 10, *Études philosophiques II,* edited by Marcel Bouteron, 11–298. Paris: Gallimard, Pléiade, 1950. Originally published in 1828.

Baum, L. [Lyman] Frank. *The Marvelous Land of Oz.* 1904. Reprint, New York: Dover Publications, 1961.

————. *Our Landlady.* Edited by Nancy Tystad Koupal. Lincoln: University of Nebraska Press, 1996. Originally published as a column appearing in *Aberdeen Saturday Pioneer*, January 1890–February 1891.

[Bellanger, C.]. *Le Falot du peuple, ou Entretiens de Madame Saumon, marchande de marée, sur le procès de Louis XVI.* In *Dialogues révolutionnaires*, edited by Malcolm Cook, 83–92. Exeter: University of Exeter Press, 1994. Originally published ca. 1792–93.

Booser, Madame. *Triomphe de la saine philosophie, ou La Vraie Politique des femmes.* Paris: Debrai et L'Imprimerie des femmes, sous les auspices de la Convention nationale, n.d., ca. 1795–97.

Bourbon, Stéphanie-Louise de. *Mémoire de Stéphanie-Louise de Bourbon . . . fille majeure légitimée, citoyenne française, à la Convention nationale & au peuple français.* Paris: De l'Imprimerie de Poignée, 1796.

Bruno, Louis de. *Lioncel, ou L'Émigré, nouvelle historique.* Paris: Chez Gaillourdet, An 8 (1800).

Burke, Edmund. *A Philosophical Enquiry into the Origin of Our Ideas of the Sublime and the Beautiful.* Edited by James T. Boulton. Notre Dame: University of Notre Dame Press, 1968. Originally published in 1757.

————. *Reflections on the Revolution in France and on the Proceedings in Certain Societies in London Relative to That Event.* Edited by Conor Cruise O'Brien. London: Penguin, 1986. Originally published in 1790.

Burney, Fanny. *Evelina, or The History of a Young Lady's Entrance into the World.* New York: W. W. Norton, 1965. Originally published in 1778.

Carlyle, Thomas. *The French Revolution: A History.* 2 vols. New York: Thomas Y. Crowell, 1893. Originally published in 1837.

Chateaubriand, François-René de. *Mémoires d'outre-tombe.* Edited by Maurice Levaillant and Georges Moulinier. 2 vols. Paris: Gallimard, Pléiade, 1951. Published posthumously in 1848.

Les Chevalières errantes, ou Les Sosies femelles. Paris: Guessier jeune, 1792.

Collection complète des tableaux historiques de la Révolution française composée de cent treize numéros en trois volumes. 3 vols. Paris: Chez Auber, An 13 (1804).

Condorcet, Marie Jean Antoine Nicolas de Caritat, Marquis de. "Lettre d'un jeune mécanicien aux auteurs du Républicain, 16 juillet 1791." In *Œuvres*, 12:239–41. Stuttgart–Bad Cannstatt: Friedrich Frommann Verlag, 1968.

Conspirations, trahisons, et calomnies dévoilées et dénoncées par plus de dix mille Français réfugiés au Continent de l'Amérique. [Paris]: De l'imprimerie de la citoyenne Fonrouge, Jardin égalité, ca. 1794. ANOM: 87 MIOM 27.

Correspondance française, ou Tableau de l'Europe. Multiple numbers. ANOM: 87 MIOM 86.

Correspondance littéraire. Edited by Friedrich Melchior, baron de Grimm. Multiple numbers.

Courrier politique et littéraire du Cap-français publié par M. Gatereau. Multiple numbers. ANOM: 87 MIOM 15.

Deraggis, M. *Adresse au peuple français, libre et souverain.* Par le citoyen Deraggis, ancien procureur-syndic de la commune de Mirabalais, isle et côte de Saint-

Domingue. [Paris]: De l'imprimerie de Pain, cloître Saint-Honoré, An 2. ANOM: 86 MIOM 27.

Desessarts, Nicolas Toussaint LeMoyne. *Les Crimes de Robespierre et de ses principaux complices; leur supplice; la mort de Marat; son apothéose; le procès et le supplice de Charlotte Corday.* 2 vols. Paris: Chez DesEssarts, An 5 (1797).

———. *Précis historique de la vie, des crimes et du supplice de Robespierre.* 2 vols. Paris: Chez DesEssarts, 1797.

Desmoulins, Camille. *Le Vieux Cordelier.* In *Collection des mémoires relatifs à la Révolution française,* vol. 16. Paris: Baudouin, 1825.

Devaines, Jean. *Lettres de la comtesse de . . . au chevalier de . . .* N.p., 1789.

Dickens, Charles. *Hard Times: For These Times.* Edited by Charles Shapiro. New York: Penguin Books USA / Signet Classic, 1980. Originally published in 1854.

———. *A Tale of Two Cities.* Edited by Richard Maxwell. London: Penguin, 2003. Originally published in 1859.

Dictionnaire chronologique et raisonné des découvertes, inventions . . . et importations en France. Edited by Une Société de gens de lettres. 17 vols. Paris: Louis Colas, 1822–24.

[Doppet, François Amédée]. *Le Commissionnaire de la Ligue d'Outre-Rhin, ou Le Messager nocturne . . .* Paris: Buisson, 1792.

Ducray-Duminil, le C. [François]. *Cœlina, ou L'Enfant du mystère.* 6 vols. Paris: Chez LePrieur, An 7 (1798–99).

Dulac, H. G. *Le Glaive vengeur de la République française une et indivisible, ou Galerie révolutionnaire, contenant les noms, prénoms, les lieux de naissance, . . . de tous les grands conspirateurs et traîtres à la patrie, dont la tête est tombée sous le glaive national.* Paris: G. F. Galletti, An 2 (ca. 1794).

Duperron, L. *Vie secrète, politique et curieuse de M. J. Maximilien Robespierre, député de l'Assemblée constituante en 1789, et à la Convention nationale jusqu'au 9 thermidor l'an deuxième de la République, veille de son exécution et de celle de ses complices. Suivie de plusieurs anecdotes sur cette conspiration sans pareille.* Paris: Chez Prévost, An 2 (1793–94).

Entretien du citoyen S.B. curé jacobin avec un maître d'école, dans la commune de ** dépt. des Hautes Alpes. Gap: Chez J. Allier, An 2 (1794).

Extrait d'une lettre sur les malheurs de Saint-Domingue, en général, et principalement sur l'incendie de la ville de Cap Français. Paris: Au Jardin égalité, An 2 (1793–94). ANOM: 87 MIOM 27.

[Femme Honoré]. *Lettres de deux habitans des frontières à tous les François.* Paris: Imprimerie de Feret, [1791?]. http://gallica.bnf.fr.

Ferrières, Charles-Elie, Marquis de. *Correspondance inédite.* Ed. H. Carré. Paris, 1932.

Feuille de correspondance du libraire, ou Notice des ouvrages publiés dans les différens journaux qui circulent en France & dans l'Etranger, & par le moyen de laquelle il met ses Correspondans au courant des nouveautés, sans se donner la peine de les recueillir. Paris: Chez Aubry, 1791–92.

[Feuille de Salut public]. "Aux Républicaines." *AM* 59 (29 brumaire an 2; November 17, 1793): 18:450.

Feuillet de Conches, Félix Sébastien. *Louis XVI, Marie-Antoinette et Madame Elisabeth,*

lettres et documents inédits publiés par F. S. Feuillet de Conches. 6 vols. Paris: Henri
   Plon, 1864.

Flaubert, Gustave. *Bouvard et Pécuchet avec un choix de scénarios, du Sottisier, L'Album
   de la marquise, et Le Dictionnaire des idées reçues.* Edited by Claudine Gothot-
   Mersch. Paris: Gallimard, 1979. Published posthumously in 1881 (*Bouvard*) and 1910
   (*Dictionnaire*).

———. *L'Éducation sentimentale: Histoire d'un jeune homme.* 1869. Reprinted in
   Œuvres complètes de Gustave Flaubert, vol. 3. Paris: Louis Conard, 1910.

Galart de Montjoie [Christophe Félix Louis Ventre de La Touloubre, dit Galart de Mont-
   joie]. *Histoire de la conjuration de Maximilien Robespierre.* 1795. 2nd ed. Paris:
   Maret, 1796.

——— [Galart de Montjoye]. *History of the Conspiracy of Maximilien Robespierre.* London: T. Egerton, 1796. ECCO (Eighteenth Century Collections Online, http://gdc.gale
   .com/products/eighteenth-century-collections-online/). Accessed August 4, 2010.

Godwin, William. *The Adventures of Caleb Williams, or Things as They Are.* Edited by
   George Sherburn. New York: Holt, Rinehart and Winston, 1960. Originally published
   in 1794.

———. *Enquiry concerning Political Justice.* Edited by K. Codell Carter. Oxford: Clarendon Press, 1971. Originally published in 1793.

Gouges, Olympe de. "Les Trois urnes, ou Le Salut de la patrie, par un voyageur aérien
   (Affiche publiée le 19 juillet 1793)." In *Ecrits politiques, 1792–93,* edited by Olivier
   Blanc, 2:243–48. Paris: Côté-femmes, 1993.

Gower, Earl. *Dispatches of Earl Gower, English Ambassador at Paris from June 1790
   to August 1792.* Edited by O. Browning. Cambridge: Cambridge University Press,
   1885.

Grande Motion des citoyennes de divers marchés. In *Marie-Antoinette: Anthologie et
   dictionnaire,* edited by Catriona Seth, 139–43. Paris: Robert Laffont, 2006. Originally
   published ca. 1792.

Grand Jugement rendu par le peuple français contre Louis Seize. Paris: Imprimerie de Le
   Gesne, [1791?]. http://gallica.bnf.fr.

Granger, C. *Les Crimes des terroristes, poème.* Paris: n.p., An 3 (1795).

Guénard, Élisabeth (Brossin de Méré, baronne). *Irma, ou Les Malheurs d'une jeune orpheline . . .* 5 vols. 10th ed. Paris: Chez Mme Veuve Lepetit, 1816.

———. *Irma, ou Les Malheurs d'une jeune orpheline; Histoire indienne, avec des
   romances.* Publié par la C.^e G.^d 2 vols. [Delhy and] Paris: Chez l'auteur, An 8 (1799–
   1800).

Henri IV et Louis XIV au petit coucher de Louis XVI à Saint-Cloud. Quatrième dialogue.
   N.p., n.d., ca. 1790.

Henriquez, L.-M. *Les Aventures de Jérôme Lecocq, ou Les Vices du despotisme et les
   avantages de la liberté, présentées à la Convention nationale, par Henriquez,
   citoyen de la section du Panthéon-français.* Paris: Célère, 1794.

———. *Voyage et adventures* [sic] *de Frondeabus, fils d'Herschell, dans la cinquième
   partie du monde.* Paris: Cailleau, An 7 (1798–99).

Histoire de Toussaint-Louverture, chef des noirs insurgés de Saint-Domingue. Paris: Pil-
   lot frères, An 10 (1802).

Histoire d'un poignard française [sic]: *Anecdote de la Révolution.* 2 vols. Paris: Capelle and G. F. Girard, An 11 (1803).

L'Histoire véritable de Gingigolo, roi du Mano-Emugi. N.p., n.d., ca. 1789.

Hoffmann, E. T. A. *The Sandman.* Translated by L. J. Kent and E. C. Knight. In *Tales,* edited by Victor Lange, 277–308. New York: Continuum, 1982. Originally published as *Der Sandmann* in 1816.

Hugo, Victor. *Bug-Jargal.* In *Histoires d'esclaves révoltés: Bug-Jargal / Tamango,* edited by Gérard Gengembre, 19–201. Paris: Pocket, 2004. Originally published in 1826.

———. *Le Dernier jour d'un condamné.* Paris: Pocket, 2004. Originally published in 1829.

———. *Les Misérables.* Edited by Guy Rosa and Nicole Savy. 2 vols. Paris: Livre de Poche, 1998. Originally published in 1862.

———. *Quatrevingt-treize.* Edited by Gérard Gengembre. Paris: Pocket, 1998. Originally published in 1874.

Johnson, Samuel. *The Rambler.* In *The Yale Edition of the Works of Samuel Johnson,* vol. 4, edited by W. J. Bate and Albrecht B. Strauss. New Haven, CT: Yale University Press, 1969.

Journal général de la littérature de France. 1800–1801. Multiple volumes.

LeBastier, C. B. *Dorbeuil et Céliane de Vadran: Leurs Amours et leurs malheurs pendant la tyrannie de Robespierre.* Paris: Chez LeBastier frères, An 3 (1794–95).

Lesuire, Robert. *Charmansage, ou Mémoires d'un jeune citoyen faisant l'éducation d'un ci-devant noble.* 2 vols. Paris: Defer de maisonneuve, 1792.

Louis XVI. *Correspondance politique et confidentielle, inédite de Louis XVI, avec ses frères, et plusieurs personnes célèbres, pendant les dernières années de son règne, et jusqu'à sa mort; avec des observations.* Edited by Helen-Maria Williams. Paris: Chez Debray, An 11 (1803). Alleged forgery.

———. *Déclaration du Roi adressée à tous les Français à sa sortie de Paris.* 1791. Reprinted in *Testaments et manifestes de Louis XVI,* edited by Jean-Christian Petit-fils, 47–84. Paris: Éditions des équateurs, 2009.

———. *Testaments et manifestes de Louis XVI.* Edited by Jean-Christian Petitfils. Paris: Éditions des équateurs, 2009.

Louis XIV à Saint Cloud au chevet de Louis XVI. N.p., n.d., ca. 1790.

Marat, Jean-Paul. *Les Charlatans modernes.* 1791. Reprinted in *Les Pamphlets de Marat,* 255–96. Paris: Librairie Charpentier et Fasquelle, 1911.

Marie-Antoinette. Directed by Sofia Coppola. 2006. DVD. Culver City, CA: Sony Pictures, 2007.

Marie-Antoinette. Directed by W. S. Van Dyke. 1938. DVD. Burbank, CA: Warner Home Video, 2006.

Maton de la Varenne, P. A. L. de. *Les Crimes de Marat et des autres égorgeurs; ou, Ma résurrection.* Paris: André, An 3 (1795).

Méhée de la Touche, Jean-Claude Hippolyte. *Les Noyades, ou Carrier au Tribunal révolutionnaire.* Paris: Marchands de nouveautés, 1794.

——— [FETHEMSI, pseud.]. *La Queue de Robespierre, ou Les Dangers de la liberté de la presse.* Paris: Rougyff [Gouffroy], An 2 (1794).

Mémoires sur l'Affaire de Varennes, comprenant le mémoire inédit de M. le marquis de Bouillé (comte Louis); deux relations également inédites de MM. les comtes de

Raigecourt et de Damas; celle de M. le capitaine Deslon, et le précis historique de M. le comte de Valory. Paris: Baudouin frères, 1823.

Mercier, Louis-Sébastien. *Paris pendant la Révolution (1789–1799), ou Le Nouveau Paris.* 2 vols. Paris: Librairie Poulet-Malassis, 1862.

Michaud, Joseph-François [M. d'Albins, pseud.]. *Les Adieux de Marie-Thérèse-Charlotte de Bourbon: Almanach pour l'année 1796.* Basle: Chez Tournesen, 1796.

Michon, Pierre. *Les Onze.* Lagrasse: Éditions Verdier, 2009.

Moleville, Antoine-François Bertrand, marquis de. *A Refutation of the Libel on the Memory of the Late King of France.* London: n.p., 1804.

Necker, Jacques. *Œuvres complètes de M. Necker.* Vol. 3, *De la révolution française.* Paris: n.p., 1820.

Nogaret, François-Félix. *À la nation, nouvel essai pindarique sur la situation de la République française aujourd'hui 10 août 1793.* Versailles: M. D. Cosson, An premier de la République, 1793.

———. *À Louis-Xavier de S. P***, malade de chagrin de voir sa fortune altérée par la Révolution.* Versailles: Cosson and Lebas, 1791.

———. *L'Âme de Timoléon, ou Principes républicains, philosophiques et moraux, auxquels on a joint quelques motifs de chants analogues aux fêtes nationales.* Paris: Delaplace, An 6 de la République française (1798).

———. *L'Antipode de Marmontel, ou Nouvelles Fictions, ruses d'amour et espiègleries de l'Aristénète français, opuscule précédé de la correspondance de l'auteur avec Parny, Palissot et autres littérateurs.* Paris: Imprimerie de Glisau, An 8 (1800).

———. *L'Appel aux nations.* Versailles: Cosson, n.d., ca. 1793.

———. *L'Aristénète français, ou Recueil de folies amoureuses.* 4th ed. 2 vols. Paris: Léopold Collin, 1807.

———. *Cantique des mille forgerons de la manufacture d'armes de Versailles.* Versailles: Cosson, n.d., ca. 1793.

———. *Contes et historiettes en prose, de Félix Nogaret.* 2 vols. Versailles: Cosson, 1795.

———. *Le Dernier Soupir d'un rimeur de 89 ans, ou Versiculets de Nogaret (Félix) sur la métaphysico-néologo-romanticologie.* Paris: Marchands de Nouveautés, l'Auteur, and Leclerc, 1829.

———. *Le Dialogue entre Solon et François-Félix Nogaret, citoyen français, domicilié dans une grande ville.* N.p., n.d., ca. 1789.

———. *Extrait du "Journal de la Société des amis de la constitution," séante à Versailles, en date du 3 juin 1791.* Versailles: Cosson, 1791.

———. *Le Miroir des événemens actuels, ou La Belle au plus offrant: Histoire à deux visages.* Paris: Au Palais Royal and Chez les Marchands de Nouveautés, l'An de notre salut, et le deuxième de la Liberté (1790).

———. *Le Réveil d'Adam: Hiérodrame en trois actes.* Paris: Veuve LePetit, An 13 (1804).

———. Letter to Benjamin Franklin, March 8, 1783. In *Benjamin Franklin Papers—Hays Calendar* 7.1. Philadelphia: American Philosophical Society, n.d. http://www.amphilsoc.org/library/mole/f/franklin/hays7.htm. Updated 2010.

Nouvelle Bibliothèque universelle des romans. Paris: Maradan, 1800–1805. Multiple volumes.

Passion de 1790, ou Louis XVI sacrifié pour et par son peuple. Paris: De l'Imprimerie Philippe Parabole, 1790.

Perrin, René. *Incendie du Cap, ou Le Règne de Toussaint-Louverture.* Paris: Chez Marchand, An 10 (1802).

Philo, histoire politico-philosophique, par grenadier N. G. N.p., 1790.

Picquenard, Jean-Baptiste. *Adonis ou le bon nègre.* In *Adonis suivi de Zoflora et de documents inédits*, edited by Chris Bongie, 1–82. Paris: L'Harmattan, 2006. Originally published in 1798.

Pigault-Lebrun, Charles Antoine Guillaume. *L'Enfant du carnaval, histoire remarquable, et surtout véritable pour servir de supplément aux Rhapsodies du jour.* Paris: Desjonquères, 1989. Originally published in 1796.

Pitt à Saint-Domingue, ou Les Crimes de l'ancien comité de Salut-public: Entretien entre le Caporal Tranche-Montagne et Brise-Raison sur les colonies. [Paris]: De l'Imprimerie des droits du peuple, [1795?]. ANOM: 87 MIOM 27.

[Pochet, A.] *La Boussole nationale, ou Voyages, aventures et anecdotes historico-rustiques de Jaco surnommé Henri quatrième laboureur, descendant du frère de lait de notre bon roi Henri IV: Recueillies par un vrai patriote.* 3 vols. Paris: De l'Imprimerie de la liberté sur la place de la Bastille, 1790.

———. *L'Héroïsme uni à l'espérance par la félicité publique à l'autel de la liberté: Fête Gymnastique et Athénienne . . . l'an troisième de la Liberté.* N.p.: De l'Imprimerie de Pain, n.d., ca. 1792.

Poissardiana, ou Catéchisme des Halles. N.p., n.d., ca. 1797.

Proyart, Abbé Liévin-Bonaventure [Le Blond de Neuvéglise, pseud.]. *La Vie et les crimes de Robespierre surnommé le tyran, depuis sa naissance jusqu'à sa mort.* Augsbourg: Chez tous les libraires, 1795.

Réflexions sur le commerce. N.p., n.d. [1789–90?]. ANOM: 87 MIOM 05.

Regnault-Warin, Jean-Baptiste Joseph Innocent Philadelphe (dit Julius-Junius). *L'Ange des prisons, élégide.* Paris: Chez L'Huillier, Delaunay, Pillet, 1817.

———. *La Caverne de Strozzi.* Paris: Au Magasin des romans nouveaux, Chez Lepetit, An 7 (1798–99).

———. *Le Cimetière de la Madeleine.* 2 vols. Paris: Chez Lepetit jeune, An 8, An 9 (1800–1801).

———. *Clémence.* 3 vols. Paris: Chez Maison, An 11 (1802).

———. *Conseils au peuple sur son salut.* Bar-le-Duc: François Duval, "La Patrie étant en danger, An 4," [1793?].

———. *Le Contemplateur.* Paris: Au Bureau général du Contemplateur, An 9 (1801).

———. *The Magdalen Churchyard, from the French of J. J. Regnault Warin.* N.p.: Nabu Publishing, 2010. (Nabu Publishing is a subsidiary of the on-demand publisher Biblio-Bazaar LLLC.)

———. *The Magdalen Churchyard.* Translated by Samuel Mackay. Whitefish, MT: Kessinger Publishing, 2008. Originally published in 1809.

———. *Le Paquet-bot de Calais à Douvres: Roman politique et moral.* Paris: Chez André, An 10 (1802).

———. *Les Prisonniers du Temple.* Paris: Locard, fils, An 9 (1800).

———. *Spinalba, ou Les Révélations de la Rose-Croix.* 4 vols. Paris: Chez André, An 11 (1803).

Le Règne du Prince Trop-Bon dans le royaume des fols, Conte oriental, ou Plutôt Histoire occidentale, par madame LA TOUJOURS COMTESSE DE * * * . Coblentz, Worms, Tournay, Aix-la-Chapelle, and Paris: Bureau de l'ami du roi, 1792.

Résurrection de Louis XVI, roi des Juifs et des François. Jerusalem: De l'Imprimerie du Saint-Sépulchre, 1790.

Rétif de la Bretonne, Nicolas Edme. *La Découverte australe par un homme volant, ou Le Dédale français.* Edited by Paul Vernière. 2 vols. Geneva: Slatkine Reprints, 1979. Originally published in 1781.

———. *Les Nuits de Paris, ou Le Spectateur nocturne.* Edited and abridged by Michel Delon. Paris: Gallimard, 1986. Originally published in 1788.

Le Réveil des dames, ou Les Femmes devenues Papes, Cardinaux, Evêques, Ministres, Magistrats, Professeurs, par un Corps académique de Dames. Paris: n.d., ca. 1791.

Révéroni Saint-Cyr, Jacques Antoine. *Pauliska, ou La Perversité moderne: Mémoires récents d'une Polonaise.* Edited by Michel Delon. Paris: Desjonquères, 1991. Originally published in 1798.

———. *Sabina d'Herfeld, ou Les Dangers de l'imagination; lettres prussiennes.* 4th ed. 2 vols. Paris: Barba, 1814. Originally published in 1797.

Riouffe, Baron Honoré Jean. *Mémoires d'un détenu, pour servir à l'histoire de la tyrannie de Robespierre.* 2nd ed. Paris: Chez Brigitte Mathé and Chez Louvet, An 3 (1795).

Rivarol, Antoine. "Lettre à M. le Président de * * * sur le globe aérostatique, sur les têtes parlantes, et sur l'état présent de l'opinion publique à Paris." 1783. Reprinted in *Œuvres complètes de Rivarol,* 2:229–35. Paris: Léopold Collin, 1808.

———. *Mémoires de Rivarol.* Edited by Saint-Albin Berville. Paris: Éditions GALIC, 1962. Originally published in 1824.

Robertson, E. G. *Mémoires récréatifs scientifiques et anecdotiques du physicien-aéronaute E. G. Robertson.* 2 vols. Paris: Chez l'auteur, 1831.

Robespierre, Charlotte. *Mémoires de Charlotte Robespierre sur ses deux frères.* Edited by Albert Laponneraye. Paris: Au Dépôt central, 1835.

Robespierre, Maximilien. *Éloge de Gresset.* 1785. Reprint, *Éloge de Gresset par Robespierre,* edited by D. Jouaust. Paris: Académie des bibliophiles, 1868. http://openlibrary .org/. Accessed March 13, 2011.

———. *Œuvres.* Vols. 9–10. Edited by Marc Bouloiseau, Georges Lefebvre, Albert Soboul, et al. Paris: Presses universitaires de France, 1957–60.

———. *Œuvres de Maximilien Robespierre, avec une notice historique, des notes et des commentaires.* Edited by Albert Laponneraye and Armand Carrel. 3 vols. Paris: Chez l'éditeur, 1840.

Le Roi trompé et détrompé ou les bonnes leçons, histoire indienne, traduite d'un manuscrit arabe. Paris: n.p., 1790.

Roland, Marie-Jeanne. *An Appeal to Impartial Posterity, by Madame Roland, wife of the minister of the Home Department; or, A collection of pieces written by her during her confinement in the prisons of the Abbey and St. Pélagie.* Published originally in Paris for the benefit of her only daughter, deprived of the fortune of her parents, whose property is still in sequestration. Translated from the French. Dublin: J. Cham-

bers, 1796. ECCO (Eighteenth Century Collections Online, http://gdc.gale.com/
products/eighteenth-century-collections-online/). Accessed 2009–11.

———. *Appel à l'impartiale postérité, par la citoyenne Roland, femme du ministre de
l'Intérieur; ou Recueil des écrits qu'elle a rédigés, pendant sa détention aux prisons
de l'Abbaye et de Sainte-Pélagie; D'après l'édition de Paris, faite au profit de sa fille
unique, privée de la fortune de ses père et mère, dont les biens sont toujours séques-
trés*. Paris: Chez Louvet; London: J. Johnson, 1796. ECCO (Eighteenth Century Collections Online, http://gdc.gale.com/products/eighteenth-century-collections-online/).
Accessed 2009–11.

Romeau. *La Tête ou l'oreille du cochon, ou Proposition faite à tous les citoyens de célébrer dans le sein de leurs familles, les époques les plus intéressantes de la Révolution*. Paris: Imprimerie de Pellier, 1798. http://gallica.bnf.fr.

Rondot. *L'Ombre de Robespierre, aux Français; ses avis aux frères et amis, sur la pere
[sic] de sa tête, et les moyens de faire triompher sa queue*. Paris: De l'Imprimerie
David, n.d.

Rosny, A. J. *Les Infortunes de La Galetierre pendant le régime décemviral* . . . 2nd ed.
Paris: LePrieur, An 7 (1798–99).

———. *Les Infortunes de Mr de la Galetierre pendant le régime décemviral. Contenant
ses persécutions, sa fuite sous Robespierre, son naufrage et son séjour dans une île
déserte, suivis de son retour en France*. Paris: Consort, An 5 (1796–97).

Roussel, Pierre-Joseph-Alexis [P.J.A.R.D.E., pseud.]. *Le Château des Tuileries, ou Récit
de ce qui s'est passé dans l'intérieur de ce Palais, depuis sa construction jusqu'au
18 brumaire de l'an VIII; avec des particularités sur la visite que le Lord Bedfort y a
faite après le 10 Août 1792* . . . 2 vols. Paris: Lerouge, 1802.

——— [Proussinalle, pseud.]. *L'Histoire secrète du Tribunal révolutionnaire* . . . *avec des
anecdotes piquantes sur les orgies que faisaient les juges et les jurés*. 2 vols. Paris:
Lerouge, 1815.

Rouy, Aîné. *Assassinats commis sur 81 prisonniers de la prison dite Saint-Lazare, le 7, 8,
et 9 Thermidor*. Paris: Geoffroy, ca. 1794.

Saintomer, C. *Jugement du peuple souverain, qui condamne à mort la Queue infernale
de Robespierre*. Paris: Guffroy, ca. 1794.

Sedaine, Jean-Michel. *Richard Cœur de lion, comédie en trois actes, mêlée d'ariettes.
Musique de M. Grétry*. Paris: Gardy, 1812.

Sénac de Meilhan, Gabriel. *L'Émigré*. In *Le Roman noir de la Révolution*, edited by Raymond Trousson, 81–432. Paris: Éditions Nathan, 1997. Originally published in 1797.

Shelley, Mary. *Frankenstein, or The Modern Prometheus*. Edited by J. Paul Hunter. New
York: W. W. Norton, 1996. Originally published in 1818, rev. ed. 1831.

———. *Frankenstein, or The Modern Prometheus*. Edited by James Reiger. Chicago: University of Chicago Press, 1982.

———. *Mary Shelley's Journals*. Edited by Frederick L. Jones. Norman: University of
Oklahoma Press, 1947.

Shields, David. *Reality Hunger: A Manifesto*. New York: Alfred A. Knopf, 2010.

Sieyès, Emmanuel Joseph, Abbé. *Qu'est-ce que le tiers état?* N.p., 1789. http://gallicabnf.fr/.

Soirées amoureuses du Général Mottier et de la belle Antoinette. Persépolis: À l'enseigne
de l'astuce et de la vérité délaissée, 1790.

Les Souvenirs d'un jeune prisonnier, ou Mémoires sur les prisons de la Force et Duplessis, pour servir à l'histoire de la révolution. N.p., n.d., ca. An 3 [1795?].

Stevenson, Robert Louis. *The Strange Case of Dr. Jekyll and Mr. Hyde, The Merry Men, and Other Tales and Fables.* Edited by Tim Middleton. Ware, UK: Wordsworth Editions, 1993. *The Strange Case of Dr. Jekyll and Mr. Hyde* was first published in 1886.

S***, Madame [Suremain, Louise-Marie]. *Melchior ardent, ou Les Aventures plaisantes d'un Incroyable.* 2 vols. Paris: Chez Lefort et Moutardier, n.d., ca. 1800.

Thomas, Chantal. *Les Adieux à la Reine.* Paris: Seuil, 2002.

Vadé, Jean-Joseph. *Œuvres choisies de M. Vadé.* Avignon: Chez Luxembourg Bonnet, n.d., ca. 1821.

Verne, François. *Le Voyageur sentimental en France sous Robespierre.* Geneva and Paris: J. J. Paschoud and Maradan, An 7 (1798–99).

Vigny, Alfred de. *Stello.* Edited by Marc Eigeldinger. Paris: Flammarion, 1984. Originally published in 1832.

Villemain d'Abancourt, François-Jean. *Le Cimetière de la Madeleine.* Paris: Marchand de nouveautés, An 9 (1800–1801).

———. *Le Cimetière de Mousseaux.* Paris: Roux, 1801.

V'la c'qui s'est dit. In *Dialogues révolutionnaires*, edited by Malcolm Cook, 73–81. Exeter: University of Exeter Press, 1994. Originally published ca. 1791–92.

Voltaire. *Œuvres de Voltaire.* Vol. 3, *Théâtre.* Edited by Charles Palissot de Montenoy. Paris: Stoupe and Servière, 1792.

Wilde, Oscar. *The Picture of Dorian Gray.* Edited by Camille Cauti. New York: Barnes and Noble Classics, 2003. Originally published in 1890.

Williams, Helen-Maria. *An Eye-Witness Account of the French Revolution by Helen Maria Williams: Letters Containing a Sketch of the Politics of France.* Edited by Jack Fruchtman Jr. New York: Peter Lang, 1997. Originally written in 1790–95.

———. *Memoirs of the Reign of Robespierre.* Edited by Frantz Funck-Brentano. London: John Hamilton, 1929. Originally published in 1795.

[Williams, Hélène-Marie, ed.]. *Correspondance politique et confidentielle, inédite de Louis XVI, avec ses frères, et plusieurs personnes célèbres, pendant les dernières années de son règne, et jusqu'à sa mort; avec des Observations.* 2 vols. Paris: Chez Debray, An 11 (1803). Alleged forgery.

Wollstonecraft, Mary. *A Vindication of the Rights of Man with A Vindication of the Rights of Woman and Hints.* Edited by Sylvana Tomaselli. Cambridge: Cambridge University Press, 1995. Originally published in 1790 (*Rights of Man*) and 1792 (*Rights of Woman*).

SECONDARY SOURCES

Abray, Jane. "Feminism in the French Revolution." *American Historical Review* 80, no. 1 (February 1975): 43–62.

Alder, Ken. *Engineering the Revolution: Arms and Enlightenment in France, 1763–1815.* Princeton, NJ: Princeton University Press, 1997.

Altick, Richard D. *The Shows of London.* Cambridge, MA: Belknap Press, 1978.

Amartin-Serin, Annie. *La Création déifiée: L'Homme fabriqué dans la littérature*. Paris: Presses universitaires de France, 1996.

Amossy, Ruth. "Fathers and Sons in *Old Goriot*: The Symbolic Dimension of Balzac's Realism." In *Approaches to Teaching "Old Goriot*," edited by Michal Peled Ginsburg, 45–53. New York: Modern Language Association, 2000.

Ancelon, E. A. *La Vérité sur la fuite et l'arrestation de Louis XVI à Varennes, d'après des documents inédits*. Paris: E. Dentu, 1866.

Andress, David. *The French Revolution and the People*. London: Hambledon and London, 2004.

———. "Living the Revolutionary Melodrama: Robespierre's Sensibility and the Construction of Political Commitment in the French Revolution." *Representations* 114, no. 1 (Spring 2011): 103–28.

———. *The Terror: Civil War in the French Revolution*. London: Little, Brown, 2005.

April, Robert S. "Representation of the Dead Body in Literature and Medical Writing during the Restoration in France (1799–1848)." In *Images of the Corpse: From the Renaissance to Cyberspace*, edited by Elizabeth Klaver, 63–87. Madison: University of Wisconsin Press, 2004.

Arasse, Daniel. *La Guillotine et l'imaginaire de la Terreur*. Paris: Flammarion, 1987.

Artarit, Jean. *Robespierre, ou l'impossible filiation*. Paris: La Table ronde, 2003.

L'Art de l'estampe et la révolution française. Paris: Musée Carnavalet, 1977.

Atkinson, Diane. *The Suffragettes in Pictures*. London: Museum of London, 1996.

Aulard, François Victor Alphonse. *Paris sous le Consulat: Recueil de documents pour l'histoire de l'esprit public à Paris*. Vol. 4. Paris: Librairie Léopold Cerf, Noblet, and Quantin, 1909.

Au Temps des Merveilleuses: La Société parisienne sous le Directoire et le Consulat. Paris: Musée Carnavalet, 2005.

Baczko, Bronislaw. *Comment sortir de la Terreur: Thermidor et la Révolution*. Paris: Gallimard, 1989.

Baker, Keith. *Condorcet: From Natural Philosophy to Social Mathematics*. Chicago: University of Chicago Press, 1975.

Barbéris, Pierre. *Balzac et le mal du siècle: Contribution à une physiologie du monde moderne*. 2 vols. Paris: Gallimard, 1970.

———. *Le Monde de Balzac*. Paris: Arthaud, 1973.

Bardèche, Maurice. *Balzac romancier*. Paris: Plon, 1940.

Becker, Ernest. *The Denial of Death*. New York: Free Press, 1975.

Beizer, Janet. *Family Plots: Balzac's Narrative Generations*. New Haven, CT: Yale University Press, 1985.

Bell, David A. *The Cult of the Nation in France: Inventing Nationalism, 1680–1800*. Cambridge, MA: Harvard University Press, 2001.

Bellanger, Claude, Jacques Godechot, Pierre Guiral, and Fernand Terrou. *Histoire générale de la presse française*. 5 vols. Paris: Presses universitaires de France, 1969–76.

Bellhouse, Mary L. "Candide Shoots the Monkey Lovers: Representing Black Men in Eighteenth-Century French Visual Culture." *Political Theory* 34 (2006): 741–84.

Berville, Saint-Albin, and François Barrière. "Avertissement placé en tête de la première édition." In Marie-Jeanne Roland de la Platière, *Mémoires de Madame Roland*, edited by Saint-Albin Berville and François Barrière, 1:ix–xviii. 3rd ed. Paris: Baudouin frères, 1827.

Bessand-Massenet, Pierre. *La France après la Terreur, 1795–1799*. Paris: Plon, 1946.

Besser, Gretchen R. "Lear and Goriot: A Re-evaluation." *Orbis Litterarum* 27 (1972): 28–36.

Bewell, Alan. "An Issue of Monstrous Desire: *Frankenstein* and Obstetrics." *Yale Journal of Criticism* 2, no. 1 (1988): 105–28.

Bianchi, Serge. "Clergé/Prêtres." In *Dictionnaire historique de la Révolution française*, edited by Albert Soboul, 229–31. Paris: Presses universitaires de France, 1989.

Bidelman, Patrick Kay. *Pariahs Stand Up! The Founding of the Liberal Feminist Movement in France, 1858–1889*. Westport, CT: Greenwood Press, 1982.

Blakemore, Steven. *Crisis in Representation: Thomas Paine, Mary Wollstonecraft, Helen Maria Williams, and the Rewriting of the French Revolution*. Madison, NJ: Fairleigh Dickinson University Press, 1997.

Blanc, Olivier. *La Dernière Lettre: Prisons et condamnés de la Révolution, 1793–94*. Paris: Robert Laffont, 1984.

———. *Olympe de Gouges*. Paris: Syros, 1981.

Boffa, Massimo. "Émigrés." In *A Critical Dictionary of the French Revolution*, edited by François Furet and Mona Ozouf, translated by Arthur Goldhammer, 324–36. Cambridge, MA: Harvard University Press, 1989.

Bongie, Chris. *Friends and Enemies: The Scribal Politics of Post/Colonial Literature*. Liverpool: Liverpool University Press, 2008.

Bouloiseau, Marc. *Robespierre*. Paris: Presses universitaires de France, 1957.

Bourdieu, Pierre. *Distinction: A Social Critique of the Judgement of Taste*. Translated by Richard Nice. Cambridge, MA: Harvard University Press, 1984.

———. *The Field of Cultural Production: Essays on Art and Literature*. Edited by Randal Johnson. New York: Columbia University Press, 1993.

Boursin, E., and Augustin Challamel. *Dictionnaire de la Révolution française — institutions, hommes et faits*. Paris: Jouvet, 1893.

Bouton, Cynthia. "Gendered Behavior in Subsistence Riots: The French Flour War of 1775." *Journal of Social History* 23 (Summer 1990): 235–55.

Boyle, David. *Troubadour's Song: The Capture, Imprisonment and Ransom of Richard the Lionheart*. New York: Walker, 2005.

Brécy, Robert. "La Chanson révolutionnaire de 1789 à 1799." *Annales historiques de la Révolution française* 53 (1981): 279–303.

Brouard-Arends, Isabelle, and Laurent Loty, eds. *Littérature et engagement pendant la Révolution française*. Rennes: Presses de l'Université de Rennes, 2007.

Brown, Howard G. *Ending the French Revolution: Violence, Justice, and Repression from the Terror to Napoleon*. Charlottesville: University of Virginia Press, 2006.

Brunel, Pierre. "Sublime et grotesque dans *Le Père Goriot*." *L'Année balzacienne* 2, no. 1 (2001): 30–56.

Buhle, Mari Jo, and Paul Buhle, eds. *The Concise History of Woman Suffrage*. Urbana: University of Illinois Press, 1978.

Burke, Janet. "Leaving the Enlightenment: Women Freemasons after the Revolution." *Eighteenth-Century Studies* 33, no. 2 (Winter 2000): 255–65.

Butler, Marilyn. "*Frankenstein* and Radical Science." In Mary Shelley, *Frankenstein*, edited by J. Paul Hunter, 302–13. New York: Norton, 1996.

Cameron, Vivian. "Political Exposures: Sexuality and Caricature in the French Revolution." In *Eroticism and the Body Politic*, edited by Lynn Hunt, 90–107. Baltimore, MD: Johns Hopkins University Press, 1991.

Caratini, Roger. *Dictionnaire des personnages de la Révolution*. Paris: Belfond-Pré aux Clercs, 1988.

Carrier, Hubert. *Les Mazarinades*. 2 vols. Paris: Champion, 1989.

Casanova, Pascale. *The World Republic of Letters*. Translated by M. B. DeBevoise. Cambridge, MA: Harvard University Press, 2004.

Castein, Hanne. "'Zerrbilder des Lebens': E. T. A. Hoffmann's *Der Sandmann* and the Robot Heritage." *Publications of the English Goethe Society* 67 (1997): 43–54.

Castelot, André. *Varennes: Le Roi trahi*. Paris: Éditions André Bonne, 1951.

Castle, Terry. *The Female Thermometer: Eighteenth-Century Culture and the Invention of the Uncanny*. New York: Oxford University Press, 1995.

Castonguay-Bélanger, Joël. *Les Écarts de l'imagination: Pratiques et représentations de la science dans le roman au tournant des Lumières*. Montreal: Presses de l'Université de Montréal, 2008.

Censer, Jack, and Lynn Hunt, eds. "Liberty, Equality, Fraternity: Exploring the French Revolution." http://chnm.gmu.edu/revolution/about.html.

Cerati, Marie. *Le Club des citoyennes républicaines révolutionnaires*. Paris: Éditions sociales, 1966.

Chapuis, Alfred. *Les Automates dans les œuvres d'imagination*. Neuchâtel: Éditions du Griffon, 1947.

Chapuis, Alfred, and Edouard Gélis. *Le Monde des automates: Étude historique et technique*. 2 vols. 1928, 1948. Reprint, Geneva: Slatkine Editions, 1984.

Chartier, Roger. *Les Origines culturelles de la Révolution française*. Paris: Seuil, 1990.

Chartier, Roger, and Daniel Roche. "Introduction: Les Livres ont-ils fait la Révolution?" In *Livre et Révolution: Mélanges de la Sorbonne 9*, edited by Frédéric Barbier, Claude Jolly, and Sabine Juratic, 9–20. Paris: Aux Amateurs de livres, 1988.

Chen, Wei-ling. "Le Père Goriot, autodestructeur." *NTU Studies in Language and Literature* (Taiwan) 11 (December 2002): 60–67.

Cherry, Christopher. "Machines as Persons?" In *Human Beings*, edited by David Cockburn, 1–24. Cambridge: Royal Institute of Philosophy, 1991.

Cioranescu, Alexandre. *Bibliographie de la littérature française du dix-huitième siècle*. 3 vols. Paris: Editions du CNRS, 1962.

Clarke, Joseph. *Commemorating the Dead in Revolutionary France: Revolution and Remembrance, 1789–1799*. Cambridge: Cambridge University Press, 2007.

Clemit, Pamela. "*Frankenstein*, *Matilda*, and the Legacies of Godwin and Wollstonecraft." In *The Cambridge Companion to Mary Shelley*, edited by Esther Schor, 26–44. Cambridge: Cambridge University Press, 2003.

Clère, Jean-Jacques. "Haute cour" and "Tribunaux." In *Dictionnaire historique de la Révolution française*, edited by Albert Soboul, 533, 1049–52. Paris: Presses universitaires de France, 1989.

Cobb, Richard. *The French and Their Revolution*. Edited by David Gilmour. New York: New Press, 1998.

Cook, Malcolm C. "Politics in the Fiction of the French Revolution, 1789–1794." *Studies on Voltaire and the Eighteenth Century* 201 (1982): 233–340.

———. "Robespierre in French Fiction." In *Robespierre*, edited by Colin Haydon and William Doyle, 224–36. Cambridge: Cambridge University Press, 1999.

Cottom, Daniel. "The Work of Art in the Age of Mechanical Digestion." *Representations* 66 (Spring 1999): 52–74.

Coudreuse, Anne. *Le Goût des larmes au XVIIIe siècle*. Paris: Presses universitaires de France, 1999.

Coulet, Henri. "Existe-t-il un roman révolutionnaire?" In *La Légende de la Révolution*, edited by Christian Croisille and Jean Ehrard, 173–83. Clermont-Ferrand: ADOSA, 1988.

Courteix, René-Alexandre. *Balzac et la Révolution française*. Paris: Presses universitaires de France, 1997.

Creswell, Robyn. "Egypt: The Cultural Revolution." *New York Times Book Review*, February 20, 2011, 27.

Crouzet, François. "French Historians and Robespierre." In *Robespierre*, edited by Colin Haydon and William Doyle, 255–83. Cambridge: Cambridge University Press, 1999.

Cuddon, J. A., ed. *A Dictionary of Literary Terms*. London: Penguin, 1979.

Curtin, Philip. "The Declaration of the Rights of Man in Saint-Domingue, 1788–1791." *Hispanic American Review* 30, no. 2 (May 1950): 157–75.

Darnton, Robert. *The Kiss of Lamourette: Reflections in Cultural History*. New York: Norton, 1990.

———. *Mesmerism and the End of the Enlightenment in France*. Cambridge, MA: Harvard University Press, 1968.

———. "The Revolutionary Character of the French Revolution: How the Spirit of '89 Mobilized a Will to Build a New World." *Princeton Alumni Weekly*, March 8, 1989, 16–23.

Daumas, Maurice. *Histoire générale des techniques*. Vol. 3, *L'Expansion du machinisme*. Paris: Presses universitaires de France, 1968.

Daut, Marlene. "Sciences of Desire: Race and Representations of the Haitian Revolution in the Atlantic World, 1790–1865." PhD diss., University of Notre Dame, 2008.

Davis, Natalie Zemon. "Women on Top." In *Society and Culture in Early Modern France: Eight Essays by Natalie Zemon Davis*, 124–51. Stanford, CA: Stanford University Press, 1975.

DeBaecque, Antoine. *La Caricature révolutionnaire*. Paris: Presses du CNRS, 1988.

———. *Glory and Terror: Seven Deaths under the French Revolution*. Translated by Charlotte Mandell. New York: Routledge, 2001.

———. "L'Homme nouveau est arrivé: La Régénération des Français en 1789." *Dix-huitième siècle* 20 (1988): 193–208.

Debord, Guy. *La Société de spectacle*. Paris: Gallimard, 1992.

DeJean, Joan. Review of *The Other Enlightenment*, by Carla Hesse. *Journal of Modern History* 75 (2003): 958–60.

De la Motte, Dean. "Balzacorama: Mass Culture in *Old Goriot*." In *Approaches to*

Teaching "Old Goriot," edited by Michal Peled Ginsburg, 54–61. New York: Modern Language Association, 2000.

Deleuze, Gilles, and Félix Guattari. *Kafka: Pour une littérature mineure.* Paris: Minuit, 1975.

Delon, Michel, and Jean-Marie Goulemot, eds. *Ballons et regards d'en haut.* Paris: L'Harmattan, 2007.

Desan, Suzanne. "'Constitutional Amazons': Jacobin Women's Clubs in the French Revolution." In *Re-creating Authority in Revolutionary France*, edited by B. T. Ragan Jr. and E. A. Williams, 11–35. New Brunswick, NJ: Rutgers University Press, 1992.

———. "Crowds, Community, and Ritual in the Work of E. P. Thompson and Natalie Davis." In *The New Cultural History*, edited by Lynn Hunt, 47–71. Berkeley and Los Angeles: University of California Press, 1989.

———. "Reconstituting the Social after the Terror: Family, Property, and the Law in Popular Politics." *Past and Present* 164, no. 1 (August 1999): 81–121.

DesBordes, G. E. "Notice sur l'auteur de l'ancien Fond du Sac." In *Le Fond du sac, recueil de contes en vers*, by François-Félix Nogaret, vii–xix. Rouen: J. Lemonnyer, 1879.

Dever, Carolyn. "Psychoanalyzing Dickens." In *Palgrave Advances in Charles Dickens Studies*, edited by John Bowen and Robert Patten, 216–33. Basingstoke, UK: Palgrave Macmillan, 2006.

Didier, Béatrice. *Ecrire la Révolution, 1789–1799.* Paris: Presses universitaires de France, 1989.

d'Orliac, Jehanne. *Les Dames de la Halle, 1181–1939.* Paris: Société d'éditions extérieures et coloniales, 1946.

Douthwaite, Julia V. "On *Candide*, Catholics, and Freemasonry: How Fiction Disavowed the Loyalty Oaths of 1789–90." *Eighteenth-Century Fiction* 23, no. 1 (2010): 81–117.

———. *The Wild Girl, Natural Man, and the Monster: Dangerous Experiments in the Age of Enlightenment.* Chicago: University of Chicago Press, 2002.

Doyle, William. *The Oxford History of the French Revolution.* Oxford: Oxford University Press, 1989.

Duhet, Paule-Marie. *Les Femmes et la Révolution, 1789–1794.* Paris: Gallimard-Julliard, 1971.

Duprat, Annie. "Louis XVI morigéné par ses ancêtres en 1790: *Les Entretiens des Bourbons.*" *Dix-huitième siècle* 26 (1994): 317–32.

———. *Les Rois de papier: La Caricature de Henri III à Louis XVI.* Paris: Belin, 2002.

Durruty, Bruno. "Les Auteurs de catéchismes révolutionnaires (1789–1799)." *Annales historiques de la Révolution française* 1 (1991): 1–18.

Duval, Georges. *Histoire de la littérature révolutionnaire.* Paris: E. Dentu, 1879.

Edelstein, Dan. *The Terror of Natural Right: Republicanism, the Cult of Nature, and the French Revolution.* Chicago: University of Chicago Press, 2009.

Ellenberger, Michel. *Cartouche: Histoire d'un brigand, un brigand devant l'histoire.* Paris: La Bibliothèque, 2006.

Eude, Michel. "La Loi de Prairial." *Annales historiques de la Révolution française* 254 (October–December 1983): 543–59.

Fabre, Jean. *Idées sur le roman de Madame de Lafayette au Marquis de Sade.* Paris: Éditions Klincksieck, 1979.

Favier, Jean, ed. *Chronicle of the French Revolution, 1789–1799*. London: Chronicle Communications, 1989.

Fish, Stanley. "Normal Circumstances, Literal Language, Direct Speech Acts, the Ordinary, the Everyday, the Obvious, What Goes without Saying, and Other Special Cases." 1978. Reprinted in *Critical Theory since Plato*, edited by Hazard Adams, 1200–1209. New York: Harcourt Brace Jovanovich, 1992.

Florescu, Radu. *In Search of Frankenstein*. Boston: New York Graphic Society, 1976.

Forrest, Alan. "L'armée, la guerre et les politiques de la Terreur." In *Les politiques de la Terreur, 1793–1794*, edited by Michel Biard, 53–67. Rennes: Presses universitaires de Rennes, 2008.

Foucault, Michel. *Discipline and Punish: The Birth of the Prison*. Translated by Alan Sheridan. New York: Vintage, 1979.

———. *The Order of Things: An Archaeology of the Human Sciences*. New York: Vintage Books, 1973.

Foulke, Jan. *Fourteenth Blue Book: Dolls and Values*. Grantsville, MD: Hobby House Press, 1999.

Frantz, Pierre. "Travestis poissards." *Revue des sciences humaines* 61, no. 190 (April–June 1983): 7–20.

Fraser, Antonia. *Dolls, Pleasures and Treasures*. New York: Putnam's Sons, 1963.

Fraser, James. "The History and Mystery of Secret Societies and Secret Political Clubs, Part Two." *Fraser's Magazine for Town and Country* 22 (August 1840): 246.

Frégier, Honoré-Antoine. *Des classes dangereuses de la population dans les grandes villes, et des moyens de les rendre meilleures*. 2 vols. Paris: J.-B. Baillière, 1840.

Freud, Sigmund. "The Uncanny." 1919. In *Collected Papers*, translated by Joan Rivière, 4:368–407. 9th ed. London: Hogarth Press, 1956.

Friguglietti, James. "Rehabilitating Robespierre: Albert Mathiez and Georges Lefebvre as Defenders of the Incorruptible." In *Robespierre*, edited by Colin Haydon and William Doyle, 212–23. Cambridge: Cambridge University Press, 1999.

Furet, François. *Interpreting the French Revolution*. Translated by Elborg Forster. Cambridge: Cambridge University Press, 1981.

Furet, François, and Denis Richet. *La Révolution française*. Paris: Fayard, 1973.

Gallez, Alfred. *Le Brigand Moneuse, capitaine des "chauffeurs du Nord."* Brussels: Brepols, 1959.

Gallo, Max. *L'Homme Robespierre: Histoire d'une solitude*. 1968. Reprint, Paris: Perrin, 1994.

Gauchet, Marcel. "Necker." In *A Critical Dictionary of the French Revolution*, edited by François Furet and Mona Ozouf, translated by Arthur Goldhammer, 287–97. Cambridge, MA: Harvard University Press, 1989.

Gay, Peter. Introduction to *The Philosophical Dictionary*, by Voltaire, 45–52. Translated by Peter Gay. New York: Harcourt, Brace and World, 1962.

Genand, Stéphanie, ed. *Romans de l'émigration, 1797–1803*. Paris: Champion, 2008.

Gérard, Alice. *La Révolution française: Mythes et interprétations (1789–1970)*. Paris: Flammarion, 1970.

Ghachem, Malick. "'The Colonial Vendée.'" In *The World of the Haitian Revolution*, edited by David Patrick Geggus and Norman Fiering, 156–76. Bloomington: Indiana University Press, 2009.

Gilchrist, J., and W. J. Murray. *The Press in the French Revolution: A Selection of Documents taken from the Press of the Revolution for the Years 1789–1794*. New York: St. Martin's Press, 1971.

Gildea, Robert. *Children of the Revolution: The French, 1799–1914*. Cambridge, MA: Harvard University Press, 2008.

Gillet, Jean. "Les Grands cimetières sous la lune." *Revue d'histoire littéraire de la France* 90, nos. 4–5 (1990): 654–62.

Gillispie, Charles Coulston. *Science and Polity in France: The Revolutionary and Napoleonic Years*. Princeton, NJ: Princeton University Press, 2004.

Girard, René. *The Scapegoat*. Translated by Yvonne Freccero. Baltimore, MD: Johns Hopkins University Press, 1986.

Glancy, Ruth, ed. *Charles Dickens's "A Tale of Two Cities": A Sourcebook*. London: Routledge, 2006.

Gobry, Ivan. *Dictionnaire des martyrs de la Révolution*. Paris: Dualpha, 2002.

Godechot, Jacques. "La Presse française sous la Révolution et l'Empire." In *Histoire générale de la presse française*, edited by Claude Bellanger, Jacques Godechot, Pierre Guiral, and Fernand Terrou, 1:456–59. Paris: Presses universitaires de France, 1969.

Godfrey, James L. *Revolutionary Justice: A Study of the Organization, Personnel, and Procedure of the Paris Tribunal, 1793–95*. Chapel Hill: University of North Carolina Press, 1951.

Godineau, Dominique. *Citoyennes tricoteuses: Les Femmes du peuple à Paris pendant la Révolution française*. Aix-en-Provence: Alinéa, 1988.

Goncourt, Edmond de, and Jules de Goncourt. *Histoire de la société française pendant la Révolution*. Paris: G. Charpentier, 1864.

Gordon, L. S. *Le Thème de Mandrin, le "brigand noble" dans l'histoire des idées en France avant la Révolution*. Paris: École des Hautes Études—Sorbonne, 1970.

Gottschalk, Louis, and Margaret Maddox. *Lafayette in the French Revolution through the October Days*. Chicago: University of Chicago Press, 1959.

Gough, Hugh. *The Newspaper Press in the French Revolution*. Chicago: Dorsey Press, 1988.

Granier, Camille. *La Femme criminelle*. Paris: Octave Doin, 1906.

Greer, Donald. *Incidence of the Terror during the French Revolution: A Statistical Interpretation*. Cambridge, MA: Harvard University Press, 1935.

Grenby, M. O. *The Anti-Jacobin Novel: British Conservatism and the French Revolution*. Cambridge: Cambridge University Press, 2001.

Gueniffey, Patrice. *La Politique de la Terreur: Essai sur la violence révolutionnaire, 1789–1794*. Paris: Fayard, 2000.

Guilhaumou, Jacques. *La Langue politique et la Révolution française: De l'évènement à la raison linguistique*. Paris: Méridiens Klincksieck, 1989.

Gullickson, Gay L. *Unruly Women of Paris: Images of the Commune*. Ithaca, NY: Cornell University Press, 1996.

Guyon, Bernard. *La Pensée politique et sociale de Balzac*. Paris: Armand Colin, 1947.

Hacking, Ian. *The Taming of Chance.* Cambridge: Cambridge University Press, 1990.

Hahn, Roger. *The Anatomy of a Scientific Institution: The Paris Academy of Science, 1666–1803.* Berkeley and Los Angeles: University of California Press, 1971.

Hamel, Ernest. *Histoire de Robespierre.* 3 vols. Paris: Chez l'auteur, 1867.

Hannam, June, Mitzi Auchterlonie, and Katherine Holden, eds. *International Encyclopedia of Women's Suffrage.* Santa Barbara, CA: ABC-CLIO, 2000.

Hardman, John, ed. *The French Revolution Sourcebook.* London: Arnold; New York: Oxford University Press, 1999.

———. *Louis XVI: The Silent King.* London: Arnold; New York: Oxford University Press, 2000.

———. *Robespierre.* London: Longman, 1999.

Hatin, Eugène. *Bibliographie historique et critique de la presse périodique française.* Paris: Firmin Didot, 1866.

———. *Histoire politique et littéraire de la presse en France.* 8 vols. Paris: Poulet-Malassis et de Broise, 1860.

Henig, Robin Marantz. "The Real Transformers." *New York Times Magazine,* July 29, 2007: 28–35, 50, 55.

Hernardinquer, J.-J. "Le Porc familier sous l'ancien régime." *Annales E.S.C.* 6 (1970): 1746–52.

Herschberg-Pierrot, Anne. *Le Dictionnaire des idées reçues de Flaubert.* Lille: Presses universitaires de Lille, 1988.

Hesse, Carla. *The Other Enlightenment: How French Women Became Modern.* Princeton, NJ: Princeton University Press, 2001.

———. *Publishing and Cultural Politics in Revolutionary Paris, 1789–1810.* Berkeley and Los Angeles: University of California Press, 1991.

Higonnet, Patrice. *Goodness beyond Virtue: Jacobins during the French Revolution.* Cambridge, MA: Harvard University Press, 1998.

Hilaire-Pérez, Liliane. *L'Invention technique au siècle des Lumières.* Paris: Albin Michel, 2000.

Houssaye, Arsène. *Galerie du XVIIIe siècle, Quatrième série, Hommes et femmes de cour.* 6th ed. Paris: Hachette, 1858.

Huber, Thomas J., and Bert T. te Wildt. "Charles Dickens's *A Tale of Two Cities:* A Case Report of Posttraumatic Stress Disorder." *Psychopathology* 38, no. 6 (2005): 334–37.

Huet, Marie-Hélène. "Living Images: Monstrosity and Representation." *Representations* 4 (1983): 73–87.

Hufton, Olwen. "The Reconstruction of a Church, 1796–1801." In *Beyond the Terror: Essays in French Regional and Social History, 1794–1815,* edited by Gwynne Lewis and Colin Lucas, 21–52. Cambridge: Cambridge University Press, 1983.

———. "Social Conflict and the Grain Supply in Eighteenth-Century France." *Journal of Interdisciplinary History* 14 (Autumn 1983): 303–31.

———. *Women and the Limits of Citizenship in the French Revolution.* Toronto: University of Toronto Press, 1992.

Hunt, Lynn. *The Family Romance of the French Revolution.* Berkeley and Los Angeles: University of California Press, 1992.

———. *Measuring Time, Making History*. Budapest: Central European University Press, 2008.

Hyslop, Beatrice F. "The Theater during a Crisis: The Parisian Theater during the Reign of Terror." *Journal of Modern History* 17 (1945): 332–55.

Jacob, Louis. *Robespierre vu par ses contemporains*. Paris: Librairie Armand Colin, 1938.

Jones, Colin. *Longman Companion to the French Revolution*. London: Longman, 1988.

Jones, Kimberly. "L'Iconographie henricéenne dans l'estampe de l'ancien régime, 1774 à 1793." In *La Légende d'Henri IV*, 307–22. Paris: Association Henri IV, 1995.

Jordan, David P. *The King's Trial: Louis XVI vs. the French Revolution*. Berkeley and Los Angeles: University of California Press, 1979.

———. *The Revolutionary Career of Maximilien Robespierre*. New York: Free Press, 1985.

Kanes, Martin. *Père Goriot: Anatomy of a Troubled World*. New York: Twayne, 1993.

Kang, Minsoo. *Sublime Dreams of Living Machines: The Automaton in the European Imagination*. Cambridge, MA: Harvard University Press, 2011.

Kaplan, Steven. *Provisioning Paris*. Ithaca, NY: Cornell University Press, 1984.

Kayser, Wolfgang. *The Grotesque in Art and Literature*. Translated by Ulrich Weisstein. Bloomington: Indiana University Press, 1963.

Kennedy, Deborah. *Helen Maria Williams and the Age of Revolution*. Lewisburg: Bucknell University Press, 2002.

Kennedy, Emmet. *A Cultural History of the French Revolution*. New Haven, CT: Yale University Press, 1989.

Kennedy, Michael. "Les Clubs des Jacobins et la presse sous l'Assemblée nationale, 1789–1791." *Revue historique* 264, no. 1 (1980): 49–63.

Kennedy, Randy. "The Free-Appropriation Writer." *New York Times*, February 28, 2010, WK 3.

Krief, Huguette. "Écriture politique et écriture des corps dans le roman sous la Révolution française." In *L'Engagement littéraire*, edited by Emmanuel Bouju, 111–26. Rennes: Presses universitaires de Rennes, 2005.

———. *Entre Terreur et vertu: Et la fiction se fit politique . . . (1789–1800)*. Paris: Honoré Champion, 2010.

———. "Parole topique et terreur sous la décennie révolutionnaire." In *Locus in fabula: La Topique de l'espace dans les fictions françaises d'ancien régime*, edited by Nathalie Ferrand, 622–39. Louvain: Éditions Peeters, 2004.

———, ed. *Vivre libre et écrire: Anthologie des romancières de la période révolutionnaire (1789–1800)*. Oxford: Voltaire Foundation "VIF," 2005.

Lafrance, Geneviève. *Qui perd gagne: Imaginaire du don et Révolution française*. Montreal: Presses de l'Université de Montréal, 2008.

Landes, Joan. *Visualizing the Nation: Gender, Representation, and Revolution in Eighteenth-Century France*. Ithaca, NY: Cornell University Press, 2001.

———. *Women and the Public Sphere in the Age of the French Revolution*. Ithaca, NY: Cornell University Press, 1988.

Langlois, Claude. *La Caricature contre-révolutionnaire*. Paris: Presses du CNRS, 1988.

———. "Counterrevolutionary Iconography." In *French Caricature and the French Revo-*

lution, 1789–1799, 41–54. Los Angeles: Grunwald Center for the Graphic Arts and UCLA, 1988.

———. *Les Sept Morts du roi.* Paris: Anthropos, 1993.

Lawrence, William. *Lectures on Comparative Anatomy, Physiology, Zoology, and the Natural History of Man.* 9th ed. London: Bohn, 1848.

Lefebvre, Georges. *Le Directoire.* Paris: Colin, 1946.

———. "Remarks on Robespierre." Translated by Beatrice F. Hyslop. *French Historical Studies* 1, no. 1 (1958): 7–10.

———. *Les Thermidoriens.* Paris: Colin, 1937.

Lemaire, Jean-François. "Le Dr Jean-Paul Marat médecin parisien." In *Marat homme de science?*, edited by Jean Bernard, Jean-François Lemaire, and Jean-Pierre Poirier, 13–63. Paris: Les Empêcheurs de Penser en Rond, 1993.

Lenotre, G. [L. L. T. Gosselin, pseud.]. *The Flight of Marie-Antoinette.* Translated by Mrs. Rodolph Stawell. London: William Heinemann, 1913.

Levy, Darline Gay, and Harriet B. Applewhite. "Responses to the Political Activism of Women of the People in Revolutionary Paris, 1789–1793." In *Women and the Structure of Society: Selected Research from the Fifth Berkshire Conference on the History of Women*, edited by Barbara J. Harris and JoAnn K. McNamara, 215–31. Durham, NC: Duke University Press, 1984.

Levy, Darline Gay, Harriet Branson Applewhite, and Mary Durham Johnson, eds. *Women in Revolutionary Paris, 1789–1795: Selected Documents Translated with Notes and Commentary.* Urbana: University of Illinois Press, 1979.

Ligou, Daniel. "Franc-maçonnerie." In *Dictionnaire historique de la Révolution française*, edited by Albert Soboul, 475–81. Paris: Presses universitaires de France, 1989.

Livesey, James. *Making Democracy in the French Revolution.* Cambridge, MA: Harvard University Press, 2001.

Loomis, Stanley. *The Fatal Friendship: Marie-Antoinette, Count Fersen, and the Flight to Varennes.* Garden City, NY: Doubleday, 1972.

Lucey, Michael. "Kinship, Economics, and Queer Sexuality in Balzac's *Old Goriot*." In *Approaches to Teaching "Old Goriot,"* edited by Michal Peled Ginsburg, 126–33. New York: Modern Language Association, 2000.

Lyon-Caen, Judith. *La Lecture et la vie: Les Usages du roman au temps de Balzac.* Paris: Tallandier, 2006.

Lyons, Martyn. *Reading Culture and Writing Practices in Nineteenth-Century France.* Toronto: University of Toronto Press, 2008.

MacLean, Ian. *Woman Triumphant: Feminism in French Literature, 1610–1652.* Oxford: Clarendon Press, 1977.

Marcus, Sharon. *Apartment Stories: City and Home in Nineteenth-Century Paris and London.* Berkeley and Los Angeles: University of California Press, 1999.

Marion, Rene S. "The 'Dames de la Halle': Community and Authority in Early Modern Paris." PhD diss., Johns Hopkins University, 1994.

Maron, Eugène. *Histoire littéraire de la Révolution: Constituante — Législative.* Paris: Chamerot, 1856.

Marshall, Alan, and Thierry Gouttenègre. "L'Affiche en révolution." In *L'Affiche en révo-*

lution, edited by Alan Marshall and Thierry Gouttenègre, 9–32. Vizille: Musée de la Révolution française, 1998.

Martin, Alex. *Enlightened Metropolis: Constructing Imperial Moscow, 1762–1855*. Cambridge: Cambridge University Press. Forthcoming.

Martin, Angus, Vivienne G. Mylne, and Richard Frautschi, eds. *Bibliographie du genre romanesque français, 1751–1800*. London: Mansell, 1977.

Martin, Jean-Clément. *Violence et Révolution: Essai sur la naissance d'un mythe national*. Paris: Seuil, 2006.

———. "Violences et justice." In *Les Politiques de la Terreur, 1793–1794*, edited by Michel Biard, 129–40. Rennes: Presses universitaires de Rennes, 2008.

Mason, Laura. *Singing the French Revolution: Popular Culture and Politics, 1787–1799*. Ithaca, NY: Cornell University Press, 1996.

Matharan, Jean-Louis. "Suspects." In *Dictionnaire historique de la Révolution française*, edited by Albert Soboul, 1004–8. Paris: Presses universitaires de France, 1989.

Mathiez, Albert. "Étude critique sur les journées des 5 et 6 octobre 1789." *Revue historique* 67 (May–August 1898): 241–81.

———. "Étude critique sur les journées des 5 et 6 octobre 1789, suite." *Revue historique* 68 (September–December 1898): 258–94.

———. "Étude critique sur les journées des 5 et 6 octobre 1789, suite et fin." *Revue historique* 69 (January–April 1899): 41–66.

———. *Robespierre terroriste*. Paris: La Renaissance du livre, 1921.

Mayer, Arno. *The Furies: Violence and Terror in the French and Russian Revolutions*. Princeton, NJ: Princeton University Press, 2000.

Mayr, Otto. *Authority, Liberty, and Automatic Machinery in Early Modern Europe*. Baltimore, MD: Johns Hopkins University Press, 1986.

Maza, Sarah. *Private Lives and Public Affairs: The Causes Celebres of Pre-revolutionary France*. Berkeley and Los Angeles: University of California Press, 1993.

Mazauric, Claude. "Terreur." In *Dictionnaire historique de la Révolution française*, edited by Albert Soboul, 1020–25. Paris: Presses universitaires de France, 1989.

McMillan, James F. *France and Women, 1789–1914: Gender, Society and Politics*. London: Routledge, 2000.

Mellon, Stanley. *The Political Uses of History: A Study of Historians in the French Restoration*. Stanford, CA: Stanford University Press, 1958.

Mellor, Anne K. "Choosing a Text of *Frankenstein* to Teach." In Mary Shelley, *Frankenstein*, edited by J. Paul Hunter, 160–66. New York: Norton, 1996.

———. *Mary Shelley: Her Life, Her Fiction, Her Monsters*. New York: Methuen, 1988.

Melzer, Sara E., and Leslie W. Rabine, eds. *Rebel Daughters: Women and the French Revolution*. New York: Oxford University Press, 1992.

Ménégault, A. P. F., and Rigobert Piquenard. *Martyrologe littéraire; ou, Dictionnaire critique de sept cents auteurs vivans*. Paris: Germain Mathiot, 1816.

Michel, Frann. "Lesbian Panic and Mary Shelley's *Frankenstein*." *GLQ* 2, no. 3 (1995): 237–52.

Miller, D. A. "1839: Body Bildung and Textual Liberation." In *A New History of French Literature*, edited by Denis Hollier, 681–87. Cambridge, MA: Harvard University Press, 1989.

Monglond, André. *La France révolutionnaire et impériale: Annales de bibliographie méthodique et description des livres illustrés.* 5 vols. Grenoble: B. Arthaud, 1931–38.

Moore, A. P. *The "Genre Poissard" and the French Stage of the Eighteenth Century.* New York: Columbia University Institute of French Studies, 1935.

Moore, Raylyn. *Wonderful Wizard, Marvelous Land.* Bowling Green, OH: Bowling Green University Popular Press, 1974.

Moretti, Franco. *The Way of the World: The Bildungsroman in European Culture.* London: Verso, 1987.

Morton, J. B. *The Bastille Falls and Other Studies of the French Revolution.* London: Longmans, Green, 1936.

Morton, Timothy, ed. *Mary Shelley's "Frankenstein": A Sourcebook.* London: Routledge, 2002.

———. *Shelley and the Revolution in Taste: The Body and the Natural World.* Cambridge: Cambridge University Press, 1994. Reprint, Cambridge: Cambridge University Press, 1998.

Napo, Tommaso, ed. *Index biographique français.* 3rd ed. Munich: K. G. Saur, 2004. Multiple fiches.

Norberg, Kathryn. "'Love and Patriotism': Gender and Politics in the Life and Work of Louvet de Couvrai." In *Rebel Daughters: Women and the French Revolution*, edited by Sara E. Melzer and Leslie W. Rabine, 38–53. New York: Oxford University Press, 1992.

Norris, Robert Standish. "The Counter-revolutionary Imagination: Edmund Burke and the French Revolution, 1789–1797." PhD diss., New York University, 1976.

Nye, Russel B. "An Appreciation." In *The Wizard of Oz and Who He Was*, edited by Martin Gardner and Russel B. Nye, 1–17. East Lansing: Michigan State University Press, 1994.

Ogle, Gene E. "The Trans-Atlantic King and Imperial Public Spheres: Everyday Politics in Pre-revolutionary Saint-Domingue." In *The World of the Haitian Revolution,* edited by David Patrick Geggus and Norman Fiering, 79–96. Bloomington: Indiana University Press, 2009.

Orr, Linda. *Headless History: Nineteenth-Century French Historiography of the Revolution.* Ithaca, NY: Cornell University Press, 1990.

Outram, Dorinda. *The Body and the French Revolution: Sex, Class and Political Culture.* New Haven, CT: Yale University Press, 1989.

Ozouf, Mona. *L'Homme régénéré: Essais sur la révolution française.* Paris: Gallimard, 1989.

———. *Varennes: La Mort de la royauté.* Paris: Gallimard, 2005.

Parent, Françoise. "De nouvelles pratiques de lecture." In *Histoire de l'édition française*, vol. 2, *Le Livre triomphant*, edited by Henri-Jean Martin and Roger Chartier, 606–21. Paris: Promodis, 1984.

Pasco, Allan H. "Literature as Historical Archive: Reading Divorce in Mme de Staël's *Delphine* and Other Revolutionary Literature." *EMF: Studies in Early Modern France* 7 (2001): 163–200.

Pastre, Geneviève. *Les Amazones: Du mythe à l'histoire.* Paris: Éditions Geneviève Pastre, 1996.

Paulson, Ronald. *Representations of Revolution (1789–1820)*. New Haven, CT: Yale University Press, 1983.

Pellegrin, Nicole. *Les Vêtements de la Liberté: Abécédaire des pratiques vestimentaires françaises de 1780 à 1800*. Aix-en-Provence: Alinéa, 1989.

Pertué, Michel. "Tribunal du 17 août / Tribunal révolutionnaire." In *Dictionnaire historique de la Révolution française*, edited by Albert Soboul, 1046–49. Paris: Presses universitaires de France, 1989.

Petitfils, Jean-Christian. *Louis XVI*. Paris: Éditions Perrin, 2005.

Petrey, Sandy. *Realism and Revolution: Balzac, Stendhal, Zola, and the Performances of History*. Ithaca, NY: Cornell University Press, 1988.

Peuchet, Jacques. *Mémoires tirés des Archives de la Police de Paris pour servir à l'histoire de la morale et de la police depuis Louis XIV jusqu'à nos jours*. Vol. 3. Paris: A. Levasseur, 1838.

Pigoreau, Alexandre-Nicolas. *Petite Bibliographie biographico-romancière, ou dictionnaire des romanciers tant anciens que modernes . . .* Paris: Pigoreau, 1821. http://www.textesrares.com/irma/irmoo.htm. Accessed September 2, 2010.

Pitts, Leonard. "Young for One, Brief Shining Moment." *South Bend Tribune*, January 21, 2011, A6.

Popkin, Jeremy. *Revolutionary News: The Press in France, 1789–1799*. Durham, NC: Duke University Press, 1990.

Price, Munro. *The Road from Versailles: Louis XVI, Marie-Antoinette, and the Fall of the French Monarchy*. New York: St. Martin's Griffin, 2004.

Quérard, J.-M. *La France littéraire, ou Dictionnaire bibliographique*. 12 vols. Paris: Firmin Didot frères, 1827–64.

Reddy, William. *The Navigation of Feeling: A Framework for the History of Emotions*. Cambridge: Cambridge University Press, 2001.

Reichardt, Rolf, and Hubertus Kohle. *Visualizing the Revolution: Politics and Pictorial Art in Late Eighteenth-Century France*. London: Reaktion Books, 2008.

Reinhard, Marcel. *La Chute de la royauté (10 août 1792)*. Paris: Gallimard, 1969.

Renan, Ernest. "What Is a Nation?" 1882. Translated by Martin Thom. In *Nation and Narration*, edited by Homi K. Bhabha, 8–22. London: Routledge, 1990.

Rendall, Jane. *The Origins of Modern Feminism: Women in Britain, France, and the United States, 1780–1860*. New York: Schocken Books, 1984.

Rétat, Pierre. "L'Ebranlement de la 'littérature' en 1789." In *L'Ecrivain devant la Révolution, 1780–1800*, edited by Jean Sgard, 17–29. Grenoble: Société française d'étude du 18e siècle and Université Stendhal de Grenoble, 1990.

Rice, Xan, Katherine Marsh, et al., "Women Have Emerged as Key Players in the Arab Spring." *Guardian*, April 22, 2011. http://www.guardian.co.uk/. Accessed on June 15, 2011.

Riskin, Jessica. *Science in the Age of Sensibility: The Sentimental Empiricists of the French Enlightenment*. Chicago: University of Chicago Press, 2002.

Röder, Birgit. *A Study of the Major Novellas of E. T. A. Hoffmann*. Rochester, NY: Camden House, 2003.

Rogers, Katharine M. *L. Frank Baum, Creator of Oz*. New York: St. Martin's Press, 2002.

Ronzeaud, Pierre. "De la Harangère à la 'harangueuse': Étude d'un stéréotype polémique forgé au XVIIe siècle." In *Ouverture et dialogue: Mélanges offerts à Wolfgang Leiner*, edited by Ulrich Döring, Antiopy Lyroudias, and Rainer Zaiser, 739–53. Tübingen: Gunter Narr Verlag, 1988.

Roudinesco, Élisabeth. *Théroigne de Méricourt: A Melancholic Woman during the French Revolution*. Translated by Martin Thom. London: Verso, 1991.

Rudé, George. *The Crowd in the French Revolution*. Oxford: Clarendon Press, 1959.

Russo, Elena. *Styles of Enlightenment: Taste, Politics, and Authorship in Eighteenth-Century France*. Baltimore, MD: Johns Hopkins University Press, 2007.

Ryn, Claes G. *The New Jacobinism: Can Democracy Survive?* Washington, DC: National Humanities Institute, 1991.

Sage, Victor. "Diderot and Maturin: Enlightenment, Automata, and the Theatre of Terror." In *European Gothic: A Spirited Exchange, 1760–1960*, edited by Avril Horner, 55–70. Manchester: Manchester University Press, 2002.

Sainte-Beuve, Charles Augustin. *La Littérature française des origines à 1870: Dix-huitième siècle*. Vol. 7. Paris: La Renaissance du livre, 1926.

Sangsue, Daniel. "De quelques têtes coupées dans la littérature du XIXe siècle." In *Crime et châtiment*, edited by Jean Clair, 75–83. Paris: Gallimard and Musée d'Orsay, 2010.

Saurel, Louis. *Le Jour où finit la Terreur: Le 9 thermidor An 2, 27 juillet 1794*. Paris: Laffont, 1962.

Schama, Simon. *Citizens: A Chronicle of the French Revolution*. New York: Alfred A. Knopf, 1989.

Scurr, Ruth. *Fatal Purity: Robespierre and the French Revolution*. New York: Henry Holt, 2006.

Secher, Reynald. *Le Génocide franco-français: La Vendée-vengé*. Paris: Presses universitaires de France, 1986.

Seth, Catriona, ed. *Imaginaires gothiques: Aux sources du roman noir français*. Paris: Desjonquères, 2010.

———, ed. *Marie-Antoinette: Anthologie et dictionnaire*. Paris: Robert Laffont, 2006.

Sgard, Jean. *Dictionnaire des journalistes, 1600–1789*. Vol. 2. Oxford: Voltaire Foundation, 1999.

Shapiro, Barry M. *Revolutionary Justice in Paris, 1789–1790*. Cambridge: Cambridge University Press, 1993.

———. *Traumatic Politics: The Deputies and the King in the Early French Revolution*. University Park: Pennsylvania State University Press, 2009.

Smiley, Jane. *Charles Dickens: A Penguin Life*. New York: Lipper / Viking, 2002.

Soboul, Albert. *Les Sans-culottes parisiens en l'an II*. Paris: Clavreuil, 1958.

Sol, Antoinette. "Trials and Tribulations: Readings and Misreadings of the Revolutionary Body in French Women Novelists, 1792–1799." *Echo*, 2004. http://www.echopolyglot.com/. Accessed August 31, 2010.

Somers, Margaret R. *Genealogies of Citizenship: Markets, Statelessness, and the Right to Have Rights*. Cambridge: Cambridge University Press, 2008.

Spivak, Gayatri Chakravorty. *A Critique of Postcolonial Reason: Towards a Theory of the Vanishing Present*. Cambridge, MA: Harvard University Press, 1999.

Stafford, Barbara Maria. *Artful Science: Enlightenment Entertainment and the Eclipse of Visual Education*. Cambridge, MA: MIT Press, 1994.

Stanton, Elizabeth Cady, Susan B. Anthony, and Matilda Joslyn Gage, eds. *History of Woman Suffrage*. 2nd ed. 3 vols. Rochester, NY: Charles Mann, 1889.

Steinberg, Ronen. "The Afterlives of the Terror: Dealing with the Legacies of Violence in Post-revolutionary France, 1794–1830s." PhD diss., University of Chicago, 2010.

Steintrager, James. *The First Sexual Revolution: Libertines, License, and the Autonomy of Pleasure*. New York: Columbia University Press. Forthcoming.

Stewart, Philip. "This Is Not a Book Review: On Historical Uses of Literature." *Journal of Modern History* 66 (1994): 521–38.

Sutherland, D. M. G. *The French Revolution and Empire: The Quest for a Civic Order*. Oxford: Blackwell, 2003.

Tackett, Timothy. "Interpreting the Terror." *French Historical Studies* 24, no. 4 (Fall 2001): 569–78.

———. *When the King Took Flight*. Cambridge, MA: Harvard University Press, 2003.

Taine, Hippolyte. *Essais de critique et d'histoire*. 2nd ed. Paris: Libraire de L. Hachette, 1866.

Thomas, Chantal. *La Reine scélérate: Marie-Antoinette dans les pamphlets*. Paris: Éditions du Seuil, 1989.

Tickner, Lisa. *The Spectacle of Women: Imagery of the Suffrage Campaign*. Chicago: University of Chicago Press, 1988.

Tilly, Louise. "Food Riot as a Form of Political Conflict in France." *Journal of Interdisciplinary History* 2 (1971): 23–57.

Tissandier, Gaston. *Histoire des ballons et des aéronautes célèbres*. 2 vols. Paris: H. Launette, 1887–90.

Tocqueville, Alexis de. *L'Ancien Régime et la Révolution*. 1856. Edited by J.-P. Mayer. Paris: Gallimard, 1967.

Ton-That, Thanh-Vân. *Lectures d'une œuvre: "Bouvard et Pécuchet"; Une odyssée de la bêtise*. Paris: Éditions du Temps, 1999.

Tourneux, Maurice. *Bibliographie de Paris pendant la Révolution française*. Vol. 2. Paris: Imprimerie Nouvelle [Association ouvrière], 1894.

Trilling, Lionel. Introduction to *Bouvard and Pécuchet*, by Gustave Flaubert, v–xxxvii. Translated by T. W. Earp and G. W. Stonier. New York: New Directions, 1954.

Vaillant, Alain. *La Crise de la littérature: Romantisme et modernité*. Grenoble: ELLUG, 2005.

Van den Heuvel, Gerd. "Terreur, terroriste, terrorisme." In *Handbuch politisch-sozialer Grundbegriffe in Frankreich, 1680–1820*, edited by Rolf Reichardt, Hans-Günter Funke, et al., 3:89–132. Munich: Oldenbourg, 1985.

Vaughn, Harold. "Hell's Desperate Cry! A Prayer from Perdition." *Christ Life Ministries Report* 26, no. 3 (September–December 2003): 3. http://christlifemin.org/publications/Newsletter/newsletter_2003-3.pdf. Accessed March 23, 2011.

Viguerie, Jean de. *Louis XVI, le roi bienfaisant*. Paris: Éditions du Rocher, 2003.

Vila, Anne C. *Enlightenment and Pathology: Sensibility in the Literature and Medicine of Eighteenth-Century France*. Baltimore, MD: Johns Hopkins University Press, 1998.

Voltaire et Henri IV. Musée national du château de Pau, April 27–July 30 2001. Paris: Éditions de la Réunion des musées nationaux, 2001.

Voskuhl, Adelheid. "Motions and Passions: Music-Playing Women Automata and the

Culture of Affect in Late Eighteenth-Century Germany." In *Genesis Redux: Essays in the History and Philosophy of Artificial Life*, edited by Jessica Riskin, 293–320. Chicago: University of Chicago Press, 2007.

Vovelle, Michel. *La Révolution française: Images et récit, 1789–1799.* 5 vols. Paris: Éditions Messidor / Livre Club Diderot, 1986.

Wagenknecht, Edward. "Utopia Americana." 1929. Reprinted in L. Frank Baum, *The Wizard of Oz*, edited by Michael Patrick Hearn, 142–57. New York: Schocken Books, 1983.

Wagner, Nicolas. "Fête et dissolution sociale: À propos de quelques notices du *Journal de Paris* (1797)." In *Les Fêtes de la Révolution: Colloque de Clermont-Ferrand*, edited by Jean Ehrard and Paul Vialleneix, 525–36. Paris: Société des études robespierristes, 1977.

Walker, Lesley H. *A Mother's Love: Crafting Feminine Virtue in Enlightenment France.* Lewisburg, PA: Bucknell University Press, 2008.

Weber, Caroline. *Terror and Its Discontents: Suspect Words in Revolutionary France.* Minneapolis: University of Minnesota Press, 2003.

Weinbaum, Batya. *Islands of Women and Amazons: Representations and Realities.* Austin: University of Texas Press, 1999.

Williams, Raymond. *Culture and Society, 1780–1950.* 1958. Reprint, New York: Columbia University Press, 1983.

Withers, Warrington. "Dickens and the Psychology of Dreams." *PMLA* 63, no. 3 (September 1948): 984–1006.

Woloch, Isser. *Jacobin Legacy: The Democratic Movement under the Directory.* Princeton, NJ: Princeton University Press, 1970.

Woodward, Lionel. *Hélène-Maria Williams et ses amis: Une Anglaise amie de la Révolution française.* 1930. Reprint, Geneva: Slatkine Reprints, 1977.

Younis, Jumanah. "Egypt's Revolution Means Nothing if Its Women Are Not Free." *Guardian*, March 9, 2011. http://www.guardian.co.uk/. Accessed June 14, 2011.

Austin, J. L., 115

automatons, 60; genre of automaton tales, 83–
87, 89–91; and *Frankenstein*, 93, 95–97;
interpretations of, 68–71; invention of,
64–66; in *Le Miroir*, 77–78, 80

Aventures de Jérôme Lecocq, Les (Henriquez),
attitudes toward writing in, 84

Baczko, Bronislaw, 193

Bailly, Jean-Sylvain: as supporter of *La Boussole nationale*, 9; execution of, 167

Balzac, Honoré de: *Les Chouans*, 141; *Du
Gouvernement moderne*, 141–42; *Le Père
Goriot*, 14, 98–99, 102, 111, 136, 140–52;
political views of, 141–42, 151–52, 202;
Souvenirs d'un paria, 202; "Sur Cath-
erine de Médicis," 210

Barbéris, Pierre, 140–41

Barère de Vieuzac, Bertrand, 191–93

Barra, Joseph, 191

Bastille: storming of, 38–39; "papers of the,"
180–81; in *A Tale of Two Cities*, 219, 222

Baum, L. Frank, 13, 21; biographical details
of, 52; as newspaper publisher, 52; *The
Marvelous Land of Oz*, 23, 55–58; *Our
Landlady*, 52–55

Beauharnais, Alexandre de, 108

Becker, Ernest, 19, 49

Bergerac, Cyrano de, 71

Bernardin de Saint-Pierre, Jacques-Henri, 6

Bidelman, Patrick, 51

Blanc, Olivier, 172

Blanchelande, Philibert François Rouxel de,
trial of, 162–63, 173

book illlustration, 2, 12; in *Le Château des
Tuileries*, 36–37; in *Cœlina*, 165–66;
dialogue between images, 202; dialogue
between text and image, 24, 113–14; in
Le Glaive vengeur, 174–75; in *Melchior
ardent*, 43–44

Boufflers, Stanislas Jean, chevalier de, 62, 64

Bouillé, François Claude, marquis de, and son
François, 104–5

Bouloiseau, Marc, 204

Bourbon Restoration: expiatory monuments
created during, 125; explanations of
Varennes during, 105; fears of, 211, 215,
217; in *Le Père Goriot*, 140–41, 144–45;
Robespierre's reputation during, 203;
satire of, 99. See also Charles X; Louis
XVIII

Bourbons: Adieux and, 121–25; in *Le Cimetière de la Madeleine*, 129, 134–35;
comte d'Artois (brother of Louis XVI,
later King Charles X), 69–70, 86, 135,
137; comte de Provence (brother of Louis
XVI, later King Louis XVIII), 69–70, 135,
137; and fathers' death, 150–51, 211;
hidden profiles of, in art, 123–24; history
of family, 99–100, 142, 211–12; images
of royal family, 122–25, 235–36; in
Irma, 211–16; Louis XVII in *L'Ange des
prisons*, 134; Louis-Charles (son of Louis
XVI, dauphin, died 1795), 121; Madame
Élisabeth (sister of Louis XVI, executed
1794), 121; Marie-Thérèse (daughter of
Louis XVI, later duchesse d'Angoulême,
died 1851), 12, 103–4. See also Bourbon
Restoration; Charles X; *Entretiens des
Bourbons, Les*; Henri IV; Louis XVI; Louis
XVIII; Marie-Antoinette

Bourdieu, Pierre, 3

Boussole nationale, La (Pochet), 9–11; Henri
IV in, 10, 11 fig. 1, 114

Bouvard et Pécuchet (Flaubert), 155–56, 161,
224–27

Bréguet, Abraham-Louis, 65

Breteuil, Louis Charles Auguste le Tonnelier,
baron de, 105, 114

brevets, for inventions, 61–62

Brissot, Jacques Pierre, 184

Brossin de Méré, baronne. *See* Guénard,
Élisabeth

Brouard-Arends, Isabelle, 6

Brown, Howard, 156–57, 194, 271n91

Bruno, Louis de, 209

Brunswick Manifesto, 139

Buffon, Georges-Louis Leclerc, comte de, 68

Bug-Jargal (Hugo), 110

Burke, Edmund, 7, 49–50, 57, 141–42; *Reflections on the Revolution in France*, 19–20,
34; *Philosophical Enquiry*, 78, 100, 121,
158

"Ça ira," 149

cabinets de lecture (lending libraries), 7–8, 41

cahiers de doléances (grievances), 39, 115

Caleb Williams (Godwin). See *Adventures of
Caleb Williams, The* (Godwin)

calendar, republican, 239–40

Candide (Voltaire), 43, 244n8

Cap-Français (Haiti), 108; slave revolt in,

Peuchet, Jacques, 132

A Philosophical Enquiry into the Origin of Our Ideas of the Sublime and Beautiful (Burke), 78, 100, 121, 158

Picture of Dorian Gray, The (Wilde), 201, 227, 272n116

pig: Louis XVI as, 116–18, 120; Mubarak as, 237

Pigault-Lebrun, Charles-Antoine-Guillaume, 165, 209

Pitt à Saint-Domingue, 189

pity, 3, 98, 100–101, 120, 129; and *bienfaisance*, 6; in *Le Dictionnaire des idées reçues*, 226; on fears of an insurrection of pity, 122; warning against "false pity," 174

Pochet, A., 9–11, 252n11

poissardes: attitudes toward the king, 109; "false *poissardes*," 33; and *femme forte*, 38–39; literary genre, 26–27, 29, 31–32; and *Our Landlady*, 52–55; satire of, 40, 48–49; and Versailles march, 17, 21, 23; work of, 33

Polignac, Auguste Jules Armand Marie, duc de (Prime Minister of France, 1829–30), 141

political clubs: Society of Revolutionary Republican Women, 39; women's, 38–40, 49, 238. *See also* Girondins; Jacobins

Popkin, Jeremy, 159, 164, 243n2

positivism, 2–3; new positivism, 4–5

Pound, Ezra, 158

Prisonniers du Temple, Les (Regnault-Warin), 134

Protestantism, 10, 28; massacre of (Saint Bartholomew's Day) in *Le Dictionnaire des idées reçues*, 226

Proussinalle. *See* Roussel, Pierre-Joseph-Alexis

Provence, comte de (brother of Louis XVI), 26, 135, 137, 145. *See also* Bourbon Restoration; Louis XVIII

Proyart, Abbé (pseud. Le Blond de Neuvéglise), 196, 198, 206, 225

Prudhomme, Louis-Marie, as editor of *Les Révolutions de Paris*, 21, 26, 159, 181

psychology: in biographies of Robespierre, 198–206; crime narratives and, 188–90; criminal, prison memoirs and, 181–83; Dickens and, 220–21; psychological profiling, 189; 227; use in fiction, 130

Qu'est-ce que le Tiers état? (Sieyès), 237

Questions sur l'Encyclopédie (Voltaire), 81

Queue de Robespierre, La, 193–94

Rabelais, François, 24; *Gargantua*, 43

Reclus, Élie, 51

Reddy, William, 115, 127, 214

Reflections on the Revolution in France (Burke), 19–20, 34

Regnault-Warin, Jean-Baptiste (called Julius-Junius), 12, 39; career as writer, 128, 134; *Le Cimetière de la Madeleine*, 128–35; police pursuit of, 101, 128, 131–33, 138, 210–11

Règne du Prince Trop-Bon, Le, 111–14

Reichardt, Rolf, 12

Religieuse, La (Diderot), 85

Renan, Ernest, 3

Republic, First (1792–1804). *See* Consulate; Directory; National Assembly; National Convention; republicanism

republicanism, 12, 141, 214; in *Le Dictionnaire des idées reçues*, 226; and Pantheon, 156, 216; rituals of, 45–46; and Madame Roland, 185; symbols of, 120, 124–25; in *A Tale of Two Cities*, 222; and women, 39

Restoration. *See* Bourbon Restoration

Rétif de la Bretonne, Nicolas Edme, 47, 71, 127

Réveil des dames, Le, satire of gender reversal in, 49

Révéroni Saint-Cyr, Jacques Antoine, 45, 49

Revolution of 1848, 20

Revolutionary Tribunal. *See* tribunals

Révolutions de Paris, Les (newspaper): fate of, 159; politics in, 180; printing of laws in, 62; reportage of Versailles march, 21–22, 34

Revue de Paris, La (newspaper), 140

Richard Cœur de lion (Grétry), 148–49

Riouffe, Honoré Jean, baron, 181–83

Rivarol, Antoine, comte de, 33, 69

Robertson, E. G., 217

Robespierre, Charlotte, 203, 209, 225

Robespierre, Maximilien: as automaton, 85–86; biographies of, 196–206; *Éloge de Gresset*, 127–28, 198; crime legend of, 189–90; and Festival of the Supreme Being, 213; in *Irma*, 210, 212–13, 214–16; in literature, 14, 209–10; in phantasma-